JON VICKERS

A HERO'S LIFE

Music advisor to Northeastern University Press · GUNTHER SCHULLER

JON VICKERS

A Hero's
Life

Jeannie
Williams

Foreword by

Birgit Nilsson

NORTHEASTERN UNIVERSITY PRESS · BOSTON

Northeastern University Press

Copyright 1999 by Jeannie Williams

Excerpt from *Peter Grimes* reprinted with kind permission of Boosey & Hawkes Music Publishers Ltd., © copyright 1945 by Boosey & Hawkes Music Publishers Ltd.

Excerpts from *Galina: A Russian Story*, English translation copyright © 1984 by Galina Vishnevskaya and Harcourt, Inc., reprinted by permission of the publisher.

Library of Congress Cataloging-in-Publication Data
Williams, Jeannie, 1942–
    Jon Vickers : a hero's life / by Jeannie Williams ; foreword by
Birgit Nilsson.
        p.   cm.
    Includes discography, videography, bibliographical references,
and index
    ISBN 1-55553-408-2 (cl : alk. paper)
    1. Vickers, Jon. 2. Tenors (Singers)—Canada Biography. I. Title.
    ML420.v367 w55 1999
    782.1′092—dc21
    [B]   99-36261

Designed by Virginia Evans

Composed in Baskerville by Wellington Graphics, South Boston, Massachusetts. Printed and bound by Quebecor Printing, Brattleboro, Vermont. The paper is Quebecor Liberty, an acid-free sheet.

MANUFACTURED IN THE UNITED STATES OF AMERICA
03 02 01 00 99   5 4 3 2 1

To my music-loving father

To Bruce Burroughs and Peter Dvarackas,
from whom I learned so much about opera

And to David Patrick Stearns,
from whom I first heard the name Jon Vickers

Contents

List of Illustrations

With Marilyn Horne in Samson et Dalila
With Hetti and their daughter Wendy
With his second wife, Judy
With Theodor Uppman
At a tribute to Maria Callas at the Lyric Opera of Chicago

Foreword

I have had many tenors. I should say, I have had many wonderful tenors on stage. There were Jussi Björling, Set Svanholm, Carlo Bergonzi, Ramón Vinay, Karl Liebl, Wolfgang Windgassen, Jess Thomas, Franco Corelli, Giuseppe di Stefano, Max Lorenz, Helge Brilioth, Plácido Domingo, Richard Tucker, James McCracken, Torsten Ralf, José Carreras, to mention a few. There was even Beniamino Gigli, when I was very young.

But Jon Vickers was different, very different, both as an artist and as a human being. He looked neither right nor left; his opinions were as strong as the rock of *Die Walküre*. He *had* to have it his way, no matter what.

I always found it very exciting to sing with Jon, because he gave not only one hundred percent but one hundred and twenty. You would have to be made of stone not to respond to his unbelievably intensive way of singing-acting. His first *Tristan*, which we sang together in Buenos Aires in September 1971, was a milestone in his great career.

I will always remember the *Tristan* film that we did together at the 1973 Orange Festival in France. I have never seen an artist perform a role more realistically, especially in the third act. His eyes! I can still see them. That was no longer make-believe, that was real drama—and I was almost fearing for his well-being.

Jon also could be quite exasperating. We gave one performance only of *Tristan und Isolde* at the Met (January 30, 1974), a performance that has taken on some sort of legendary status—and that almost did not happen.

Jon had been singing the opera with another soprano, and I had been doing some concerts, coming to New York only two days before the performance. Upon my arrival, the Met rang immediately and I was told that "since we cannot find Jon Vickers, we have arranged for you to rehearse with Jess Thomas, who has generously offered to replace Jon at the rehearsal." I found it indeed very kind of Jess to offer this, but I replied, "I tell you one thing: The one I am rehearsing with tomorrow is the one who is going to sing the performance of Tristan; otherwise you have to look for another Isolde."

The next morning at 10:30, Jon was there to rehearse.

After our first *Walküre* together at the Met, in January 1960, the critics wrote that Nilsson had finally found the right "playmate" for the great

Wagnerian operas. I too somehow felt that I was destined to sing the big Wagnerian roles with Jon, and I believe that in his heart of hearts he felt the same way toward me.

However, Jon was not easy to convince. He accepted a date and he canceled it, only to repeat the same, over and over. I waited and waited for my Tristan for fourteen years, just as long as Jacob waited for Rachel in the Bible.

Believe me, Jon was worth waiting for!

Jon is a wonderful and never-a-dull-moment colleague and friend. Therefore, this book by Jeannie Williams is all the more interesting in explaining what motivates him, not only as an artist but also as a human being.

BIRGIT NILSSON

Preface

Then shall the righteous shine forth.
—Matthew 13:43

The great Canadian tenor Jon Vickers holds a continuing fascination for public and colleagues alike, and he is secure within the circle of opera singers whose art burned brightest in this century. His work was so original, his personality so vivid—and so baffling, both on- and offstage—that those who knew him needed little temptation to slip into analysis.

The most famous Isolde to Vickers's Tristan was Birgit Nilsson, who told me bluntly, "He was almost always unhappy. . . . His nerves were outside the skin, not inside the skin." Those are the last attributes to be associated with the cheerful Nilsson, and she could not understand them in one who had reached heights equal to her own. She recalled that after his early successes at the Metropolitan Opera (with her in *Fidelio*) and at La Scala, Vickers was anything but cheerful. "He was like he had the whole world on his shoulders. I said, 'Try and be happy! Think how wonderful a career you have ahead, and be thankful.' . . . He's his own worst enemy," she sighed. "He's a dear soul . . . but he's a bit difficult, and not wanting to be."[1]

Regina Resnik played a key role in Vickers's early career in the 1950s and later was among the singers who feared him onstage, particularly in *Carmen*. An insightful, incisive observer, she took an even more somber view of Vickers. "I always had a feeling that there was something—as a man and as an artist—that's unfulfilled in Jon. Somewhere there was a void he did not fill. . . . And I thought that that was probably one of the reasons for this edge of fear and excitement that was onstage [with him] all the time. It just went a little tiny bit overboard, and that 'overboard' is in my estimation some sort of inexplicable insecurity. Because somebody who is completely sure does not have to traverse that line of fear, or create it. To me, it's still to this day unfathomable."[2]

It has been said that it is dangerous, and sometimes unrewarding, to come too close to a mystery, and a great singer is very much a mystery. To discover the inner workings of that singer, to poke and pry at the ways he may produce in us powerful and beautiful, painful and exalting emotions, can reduce or even destroy his mystery and power. But it also may be true that such discoveries leave us with greater respect for the phenomenon we explore.

In Vickers's case, more mystery than usual surrounds him because of his aversion to publicity. This was crystallized on a weekend in November 1987, toward the close of his career: he and Luciano Pavarotti were scheduled to appear at Carnegie Hall one Sunday—Vickers in the afternoon, Pavarotti in the evening.

Pavarotti's time in New York was massively publicized, as usual. He was there chiefly for a new production of *Il Trovatore* at the Met, and was one of several superstars on the bill for an AIDS benefit later at Carnegie Hall. For that event, he appeared at a press conference on the Carnegie stage a couple of days before his recital. Questions were divided between the benefit and the tenor's eighty-five-pound weight loss, which he said was necessary so that he could both ride a horse comfortably and perhaps cut a slim enough figure to sing the fatally lovesick young Werther onstage. Photos in newspapers the next day displayed Pavarotti's beaming smile and newly baggy suit.

That two of the world's greatest living tenors were to sing at the same hall on the same day went unremarked by the media. As usual, no interviews with Vickers, nor any mention of him other than in Carnegie ads, appeared. It was as if the two inhabited different musical worlds. The Carnegie staff was abuzz about the Pavarotti events; but Vicker's appearance caused no particular stir, since he could be expected to do no more than his job of singing.

As it turned out, he canceled that appearance because of illness at the last minute. Revieweres were left to mourn that the *Peter Grimes* interludes were all they had to recall Vickers on the program at Carnegie.

Pavarotti, fifty-two on that weekend, had no final stage appearance in mind when this book was written. But we can be sure it will not come to pass in obscurity. For Vickers, the end came at age sixty-one in the little Canadian town of Kitchener, not with a huge gala in New York or London, as may be expected for Pavarotti or Plácido Domingo, but with two other singers far from famous and the local symphony. I was there in 1988, and this Act 2 of *Parsifal* must have been as consummate a performance as he had ever given.

Many mysteries remain concerning Vickers, and many persons who knew him address those mysteries in this book. From what sources sprang his astounding ability to create such indelible stage portraits? Why did he express surprise throughout his life that anyone should think him difficult to deal with? He admitted to a major problem with Sir Georg Solti, but blocked out, at least publicly, the scores of other disagreements and genuine rages that kept his colleagues talking years after they occurred. How did these problems relate to his artistic abilities? What was the story behind his cancelation of a much-heralded *Tannhäuser* at Covent Garden? Most of those I interviewed believed that Vickers withdrew because of vocal obstacles. Many also disbelieved his public statement about moral aversion to the role, citing all the other objectionable characters he portrayed. But Vickers never once departed from that public statement. How did he reconcile himself to that situation? How did he maintain his very private—and genuinely religious—persona in the cauldron of the international opera world?

Was he a wise conservator of his talents? Or could he have been an even greater artist had he taken more chances with his repertoire (where were the Siegfrieds of the *Ring*, and the *Wozzeck* that Karajan asked from him?), and had he worked more willingly with some of his conductor and director colleagues? Covent Garden's former chief Sir John Tooley is one who believes strongly that the latter is the case.

The American tenor Richard Cassilly summed up the bafflement of many fellow artists about the Vickers mode of operation: "I never understood how Jon intimidated so many people. . . . He ran his world. He told people the rules by which he would play, and they did it."[3] But the late, longtime Metropolitan Opera press and tour director Francis Robinson, who saw so many great ones pass by, said that Vickers was "the kind of artist who ends up being an opera hero forever."[4]

Vickers read widely in psychology, among other fields. As he portrayed the greatest heroes in opera, he may well have contemplated how the ubiquitous hero myth applied to those roles as well as to his own life. The Jungians describe the hero's miraculous but humble birth (Vickers's birth indeed was something of a miracle to his parents), his early proof of strength, his rapid rise to prominence, his struggle with the forces of evil, his fallibility to the sin of pride, and his fall through betrayal or a heroic sacrifice.[5]

My fascination with Vickers grew as I worked on a different book about tenors. He clearly stood out for his passion, commitment, artistry, and unique vocal quality. I well remember the first major impression he made upon me. I had come late to opera and missed much of his career onstage. I had seen him in *Fidelio*, in *Peter Grimes*, a revelation in its totality, and even as Tristan in Chicago (there was a great amount of coughing). It was his final full *Tristan*, although most of the world didn't know that at the time.

Then he appeared in *Die Walküre* when the Met visited Washington, D.C., on its centennial season tour in spring 1984. I had an excellent front-and-center seat in the Kennedy Center Opera House, in which the pit is smaller than the Met's. The singers seemed very close, and I received the full impact of the Vickers voice and presence. The first act was shattering. I had never imagined such intensity in opera. In Act 2 the spotlight went out during the scene with Siegmund and Brünnhilde when it was supposed to be on Vickers. The stage was black for a long minute or so, but Vickers's voice never faltered. Today the phrase "old horse" resonates in my mind. That's what he called himself on occasion in later years, and it would have been impossible for that old horse, at the top of his field for a quarter century, to have been thrown by such a detail. I went backstage after Act 3 to look for this amazing person, not knowing that the tenor often leaves the house after Siegmund's death in Act 2. Only soprano Johanna Meier was left, surrounded by admirers.

That tour was the last time Vickers would sing a complete Siegmund. But it was just the beginning of Vickers, and of Wagner, for me.

So few—are there any?—singers today possess the commitment, passion, risk tolerance, and transcendent communication that distinguished this artist. I feel fortunate to have experienced all this before his career closed. It is a rewarding responsibility to be able to tell his story. Vickers has not cooperated with the writing of this book, but that will be no surprise to those who know him as a private man. I regret any errors that may result from my inability to verify information with persons whom he discouraged from speaking with me. Similarly, I have been able only to paraphrase, not to quote directly, his archival correspondence because I lacked his approval. Nonetheless, I hope this book will be received, despite these limitations, as a worthy attempt to gather together for the first time the crucial details about the life of a great twentieth-century singer.

JON VICKERS

A HERO'S LIFE

Prologue

T HE EARLY-MORNING SUN GLINTS OFF COUNTLESS LAKES AND PONDS that dot the green-gold checkerboard of fields surrounding Prince Albert, the little gateway city holding back the northern wilderness of Saskatchewan province. A red fox stalks near the small airport's landing strips, where young Canadians and other British Commonwealth airmen learned to fly Tiger Moths in the war years of the 1940s. Hay bales squat just yards from the runways. Southward across the North Saskatchewan River lies Central Avenue, and the spire of St. Paul's Presbyterian Church pokes above the downtown business district.

The town turned out in September 1977 for a full-scale tribute to the most famous of its "three Johns," as some residents speak of them. Prime Minister John G. Diefenbaker and star Maple Leafs goalie Johnny Bower lagged far behind in the international recognition achieved by Jonathan Stewart Vickers, who had sung in the St. Paul's choir.

Vickers flew in on a small plane and ruminated: "So many people never have the thrill of getting up on a beautiful day and looking down on the magnificence of nature, all the fall colors, the harvest having come in. You see all these wonderful patterns of the farm machinery that have moved on the earth."[1]

The muscular man who had once helped farm those fields gave a brief dinner speech on Tuesday, September 27, at the Sheraton Marlboro Motor Inn. He joked that returning to St. Paul's for his concert the following night would be "much more terrifying" than singing at La Scala or on any of the world's great opera stages. "You feel rather exposed, you know, rather naked, and it's very difficult to sing for your friends."[2]

He spoke more truth about his life in music than his old friends, some the descendants of trappers and traders, farmers and early Mounties, probably realized. Vickers was continually exposed, emotionally naked on stage, because light roles and one-dimensional parts were not his destiny. He became

Otello in extremis, Peter Grimes in the deepest agony of mind, Tristan flayed by desire, heroes and outsiders alike. Sensible people—Vickers himself—say that singers must remain in control, must master such emotions on stage. Some who sang with him suggested that this singer came perilously close, closer than almost any singer they could recall, to naked reality.

But the citizens of his hometown, who had seen little of that, now saw only the genial, dapper man who had sung in their churches and worked as a salesman and store manager in western Canada. He might have become a civic stalwart like Jack Matheson, the personable menswear shop owner who presented Vickers with a top hat, Prince Albert's city symbol, as worn by the man for whom it was named, the husband of Queen Victoria.

Vickers, in typically Canadian fashion, always tended to downplay his drive toward a career, saying he could just as happily have been a doctor or a farmer. All his siblings sang well, he said; his brother Arthur also could have succeeded as a singer. Greatness often springs from unassuming seeds. But it remains a matter of fascination to contemplate what hidden restlessness, what deep consciousness of having a gift to nurture, what fierce will or passion led Jonathan Vickers to the summit of the byzantine world of opera—and what kept him, in many ways, on a separate peak.

At St. Paul's, Vickers, accompanied by the New York pianist Peter Schaaf, gave the townspeople a program organized chronologically. All the music was long familiar to him, if not to his audience. He began with the soothing "Where'er you walk" from Handel's *Semele*, followed by an aria that some present might never have heard, the agonized "Total eclipse" from Handel's *Samson*. The Prince Albertians heard the short and accessible "Winterstürme," from *Die Walküre*, and some lighter music by Purcell, Vaughan Williams, and Dvořák. But they also experienced Vickers in Grimes's final scene, a startling piece in any setting, and one Vickers has said is difficult to present out of its operatic context. He was never one to condescend to his listeners. In fact, his audience was wider; the concert was broadcast later by CBC Radio.

Vickers claimed always to be at one with Prince Albert, "native, rooted here," as Grimes tells Captain Balstrode, even when not physically present. "I am so damn Canadian, so Canadian through and through, that it's ridiculous. I am tied to this country," Vickers mused a few years later.[3] Canada, said Robertson Davies, one of its most successful authors, is a country torn between "a very northern, rather extraordinary, mystical spirit that it fears, and its desire to present itself to the world as a Scotch banker.

This makes for tension. Tension is the very stuff of art."[4] He might have been speaking of Vickers, so well does this apply.

Canada derives its name from a Huron-Iroquois word for "settlement." Vickers was to suffer much misunderstanding and pain at the hands of his fellow settlers, while reigning as an operatic hero in other nations, not his own.

PART
1

1926–1956
The Early Years

No matter what we did in this pursuit of
excellence, we did it for the glory of God.
I have never lost that.
—*Jon Vickers*

1

Prince Albert

JON VICKERS'S PARENTS WERE CANADIAN, OF ENGLISH AND IRISH descent. If they had not been driven by poverty to seek a better life in western Canada but had remained in Ontario, close to Toronto, Vickers might have found it easier to begin his music studies and career. Yet his drive makes it impossible to conceive of his failing to follow his gift no matter where he might have found himself. And it is certain that the small-town associations and the eleven summers of farm work in his early days did much to nourish the artist he was to become.

His father, William Stewart Vickers, was born in Kirkton, Ontario, in 1890, the son of a Methodist carpenter and grain thrasher whose father had emigrated from England in the mid-nineteenth century. William had a grandmother of Irish heritage. A short, burly schoolteacher with a large head, William Vickers in 1914 married the petite sixteen-year-old Frances Myrle Mossip, known as Myrle (and in early records spelled Merle), the daughter of a dairyman from London Township, Middlesex County, Ontario. Bill Vickers (as his neighbors called him) first taught in Dryden, Ontario. The couple began having children almost immediately, and the young family moved west in 1920 to Melfort, Saskatchewan. Bill apparently had relatives in the area; his brothers also moved west. He taught and was town bandmaster until 1925, when he and Myrle settled in Prince Albert, some sixty miles northwest of Melfort. There, Bill became principal of the Connaught School. In 1941 he took over as principal of the King George School, a grade school attended by his children, and held that post till he retired in June 1956. He taught briefly after that at a Bible college in Three Hills, Alberta. He was also throughout his life a lay minister in the Presbyterian and Methodist traditions, which had a profound impact on his fourth son.

Jonathan was the sixth in a brood of eight blondly handsome children. His mother spoke of having two families because of the break of more than three years between her first five children and the last three. In that sense Jon was also an "oldest" child, with all the dominating aspects of that place in the birth order. Myrle's doctor told the couple that she should have no more children after her fifth was born in December 1922. Twenty-four years old at that time, she was small, four feet ten inches and ninety-two pounds. The doctor said, "This young woman's body has had enough, but it's not my decision."[1]

Sterilization was suggested, but after Myrle and Will, as she and family members called her husband, had talked and prayed, they decided against it. "And the next one was you!" Myrle told Jonathan many years later, bursting into tears as she recounted the story to her son while on a plane trip.[2]

Jon was born on October 29, 1926. Bernice was born in 1928, and Arthur Henry in 1932. Myrle also may have had a miscarriage after Arthur's birth. The older five were Frances Margaret; William David, known as David; John Wesley, known as Wesley; Albert Harvey, called Ab; and Ruth, the last two born in Melfort. The family recalled the children's birth order by a memory device: "Margaret Does Well At Reciting Jokes By Aristotle."

Bill Vickers was at band practice and Myrle Vickers was alone when Jonathan was born. "It was a very cold wintry night late in October. There was no running water or electricity in the old house, only a well in the backyard," Vickers told John Ardoin.[3] That house was a yellow, two-story frame dwelling, probably at 1135 First Street East.

Myrle would say "she must have had a premonition that [Jon] was going into show business, because of the name she gave him," recalled a close family friend, Jean Anderson Turnbull. "Jonathan, instead of John. It just sounds showbiz."[4] Blue-eyed Jonathan would grow to look much like his father, with a wide, strong chin, large-domed forehead, massive hands, and stocky build. Both had huge barrel chests and bowed legs. He described his father as "a steady, velvet-covered rock" and his mother as "a little bubbling bottle of champagne." They complemented one another to give the family "a magnificently happy home life," he said, and despite Bill's firm rule and their slim finances, this seems to have been the case.[5]

Prince Albert was a city in which religion was important, as can be seen in its heavy vote in favor of Prohibition in 1916. It had been settled in 1866 by a Scots-born Presbyterian missionary from Ontario, who persevered even though he was not well received by the Cree Indians. Prince Albert's economic future would rest on the area's scenic beauties and on the lumber and agriculture industries that developed. The city had serious financial problems even before the 1929 crash and Great Depression, problems tempered somewhat by the opening in 1928 of the Prince Albert National Park, thirty-five miles north of the city, a major spur to employment.

So while the Vickers family had sturdy religious support in a setting of outdoor splendor—both strong influences on Jonathan—the depression years were devastating to the area. Jobless farmworkers flocked to Prince Albert, and in 1930 work camps were set up in the park. By 1939 the city had just over eleven thousand residents. Canada entered World War II that year, and one of several flight training schools was set up in Prince Albert; meanwhile, a number of Mennonite objectors worked in the park. The city was then on the road to growth and economic health.

But the 1930s were difficult for the Vickers family. They moved shortly after Jonathan's fourth birthday, in 1930, and in the depth of the depression, had to move again because they could not afford that home. He says that at that time his father went to work for a friend, "not so much to earn extra money as to ensure one less mouth at home to feed."[6] Jonathan was just five in November 1931 when Bill's teaching salary was cut from $254 to $119.54 a month. But Jon remembered his father's dignity when he asked town officials for the right to farm a vacant lot adjoining his home.[7] It became the Vickers vegetable garden: "My older brothers pulled up roots; all the sod was broken by hand," Vickers recalled. "I remember the happiness in that family when the harvest came in!"[8] The lot was one of two adjoining the old frame house at 305 19th Street East, where Jon grew up. The Vickerses had three-quarters of the roomy two-story duplex, with fireplaces and a long veranda, and finally had modern utilities. Another resident lived in the back, and the other vacant lot was used as a maple-shaded play yard.

Myrle Vickers "never complained," recalled Eva Payne Furniss, a Prince Albert native and family neighbor. "She was hardworking and honest as the day was long. She would make all these breads, take huge loaves out of the oven. When she came to shucking peas, she'd do mountains of them [to put up for winter meals]. They had a small garden that ran into the next block. . . . And there were no wash machines then. She'd have lines full of clothes." As one might expect of a hardworking, religious homemaker with no money for luxuries, she never cut her hair and wore no makeup.[9]

Jean Turnbull recalled, "I can remember the kids all having their chores. I would go home with Bubs [Bernice] after school, and there was always an apple in the pantry. The children all helped, setting the table and getting the vegetables ready" for dinner.[10]

Myrle was a fastidious housekeeper, and the home had to be especially clean for Sundays. On Saturdays the Vickers children helped scrub, wax, and polish the floors while listening to the afternoon radio broadcasts of the Metropolitan Opera, which had begun in 1931. Vickers specifically recalled the February 26, 1938, *Aida* at which Giovanni Martinelli became ill and collapsed halfway through "Celeste Aida," to be replaced by Frederick Jagel.[11] Young Jon was eleven years old, and that season he also might have heard Richard Crooks as Des Grieux and Don Ottavio; Melchior doing heavy duty as Siegmund, Lohengrin, Parsifal, and Tristan; Martinelli as Otello; and René Maison as Don José.

Bill Vickers was a strict man; as Eva Furniss recalled, "he was a school principal. It went with the job." On occasion he could become angry with his own children.[12] A dominant community figure, he expressed himself forcefully at teachers conventions, often on controversial subjects. If these became dinner table fodder at home, he clearly set an example for his brood. A former vice principal with Bill, H. A. Loucks, recalled at those conventions that "even if the majority failed to agree with him at first . . . as often happened, he was able to convince his fellow teachers that he was in the right."[13] This insistence on his views was a trait his son Jon would share.

William Powell, who went through school with Jon, recalled a winter day when they were in a group riding a homemade plank bobsled, racing dangerously down a hill near the Vickers home toward the railroad tracks, where the road curved. "Jon had difficulty sitting down next day in school. His dad gave him a blistering," although probably using just one big hand.[14] Young Jon actually enjoyed the strictures of his life, but admitted later that "a couple [in the family] did rebel against it."[15]

The family attended First Baptist Church, where Jon sang as a boy soprano and a sister later ran the Sunday school. Bill, although not ordained, filled in as preacher there, as well as at St. Paul's Presbyterian, particularly when it was between ministers, and at other area churches. "He had a tremendous voice, which I suppose he passed on to Jon, a bull voice. He would hold forth at great length," recalled John Victor Hicks, a Prince Albert resident who was an organist as well as an eminent poet.[16] Bill kept a daily diary, knelt with his family to say grace at meals, and read the Bible through each year. He conducted Bible study sessions in a quite scholarly manner in his home as well as in churches. His favorite biblical book was Revelation, and he loved to talk of things to come as revealed there, perhaps imparting hints of life's mystery to some of his children.

"My father said the responsibility of a human being was to take whatever talent he has—whether to be a gardener or a president—and do that job to the utmost of his ability. That is the fundamental philosophy of my life," Vickers recalled. "Over and over again he would say, 'You will do with your might what your hands find to do. You will do it to the best of your ability.' He pounded that into our heads; no matter what we did in this pursuit of excellence, we did it for the glory of God. I have never lost that."[17]

Bill took his family on many preaching jobs with the Salvation Army, the Plymouth Brethren, and the United Church; the children would help provide music. Bill and Myrle played the piano, and Bill the horn in the city band. Myrle also had a pretty voice. The children played various instruments and all sang, both solo and in duos, trios, and quartets. This "poor man's Trapp family," as Vickers later called it, helped raise money for war bonds and for the Red Cross and was heard on local radio.[18] "My first recollections of singing in public was when I was about five years old," said Vickers, then "a curly-haired little fella" who did some radio solos.[19] The family sang at the jail and the Saskatchewan penitentiary. "I suppose it must have sounded pretty funny, but we gave pleasure," Vickers recalled. "I have a very clear memory of going into a prison on Mother's Day when I was six or seven" and the men whistling at his sisters. "I sang 'Don't Forget the Promise Made to Mother' and couldn't understand why all the men were bawling."[20] He also recalled a public Christmas concert in which he sang at age three.

His older brothers were in the city band and took music lessons, but Vickers never did, though he picked up a little piano playing. This, he said, was because his chief interest was singing. "I guess everyone thought of singing as a natural talent; you just opened your mouth and sang."[21] Vickers claimed to have been extremely shy as a child, although this is not how others recall him. Singing, he said, was a way out of that shyness. But he added years later: "To begin with, I sang because I had to sing. It was part of me . . . an absolute necessity, fulfilling some kind of emotional and even perhaps physical need in me."[22]

When Jon sang as a teen at St. Paul's, the parishioners noted the tremendous size of his voice. The windows would rattle as he hit the final *fortissimo* of "Jerusalem" at full blast.[23] Once, a visitor told the boy he had a remarkable voice and should be trained. His mother politely but firmly said, "No, Jonathan sings along with the rest of us." It was just a comment, but it became a seed of future conflict in her son as his interest in singing progressed.[24] (Myrle never shortened his name to "Jon.")

The Vienna Boys' Choir passed through on a Canadian tour, and little Jon was introduced to its leader. "There were always people trying to push me. My mother and dad just pooh-poohed it. . . . I was just one of the family—and it's true, they were all very good singers."[25] Indeed, his family later seemed to take his career somewhat casually; his sister Bernice, with whom he was close, never heard him sing at the Metropolitan Opera, though his parents did once.

Moviegoing was frowned upon, and there was no money for it anyway; card games were forbidden. But singing around the piano was a popular family pastime, with church friends and visiting servicemen joining the songs. "The piano bench never got cold," Vickers recalled.[26] On Sundays only hymns could be played, and neighbors could hear the family in full voice.

Myrle was always ready to pack for a family picnic at Little Red River. Her older sons loved to tease her, and she enjoyed it all. A grade school friend of Jon's, Robert Motherwell, recalled rousing games of croquet on the big front lawn and a family that found lots of fun among themselves. Motherwell, who lived a few doors away, said there was always an extra chair at the Vickers dinner table, despite their skimpy budget. In return, he would sometimes use an extra nickel to take Jon to a matinee at the Orpheum, a western or a Flash Gordon serial. Jon's father, he thought, probably was unaware of those outings.[27]

The Vickerses were far from the poorest family in Prince Albert, but "for a long time, I never thought that life was anything else but working to survive and eat," Vickers said.[28] From ages eight to eighteen he worked every summer with his brothers on the farm of Frank White, in the Tisdale area. White was his father's best friend, and no one other than his father influenced him more, Vickers said.[29] The young people always asked Jon to sing at get-togethers, White recalled. "He never hesitated, though I recall one time they accused him of showing off a bit, and so he said he wouldn't. But I went to him and asked, 'Who gave you your voice anyway, Jonny?' 'Well, God did,' he answered. 'Then,' I said, 'sing, sing, sing!' And he sang and kept on singing."[30]

That farm was where the famed Vickers physique developed, based solidly on his genetic heritage from his father. He ran tractors, fed pigs, hauled water, cleaned chicken houses, brought in hay with horse teams, and worked with threshing crews. "I learned a love of the soil, and the sheer physical satisfaction of working against time and weather to plough the earth and prepare a crop. When you have experienced all these things in your most formative years, you can never take it out of yourself."[31]

He usually returned a little late to the classroom each autumn "because they had to drag me off the farm to get me back in school."[32] Helping with the harvest was encouraged in the war years. "They were some of the happiest days of my life," he said much later, recalling big country breakfasts with a happy crowd of workmen.

I realize my whole philosophy of life was formed in those years. In this rural setting I came to the conclusion the only meaningful thing in this life is contact with other human beings. It was there too that deep and profound Christian convictions settled in me which have been an influence all of my life.

The understanding, which slowly and surely developed in me, of the necessity of human contact and an understanding of the needs of others and their problems has probably, more than anything else, given me the ability to analyze my roles, to come to grips with a score, to study a drama, to project my feelings into the life of someone I've never met except on a piece of paper. It enabled me to put myself into that person's life and their feelings to the point that I can put the person on and wear him for my stage life.[33]

He found more physical work at home: Bill Vickers would order fifteen cords of wood, which he and his sons would saw into sixteen-inch stove-length logs. For three springs Jonathan dug the garden of the Vickerses' next-door neighbor while her husband was overseas at war. The family had no car in the 1940s; Bill bicycled to his work at school and to make deliveries of Fleischmann's Yeast, a baking and medicinal staple that he sold to supplement his income. (He would have done well to make $2,500 annually at King George.) One of the boys, often Jon, would accompany him on his rounds. Even then Jon was spoken of as a lad with a good business head. He also worked after school at the local Safeway market.

The lawyer and budding politician John G. Diefenbaker was a family friend who also attended the Baptist church. At one point he offered to take in Jon to give Bill Vickers one less mouth at the table. The Vickerses appreciated the offer but "wouldn't hear of it," Vickers said later.[34] Nevertheless, the Diefenbaker friendship was to endure until the future prime minister's death. The senior Vickerses themselves took in boarders after the older children left home; after 1946 they lived at 115 24th Street East (the 19th Street house has since been torn down).

Jon graduated in 1941 from King George, where his father had become principal that fall. (Jon may have begun grade school a year later than most because his father believed a child should be six before entering and Jon had an October birthday.) He then attended Prince Albert Collegiate Institute, a public high school. He was a high C or low B student but could have done much better had he not missed school on occasion because of his other jobs, recalled then-principal R. D. Kerr. "He was a smart boy . . . with an analytical mind. He was nobody's fool, down to earth." At the time, the school was so crowded that it had morning and afternoon shifts. A shorter day gave Jon time to work, but Kerr had to talk with Jon about his absences.[35]

The yearbook for his graduation year, 1945, listed "Johnnie 'Look for the silver lining' Vickers" with the lines:

> Our blond-haired tenor is always there
> With a merry laugh and never a care.
> He's willing to try out any new sport
> Is at home in the gym or basketball court.

He played football and basketball his senior year; the only school award he ever won, he said, was "most outstanding athlete" that year. He also did weightlifting, just for fun. He excelled in chin-ups and other school exercises, recalled Powell, and was very competitive on the basketball court.[36] In the late afternoon Jon could often be seen striding down the street, smacking a softball into his glove, on the way to strike out a few more batters (but never on Sundays). John Hicks joked at the tribute more than three decades later that "had he but exercised a bit more singleness of purpose, he might have become one of the finest softball pitchers in northern Saskatchewan."[37] Speed skating also became a Vickers favorite, with its daring, dramatic qualities, and he was urged to consider aiming for the Olympics.

Jean Turnbull recalled that Jon "was a real happy-go-lucky kid, very well liked. I can remember going ice skating with him down at the Minto Arena, and in those days ice skating was really something. That was one of the few things that your parents would let you do! They had one of those great big silver balls with mirrors on it that they use in ballrooms," turning with colored lights. Turnbull recalled visits when she was in third or fourth grade to the Vickers home, "playing hide-and-go-seek in that house . . . with Arthur and Bubs [Bernice] and Jon. It was scary, because it was a big house." Jon was "a real teaser," far from shy. The high school students socialized as a group, so she never recalled his having a steady girlfriend. The Baptist church was very important in his life, and there was always a young people's group. They enjoyed cross-country skiing, sleighrides (after which Jon would sometimes sing), and swimming in the river.[38] Vickers's IOA form teacher, Arnold Friesen, recalled him sitting in the back of the class, enjoying being surrounded by admiring girls.[39]

Some pursuits were on a humble level. Vickers idolized his tall, handsome oldest brother, Dave, throughout his childhood, and recalled that Dave was a great player of "dibs." A dib was a small round piece of baked clay, "as opposed to those luxurious objects of childish wonder—glass marbles." Players bounced dibs off a wall, trying to land them within a handspan of another player's and thus win the other's dib. Dave won a total of one thousand dibs, and "I still recall the thrill when he staked all his little brothers to a hundred dibs apiece so that we could get going in that most exciting of games. How much more satisfying than to be given a dime to go and buy a hundred dibs!"[40]

Vickers looked at his childhood poverty through the prism of the years in 1968 on a British radio program. He said that the sole object he would take to a desert island would be "a big, pretty child's ball." He had been given a rubber one for Christmas at age four or five: "I bounced it on a nail and it was destroyed." He recalled the incident vividly, "how sick this thing went in my hands." And his father "thought that I had broken it on purpose, and somehow I could not even have the courage to try to persuade him that I hadn't. I just accepted it."

The "it" referred to his father's stern judgment of his children. But the lesson later for Vickers was one of simplicity, a quality he would retain that served him well in his art. That ball reminded him "of the precious things that sometimes we can destroy without even thinking . . . the simple, beautiful things of life, no matter how ordinary they may seem, they are very, very beautiful, that we should keep this childlike love of them, wonder of them, and as an adult protect and shield those things." Vickers had taken the interviewer's question more seriously than most guests would do. "You'll laugh when I tell you," he said, displaying the open, almost naive facet of his personality that was one of his most appealing traits.[41]

That sternness of his father's left "an indelible imprint on my whole personality," Vickers later recalled. It made him uncompromising in his demands upon himself, and when he fails, "I feel I've let God down, I've let myself down, my profession down, my talent down. That's a natural product of my upbringing."[42]

Jon had a seventh-grade music teacher, Nancy Larson, who gave many youngsters the joy of music. Robert Motherwell recalled that she particularly encouraged Jon, giving him solo parts and much instruction. "She had him picked as a winner." Her choirs always did well in town music festivals. At one, Jon's voice broke in the middle of the event. He was then about twelve years old.[43]

The 1906 St. Paul's Church had been given a two-manual Casavant pipe organ in the 1930s. The church's organist, an Englishman named Luther Roberts, listened to young Jon sing "just after puberty," Vickers recalled. "He threw up his hands in horror and said this is too good a voice, you mustn't hurt it. He implanted in me perhaps too great a fear of hurting my voice." Roberts warned against trying to extend Vickers's range at his age. "He thought I was a baritone" because of the dark color of the boy's voice and its baritonal solidity in the lower registers.[44] During his last year of high school Vickers took three or four months of vocal lessons with the organist. "He didn't profess to be a voice teacher, but he was a superb musician."[45] Roberts kept the boy on pieces from oratorios—*Elijah* was one, no doubt "Then shall the righteous shine forth," transposed down so his voice would not be strained.

And that, as Vickers put it, "was the very beginning of, how shall I say it—singling out of me from the rest of the family."[46]

On the popular side, Vickers learned "Cherry Ripe," coached by John Hicks's wife, Marjorie, for an amateur concert at the Orpheum Theater. Marjorie also taught piano to his sister Bernice.

The Vickers family was in the audience when an evangelist appeared at St. Paul's. John Hicks played the organ for the event but doesn't recall what, if any, religious affiliation the man had. But the Vickerses thought he was wonderful, and the gospel-style music seemed to have had a strong effect on them. Hicks said, "If Jon hadn't moved [away], he could have become" an evangelist.[47]

One autumn, in a Prince Albert Collegiate history class, the teacher, Arnold Friesen, asked students to talk about something that interested them. "I was fascinated with a little bit of Greek history . . . the construction of the Acropolis," Vickers recalled.

> But having never heard it pronounced before, I got up and made the marvelous mistake of pronouncing it the 'Acro-PO-lis.' Everyone in the classroom howled with laughter, and I was reduced to falling into my shoes. And Mr. Friesen was marvelous the way he rescued me and made me feel reasonably comfortable.
>
> Many years later I was invited to the Athens festival to sing in the Herodes Atticus, which is a great amphitheater in Athens. I was singing *Otello*, and it was quite an impressive sight. Princess Irene was in the front row. And as I stood and sang the opening bars, just on the horizon I saw the lighted Acropolis.

He laughed gently as he described the moment at his Prince Albert tribute. "It was quite, quite something."[48]

Jonathan Vickers's road to the Greek monuments took him next to the music-loving Canadian towns where he got his first taste of the life onstage, a life that would consume him for almost forty years.

2

Footloose

THOUGH VICKERS CONSIDERED BEING A FARMER, HE ALSO HAD HIS eye on medical school through his years in high school, where he did well in science and studied Latin. He had been too young to join the army, although like some his age he could have received a draft notice after turning eighteen in October 1944. His elder brothers, David, Wesley, and Ab, served; Ab, who later became a minister, was shot down over Germany and held prisoner for ten months until freed by the Russians.

But with war's end in 1945, the year Vickers finished high school, "All the boys came back from overseas. Anyone who had served in the army automatically had preferential treatment in the university over any new graduate from high school," he recalled. He was asked to wait two years to enter. Many young people with few means did find their way to college at the time. But "I just became impatient and said, well, I won't wait. . . . And so I went into the business world."[1]

As a follow-up to his Standard Brands yeast-selling days in Prince Albert, he had been asked to learn Spanish and set up a wholesale operation in Cuba for that company.[2] But he turned down that offer to become a fruit sorter and butcher boy at the Safeway, where he had worked summers in Prince Albert. In a year, he had worked his way up to store manager. Then F. W. Woolworth Co. offered him employment and for three and a half years transferred him "from one dirty store to the next," Vickers recalled.[3] Of giving up his hope for medical school, he said: "Maybe it was my own fault for not being a little more determined. . . . [But] I've always walked through doors that have opened and not tried to force ones that were closed."[4]

Woolworth used Vickers as a troubleshooter, "usually landed with the awkward branches and told to pull them together," he said.[5] Vickers has sometimes said he went first to Flin Flon, Manitoba, then to Port Arthur, Ontario, but others place him in Port Arthur in 1946, and he certainly was in Flin Flon in 1947. Be that as it may, he was sent to the small store in Port

Arthur (now Thunder Bay), in northwestern Ontario province, on Lake Superior. It was a lengthy thousand miles by rail from Toronto to the south. As assistant manager, his task was to clean up inventory theft and train new staff to replace those fired.

He joined the choir at First Baptist Church, whose organist, Alma Madill, put him in touch with the Bocking family; he rented a room from Lyle Louise Bocking, a fine contralto who sang at Trinity United Church. Vickers sang there as well. Her son Richard, then about sixteen, would study at the University of Manitoba in Winnipeg, remain friendly with Vickers, and become a CBC producer who worked with the tenor on two notable occasions. Richard recalled that Vickers's booming laugh could be heard all over the house, and that he was always singing.[6] This was a hallmark of the Vickers gift: Music was as much a part of him as blood and bones; it circulated through him always, and he could not help bursting out with it.

In fall of 1946 Vickers hired Winnifred Harpell to run the Woolworth notions counter. She turned seventeen that October and had just won the Canadian junior ladies tennis championship. She also was in the First Baptist choir, and Vickers often walked her home from practice. Dark-haired and petite, she was a mature teen, but the relationship wasn't passionate. She found Vickers to be full of fun and music. He enjoyed light opera at a time when, as Winnifred recalled, the popular *Oklahoma!* song "Everything's Up to Date in Kansas City" was considered racy, with its line "She's gone about as far as she can go." As they walked home on a night when brilliant stars filled the winter sky, Vickers, a religious-minded young man, told her, "When I was a little boy, my mother used to say the stars were the windows of heaven where the angels peep through."[7] Visiting the Bocking home with Vickers, Winnifred met Richard Bocking, whom she would marry in 1953.

Among the homes in which Vickers and his voice were welcome was that of respected lawyer Lloyd Seaman, whose daughters, Mary and Elizabeth, were musical. The family played host to visiting musical luminaries; the tenor Jan Peerce was one of those who gave concerts in their home. The Seaman daughters have no memory of this, but it's said that one Sunday afternoon when Vickers sang at their home, the guests included an Ontario chief justice from Toronto, James C. McRuer. The judge asked how the young man was furthering his singing career. Told that Vickers wasn't doing any such thing, McRuer said he would contact a friend, George Lambert, a baritone who taught at Toronto's Conservatory of Music (yet to be dubbed Royal). If this anecdote in a legal book is true, it may have been how Vickers first came to Lambert's attention.[8]

Elizabeth Seaman accompanied Vickers on the piano, and he went out with her for a time. Mary, a violinist, was one of the first women to encounter what would be a lifelong Vickers habit: lifting them into the air in a show of strength. At a picnic he came up behind Mary, a tall girl, grasped the belt of her slacks, and hoisted her off the ground with one arm. Mary recalled him as a bull of a young man.[9]

Woolworth also sent Vickers to what he later called "a funny little place." Flin Flon, northwest of Prince Albert, not only had a lively musical life but also was named for a fictional hero: one Joseph Flintabatty Flonatin, prospector. In *The Sunless City* he has adventures, rivaling any in Alberich's underground, in a realm of gold mountains ruled by women, from which he escapes via an extinct volcano. The prospectors who read this battered dime novel in a lonely Manitoba winter in 1915 named their rich ore claim "Flin Flon." A statue in Flin Flon that immortalizes this hero depicts him not as tall and dashing but rather as a short, stocky figure. The designer was the cartoonist Al Capp, best known as the creator of Li'l Abner, a character to whom Vickers later would compare Wagner's young Siegfried.[10]

The mining of minerals, including gold, copper, and zinc, was Flin Flon's chief industry, although it was served only by steam trains and small planes. No highways led there; the airport was built in the 1960s. But the mining drew workers from Central Europe, including Croats, Serbs, French, and Jews from various countries. Although Prince Albert had had a varied population especially in the war years, this was even more of an introduction to the world for Vickers, described as a naive young man at the time.[11] In this bustling town of twelve thousand, Vickers worked in the good-sized Woolworth store on Main Street, for a company that had codes for everything from dress to grammar. He was an assistant manager and general dogsbody, sweeping floors when necessary. James Goodman, a founder of the Flin Flon Glee Club, estimated that Vickers wouldn't have made more than thirty or thirty-five dollars a week at Woolworth. Miners made more; Goodman as an engineer for Hudson Bay Mining and Smelting Co., Ltd., took home about two hundred dollars monthly.[12]

Flin Flon had some fourteen churches, and Vickers joined two choirs, at the First Baptist Church, which he attended, and the United Church. "He'd sing one service [at United], then run down the hill a mile to sing at the other. We didn't have cars or buses," recalled Dorothy Young Liss. Her mother, Jean Young, was the first to publicly accompany Vickers when his boss at Woolworth invited him to sing at the Rotary Club. "Mother said she never heard a voice like it in her life." What Mrs. Young heard was a very baritonal Vickers. "He had been singing as a baritone. He didn't realize he was a tenor."[13]

Goodman recalled first hearing Vickers sing, as what Goodman also said was a baritone, in the old 480-seat Jubilee Hall, at a Glee Club practice.

"The windows seemed to be rattling, there was such a reverberation . . . from this young guy. He was singing a religious song, 'Night of Nights.' It sure rang the hall." Vickers was so good as a baritone, Goodman felt at the time, that it was a shame he was going for tenor parts.[14]

Vickers rarely publicly acknowledged it, but the club's production of *The Pirates of Penzance* was his first stage performance, on March 20, 21, and 22, 1947. He had turned twenty the previous October. It was an amateur production, put on by the club formed the previous November. Vickers's Mabel was Cecelia Sukke Allen, a married woman ten years his senior. A brunette of Norwegian-Swedish descent from a Saskatchewan farm, she was his first leading lady. When Vickers was learning the role of Frederic, the naive young pirate apprentice, he sang in head voice or falsetto on a B-flat. Doris E. Bell, the club's music director, had attended the Toronto Conservatory and sung with the Toronto Mendelssohn Choir. She was a curmudgeon, related Liss, and would have none of falsetto. "She said, 'Jon Vickers, you sing that note!' He said, 'I can't!' She said, 'You can!' So he sang it the way she wanted it."

In addition to discovering more about his top range, Vickers displayed his social charisma and growing attraction for women. After hitting that note, "To our astonishment he walked over to this person I called Mrs. Bell and put his arm around her and said, 'Oh, you're not mad at me, Doris!' Everyone almost fainted. Oddly enough, she seemed to like it," Dorothy Liss recalled.[15] Another Glee Club member, Kit Cole, recalled that Bell told Vickers he must leave and take singing lessons, because she recognized his gift.[16]

Ron Price, who played a pirate and worked on the production crew, also said that Vickers "at that time was a baritone who was able to sing tenor. And he could crack on a high note like anybody else." Price's wife, Jean, played piano for *Penzance* with Jean Young; their two pianos were the "orchestra."[17] These recollections of Vickers's singing baritone run directly counter to what Vickers himself has said: that he was always a tenor.

Dorothy Liss recalled that the *Penzance* cast and chorus had many big men, including a six-foot two-inch Pirate King. But when they were being measured for costumes, "Jon had a bigger chest than any of them." Vickers decided not to wear the first-act costume "because it made him look so bow-legged, which he was. It was the white stockings to the knee to which he objected. He was eventually outfitted in a pillbox hat, short double-breasted jacket, breeches, and knee-high boots." Those boots would be the first of many efforts to camouflage his legs for a better stage appearance. She was amused by the idea of "this little Baptist boy mixed up in that bunch of pirates, fellows from all over the world. They were miners, plumbers, businessmen, and not many read music." Vickers could read and was a quick study, but she didn't recall his playing the piano.[18]

Penzance has a song about sherry drinking, and on the first night a Hungarian cast member took a case of the real thing to the dressing room for all to partake. It was a hot evening, and the doors behind the stage were open. The odor of sherry wafted into the hall, but Liss is certain that Vickers, true to his upbringing, drank none of it. He never even smelled a cork, one of the men said. Her mother had invited him over on a night when she had a group of curlers there. They downed beer and whiskey, "and Jon got on famously with them. He had a way with people; he was never a snob. But he did not drink beer. He didn't apologize, he just didn't do it." Liss also recalled Vickers singing for a banquet of four hundred rowdy curlers in a gymnasium. He was able to bring them to stillness merely with his presence.[19]

Cecelia Allen recalled Vickers's having difficulty with high notes and clearly being unused to the stage. "He would turn his back to the audience," and she would correct him. "He took everything graciously," including her corrections.[20]

Vickers could be a cutup, and was one Saturday night when the *Penzance* principals gathered for an informal runthrough at the Price home. British-born drama director Dorothy Ash didn't like Vickers much. "She thought he sort of fancied himself. He gave that impression; he was a pretty sharp kid," Dorothy Liss said. Walking home that evening, she couldn't resist asking, "'Jonny, you know how Mrs. Ash feels about you. Why did you behave like that?' He said, 'You know, when somebody thinks I'm cocky and conceited, I really hate to disappoint them.'" But Dorothy, whose grandfather was a Presbyterian minister, saw his serious side and heard Vickers speak of his voice as he would in decades to come. "I always knew that he was so deeply religious in the best possible way. He was never vain. He felt his voice was a gift, that it was his responsibility to develop that talent as much as he possibly could."[21]

Goodman stepped in for a time to help direct *Penzance*, after Bell's husband died unexpectedly. Vickers had his own mind, but "if you would tell him a different way, he would try it out." He seemed to treat some of his music with Mabel as more of a solo than a duet. And Goodman recalled significantly, "We all knew he hated Wagner." Vickers then viewed heroic tenor music as "high-voiced screaming . . . he wasn't going to do it, to ruin his voice to be famous, to burn himself out. This was his attitude, we all knew that."[22]

Vickers found other entertainment in Flin Flon. He certainly attracted notice: "We all knew him. He was an eligible bachelor," recalled Joyce Guymer Henderson. She was a teenager when she saw Vickers at the town skating rink. "We used to skate as couples, round and round." He asked her to be his partner, among other girls, and Henderson recalled he wore his speed skates.[23]

Dorothy Liss and Vickers were chums, not really romantic. "But I don't think he took anybody else out" in Flin Flon, and they shared "a kiss here and there, probably." Vickers "was handsome, had a lot of blond curls, and was well built." She recalled his enthusiasm on a movie outing, and thought he hadn't seen many films. "I was so embarrassed. He was pounding my knee and jumping up and down like a three-year-old. I was hoping nobody thought he was with me. He was lots of fun," she recalled warmly. "You ran when you walked with him. He always ran, and he grabbed you by the hand and you'd run too."[24]

Cecelia Allen noticed that Vickers was "very gentlemanly. I think he was brought up in a very good Christian home. He did his parents proud . . . great morals he had. I wasn't a young girl, but I noticed him with the girls. He was nice to everybody." A number of them, she recalled, were extremely interested in the likeable young man. But he seemed far from ready for any serious romantic interests.[25]

Vickers soon moved on. Jim Goodman said Vickers made it clear when he left Flin Flon that his goal, whatever Woolworth might have in mind for him, was to study with "Jimmy Wood, J. Roberto Wood," in Winnipeg.[26] And that was his next teacher, in a town where Vickers would take a major step toward a singing career.

Transferred first to Winnipeg, then to Brandon, west of Winnipeg, Vickers continued to sing and cut a swath at the First Baptist Church in Brandon, where he never charged for singing, although other tenors did. He and the red-haired choir director and organist were much attracted to one another, church members recalled, although she was married. He had little money while working in Brandon, but scrimped so he could travel regularly back to Winnipeg for voice lessons with Wood, probably going the 145 miles by bus. Doris Hunt, a First Baptist member, recalled him as being seriously devoted to his singing. His voice was continually heard as he stocked the Woolworth basement.[27]

But his Woolworth bosses finally told him to stop singing at so many weddings, funerals, and other jobs and concentrate on his retail career.[28] Vickers decided he was tired of troubleshooting and felt exploited as a single man who could be relocated with little notice.[29] So with a bank balance of just $225, he sent his résumé to the Hudson Bay Company and in 1947 was hired by them to sell tools in the basement, back in Winnipeg, at $40 a week.

Vickers had talked with Dick Bocking, then a University of Manitoba agricultural economy student, about how he could make very good money if he worked his way up to manager with Woolworth. Given Vickers's excellent business head, it is indicative of how much his singing meant to him that he would quit the chain after putting in several hardworking years with it.

In 1947, in Canada's heartland, Winnipeg was a town of quite some musical sophistication, and James Robert Wood was among the best-known church music directors, joining Knox United Church in 1944. He was born in Scotland, but, as was the fashion, his name metamorphosed into Roberto after a trip to Italy, even as Edward Johnson, the Canadian tenor who later ran the Metropolitan Opera, had once become Eduardo Di Giovanni. Wood, an excellent baritone, was a CBC Radio soloist (Vickers probably had heard him) and did much concert work in western Canada.

Wood made Vickers a tenor soloist at Knox. In return he and his wife, Mary, an excellent organist and coach, gave him voice lessons, which normally cost two dollars, a large sum at the time. "It was a tradeoff," recalled Dorothy Liss, who visited Vickers with her husband there in March 1948.[30] Doris Bell also went to Winnipeg to be sure that Vickers met the right music people. "He was living on next to nothing, just scraping by," Liss said. Home was the big front room of an old house downtown, the kind where you might find a pulldown wall bed. The granddaughter of a woman who rented to Vickers said later, "He was the most conceited man. He always sang in the shower."

Choirs and ensembles led by Wood and his wife won many competitions, and the couple also were festival judges. Wood emphasized vocal production, placement, and technique, and urged young singers to gain a solid background before beginning a career.[31] That turned out to be exactly what Vickers did. In 1948 the Woods moved to Victoria, B.C., where they ran the First United Church choir and revived the Victoria music festival.

If Vickers had tuned in on March 12, 1948, he would have heard the Met radio broadcast of *Peter Grimes*, which had had its first production in the house on February 12, with Frederick Jagel as Grimes. (Regina Resnik, who later would be important to Vickers's career, was the first Ellen at the Met but did not sing the broadcast.)

Vickers's singing in the Hudson Bay Co. chorus at the store at Christmas probably helped attract the notice of another top church music man, Davidson Thomson, who had moved from Knox to Augustine United Church in a 1944 general shakeup. Also an insurance man, Thomson directed the Bay choir; its annual Christmas concert on the stairs of the elegant store's mezzanine was a popular holiday event, also broadcast on radio, then in its heyday.

But Vickers had yet to receive any money for his singing. His religious background had taught him he had a God-given talent, "and to be paid for it is unthinkable," he recalled. "It was an immense drama for me the first time I was ever paid to sing." At Knox, "I think they just decided because I was a person who didn't expect any money, and wouldn't think of taking it—they said, well, tenors were scarce—why not hire another one." Vickers didn't mind at first, "but with all modesty I don't think he was as good as I was. And he was given all the solos. I thought, well, you know, there's something wrong here."[32] That tenor was George Kent, a well-established singer who also became Knox choir director in fall of 1949 and said that he taught Vickers "Total eclipse" from Handel's *Samson*.

Thomson, with whom Vickers already was studying, had been asking the tenor to join Augustine, "and when this happened, I said, 'Okay, I'll be paid,' and I accepted my first paid job as a church soloist in Winnipeg." It was announced on December 10, 1949, in the Winnipeg newspaper. He was paid a mere three hundred dollars a year. But it took some immense wrestling with the idea that his first music money came "from the church of all places!"[33]

Young Jon found a home away from home at the handsome stone Augustine church, where he was welcomed by the Scottish-born choir director and baritone soloist Thomson, who was a friend of the conductor Sir Ernest MacMillan (who also had led Toronto's Conservatory of Music, which added Royal to its name in 1947). Jon sang solos from *Messiah*—"Comfort ye" and "Ev'ry valley"—and from *Elijah*, including "Then shall the righteous shine forth." And he was fussed over by the older women of the choir.

Stewart MacMillan Thomson, the youngest of Davidson Thomson's four children and four years younger than Vickers, recalled, "He was quite wonderful-looking in those days—a husky, square build, that blond, wavy hair. And he was a very nice fellow. It came from his background. He was right at home when he came into that atmosphere. He looked good and he spoke well . . . always a broad smile." Stewart had no recollection of Vickers's doing any proselytizing in those days. "He didn't flaunt [his religion] in any way. . . . But I think he was a serious person . . . a spiritual person."[34] Phyllis Cooke, who later married Stewart Thomson, was seventeen and new to the church choir. "I'd never seen anyone with such a big chest," she said of Vickers. "And the sound that came out of him—it would take the top of your head off." He was "focused, with huge energy and warmth." She felt, "He sings the way he is—highly spiritual."[35]

Vickers became a regular guest at the Thomson home at 584 Broadway, sharing Sunday dinners and visits to their camp on Lake Winnipeg. In later years he always boasted of having had only one teacher, in Toronto. But in addition to lessons from Wood, he had some studies with Thomson. Stewart, who became an architect but was immersed in music all his life, said his father taught Vickers perhaps once a week, at home in the front room. "It was vocal production," not just coaching. "I recall that when Jon would sing something like 'Comfort ye,' father would tell him, 'Put away your cloak and dagger. This isn't opera!' Jon was just inclined to dramatize it more than father thought Handel should be."[36] Perhaps Vickers still was emulating to some small extent those gospel singers who had so impressed his family in Prince Albert with their overt emotionalism. And it could be that Thomson planted seeds for the control that Vickers exercised in later years over some of the most dramatic roles in opera.

But the lessons next to the Thomson upright piano may have frustrated Vickers because of Thomson's insistence on vocal exercises rather than learning music. Thomson also was a moody and difficult man, by his children's accounts, peculiar and bombastic by others. "Jon was busting with dramatic energy," said Stewart. Davidson "tried to take the cutting edge off, but that didn't suit Jon. He didn't buy it for long." And Vickers was still trying to control his big voice. At one Augustine concert, "Jon just swamped the whole choir with his output. It kind of took the whole thing out of proportion. He hadn't learned to modulate it," Stewart recalled.[37]

However much in later years Vickers would downplay his early ambitions, he seemed in his twenties to be calculating how he might make a singing career. Another Thomson brother, Ed, thirteen years older than Vickers, recalled that Vickers voiced to Davidson his desire to sing at the Metropolitan Opera.[38] The Italian tenor Ferruccio Tagliavini, then singing principal roles at the Met, gave a Winnipeg concert, which Vickers attended. Later he recalled thinking, "Gosh, I'd like to be able to sing like that."[39]

Vickers also became acquainted with Kathleen Morrison, a busy soprano two years his junior who already had been chosen a "Singing Star of Tomorrow" in a Canadian national radio competition. She and her family were of the Scots Wee Free persuasion, strictly religious. She was also a Knox soloist and later became protocol chief for Manitoba Province. Kathleen, brunette and vivacious, said Vickers was a particular favorite of her mother, Louise; he seems to have appealed to many maternal instincts. He often was invited for dinner and enjoyed the plain home cooking. Characterizing her own relationship with him as "good friends," without denying a little romance, Kathleen viewed Vickers at the time as "very pure," a product of his upbringing. They had music in common and would often go out together, perhaps to a movie. Vickers didn't dance. "He was very good looking. You could tell he was a tenor 'cause he was short! However, there was no doubt about the voice, ever. The minute you heard him, you knew he could really sing."[40]

Kathleen was active with the Kelvin Grads Glee Club, formed in the early 1940s, which looked citywide for its singers. This group provided two significant opportunities for Vickers to gain more experience in light opera. First, he sang Nanki-Poo to Kathleen's Yum-Yum in a December 1948 production of *The Mikado* at the 4,200-seat Civic Auditorium, for four performances (December 9, 10, 11, also with a matinee on the 11th). The *Winnipeg Tribune* wrote that he was "a find. . . . He has a natural ease of manner and uses his lyric tenor voice with unusual skill for one so young. His wandering minstrel song was rendered with an unaffected sincerity."[41]

Vickers was still learning the range of his voice; Kathleen had helped him master high notes above G for the part. They would sit on her front veranda and the neighbors would have to listen as they practiced. "But we had no problems by the time we were in *Mikado*. It was there, and beautiful." Unlike his acquaintances in Flin Flon, she never thought he sounded baritonal. "I had sung with tenors, and there was a different tone in Jon's voice than a lyric baritone. It was a heavier sound." That would have been the young heldentenor in the making, which also may be what was heard in Flin Flon. "I felt Jon really knew what he could do, he just needed the opportunity to do it. And in Winnipeg he didn't always get that opportunity, other than in the church, with his teacher. I think Davidson Thomson knew the potential of the voice."[42]

Rene Hoole apparently was Vickers's first professional director, for *Mikado*. Born in England, Hoole taught high school English and French, was a school principal, and had sung many Gilbert and Sullivan comedy parts. Vickers, like the other leads, was chosen for his voice, but Hoole always hoped dramatic ability would manifest itself in his casts. "As it turned out, he was delightful to work with." Hoole, who also played Koko, insisted no mikes be used, "so they needed the ability to speak, to enunciate," and Vickers responded well, though all this was clearly new to him. Hoole also showed the tenor "how to turn, to balance the stage when two people were on it . . . in a duet, how to stand and change position, and embrace so as not to make the lady look awkward." Vickers was extremely eager to learn. Hoole tried to orchestrate Vickers's movement so his bowlegs wouldn't be emphasized in his tights. "But I never mentioned it. I didn't want to make him overconscious of it."[43]

Many Kelvin Grads who were studying music were convinced that Vickers would "make it big," as Kathleen said. "It was exciting to go to rehearsal and listen to him. Whenever he sang, everyone just stood and listened." Vickers was fun to work with, "and if there was a mistake, well, it was a mistake. He didn't worry about it in those days. He was a happy fellow, he really was. Then you used to read write-ups about how critical he was about everything. That wasn't the Jon we worked with."[44]

Almost a year later, in 1949, came the lead role of Captain Dick in *Naughty Marietta* and a major turning point: Vickers's meeting with Mary Morrison, Kathleen's elder sister. She was a soprano studying at the Royal Conservatory of Music in Toronto, having left Winnipeg at age seventeen in 1945. (She later married the Canadian composer Harry Freedman.) Mary, the Kelvin Grads' best-known young artist, was in Winnipeg for three weeks for *Marietta*, which ran November 15–19, 1949, at the 1,450-seat Playhouse Theater. She was the bouncy Italian contessa seeking to escape a forced marriage back home. Vickers played an American, the doughty Rangers chief, a man determined never to wed. Since the Nelson Eddy–Jeanette MacDonald movie in 1935, the Victor Herbert score had found renewed popularity, with its memorable "Tramp, Tramp, Tramp" (which includes a reference to a "Canuck," or Canadian), "Falling in Love with Someone" (the tenor's aria), and "Ah, Sweet Mystery of Life."

"What I remember very vividly [at the first rehearsal] was this really unique voice, like a diamond in the rough. You knew there was something very special there," Mary recalled. However, Vickers still lacked the music theory and piano background of many other singers his age. Mary was just twenty-three, like Vickers, but she was able to compare this tenor to the voices she was hearing in Toronto. "He was very concerned about the high notes because there's a C in it, if the tenor wants to take it, and there's a C for the soprano. But he was a little apprehensive about it. . . . We finally decided we would practice it and if it worked, it worked, if it didn't, he'd sing the A."[45]

Hoole recalled criticizing Vickers for using falsetto in "Someone." The *Winnipeg Tribune* called him "one of the most promising 'finds' in many seasons," adding that Vickers's "lyric tenor is rich and resonant and his speaking voice of fine clarity. He has improved tremendously as an actor as well and his duets with Miss Morrison were highlights. . . . Once in the final measures of *Ah, Sweet Mystery of Life* . . . and in his solo, *I'm Falling in Love,* could one find fault . . . when he resorts to falsetto to achieve the highest of tone[s], which as yet do not come easily to him."[46]

Kathleen had been married on September 3, 1949, and Mary had returned to Winnipeg to sing at the wedding, before *Marietta*. Kathleen recalled asking Vickers to come to their home and sing for Mary, "and as soon as she heard him, she said I think I should take a record back to Toronto." Mary didn't recall this meeting with Vickers but bowed to her sister's memory, so that could have been her first hearing of the tenor. Mary's recollection was that closer to her departure after *Marietta* she told Vickers he had great potential and should study seriously, and urged that he have a record made.

In those days of limited technology, it was difficult to make such a demo disk, and expensive. In fact, Winnipeg probably had only one studio where it could be done. Vickers recorded "Total eclipse" from Handel's *Samson* on one side of the disk, on the other "King ever glorious" from Stainer's *The Crucifixion*. Mary didn't recall just how Vickers got the record to her in Toronto, but she took it to the conservatory principal, Ettore Mazzoleni, who passed it to George Lambert.[47] Vickers waited and wondered, and in the meantime continued to sing. Christmas Day 1949 found him the soloist at the Augustine Church, in *Night of Nights* by B. Van de Water.

At some point in 1950 Lambert, who traveled around Canada as an examiner of students for the conservatory, auditioned Vickers in Winnipeg. The *Messiah* arias were on Vickers's list, and Lambert asked for them. "Mr. Lambert said he never saw anyone look so cross because [Vickers] didn't want to sing that music, it's so difficult," recalled Nan Shaw, who accompanied Lambert students in Toronto. "Anyway, he did, and Mr. Lambert gave him a scholarship." At five hundred dollars, it was "the big scholarship of the year."[48]

Vickers later portrayed his younger self as taking the scholarship for a lark. But all the evidence of his focused work in his church, concert, and light opera singing points to his faith in his own potential, and a strong desire to explore where it could lead him. Later, he admitted to "this terrible need to sing" at that time.[49] His final appearance in Winnipeg was at a concert at the Augustine Church in early fall 1950, to a packed audience.

The Kelvin Grads offered Vickers one more role after he had entered the Toronto Conservatory. Rene Hoole recalled being short a tenor when the group planned *The Student Prince* in 1952 or 1953. The operetta has roles for three tenors, but a Prince Karl Heinrich who could hit the necessary high Cs, with no mike, was a particular problem. Hoole sent a score to Vickers in Toronto. The tenor phoned a few days later to say that he would very much like to do it, but his teacher, Lambert, felt he had still not reached the stage where he should be singing those high notes, and that taking the role would be a mistake. "He was really not fully prepared at that time to sing in that range," said Hoole.[50]

In fact, the difficulty of that C would be an issue throughout Vickers's career, contributing to a number of decisions about the roles he would sing.

3

Beginnings at the Conservatory

I N THE 1950S THE OPERA WORLD WAS REGROUPING AFTER THE NIGHT-
mare of the World War II years. Change and opportunity would be the
watchwords of the decade. For Jon Vickers, the timing could not have
been better. He was able to learn from and work with many Europeans with
topflight musical credentials, and to take advantage of the demand for new
talent on both sides of the Atlantic.

A major change in leadership was under way in the autumn of 1950 at
the Metropolitan Opera: Rudolf Bing took the reins from Edward Johnson,
a Canadian who had been general manager, mediocre by some accounts,
for fifteen years after a prominent career as a tenor. Bing, that chilly, sharp-
tongued, but knowledgeable Viennese, fresh from Glyndebourne and Edinburgh, took on a myriad of problems both out front and backstage. But he
had a galaxy of golden voices to deploy: Kirsten Flagstad, Zinka Milanov,
Jussi Björling, Richard Tucker, and Leonard Warren were just a few (Lauritz
Melchior wasn't asked to return by Bing).

In London, onetime haberdasher David Webster had his own problems
at Covent Garden, still emerging from its war years as a candy wrapper–
strewn dance hall. Conductor Erich Kleiber arrived in 1950 to further
develop the first permanent opera company, with many fine voices. And in
1951 an awkward Australian filly named Joan Sutherland would first set foot
in England.

In Italy's houses, Maria Callas, who was singing Aida, Norma, Isolde,
and Kundry in Italian, was still new to La Scala but beginning to receive
the startling reviews that would become a crescendo of adulation. Renata
Tebaldi was the cool, established diva who would face off against Callas's
visceral style. Among the tenors of renown, Ramón Vinay was singing
Otello and Ludwig Suthaus was Tristan. Beniamino Gigli, Giacomo Lauri-
Volpi, Mario Del Monaco, and Giuseppe di Stefano led the Italian tenor
wing. Baritone Tito Gobbi was already a star of some magnitude. Young

Franco Corelli had lost his voice by overuse at school but would make his remarkable debut with Callas in 1954 at La Scala.

At Bayreuth, Richard Wagner's grandsons, Wieland and Wolfgang, had taken the festival's postwar helm, although the stains of Hitler connections would remain. Wieland in particular was working out the simpler, more human stagings of Wagner operas that would open to controversy in 1951.

Canada was far from the international music circuit, and a backwater in general, with a population of only about 13 million. A wartime *Punch* cartoon had portrayed a London woman asking what it was that C-A-N-A-D-A stood for on the armbands of certain soldiers from abroad. The lakeside city of Toronto was still very much a white, Anglo-Saxon, Protestant enclave of 1,200,000. Most of the immigration that was to transform it into a thriving cosmopolis was yet to come. Churchgoing was strong, and opera was in its infancy. The Royal Conservatory of Music (RCM) Opera School had been founded in 1946, and its opera company gave its first Opera Festival in 1950. The Canadian Opera Company soon grew from these roots, proudly recording words of encouragement from Mr. Bing, as he was known.[1]

And in the autumn of 1950, in the halls of the old brick Toronto Conservatory of Music, Jonathan Vickers, fresh from western Canada, was easy to spot. At twenty-five, he had blond curls standing up on his big head; his face was ruddy and his white teeth and dark blue eyes flashed. He frequently wore a favorite sweater of golden yellow, a color that did nothing to minimize his barrel chest and hugely muscled arms and shoulders. "You could hear him all over the place, whether he was laughing or singing," recalled Nan Shaw, the petite pianist who accompanied Vickers's lessons with George Lambert for most of his conservatory years. "He was very outgoing."[2]

The conservatory, founded in 1886, was a burgeoning music center in Toronto, with many faculty members who were born or had studied in Europe—in London, Leipzig, or Berlin. The conductor Ernest MacMillan, later Sir Ernest, was principal in the struggling 1930s. The school received its royal charter in 1947. The principal from 1945 to 1968 was Swiss-born, Oxford-educated Ettore Mazzoleni, who had been a protégé of Ralph Vaughan Williams. And the trustees' chairman from 1947 to his death in 1959 was that Canadian tenor Edward Johnson.

The cafeteria of the building at the corner of University and College (since demolished) was an egalitarian meeting spot for the students, a varied lot. Out of their numbers would come the pianist Glenn Gould, soprano Lois Marshall, bass-baritone Victor Braun, musical theater star Robert Goulet, and incandescent soprano Teresa Stratas, one of a handful of singers who would be on Vickers's artistic plane. "It was a marvelous place for cross-pollination," recalled the conductor Victor Feldbrill. In that cafeteria "a violinist would sit down with two singers, we exchanged ideas . . . it was a beehive of activity, an atmosphere that no longer exists," especially just after World War II, but continuing into the 1950s.

Feldbrill said of Vickers: "We used to think of him as sort of a cowboy from the west; he even spoke the way we associated with ranch-type guys. He had even then this squat body with a slightly bowlegged appearance, as if he had been riding horses. We saw him as a kind of a hayseed who had a marvelous voice. I don't think he tried to cover up [his background], put on any act."[3]

Vickers's years of business travels should have given him some sophistication. He was older than many students, and poor; dinner was often a box of Kraft macaroni and cheese, ten cents for two boxes, or a tin of tomato soup. And although he did not work during school hours as many students did, he had a variety of jobs afterward. One night job was backing brewery trucks into position so they would be ready to go in the morning. His character was clear when he told Nan Shaw, "If I had to do it, I decided I would be the best backer of all—and I was." She said loyally of such bravado, "I always thought of him as more confident than arrogant."[4]

For the first two summers in Toronto, he earned fifty-two dollars weekly as a night truckdriver for Carling and O'Keefe breweries, hauling empty bottles to their plants. Dr. G. Roy Fenwick, superintendent of music for the Ontario school system, arranged for him a soloist job at Glenview Presbyterian Church that paid five hundred dollars a year, as well as out-of-town concerts sponsored by the provincial education department.[5] The thirty concerts he sang in area high schools in 1950–51 constituted Vickers's first "tour."

Vickers lived for a time with his younger brother, Arthur, in a large residence on Yonge Street that housed the office of a Dr. Park, whose daughter Helen would become the first wife of their brother Ab.

Vickers won another scholarship for 1951–52, after that 1950–51 season. In spring 1951 Mazzoleni chose him to sing the demanding tenor solo in Bruckner's Te Deum, in its Canadian premiere (with the Symphony No. 9) in Massey Hall, with the RCM Symphony Orchestra. The other soloists on April 17 were Lois Marshall, Margaret Stilwell, and James Milligan, conducted by Mazzoleni (brother-in-law of MacMillan). MacMillan may well have heard Vickers for the first time in that work, and the tenor became a soloist with the Toronto Mendelssohn Choir, which MacMillan directed as well as being permanent conductor of the Toronto Symphony Orchestra.

The conservatory was a place to take classes but not to receive a degree. Vickers's RCM schedule in 1952 included twelve hours a week of music coaching; two language lessons weekly, covering French, German, and Italian; and weekly classes in fencing and stage deportment. Vickers described this schedule during an October 1952 visit to Prince Albert. He said under the so-called block system he was given perhaps twenty pieces of varied music to "just plough" through. His list that autumn included seven gypsy songs (probably Dvořák), three Irish ballads, four English folk songs, four French songs, and eighteen opera arias in three languages. He said he had completed work on that group in five weeks. Lambert also put him through major song cycles, including Beethoven's *An die ferne Geliebte* and Schubert's *Die Winterreise.*[6]

Because the conservatory at that time did not offer an academic curriculum, Vickers never studied the usual liberal arts subjects, other than languages, on the college level. He seems not to have taken any University of Toronto courses, being too busy with music lessons, concerts, and opera, and with earning money to support himself and later his family. His formal education, other than in music, consisted of his high school diploma from Prince Albert. But his lively mind, eager to delve below the surface of anything on which he focused, led him to become a lifelong autodidact. He read widely, especially in history, classic literature, philosophy, theology, and psychology. This was all food for the creation of his roles, as well as the building of his worldview.

Despite his lessons with Wood and Thomson in Winnipeg, Vickers made a point throughout his career that his sole teacher had been George Lambert, the conservatory faculty member who had auditioned him in Winnipeg. Lambert was an English baritone who had studied in Italy and arrived in Canada as an established opera and oratorio singer. A French student had called the distinguished Lambert "Papa," and, with that title anglicized, "Poppa" he became to everyone. He and Vickers hit it off, perhaps in part because both had large voices to contend with. The young singer plunged into Poppa's plan that he should learn as much music as possible.

Irving Guttman was a conservatory student from 1947 to 1952 and became Canada's major pioneering opera manager. He recalled that Lambert "was a dear old man, not a great teacher. But he never hurt anyone." Glenn Gould's Chilean teacher, Alberto Guerrero, said that Gould would have become famous regardless of whom he studied with, and that the same was true of two other RCM students, Vickers and the soprano Lois Marshall.[7] The baritones Victor Braun and Robert Goulet also studied with Lambert.

Lambert does seem to have helped Vickers to some extent. One of the first tasks was teaching the young tenor to handle his enormous sound and to produce the soft high notes at which critics later would marvel. "The thing that really helped him to tone down the voice was studying the narrator's [Evangelist] part in the *St. Matthew Passion*," Shaw said. "He sweated gumdrops over that, they both did, but he got it, so he could sing those high notes softly." Some falsetto entered into those notes: "It was a mixture," she recalled.[8]

Vickers had an excellent ear and was like a piece of blotting paper, Lambert was fond of saying. He soaked up everything Lambert had to teach, and both men liked to work hard. Vickers's ferocious concentration was apparent even then. When he arrived for his lessons, he was always exact about what he wanted to work on: "This is what I have prepared," he would say, unlike many other young musicians who lacked specific goals. Vickers's business background must have been helpful in giving him the maturity to meet these new challenges. "Jon was a fine person," Lambert recalled. "He was honest, dependable. He had this very strong characteristic, that he knew what he was going to do. And you didn't butt him. Perhaps you might steer him."[9] And Vickers said that when he first met Lambert, "I told him, 'The moment you think I have reached a limit, let me know. I have no intention of beating my head against the wall if there are limitations to my voice. Tell me at once and I'll pack it in.'"[10]

Oddly, Lambert rarely went to hear his students sing and had nothing to do with the opera world. "He said, 'I prepare them in the studio, that's all I want to know,'" recalled Ezra Schabas, then the conservatory concert bureau manager.[11]

Ian Garratt, a tenor also at the RCM in the 1950s, said that Vickers would grab Shaw or any other accompanist he saw free to play for him, even if just for ten or fifteen minutes. "He had an insatiable appetite to learn the roles, to practice his songs. Very few people have the sort of drive that I saw with him. . . . Stratas was the only other one there who had the drive and determination that nothing would ever have stopped them from pursuing their goals."[12]

The vocal coach and writer Stuart Hamilton was a Regina, Saskatchewan, native who went to the conservatory in 1948, studying piano. He recalled sitting in the school lobby one day when Vickers came up to him with, "Hey, you, you play the piano, don't you?" He wanted to work on the *St. Matthew Passion*. "He was very brusque. Even before he was anybody, he scared everybody to death." Hamilton wouldn't have dared say no. "He was loud, he would yell, he was constantly asserting himself in a way that made people afraid of him." This Hamilton attributed to the fact that "he was a hick from the prairies, like I was." The assertive personality was his way of dealing with feelings of inferiority.[13]

Before he arrived in Toronto, Vickers's music training had been minimal, hardly extending beyond his church choir work and the operetta appearances. He could play the piano just well enough to work on his own music. Despite hearing those Met broadcasts, he must have lacked a full conception of the huge international panorama of opera and the song literature before arriving at the conservatory. There was much to learn, and he recognized that. Later he often spoke of the awe that the conservatory library inspired in him, of the "privilege" of just being able to look at the score of Bach's *St. Matthew Passion*.[14]

There seems to have been recognition from the beginning of his conservatory years that the Vickers voice was special. Other students would listen outside the studio to hear him, and often Poppa would be singing along. Nan Shaw recalled that the voice was "really tenor, an exciting sound, but awfully big. It was simply huge. So one of his main problems was to get it toned down. Now, a lot of the other singers had big voices. They loved to shout. He didn't do that. It was just big."[15] Leo Barkin, a good friend of Lambert's who accompanied Vickers in a number of recitals, was struck by the evenness of his range. "Forget artistry—he was very young. But his range was so even—the low notes as full and firm" as the high notes. Many dramatic tenors have this solidity in one part of the range, but few have it throughout. "It was a natural thing, nothing to do with teaching," said Barkin.[16]

Nicholas (Niki) Goldschmidt, the first music director both of the Conservatory Opera School and of the CBC Opera and Festival Opera Association, was to become a close friend of Vickers's. Early on, he was struck by the warm quality of the voice, in spite of its magnitude. As the years went on, Goldschmidt continued to find this quality unique among heldentenor voices past and present.[17] He had the opportunity to see it at work as early as 1955 and 1956, when he coached Vickers in his first Wagner parts for the CBC Opera—the first act of *Die Walküre* and the third act of *Parsifal*. However, Morley Meredith, the Winnipeg-born baritone who went on to a Metropolitan Opera career, echoed friends of Vickers's in earlier days when he said the tenor had studied low-voice roles at the conservatory. Vickers, he said, made a transition to tenor with Lambert.[18] The Canadian mezzo-soprano Maureen Forrester recalled, "I always thought he sounded like a baritone in the tenor range."[19]

The voice was big, but Vickers was smart enough to turn down *Otello* when it was offered in 1952 by the CBC. He did agree to cover the part and do some rehearsals; he needed the hundred-dollar understudy fee. And he learned the entire opera, probably already having an inkling of its future importance to him.[20]

On February 27, 1952, CBC Radio's Wednesday night program presented *Peter Grimes,* which had premiered in London in June 1945. William Morton, from Vancouver, was the fisherman. Vickers sang in the chorus of townsfolk for this, his first experience with the work. He thought Morton was excellent, and even then was struck by the contradiction of the brutish Grimes singing lines of such poetry as the "Great Bear and Pleiades" in the Pub Scene. He ruminated on this over the years, and it seems fair to judge that he had filed it away as a role he wanted for himself.

In his Toronto years, then, he began a singer's always difficult process of discovering which roles were right for him. In February 1954, for instance, he sang the Duke in *Rigoletto* for the Toronto Opera Festival, a tricky high part he would never do later. He tested himself in *Tosca, Il Trovatore, Così fan tutte, Manon Lescaut,* and more operas for which he decided he was unsuited. Lambert warned his voice wouldn't mature till he was thirty, at least.

His acting was striking even in those early days, building on the basics he had picked up out west. On August 1, 1954, he appeared on television in *Down in the Valley,* a short Kurt Weill piece based on that folk song. His role was that of a cowboy unjustly jailed for a murder, and observers recalled that he lit up on stage, even made them shiver. "He did it a little bit like he did Peter Grimes," recalled Franz Kraemer, a CBC producer who told the author he had been Alban Berg's last composition pupil. "He's sort of a hero, a bit like *Fidelio.* He was excellent." This hero was a victim in the end, like Grimes.[21]

Kraemer placed Vickers in a category with Stratas and Callas as singers who had inherent and very individual vocal problems. "They had to come to the top by using their voices the right way [for them], and nobody could tell them how to do it, because nobody else would sing that way. The line, the breathing, everything has to be adjusted. Stratas had faults on the top, Callas had faults on the top." To Kraemer, Vickers's problem had to do with the fact that "the voice came too late to sing opera," and that he had sung too much oratorio, with its declamatory style. "To sing bel canto, which he tried to do, was very difficult. So he adjusted, and in the end, he had to adjust more and more."[22]

Nan Shaw retains her most indelible picture of Vickers in the studio with Lambert: "He would plank his feet down, put his hands onto the back of the grand piano—he always held on to the piano, leaning across looking at me—and fill up and nearly blow me out of the studio. He always sang holding onto the piano. He did it like he was milking a cow.

"He was a very quick study, a very quick ear for languages," Shaw recalled. "The first time he came back [to Toronto], he was speaking German fluently." His sightreading was good, and he played the piano well enough to help himself: "I remember walking into the studio and he was playing and singing lieder."[23]

Like Meredith, Robert Goulet, the American-born baritone who went to the conservatory in 1953 on scholarship, insisted that Vickers was a high baritone when he began at the school. "He wanted to work himself up so he could become a tenor. . . . Everybody knew that. . . . He looked like a lumberjack, he was built like a bull, and he didn't smile too much. He was always very serious about his craft."

Goulet was backstage calling lighting cues for *La Traviata*, a February 1955 production with Vickers as Alfredo and James Milligan as Germont. "At the end of the second act, Jon had a high A-flat. He was nervous, and he cracked. Milligan, who had a glorious voice, was supposed to sing the same note. As Jon walked off, Jimmy took the A-flat, and the place erupted. So Jon, I figured, that was the end of his career, after the baritone showed him how to do it."[24]

Milligan's wife, Edith, said Milligan had an alternative A-flat marked in his score and usually took it. Edith maintained that Vickers was always a tenor.[25]

During the Royal Conservatory years, Vickers met Henrietta Elsie Outerbridge, a child of missionaries with Saskatchewan ties, but also associated with the more exotic climates of Bermuda and China. Petite, shorter than Vickers, Hetti was very pretty, with wide-spaced blue eyes and a ravishingly warm smile. Her long dark hair was worn in a bun or braided coronet, echoing her own mother's and the long hair Vickers's mother had kept. For two years Hetti had studied medicine, the field Jon had once hoped for, with the idea of becoming a medical artist. She taught English and art at the Forest Hill Collegiate Institute.

Vickers first heard of her through friends. James Milligan was another conservatory student destined for Covent Garden, but in 1961, when he was thirty-three, a highly promising career was cut short by his sudden death in Switzerland from a heart condition. Milligan sang often with Vickers at concerts and in the Toronto Festival operas. In 1951 he married another RCM student, Edith Scott, a pianist and singer who became a respected educator. During the summer of 1952, Vickers would drive to visit them in Algonquin Park, where they worked as music counselors at the Taylor Statten Camps.

Edith recalled it as a fair trip through the park, with many steep roads. "Jon never could take hills, he can't take elevators. He's had problems with that all his life, turns his stomach inside out. He had bought himself a second-hand Chrysler, I think, a '48 or '49, a fairly big car. And he took those roads as fast as he possibly could, because he felt that the faster he went, the more he had to concentrate, the less vertigo. When he arrived, he would be absolutely white, just green-white from this trip."

The friends stayed on a small island apart from the camp, where the waterfront instructor, William Outerbridge, became a good friend of the Milligans. Edith recalled, "We were the only cottage on the island. And we'd have a bonfire, put on a great big pot of coffee and drink it till the middle of the night, talk philosophy and religion. On one of those occasions, when Jon was up, Bill said to him, 'You should meet my cousin Hetti. I betcha you'd really hit it off.'" Edith didn't recall Vickers seeing any other young women around that time. "Because during the 51–52 season, and 52–53 season, part of it, when Jim was [singing] in Montreal, Jon was often over at the apartment, my place. He'd take me to a movie, go for a walk, shopping and so on." Vickers also may have learned of Hetti through her friend Patricia Wickstrom, who was at the conservatory and played piano, and who later would marry Hetti's brother, Ian.

It was probably in the autumn of 1952 that Jon and Hetti finally met in Toronto. And it was obvious, Edith recalled, "that there was nothing else, just the two of them" after that. Hetti wasn't involved with anyone, and Edith was quite sure Vickers still was not.[26]

Hetti's paternal family was one of the earliest British families of Bermuda, a line of shipbuilders and traders that was part of a huge clan with many branches and many prominent island leaders. Her father, descended from patriarch Joseph John Outerbridge, was Dr. Leonard Mallory Outerbridge, a minister of the United Church of Canada, then of Lennoxville, Quebec. Born in Longford, in Warwick parish, Bermuda, Leonard was educated at Wabash College, in Indiana, and studied theology at Queen's University, Kingston, Ontario. He later got his master's and doctorate at the University of Chicago, where he studied religion and philosophy related to the Far East. He was ordained in 1925, and in June that year married Christena Henrietta Martyn, known as Tena, one of thirteen children of John B. and Henrietta Effie McIver Martyn, a Ripley, Ontario, couple. John was in several businesses, including selling Singer sewing machines and pianos and running undertaking and millinery establishments. Tena, a Queen's University graduate, was a high school teacher and principal in Ripley.

Shortly after the wedding, the couple sailed for China to work with northwestern rural churches. Also a botanist, Leonard helped develop strains of cold-resistant corn and rice to ease the hunger of the Chinese.[27] They arrived as the rise of the Nationalists led to attacks on the missionary establishment as representatives of imperialism. Outerbridge traveled widely in China, but he and his family had to flee from the interior in 1927 when foreigners came under attack.

And so Henrietta was born in an open cattle boxcar on a train on April 7, 1927. Behind them, another child of Leonard and Christena, a daughter named Lydia, had died, possibly killed by a household servant. Christena went into shock and gave birth prematurely. The family finally reached Beijing, which Hetti listed as her birthplace. In 1929 Hetti's brother, Ian Worrall Outerbridge, was born, also in China; he would become a well-known Toronto corporate lawyer who often dealt with Jon Vickers's business affairs. A couple of years later, the family returned to Canada.

In 1940 Dr. Outerbridge became minister of Metropolitan United Church in Regina, Saskatchewan, and his family lived in Moose Jaw for some time. This meant that Hetti and Jon, in their teen years, had lived in that province during the same six years in the 1940s. Hetti (the shortened name began as Hettie, before she dropped the *e*) had learned Chinese as her first language from servants who cared for her while her parents were working, and she was teased as a child in Canada because at first her English was not very good.[28] Leonard also was an aircraft carrier chaplain in World War II, returned to China in 1949 and eventually received the highest honor from Chiang Kai-Shek. He later wrote a column on religion for the *Toronto Globe & Mail*.

Hetti's was an excellent background for her husband's constant travels. "I had that sort of life before I married," she said in 1959. "We were always on the move."[29] A Forest Hill yearbook lists her as educated in Beijing, Boston, Bermuda, New York, Cheyenne (Wyoming), Regina, Vancouver, and Toronto. She received a bachelor of arts degree from the University of British Columbia, Vancouver; back in the Toronto area, she taught at Port Credit High School in Spadina in 1950 and then at Forest Hill. In 1952 she was paid $3,700 annually and listed by the Ontario Department of Education as an assistant principal with a specialty in arts and crafts. Forest Hill's student body was almost entirely Jewish; Hetti was extremely popular with the students and brought a spark to her teaching. She was outgoing, energetic, and full of joie de vivre, and she dressed in a bright, theatrical, but smart fashion.

Her colleagues knew of her relationship with the blond music student from Saskatchewan. In the women teachers' lunch room, "her face lit up when she talked about him," recalled May Hambly, another Forest Hill teacher. Vickers attended school picnics, and Hambly recalled him as "huge through the shoulders" and batting brilliantly in the baseball games. On occasion he would break into a snatch of opera during play.[30] Jon and Hetti double-dated with his brother Arthur and Arthur's future wife, Lillian Senick, from Saskatoon.

The couple wasted no time in marrying. On July 31, 1953, George Lambert sang at their wedding in Timothy Eaton Memorial Church—"Jesus, the Very Thought of You," written by Eric Thiman in 1926, the year of Vickers's birth. Hetti's father performed the ceremony, and an Outer-bridge uncle gave her away. The bride wore ivory taffeta and carried a Bible and orchid. Arthur Vickers was best man, Albert Vickers an usher. Hetti's brother, Ian, also was a newlywed, having married Pat Wickstrom on June 18. The honeymoon trip took Jon and Hetti to the Prince Albert area, visiting friends along the way, driving up in a big black Packard. They stopped to see the Bocking family, with whom Vickers had roomed in Port Arthur. Dick Bocking and Winnifred were to wed in early August, and Jon, in a naively proud gesture, brought out Hetti's wedding gown for them to admire.[31]

Vickers had a fondness for a Bing Crosby song, "Welcome to My Dreams." "It's a sentimental song, but it's a very beautiful little song that Bing Crosby sang in this movie around the time I met my wife," he recalled. (Actually, it was from a 1945 movie, a Klondike caper titled *The Road to Utopia*.) "And I like to think that my wife and my own relationship is one that is still full of lots of romance." But when they met and married, "I had nothing else to welcome her with, because my dreams were all that I had."[32]

Their apartment at 65 Crescent Road, in a pleasant residential area, was described by Vickers as a garret, and there was little money for decorating. But the couple's furniture included attractive pieces from Hetti's family, such as two beautiful Chinese rugs and black lacquer furniture. Hetti's artistic flair was announced by the rainbow painting she did on their front door at the top of the stairs. A number of her paintings, some of flowers, adorned the apartment, along with other art. Candles were much used, in an atmosphere guests called romantic.[33]

Vickers keyed remembrance of those days to another piece of music. "The people down below had a tape recorder or a record player, and we didn't have one. Every once in a while we'd hear 'Jesu, Joy of Man's Desiring,' and it had a very special sort of quality to it, a spirituality. . . . My wife and I were compelled many times to stop and just sit on the stairs and listen to it play." Later they found it was played by the Romanian pianist Dinu Lipatti, who died at age thirty-three in 1950.[34]

May Hambly recalled that when Hetti was pregnant in 1954 with her first child, Allison, her husband encouraged her to wear a bright red maternity dress, at a time when expectant mothers stuck to concealing navy and black. He told her, "Everybody knows you're pregnant, so you might as well be happy about it and show off."[35] Hetti taught well into her first pregnancy, though it wasn't long before then that teachers who married had to quit. Friends believed that Hetti's family, while not rich, must have helped the young couple financially. She was making $3,900 by the end of 1953, while Jon struggled with his classes and part-time jobs.

Jon and Hetti were a perfect match, by all accounts. Teresa Stratas, a frequent Vickers stage partner, said later, "Theirs was one of the great love stories of our time." The soprano remembered Hetti's beauty and simplicity, the clarity in her blue eyes: "She was a spectacular human being."[36] Hetti was warm, sweet, and devoted to her husband and children, as had been Vickers's mother. She and Jon saw eye to eye on religious and moral matters. She also was intelligent and strong-minded enough to damp down some of his angry moments.

As his father's had been, Vickers's household was a patriarchal one. "Don't think that Hetti ruled the house. Jon ruled the house and set the standards," recalled the English baritone Peter Glossop. "Hetti was a sweet woman who went along with Jon, and if he said, 'I want it to be this way when I'm gone,' she would ensure that it was that way. She would say, 'This is your father's wish, that you should not be in later than ten o'clock, and I cannot go against your father's wishes.'"[37]

Hetti continued to paint, and she broadened her husband's interests to include art. He admired her scholarly father and developed an interest in the great Chinese writings, among his voracious reading habits. She also handled her husband's business and investment dealings, all on instruction from him via phone when he was away. And she took a deep interest in his background preparations for his roles. Although not a musician, she readily discussed the characterizations so vital to him. He might be having a talk with his agent at home, and Hetti would sit in a corner knitting, piping up once in a while with her insightful comments. He often deferred to her, and he always listened, which was far from the case with others trying to give him advice. The soprano Roberta Knie recalled Hetti as "lovely, independent, incredibly intelligent." Jon, she said, "was terribly [male] chauvinistic, and when he'd get on one of his [rants], Hetti and I would literally tease him out of it."[38] But Hetti would not be heard from in public in the years to come. She did no interviews; when her husband talked with journalists at their homes on occasion, she was not part of the on-record conversations but supplied tea and cookies. Only a few comments from her saw print.

Her husband was fond of surprising Hetti with gifts (something he also did with friends). She loved shoes, and he once had a particular style that she liked delivered in every color. He also surprised her with an expensive diamond ring from Garrard's in London. He was a romantic in his personal life, and the gifts also were thank-yous for all her support, for the arduous time she spent on the road with him, for her frequent times alone, for the five children she bore him.

She was "the perfect opera wife," recalled Covent Garden's Sir John Tooley. She endured much when her husband was fighting his many artistic and financial battles. But she was supportive, knew when it was best to let him get his temper out of his system, and unlike some opera spouses, was "never in the wrong place at the wrong moment, but always in the right place at the right time. She just knew when to be there and when not to be there," said Tooley.[39]

"She was the most wonderful, warm woman," recalled John Miller, former executive director of the Canadian Music Centre. He summed up what most saw as a major ingredient of the relationship: "The thing that struck me was how often she was kind of an antidote to Jon's brusqueness." He recalled walking with the couple on the Upper West Side of New York, near the Met. "Jon was full of beans and energy and aggression and he walked on way ahead," through the winter slush. "She said, 'Just let him be, he'll be absolutely fine.' She was so absolutely calm and collected, no matter what situation Jon was in, a constant contrast to Jon's energy and forthrightness. And I was always struck with Jon's tenderness toward her. I never heard him speak brusquely or any way other than with tenderness and great affection to her. With Jon, you could always misinterpret his style, always think he was angry with you." The impression was that "he had little time to spend with you, that you weren't the most important thing happening with him. I don't believe that was the case with him at all, it was just his style. She, on the other hand, would always inquire how you were, with one or two questions about your activities. He quickly came right to the point, with no flowery minutes. It was a constitutional difference between their two styles. But underlying it all was their love and his tenderness for her. It was quite wonderful to see."[40]

Vickers was indeed lucky in his wife. Miller's analysis of the relationship held true for the thirty-eight years of their marriage, during which Hetti's calm would be greatly tested.

4

A Tenor in Toronto

Y THE TIME OF HIS MARRIAGE, VICKERS HAD HAD A FALLING OUT
with his good friend and colleague James Milligan. Milligan's wife
believed that, for some reason she never knew, Vickers spread word
that Milligan was difficult to deal with, and this false report dried up jobs
Milligan might have had in Stratford and London, Ontario. She recalled
that the Milligans were not invited to Vickers's wedding, although a newspaper clipping lists Milligan as an usher.[1] The estrangement didn't last, but
is notable as one of a series of instances of coldness to friends and acquaintances that dotted Vickers's life. Such episodes seemed to stem from self-
centeredness, an oversensitivity to the demands of his own image, and his
long memory for slights, real or imagined—traits to which he would never
admit.

Despite his busy life of lessons and singing jobs, Vickers nevertheless
continued to display the warm, kind side of his personality to his conservatory teachers and fellow students. He always enjoyed large automobiles and
somehow usually managed to own one, however old, during his student
years. It was his pleasure to drive any who needed a lift in his Chrysler. Nan
Shaw recalled that frequently he would go home for dinner, then return to
the school to drive home those who might be working late, although as he
sped off they might pray for a safe arrival.[2] Mary Morrison recalled Vickers
driving her and other competitors to the semifinals of the prestigious Montreal singing competition, Nos Futures Étoiles (Our Future Stars). "Jon had
a big car, and we just laughed from the minute we got into it. Here we all
were going to compete against each other, but we had a splendid time! I
remember Jon as being great fun. . . . That was at a time when none of the
rest of us had cars."[3]

The story of Vickers's winning of a major national singing contest dis-
plays his business shrewdness and his willingness to gamble on his future. On
January 20, 1952, he was none too happy about taking only an honorable
mention in Toronto's Singing Stars of Tomorrow, a popular CBC national

radio competition. (It ran from 1943 to 1956, lucky timing again for Vickers.) But on April 13 he became a semifinalist, winning $500 as second male voice winner, and a place in the Grand Award broadcast on April 20. However, he also was a semifinalist for Nos Futures Étoiles, the French version in Montreal, with a $500 prize, also on April 20; it had the added attraction of a six-month CBC Radio contract, beginning in October, for about $125 weekly. Vickers cannily sought to do both, by entering a taped aria for Toronto so he could go to Montreal. But Singing Stars officials threw cold water on that idea. They suggested, in the Canadian way of discouraging striving for success, that it was vain of Vickers to try such a ploy.[4]

So Vickers gave up the Toronto finals, and a possible $500 top soloist prize (he did get $100 as a semifinalist). He knew it was his last chance for that competition, as the next season he would be older than the maximum age (he turned twenty-six on October 29, 1952). He went to Montreal to sing "O Paradis" from Meyerbeer's *L'Africaine* and Tosti's "Mattinata," and he won. The prize included a recital, for which he got another $500, and an audition in Montreal by the Metropolitan Opera's Rudolf Bing. On May 31 Vickers sang Walther von Stolzing's Prize Song from *Die Meistersinger*, Federico's Lament from Cilea's *L'Arlesiana*, and "O Paradis."

Bing's report: "Good material, not quite even and too 'ingolata'—top problematic; highest note he sings is A, and this is not well-produced. Sang later *O Paradiso* with B-flat which he produced badly." The Italian *ingolata* means the sound is produced back in the throat, not desirable in a voice. Bing wrote to Vickers: "You have a very heavy dramatic voice, but are three or four years too young to really concentrate on the heavy dramatic roles." Nevertheless, he commended Vickers on his stage bearing, personality, and powers of interpretation.[5]

Vickers benefited from good timing, as Toronto's first Opera Festival was organized in 1950, the year he arrived at the conservatory. The conservatory senior school and the Opera School collaborated for a highly successful eight days, offering *Don Giovanni*, *Rigoletto* and *La Bohème* at the Royal Alexandra Theatre. Nicholas Goldschmidt conducted, and Herman Geiger-Torel directed. By 1954 the Opera Festival Company of Toronto was fully professional and under Ettore Mazzoleni's direction. In 1959 it became the Canadian Opera Company and established a touring company, taking opera to parts of Canada and the U.S. where it was generally unknown.

In addition to his schoolwork and CBC and festival performances, Vickers had a hectic schedule of appearances with churches, orchestras, and choral groups of all sizes, as well as organizations such as Rotary Clubs, businesswomen's clubs, music clubs, and community groups in many parts of Canada. Ian Garratt recalled that Vickers was able to command a fee of one hundred dollars for church solos, quite high for that time.[6] Although the chief purpose was to earn a living, Vickers also was gaining experience in all kinds of musical circumstances. Churches had to be reminded to tune cranky upright pianos. Often he would sing several days in a row after tiring travel on trains and small planes. (The American mezzo Risë Stevens recalled meeting Vickers on such a train during a tour; he recognized her and gallantly offered her a seat in the dining car.) If it was a local concert, he might not arrive home till close to midnight. Hetti awaited him with a steak dinner.

Vickers's out-of-town jobs were arranged chiefly through the conservatory's Concert and Placement Bureau, which solicited and planned extensively for its best students. Vickers was often recommended as being of the caliber of Milligan and Lois Marshall. Sometimes he would sing alone, sometimes in a joint recital with a soprano. The bureau took a 10 percent commission. Singers set their own fees according to size of the hall and potential audience, said Ezra Schabas, the future MacMillan biographer who ran the bureau in the 1950s.[7] The fees covered travel, hotels, meals, and sometimes an accompanist's fee. Vickers's price in 1953 was basically three hundred dollars, but he suggested four hundred for a Flin Flon concert, the town being difficult to reach, as he well knew from his Woolworth days there.

Schabas wrote countless letters to secure bookings for Vickers, and these show that the tenor sometimes would ask for 60 percent of the gross receipts, sometimes for a fifty-fifty split, with a minimum guarantee. These letters frequently seemed to apologize for asking high fees, stating that Schabas was just passing on Vickers's demands. A 1953 western tour grossed just $2,397 for eleven stops, with Vickers's fees ranging from $300 down to $100. He would receive checks for odd amounts such as $212.85.

In 1955 he was being billed by the concert bureau as the "leading tenor at the Toronto Opera Festival now for some years," or "perhaps Canada's leading tenor." But he still was getting fees of $75 or $100 from churches or small orchestras closer to Toronto, and perhaps $150 for a *Messiah*.[8] It is easy to see how Vickers and his wife would feel they were living hand to mouth, waiting for the next job or check. Yet this was true for many young singers.

Vickers's recital repertoire in 1952 and 1953, when he was often accompanied by Earle Moss, included ballads such as "Must I Go Bound," "Lord Randal," and "A Ballinure Ballad"; Beethoven's "Adelaide" and "I Love Thee"; the Dvořák Gypsy Songs; Federico's Lament from *L'Arlesiana;* French songs, such as Fauré's "Lydia" and Massenet's "Ouvre tes yeux bleus"; and

"Total eclipse," with the preceding recitative, "O loss of sight," from Handel's *Samson*. In later years, probably because he was so busy learning major opera roles, Vickers tended to cling to many pieces for his concerts that he had sung in his student days.

A program he sang at Baltimore's Peabody Conservatory of Music on April 15, 1953, is typical, and much of it would be repeated in Vickers concerts into the 1980s. He began with five Scarlatti songs (which he would record in 1969): "Difesa non ha," "La speranza," "O, dolcissima speranza," "Cara e dolce," and "Toglietemi la vita ancor." Then he offered four Purcell songs arranged by Britten: "If music be the food of love," "There's not a swain of the plain," "Not all my torments," and "Man is for the woman made." These would be sweet fillers for recitals after his career began in earnest, and the type of song criticized as a waste of his more serious talents. There is, however, delight to be found in hearing this big voice negotiate their turns and twists. (The Scarlatti and the Purcell would open his 1967 Carnegie Hall recital.) Then came Beethoven's "Song of Penitence" and "Adelaide," followed by the Flower Song from *Carmen*. The pièce de résistance was Janáček's erotic *The Diary of One Who Vanished* (Vickers also sang it on the CBC International Service). Wrapping it up were Roger Quilter's "Go, Lovely Rose" and "Fair House of Joy," and two Vaughan Williams songs that became particular Vickers favorites, "Bright Is the Ring of Words" from *Songs of Travel* and "Song of the Road" from the opera *Hugh the Drover*.

In 1955 he was singing Don José's Flower Song, in French, and "Vesti la giubba" from *Pagliacci*. His sacred repertoire was large, including "In native worth" from Haydn's *Creation* and Dvořák's "Hear my prayer, O Lord." In the same year some churches were told by the bureau that while Vickers had Handel's "Deeper and deeper still" from *Jephtha* and Mendelssohn's "Be thou faithful unto death" from *St. Paul* on his list of selections, he was "not anxious to do [them] first thing in the morning." A recital at St. Paul's in Prince Albert that year included four spirituals (two were "Deep River" and "I Got a Robe").

In 1953, of a November recital at the Toronto Art Gallery, John Kraglund wrote of the "ringing lyric quality" of Vickers's voice and said his oratorio training had served him well in the *Samson* arias (not "Total eclipse"). But the critic suggested that Vickers was not yet familiar enough with the demands of opera arias. The *Rigoletto* arias "Questa o quella" and "La donna e mobilè" showed "a tendency to force high notes and slip over coloratura passages."[9]

Vickers repeated many times in later years that his leap to fame was made from a solid foundation. He had learned his trade in Canada, where he had sung thirty-two oratorios and twenty-eight operas and given five hundred concerts. "Playing a series of one-night stands, in a state of exhaustion, with a third-rate conductor and a fifth-rate orchestra—and I don't mean the Toronto Symphony or the CBC—after that, it's no problem at all to sing with first-raters. But without that backlog of experience, I'd never have been able to stand the pressure. It's like a ski jump. If you go off the big jump without experience, you break your neck. You have to do lots of small ones first," he said six years after leaving Canada.[10]

Relatives of Hetti's in Bermuda made it possible for Vickers to sing a few concerts there about 1955, in a small hall of three hundred to four hundred seats. The pianist and future conductor Mario Bernardi accompanied him. Closer to home, Vickers sang a number of engagements in Buffalo, New York, just across Lake Erie from Toronto, including Handel's *Samson* with the Buffalo Philharmonic under Josef Krips and the same composer's *Saul* at Westminster Presbyterian Church, where Hans Viegland was choirmaster and organist. The state of the Vickers finances was such that he had to ask for part of his *Saul* fee on the spot in order to buy new tires for his truck so he and Hetti could make it back to Toronto.[11]

Vickers did more work with the Canadian Broadcasting Corporation chiefly because it paid better, and it was a wonderful outlet for Canadian premieres and new works. The CBC had its own symphony, with 60 percent of the personnel the same as that of the Toronto Symphony. A Wednesday night program devoted to music and drama gave young artists a wide audience.

Victor Feldbrill recalled the May 1954 CBC Opera Company's premiere of *A Tale of Two Cities* by Arthur Benjamin, in which Vickers sang Charles Darnay. "We began to notice he was eating dozens of oranges during rehearsals. We said, 'Jon, what the heck is that about?' And he said, 'I need this stuff. It's good for the voice, good for everything.'"[12] It was a habit that was to continue throughout his career; getting ready to go onstage for Vickers often meant sitting in the bathtub swigging orange juice, and he ate the fruit in his dressing room throughout performances. (Later, colleagues would say he did it to keep his blood sugar levels up during the strenuously long operas he sang.)

In 1954 for the Canadian Opera Company he sang four performances of *Rigoletto* at $125 each and three performances of Wolf-Ferrari's comic opera *The School for Fathers* at $50 a night, for a total $650. In 1955 and 1956 he almost doubled his COC income, to $1,000 per year total. In 1955 he got $60 each for two nights of *Fledermaus* and $110 per night for eight *Traviata*s. In 1956 he was paid $125 each for eight *Carmen*s.[13]

Although the Duke of Mantua was his professional opera stage debut, on

February 25, 1954, it was not among the roles he would pursue in years to come. Apart from his tricky arias and high tessitura, the Duke has a caddish character to which Vickers did not relate. Milligan was the Monterone in that 1954 performance, and Goulet had a small part. A review praised Vickers's insight: "In *Questa o quella* he showed a sly humor that later on, in the *La donna e mobilè*, became a presentation of complete charm. In his third-act aria, unfortunately, he encountered some difficulty in his singing, but this gave way to some beautiful work." The next day, at a dress rehearsal for *School for Fathers*, he sang barely above a whisper.[14] He had "sung himself out" the previous night and was resting his vocal cords for the following night's opening of *School*. Of the *Rigoletto* John Kraglund wrote, "his brilliant voice carried both [arias] well and at times reached heights of lyricism. Mr. Vickers was robustly swaggering and indicated he won his women more by force than by charm." Kraglund said, however, that his "Parmi veder" was hurried and lacked tenderness, and throughout "there was a tendency to force high notes."[15]

For *Fledermaus* for the CBC, director Franz Kraemer had to deal with the size of Vickers's voice. For the opening serenade, "I put him outside the studio, then I finally put him into the gangway outside, and it was still too loud. Normally you'd just give him no mike and put him farther away."[16]

Vickers was still trying to deal with his lack of a secure high range. When he was asked to sing the *St. Matthew Passion*, he told Milligan he couldn't take on the Evangelist because of all the high notes, recalled Milligan's wife. "At that time he was funny; he used to imitate a woman with this wonderful falsetto he had, but he never used it in his singing," Edith Milligan Binnie said. Milligan had told him he should find ways to use it. "We told him, 'Why don't you talk to Emmy Heim, Jim's teacher?' She was Viennese, had been quite a well-known contralto, brought up by Sir Ernest. So Jon did, and Emmy cultivated the falsetto so he could sing the Evangelist. Because basically Jon didn't have a high C."[17] Vickers himself recalled a 1953 concert with Britten's *The Ballad of Heroes* in which the choir's pitch went up a tone during an a capella section, and he feared he would have to sing a high C-sharp if they continued in that key. "My heart was pounding," he said. Fortunately, the orchestra came in at the right pitch in time to save him.[18]

On April 27, 1954, MacMillan led the Mendelssohn Choir and seventy members of the Toronto Symphony in *Messiah* at Carnegie Hall; the next night they presented the *St. Matthew Passion*. It was Vickers's New York concert debut; soloists also included Lois Marshall, Mary Morrison, Margaret Stillwell, and Milligan. Olin Downes wrote that Vickers "occasioned admiration for the clarity of his enunciation and diction, and the richness and ring of his voice."[19] The audience for *Messiah* included the conductor André Kostelanetz; Friedelind Wagner, a granddaughter of Richard Wagner; and the baritones Igor Gorin and William Warfield.

In 1954 Vickers became a father for the first time. Hetti gave birth to a daughter, Allison Henrietta, on October 8, 1954, in Toronto.

The next month, Vickers tried on the poet Lensky in *Eugene Onegin* for a November 17, CBC broadcast, sung in English and conducted by Goldschmidt. It was a role he would never sing again, although he kept it on his list and received offers for it in the late 1950s. By then he would have bigger characters with which to contend.

"Jon Vickers, Heroic tenor," Vickers handwrote as the heading of a two-page biography for the conservatory concert office in 1954. Yet the heldentenor roles still lay in his future. Instead, on November 3, 1955, just after his twenty-ninth birthday, he sang his first Canio, a major *verismo* part that would become one of his most admired roles in the three decades ahead. This first performance was for a CBC-TV broadcast from a Montreal studio. Vickers later recalled: "In those days, a live broadcast was really murderous. You started at eight in the morning and had two full orchestral rehearsals, a dress rehearsal, and you did a show that night—if you had any voice left. And the circumstances were very difficult because of the primitive quality of the electronics, compared with today."[20]

That broadcast also offered the Canadian baritone Louis Quilico as a smooth-voiced Silvio. The Nedda was the vivacious, Czech-born soprano Eva Likova, who in 1954 was with the New York City Opera and became known for her Violetta and Gilda. She had ballet training and danced *en pointe* as Columbine for the TV broadcast. Later she recalled Vickers as serious, courteous, and artistic, a wonderful colleague.[21]

Vickers used no sobs for "Vesti la giubba," and he never would do so. His reading of the final "La commedia è finita" was a quiet one. He would say later, "I find Canio one of the truest tragic characters I've ever played, just as true and just as tragic as Peter Grimes. There's a void of emptiness and heartache that is far beyond tears."[22]

At Christmas 1955 Vickers was a soloist in *Messiah*, airing December 28 on the CBC, also with Lois Marshall, Irene Loosberg, and James Milligan, MacMillan conducting. He had his only brush with *Il Trovatore* on CBC-TV's "Concert Hour" of January 5, 1956. He sang the fourth act, thus avoiding Manrico's "Di quella pira" in Act 3 with its high Cs; Louis Quilico was Count di Luna.

A year before Vickers left Toronto, Lambert said he could no longer charge the young man for lessons, Vickers recalled, "because you know more about singing than I do."[23] This tribute to the tenor's progress was a sign that it was time for him to move on.

The Opera Festival's *Carmen* in February 1956 was an important one for Regina Resnik, one of opera's most intelligent and insightful artists. At thirty-three, she had sung the gypsy as a soprano some fifty times and was switching to the mezzo-soprano repertory. Herman Geiger-Torel was very interested in having her debut with her new sound. Ten years later, she would sing Carmen to Plácido Domingo's first José, in Santiago, with Ramón Vinay, returned to baritone roles, as Escamillo, watching with tears in his eyes that new young tenor.

Irving Guttman recalled that some with the festival had not wanted Vickers for Don José. Vickers later ascribed his difficulty to a conspiracy of sorts: "Lambert warned me, 'There are people here who are afraid of you, afraid of your talent, the potential you offer.' I didn't believe him—I couldn't—at first." Ezra Schabas, however, found it hard to believe that such words had come out of Lambert's mouth; the teacher was ever the gentleman.[24]

The first Toronto stage rehearsal for some reason began with the second-act duet of José and Carmen, Resnik recalled. "Of course, the first thing is 'Enfin c'est toi' [At last you're here, Carmen says], and they're in each other's arms. [Vickers] was a bit shy. I started to laugh, and we both laughed, and I said, 'Well, this is a way to meet a colleague—in each other's arms the first second.' Someone out front quipped, 'That's life,' and I said, 'Well, that's opera.'"

During the next two hours, Resnik said, "I was so astounded by just the natural sound of his voice." At a break, she asked where he'd been hiding. "He said, 'I'm just a farmer, and I have a feeling that's what I'm going to do the rest of my life. I'm going back to Saskatchewan and get me a farm.'" Not before this *Carmen*, she said, as they bantered back and forth.

"He did two kinds of singing: he either sang with this huge voice, which was already sounding like Otello, or he sang *pianissimo*, crooning, a kind of *mezza voce* that he sings." As rehearsals went on, "he was very curious about what I was thinking, because I was so enthusiastic." Going back to Saskatchewan was ridiculous, she told him. Resnik saw presence, charisma, and a big, promising sound. But Vickers remained unsure of his future, she said. "We always talked about what we were doing, how he sounded, what I was doing, what we wanted to do together onstage. He was very cooperative, he listened a lot, had a big boisterous temperament, and then, as now, [was] very impulsive, and very impulsive about his singing."[25]

Joanne Ivey Mazzoleni, who sang the festival's Carmen in London, Ontario, recalled that Resnik gave Vickers "a lot of pointers. He had trouble with the Flower Song, because the tessitura is high. She said, 'You've got a fabulous falsetto. Sing it falsetto.' He did, and it was fabulous. I knew his voice very well. It was a strong falsetto and that made it beautiful. And it was much easier for him."[26]

In the Royal Alexandra performances, Resnik's mezzo was praised, as was her memorable acting. Hugh Thomson called her "pure alleycat," but with a "rough nobility." Of Vickers, Thomson noted a facet that would become critical to the tenor's portrayals: Rather than use his voice "with unmitigated force" as in the past, "he had learned that he can generate more intensity often by holding back the power. He sang most affectingly and softly after his meeting with his first love, Micaela [Marguerite Lavergne]." Vickers's stage presence evidently needed work. "Once he has straightened up his deportment, as befits a dragoon in this opera, and stops lurching about stage, he will have an absolutely first-rate Don José to his credit." Vickers showed a new sincerity and new vocal control that another reviewer found "free from the over-loud tones he used to employ," with his softest sounds still quite audible.[27]

During the run Resnik called her manager, William L. Stein, in New York and urged him to hear Vickers. When Vickers told her of his skimpy finances, she said he could put up at the YMCA in Manhattan and take meals with her family. He made the trip and sang about a dozen arias for Stein, including Florestan's aria, which she suggested he include. Stein, apparently impressed, passed along to Bayreuth an air check of Vickers singing Act 1 of *Die Walküre* with the CBC Symphony Orchestra, in either a February 6, 1956, broadcast or an earlier one from 1955.

Resnik had more advice for Vickers. While visiting his home, she told him: "You will be, and very soon, I guarantee you, a great Parsifal and the perfect Siegmund." Vickers began to laugh. "German repertory?" he said. "My God, I'll never sing German repertory." Resnik insisted he would, and he asked how he would go about doing that.

> I said, "Well, I think that if I or Mr. Stein or both made the recommendation to Wieland Wagner to hear you, to audition——." He said, "What do I audition with?" I said, "Federico's Lament and Don José. You don't have to sing anything German for them."
>
> He said, "Well, that should come later. I should try the water somewhere else." I said, "No, I don't think so, in your case. I think you should try there, because there is where you'll learn, and they will teach you what you need. All you have to do is brush up on your

German; make sure when you start learning it that you have a good German coach. But there, if you're in the hands of [Hans] Knappertsbusch and Wieland Wagner, it will be your source. It will be *the* source for you, for what you're going to learn the rest of your life, maybe as an actor, as a singer, even as a musician, who knows."[28]

Things didn't go quite that smoothly with Bayreuth and Vickers, but Resnik was right about the importance of Wieland Wagner and Knappertsbusch for the tenor.

A significant step for Vickers was an appearance in July 1956 as the Male Chorus in Britten's *The Rape of Lucretia* at the Stratford Shakespearean Festival of Canada. This was the first operatic production at Stratford, and the six performances were Vickers's first in a major production beyond the fledgling COC and its festivals. It was his next major work, after the *Carmen*, with internationally known, non-Canadian artists. Later that year would come his first *Fidelio*, a concert in New York, and a concert version of Cherubini's *Médée* in the standard Italian translation, with Eileen Farrell in Philadelphia.

The two-act *Lucretia* was not to be an opera Vickers would sing again, except in 1974 in Guelph. But his part was ideal for him, with its declamatory function, its authoritative observations on evil, and its emphasis on the Christian ethic. Vickers's superb diction and word coloring were given play. "The pity is that sin has so much grace," the Male Chorus notes. Vickers, on a 1974 private recording, fills the line with elegant regret, a striking upward emphasis on the word "much."

Herman Geiger-Torel, then head of the Toronto Opera Festival, directed *Lucretia*. The cast included Jennie Tourel as the Female Chorus, with Resnik as Lucretia. Vickers received eleven hundred dollars in payment for six performances, an excellent fee at the time and "the biggest money I'd ever been offered."[29] But some sparks flew concerning the casting of Vickers, in a flap that, by one interpretation, shows Vickers's typical vulnerability to perceived slights.

Final casting was up to Geiger-Torel , who knew Vickers's work well from the conservatory, and Louis Applebaum, Stratford's director of music. The other person dealing with casting was Ezra Schabas, who knew the work only from the score and thus felt it necessary to turn for advice not only to Resnik, who had sung the Female Chorus in the first U.S. production, in Chicago in 1947, but also to Aksel Schiøtz. This Danish tenor, who had just come to Toronto, had sung the Male Chorus on the premiere tour of Britten's work in England in 1946; he alternated on tour with Peter Pears, who had sung in the Glyndebourne world premiere that year. Schiøtz knew of Vickers and told Schabas he would be excellent for the part. Vickers was also the first choice of Resnik, who talked with Schabas in February of that year, while she and Vickers were singing in *Carmen*. "I probably would have pushed [Jon] anyway," said Schabas, who was still heading the Royal Conservatory's concert bureau.[30]

Things became dicey when Vickers learned of Schabas's confidential conversation with Resnik. "He was offended and hurt," recalled Schabas, "because to him, it seemed as if I had not enough confidence in him, that I had to ask other people." Vickers for some time had been very conscious of his position as a leading tenor. "He probably felt that in view of his record, I should have just gone out and said, 'Here's your tenor, made to order.'" Moreover, Vickers refused to pay the usual 10 percent fee to the RCM, saying that Schabas had represented Stratford and not Vickers, even though Vickers had signed the standard RCM contract through Schabas as usual. Vickers also was miffed because, he said, Schabas hadn't mentioned to him that there would be a radio broadcast of *Lucretia* for which no extra payment would be made. The Canadians in the cast, used to performing on the CBC and receiving fees, felt as Vickers did that they should have received payment. Schabas says that Stratford simply wasn't in a position to pay for that on top of performance fees, as the singers were informed in a note.[31]

Vickers wrote Schabas from New York on November 28, 1956, a letter that embodied the tone of many of his future financial dealings. He said truculently that if Schabas had been acting in his interests, Schabas would have told him that the broadcasts were scheduled rather than concealing the plan from him.[32] Records show Vickers never did pay the $110 to the RCM.

As for Resnik's role, she knew she "was not in a position to be a discoverer or an impresario or an entrepreneur. But I was in the position of being a friend and colleague."[33] In fact, she did help "discover" Vickers. As Mary Morrison had influenced his arrival at the Toronto conservatory, so Resnik was a factor in giving him confidence at a crucial time that he could find a place in the larger world of opera. And her connecting him to Stein, who had become his agent in spring 1956, helped set his feet on that road.

Access to the international opera scene would come none too soon for the young married couple who had to borrow a few thousand dollars from Vickers's mother to buy a house at 77 Orchard View Boulevard in Toronto, where they took in boarders to make ends meet. Adding joy and further responsibilities, on August 30, 1956, Jon and Hetti welcomed their second child, William Leonard, who was named for his grandfathers and who inherited some of his father's innate dramatic talents.

Although the number of singing engagements had grown impressively, by the end of his sixth year at the conservatory, in 1955, Vickers had made serious plans to seek another career. "I didn't want a hand-to-mouth existence, and I knew that unless you touched the world scene the picture would always be pretty bleak," he recalled. "I knew that I had enough jobs to fill out the year, but that it just couldn't go on. I told Hetti and Poppa [George Lambert] that I had decided to quit the next June and return to the world of stores and business." Lambert agreed that it was the right decision.[34]

Vickers would tell the story of how he had almost quit with relish throughout his life, marveling at the chances that shape one's fate. It happened that the fledgling director Irving Guttman made his first trip to Europe (in 1954), visiting Terence McEwen, then with Decca. One night, Guttman went to a *Carmen* at Covent Garden with house tenor James Johnston as Don José. Guttman was introduced to Covent Garden's general administrator, David Webster, and immediately said he knew of a much better tenor than Johnston in Canada, namely, Vickers. Webster said he planned to visit New York with the Covent Garden Ballet in 1955 and asked Guttman to set up auditions in Montreal for some young Canadians.

Guttman got together a group including Louis Quilico, Joseph Rouleau, and André Turp. But Vickers declined to go to Montreal. "Jon said, 'If he wants to hear me, he can come to Toronto.' David said, 'The audacity of this young man! Who does he think he is?' I said, 'I know it's rude, but it's worth it.'"[35]

Politics may have played a part in Webster's plans. Montague Haltrecht's book on Webster says that Canadian officials weren't happy that the Royal Ballet had neglected Canada on tour. Webster had written in 1955 that he'd like to take his opera to Canada but suspected that "operatically speaking, Canada is still inclined to be a little old-fashioned." However, since Webster's house relied on government subsidy, he felt it would be at least tactful "to acknowledge an obligation of a kind" to Canada. Apparently this included looking at promising Canadian singers. Webster wrote Vickers that he would visit Toronto, but Vickers responded that he had decided to quit. He was continuing till the following summer only to honor commitments.[36] "He didn't want to take the audition in the first place. Mr. Lambert talked him into that, because he was all set to give up," Nan Shaw confirmed. But Lambert urged him, saying he had nothing to lose.[37]

A few days after writing, on November 27, 1955, Webster, by then in Toronto, called Vickers at 8 A.M. and asked to hear him at 10 A.M. But Vickers had sung the night before and didn't want to sing that day. Shaken but determined, Webster called back. This time, Vickers agreed to a 4 P.M.

audition and, as he later put it, became "a tenor discovered by David Webster one rainy Sunday afternoon in Toronto."[38]

As Lambert recalled it, "He came to see me in my studio and said, 'Well, I don't think I'm going to bother because I suppose it's just going to be another audition.' I said, 'Get down there!' And I said, 'Have you chosen your accompanist?' He said, 'No, I can't get'—whoever he'd thought of [probably Mario Bernardi]. 'Very well, we'll get somebody else.'"[39]

At the audition in Massey Hall, Goldschmidt sat with George Schick, soon to become a Metropolitan Opera conductor and coach. Vickers sang two or three opera arias; when Webster asked for something in English, he offered an aria from Handel's oratorio *Judas Maccabeus*. Goldschmidt said, "After ten minutes David Webster went up to the stage, and I remember saying to Schick, 'That's good-bye to Jon Vickers in Canada.'"[40] He could not have been more prescient.

Webster marked the tenor down as "quite something" and had a long talk with him in the Massey greenroom about opera's economic realities. He urged Vickers to move to London instead of quitting. He'd certainly offer a contract. "Then it will have to be a good one," was Vickers's response. He wanted a guarantee that if after eighteen months in England he'd failed, he could return to Canada no worse off financially. Webster told him a contract with Sadler's Wells would be no problem, but Covent Garden was a question mark. Vickers said, "Unless you think I'm too good for Sadler's Wells, I wouldn't dream of coming," to which Webster replied, "You strike me as a man who knows the value of a dollar."[41]

But Vickers heard nothing from Webster until the following spring, shortly before his self-imposed deadline to quit singing. On May 7, 1956, he jumped out of bed at 7:30 A.M. to answer the persistent ring of his doorbell. It was a long cable asking him to audition in London the following week, all expenses paid. "Haven't forgotten big impression you made," Webster wired. "Grateful if you could work in London week May 14 view future engagements."[42]

The next day, Vickers contacted Stein, with whom he had just signed for management (an action at odds with his plan to quit). Stein immediately sought to know from Webster what specifically he had in mind for Vickers and noted that Vickers was definitely developing into a Wagnerian. Webster assured him that the idea was for the young man to join the company.[43]

Vickers, who seems to have contacted Lambert even before Stein, recalled that "we agreed that it would be a mistake to go immediately." He went to New York and worked for a month with Leo Taubman, a respected accompanist and coach recommended by Stein and Resnik, on arias from *Fidelio*,

Die Zauberflöte, and *Der Freischütz,* among others.[44] He worked every day with Taubman, while staying at the YMCA.

Taubman invited a number of guests to the coaching sessions. Vickers didn't know that many were reps of major opera groups. Before leaving New York, he had a flush hand of other offers: *Aida* in Miami, *Boris Godunov* in Barcelona, *Carmen* in San Francisco, a *Das Lied von der Erde* recording with Fritz Reiner and the Chicago Symphony, and two offers that he accepted for that winter.

A list circulated by Stein of Vickers's repertoire at age twenty-nine included *Carmen, Pagliacci, Rigoletto, La Traviata,* Ferrando in *Così fan tutte,* Don Ottavio in *Don Giovanni,* Lenski in *Onegin, Aida,* and *Otello* (the last two listed as having been done on radio, although Vickers had covered only *Otello*), and a slew of oratorios.

In early June, probably June 12, he flew from New York to London. He sang "a big audition" for Webster and Rafael Kubelik onstage at Covent Garden on Friday and returned on Monday for more, with his bags packed for his return to Toronto. After Canio's "Vesti la giubba" and Don José's Flower Song, Webster asked for the *Tosca* arias. Vickers hadn't sung them for some time: "I'm terribly sorry. But I feel I've made a fantastic impression and I don't want to spoil it." Webster was all graciousness. "That's all right, Mr. Vickers. We were only asking for our own pleasure."[45]

He was offered a three-year contract with the Covent Garden Opera Company (not to become the Royal Opera until 1968). He agreed to try it for just eighteen months. Ever savvy on finances, he didn't want to become a resident in England subject to U.K. taxes.[46] Webster wanted him for *Carmen, Pagliacci, Die Walküre,* and *Tosca* (the last never came to pass). He also told Vickers he and Rafael Kubelik wanted him to sing Aeneas in *The Trojans.* Vickers said he'd never heard of Berlioz's masterwork, but he got the idea from Webster it must be important. "I'd have to see the score," he said firmly. He thought it was cunning of Webster not to show it to him until after he got to London. "I would have died!"[47] Webster was "a cagey fox," Vickers said. "He wanted to get as much as he could for as little as he had to pay," and the equally cagey Vickers found this simply the attitude of "a good business man."[48]

John Tooley, then Webster's deputy, recalled that Vickers was determined to go for the big leagues. That determination, he believed, harked back to Vickers's deeply held faith, his conviction that his voice was God-given. "Jon could not conceive of aiming for anything other than the very top. It's part of Jon."[49]

It was not until the end of July that Vickers, busy with the Stratford *Lucretia,* received the contracts signed by Webster. He and Hetti (eight months pregnant with William), twenty-two-month-old Allison, and bass Jan Rubes, who was singing the role of Tarquinius, celebrated the day he heard from Stein. Webster gave Vickers seventy-five pounds a week for work from January to July 1957, with an option for all of the following season. Performances for the first season would include *Carmen* and a new production of *The Trojans;* Webster also offered to "do best to introduce [him to] concert world here so that he cashes in second season."[50] "Cash" was a word that Webster, Stein, and Vickers could all appreciate.

The contract negotiations went on for four more months, however, and it wasn't until November 30 that Stein delivered the contract with Vickers's signature to Webster, who was staying at the St. Regis Hotel in New York. In the meantime, Stein was busy with more plans for Vickers and apparently was talking with Bayreuth, although Vickers had never sung a complete German opera. In a July 28, 1956, letter from Austria to Webster, Stein asked to end Vickers's 1957–58 season on June 15, 1958, "so that he could fulfill an engagement in Bayreuth (if so requested)."[51]

Getting a contract signed by Vickers would always be a feat. His London agent, John Coast, would say later that "a contract is not a contract [to Jon] unless he can cross something out."[52]

Stein wanted Vickers's roles specified in the Covent Garden contract; he also wanted to know if Webster planned to present both sections of *The Trojans,* a work with which Stein also was unfamiliar. "What he needs," Stein wrote Webster from Salzburg, where he was paying his various summer musical respects, "is a theater that treats him comfortably and with understanding. I am convinced Covent Garden will do just this for him. May I point out that New York is one place Vickers should not sing, at least not for three years, and I will exercise all my powers of conviction to dissuade Vickers from such an intention even if he should nurture it."[53]

By "New York" Stein apparently meant specifically the Metropolitan Opera, because Vickers indeed sang a concert in New York before leaving for London, one of two appearances Stein had booked for him with the American Opera Society. The prestigious organization, just three years old, was run by two young men, Allen Sven Oxenburg and Arnold U. Gamson, who was a conductor. After a trial run, probably on November 18, 1956, at the Metropolitan Museum's subscription concert series, Vickers sang in the society's concert version of *Fidelio* at Town Hall on November 20, with Inge Borkh. (It was not his U.S. concert debut, since he had been at Carnegie Hall with MacMillan.) On November 18 the *New York Times* ran a photo of Vickers probably for the first time in New York, a rehearsal shot of him with Gamson and Sarah Fleming, who sang Marzelline. Other cast members were Lawrence Avery as Jacquino, Paul Schoeffler as an excellent Pizarro,

Alexander Welitsch as Rocco, and Enrico di Giuseppe and Thomas Pyle as the two prisoners.

Borkh, who recently had sung Salome under Georg Solti at the reorganized Lyric Opera of Chicago and given a Carnegie Hall concert, was praised for scaling down her big voice to Town Hall's size. Gamson, wrote Howard Taubman, "drove the piece too hard, not letting it relax and sing often enough." That might have accounted in some part for Taubman's assessment of Vickers: He "unleashed a voice of size and power. He is too prodigal in his outlay of volume, but he has the makings of a capable dramatic tenor. His Florestan, however, only scratched the surface of the part's emotion."[54]

Town Hall's balcony is close to the stage. To Vickers, "It looked like it was three feet away," because in the front row were Renata Tebaldi, Zinka Milanov, Cesare Siepi, Cesare Valletti, Max Lorenz, and Rudolf Bing (and possibly Maria Callas). "They weren't there to hear me, they were there to hear Inge Borkh," recalled Vickers.[55] But Bing was hearing a tenor he had let slip through his fingers, a fact of which David Webster later would remind him.

Other tenors were busy in New York. Richard Tucker, forty-three, sang a Met Rodolfo to cheers on November 21, and also was doing *Les Contes d'Hoffmann*. Jussi Björling, forty-five, gave a concert that week at Hunter College. Jan Peerce, fifty-two, was doing *Rigoletto* at the Met, Kurt Baum, fifty-seven, was due in *Aida* in December. James McCracken, like Vickers in his thirtieth year, was a soloist at a singing teachers' event.

Philadelphia also boasted a busy fall, with excitement centered on Callas's first appearance there, as the Met visited with *Norma* on November 27, with Baum as Pollione and McCracken in the smaller role of Flavio. For the second American Opera Society engagement, Vickers appeared there November 29 as Jason in a concert *Médée*, with Eileen Farrell, also conducted by Gamson. In just two years he would be repeating the role opposite Callas herself, whose visit got massive reporting in the *Philadelphia Inquirer*. Stories began on the front page, with coverage of Main Liners dripping mink for this social event. The diva, slim and imperious, triumphed at the Academy of Music. She was no Bernhardt but a prima donna assoluta who could act, opined Edwin H. Schloss. Baum's bright lirico-dramatic tenor was admirable, but his dramatic contribution was "a series of marmoreal poses." Two days later, Farrell was nobly tortured as Médée, with a voice of thrilling power, wrote Schloss. Vickers was included in mention of a high-level cast, with Eva Likova as Glauce, Miroslav Čangalović as King Creon, and Martha Lipton as Neris.[56]

Also in November, Rafael Kubelik wrote to Vickers, saying the plan was for him to work with the Covent Garden music staff for six weeks, then to tour for six weeks, and return to London for his debut. On tour he was to sing *Carmen* and *Un Ballo in Maschera*.[57] This was the first Vickers had heard that they wanted *Ballo*. He rushed to a music store in New York to get a score and began learning it. English was then the Covent Garden preference.

Back in Toronto, two days before Christmas, he got a telegram asking if he would be willing to make his debut February 8 as Walther in *Die Meistersinger*. Vickers was astounded; he called Stein to say, "These people at Covent Garden are insane!" But John Coast, his London agent, admitted it was partly his fault that the tenor had been asked for two roles he had yet to learn: Coast had told Webster that Vickers was a quick study. Vickers knew that Walther was long and difficult: "I'm not sticking my neck out that far!"[58]

There is a story that Vickers sought three thousand dollars to pay for his family's move to London, asking a socially prominent Toronto doctor for a loan. The doctor and friends agreed to do so only if he would return to sing anything asked for by the COC, at any fee offered. Vickers, contract in hand, rejected this quid pro quo and had no trouble getting the money from a bank.[59]

Vickers recalled that when George Lambert said good-bye, he had advice for his pupil: "Always remember that your voice is like a big, juicy orange. And every conductor and every producer and every impresario who can get his hands on it will suck every bit of juice out of it that he can. And never you forget what they do with an orange peel!" The other side of the coin: "If you ever get to the point where you really think you know how to sing, please, open the score of the Bach *St. Matthew Passion*."[60] Vickers kept these as words to live by.

In October, Vickers had taken on a lighter role, displaying his physique in a tight Popeye-style T-shirt for a CBC production of Gilbert and Sullivan's *H.M.S. Pinafore*.

On Boxing Day, December 26, 1956, he appeared in *Gianni Schicchi*, with Mary Morrison, on CBC-TV (a tape survives). It was his last performance in Canada before departing for London a few days later. The light lyric role of Rinuccio was a reversion from the dramatic Jason and the Florestan he had sung the previous month. But this tale of the Renaissance was a good omen for the flowering of Vickers's career.

1957–1959

The Career Begins

He was not an opera singer.
He was a huge operatic animal.
He was born that way.
—*Ande Anderson,*
Royal Opera House general manager

5

Covent Garden and Battling the BBC

A RAINY NEW YEAR'S EVE 1956: JON AND HETTI VICKERS HAD arrived in London on December 29 via BOAC and on this night were strolling along the Edgeware Road, wondering what lay ahead with the Covent Garden Opera Company. The rest of the decade would be tumultuous for them, and every bit of Vickers's native shrewdness would be put to use as the music world opened up to him.

They took a flat in the Earl's Court area but that summer would find a house at 7 Draycott Avenue in Kenton. Of stucco and brick, with modest columns in front and a large rear garden, the house was close to an underground stop and in the neighborhood of the well-known Harrow School. Daughter Allison was then two, son Billy four months old.

Just sixteen months earlier the English had finally come off wartime rationing. "I sang to the British public with bomb craters still all over the place, and buildings grimy, not painted for years," Vickers later observed.[1] Nor was life easy for the young singer and his family. "They didn't have electric kettles, a refrigerator, anything we take for granted," Mary Morrison recalled from letters that Hetti wrote her. They found the transition a struggle and a major gamble.[2] Unsure of the future, they had rented their Toronto home to a friend from Port Arthur, Mary Seaman Copeland, and her husband, William, at whose wedding Vickers had sung. But they would never return to live at that house on Orchard View Boulevard.

On January 31, 1957, Webster wrote to Vickers at 6 Wetherby Gardens in London that he would be advised no later than the second Saturday in February of the date the season would terminate. Vickers signed a contract for 1957–58 that gave him a raise to one hundred pounds weekly.[3]

John Tooley, then deputy to David Webster, found Vickers a serious young singer who was apprehensive rather than nervous about his future at a major opera company, albeit one just beginning to take shape. His timing was good. "Covent Garden had a desperate need of a voice of that kind," said Tooley.[4] House tenor James Johnston, a fine singer but in his midfifties, had his nose extremely out of joint at the arrival of Vickers. He huffed to Webster that he would resign since he was no longer the first tenor. Vickers will never sing *Turandot* for you, he told Webster, and he was right on that count. Vickers was a very different kind of tenor.

The Canadian had much to learn, and he knew it. He did many long coaching sessions and admitted to leaning heavily on Webster, asking advice, picking his brain. Webster was a latter-day Diaghilev, the conductor Edward Downes later said. He watched over the company "like a benevolent spider," and he had the all-important quality of making artists feel at home, happy, and welcome.[5] This was essential to Vickers in those early months in London, and the impresario's visage with its pale blue eyes and smooth gray hair would become as familiar to him as that of a family member.

The opera house then was still surrounded by market stalls brimming with vegetables and fruits. Vickers, man of the soil that he always would be, appreciated leaving the unreality of the stage and stepping out on cobbled streets surrounded by the odors of produce, with perhaps a squashed tomato in the gutter.

Alan Stanley Anderson, known as Ande, a stage manager named resident producer in 1959, later general manager, worked in hundreds of performances with Vickers, in England and elsewhere. He said that offstage the tenor was "a very relaxed man. . . . He wanted to belong to the company. At breaks, he didn't nip out to a restaurant, he'd go to the canteen, talk with everyone, stagehands, choristers—he was a part of the theater."[6] This was true of most of the Covent Garden singers. But it became a career-long habit for Vickers, who spoke warmly of chorus, crew, and support staff in certain houses after relations with their directors had frosted over.

He was popular with Covent Garden colleagues from the beginning. Ron Freeman, later makeup chief, recalled: "Whenever he walked into the canteen, everybody's face lit up. They always were desperate to see him, he was such a lovely guy. Always cheerful, always got something to say, *adored* company!" He retained the big laugh that had echoed in the halls of the Toronto conservatory. "A man, through and through," summed up Freeman. "And a ladies' man too. The ladies adored him." Freeman, who in the dressing room saw more of Vickers's unclothed body than most, noted, "He's built like a lumberjack, he's a *huge* man. And the whole physique lights up when he sees a woman and charms the pants off her." The makeup man had appeared as a youngster at Covent Garden in Vickers's earliest days. "We had a teacher named Kathleen Robson, and he used to lift her off her feet, and she would go weak at the knees!"[7]

The first item on Vickers's agenda was telling Webster that he liked Kubelik's plan of twelve weeks of coaching and touring so much that "it's crazy for me to learn *Meistersinger* in such a short time, and jump into the operatic scene at the deep end."[8] Webster relented but urged Vickers to attend the rehearsals. Vickers's refusal to add the role to his repertoire caused tensions. As the tenor saw it, "When I came to London, there were people in the opera house who really, really, really did resist my being there, and they were people of some power and some position." Downes, who was coaching him in *Un Ballo in Maschera,* "came to me one day and said, 'What did you do to Mr. So-and-So,'" who had suggested at a staff meeting that Vickers's contract be bought out and that he be sent home "before you disgrace us all."[9] It was Norman Feasey, a popular répétiteur and the house's chief Wagner coach. Downes said that Webster himself was so worried about the situation that he contemplated sending Vickers back to Canada.[10] Vickers fought back, his stubborn side coming into view. He told Downes he would attend no *Ballo* calls for ten days. Downes asked why. "None of your business," Vickers told him.

The tenor went out and bought a piano for his small apartment. "I got up at seven o'clock in the morning and I went to bed at eleven o'clock at night, and I memorized *Meistersinger* in ten days." Of course, he had sung the Prize Song in 1952 for the Canadian Singing Stars competition, so he wasn't starting from scratch. He then went to the conductor Reginald Goodall and asked to go through the part with him. Goodall was all eagerness, and they did so immediately. Goodall asked why he wasn't singing the performances, and Vickers said, "'Cause I don't want to, Reggie." Said Goodall, "Oh, but you must!" The conductor rushed to Webster, who told him it appeared that Vickers couldn't learn the part. Goodall gave him the updated news on Vickers. Of this trick, Vickers said in recalling it, "Nasty of me! . . . I *am* a quick study."[11]

But Vickers's telling of the episode in a 1981 talk ignored an important detail of the version in the 1993 biography of Goodall by John Lucas: that Vickers had agreed previously with Webster to study the part with Feasey. They disagreed on some matters of phrasing, and two days later Vickers heard from Downes of the staff meeting attack by Feasey.[12] So it did not come from out of nowhere.

After proving that he could master Walther, Vickers went back to work on *Ballo,* but never did sing *Meistersinger,* then or ever, although San Francisco's Kurt Herbert Adler would pressure him heavily to do the part in 1958. He did sing the Prize Song for a BBC radio broadcast of excerpts recorded on May 7, 1957, under Kubelik, with Joan Sutherland as Eva and James Pease as Hans Sachs, a tape of which survives.

But the incident with Feasey caused tension in his beginning months at the house. "Jon was never without an element of arrogance. He always had that," the Earl of Harewood, the founder of *Opera* and a Webster aide, recalled of Vickers's early days. However complimentary one was to him, "he always thought he ought to have one degree more regard or compliment." Such feelings in singers stem from insecurities, the earl believed.[13] Downes said he and Vickers "fought like mad" on *Ballo* but soon became friends. Downes insisted he learn the role in Italian first, then in English.[14]

Vickers's first performance with the company took place March 4, 1957, in Cardiff on the spring tour, in an English-language production of *Ballo*. But April 27, at Covent Garden, is listed by the house as his official debut date, also as Gustavus III in *Ballo*. He also had been scheduled for a series of *Carmen* performances in April 1957, one of which fell before the *Ballo* performance that the house had agreed would be his official debut, to which the critics would be invited. So his actual first performance on the boards at Covent Garden was as Don José on April 24, 1957.

He sang his first José "very acceptably indeed," Webster wrote Stein on April 26, "and he is busy preparing Aeneas for *Trojans*. His work is extremely satisfactory and we look forward to his long connection with us."[15] In fact, Vickers first had asked to make his debut in *Carmen* but was disappointed in the production after seeing it. Covent Garden management agreed it was poor, but it sold, so it was kept. After a sleepless night, Vickers boldly tackled Webster, who agreed to change the debut to *Ballo*.[16]

The tenor also coached for *Ballo* with a Dr. Salomon and was able to warm up as Gustavus with six performances on tour in Cardiff, Manchester, and Southampton, although he was alternating as Don José. Ramón Vinay sang *Otello* in Manchester, with the Dutch soprano Gré Brouwenstijn, and Vickers always took any opportunity to watch and learn from a tenor then acknowledged as one of the world's greatest Otellos. While Vickers studied in Toronto, Vinay had been Tristan and Tannhäuser at the new Bayreuth, and the Chilean tenor would do Siegmund in 1959 at Covent Garden.

Vinay was a singer with a public panache Vickers would never achieve or aspire to. He sang those Otellos carrying a stick because he had injured some knee cartilage while strangling Desdemona. Interviewed in bed, drinking a Napoleon shandy, he said he had learned to use a stick by watching Olivier in *Richard III* but didn't want it thought it was only for effect.[17]

As Gustavus, Vickers displayed a "powerful, easy, unforced tenor, with a slightly Martinelli-like trumpet ring in heroic phrases," wrote the *Financial Times*. His "demeanor is confident and attractive" in a "pleasantly old-fashioned way."[18]

His official appearance in *Ballo* was greeted warmly by some critics as a boon to the Italian wing of the house repertory. He had the chief attributes of a leading Verdi tenor, wrote Desmond Shawe-Taylor: "a well-placed voice of robust and penetrating quality which does not tighten unpleasantly in the upper range; a good appearance; dramatic ability and stage presence; clear, incisive articulation." Although he fully conveyed Gustavus's high spirits, "he falls short in depicting the more regal attributes of the Swedish king." But as a lover, in the big second-act duet, "he carried all before him by the sheer ardour of his singing; and it was noticeable what a difference his presence made to the Amelia of Amy Shuard, who never before to my knowledge [had] sung Verdi with so warm a tone or so pure a line." Shawe-Taylor was more prophetic than he knew. Vickers is "not yet a world-shaking phenomenon—which is just as well or he would soon be lured away."[19] But Downes told Webster and Harewood how good Vickers was, and they began to make more big plans around him.

Opera's Harold D. Rosenthal, who followed virtually all of Vickers's career, applauding most of the way, spotted him as a future Otello and Siegmund. He recognized his durable qualities of intelligence, excellent breath control and diction, and a voice "not inherently beautiful but of exciting timbre."[20]

Downes recalled that at the first performance, in a Cardiff theater, after the Act 2 love duet with Vickers and Shuard "the place exploded. We couldn't go on—the applause would not stop! And from then on, this was Jon Vickers." That was one view. Noël Goodwin reported, "His reception was kindly—no more. If his name had been Mario Spaghetti there would have been such a stampede."[21]

Montague Haltrecht had the most interesting take on Vickers at this point. The Canadian, he said in his Webster biography, had "an uncanny instinct for hitting off neurotic heroes with a propensity for being dominated by women with a strongly maternal aspect." Vickers interpreted the king as "a somewhat masochistic character who brought poignant doomed yearning to the guilty ecstasy of his love scenes with Amelia."[22] In the future, Vickers would have equally complicated relationships with many of his stage partners, whether lashing himself as Samson for desiring Dalila or painting Isolde as not a nice girl because she lured Tristan to betray his king.

To sum up, Vickers's first Covent Garden appearances, in the second half of the 1956–57 season, included six performances of *Ballo* and two of *Carmen* on tour in March and April in Cardiff, Manchester, and Southampton; four *Ballo*s in the house in April and May; and five *Carmen*s in April, May, and July. (The season also included two performances of *Norma* with Callas, led by John Pritchard.) And that summer there would be *The Trojans*, another major turning point for Vickers. In late March Vickers had auditioned for Sir Malcolm Sargent and was signed to sing Samuel Coleridge-Taylor's *Hiawatha's Wedding Feast* that August and a *Messiah* on January 4, 1958. Webster approved those, but declined to release Vickers for four performances of *L'Incoronazione de Poppea* in New York and Philadelphia and at Cornell University in Ithaca, New York.

On May 1, 1957, Vickers wrote to Herman Geiger-Torel, who had directed him in so many Toronto productions in the 1950s, expressing his happiness about his debut in *Ballo*. He was delighted that for once he had received unanimous praise in the press, compared with his Canadian experiences. The six tour performances enabled him to be at ease for London, with, he claimed, no nerves at all. He thanked Geiger-Torel heartily for his past drilling, giving him stage technique that was vital because he had had little rehearsal for the tour *Ballo*s. He worried that his lack of experience also would be a disadvantage in working with the distinguished Sir John Gielgud on *The Trojans*, which was to open June 6. But again, he reported Gielgud's complimenting him on understanding the stage directions so well. And he admitted to Geiger-Torel his fear of *Trojans*. But the total confidence of all the Covent Garden leaders eased his tension.[23]

Throughout a correspondence that would last many years, Vickers would often ask Geiger-Torel's advice on important roles, particularly during the hectic late 1950s, after his Covent Garden triumphs brought all kinds of offers. In this ten-page letter, he essayed a metaphor about Geiger-Torel's having helped him to find his stage legs—noting that physically they were bowed—and saying that now he must find his way alone. This he was already doing, and the triumph that would open the world's doors to him lay just ahead.

Les Troyens is an epic covered in the blood of Hector Berlioz, whose life's work it was, and who died embittered that he never saw the entire huge opera staged, much less staged as he envisioned it. The barbarians at the Théâtre-Lyrique in Paris, presenting the second section in 1863, cut even Hylas's lovely song and the wonderfully human grumbles of Énée's soldiers before their leader's great aria about his coming farewell to Didon.[24] Apart from a few performances of all five acts in Germany in the 1890s, the opera was known only in mutilated shortened versions, and not until the virtually complete 1957 Covent Garden performances did the work come to be acknowledged as Berlioz's crowning masterpiece.

Vickers was not to know in the summer of 1957, as he and Covent Garden made a stunning international success of their English-language production, that forty years later no tenor would have matched his characterization of Énée, a role he would sing in both English and French over the next sixteen years. When he throws off his disguise in the third act and sings, "Reine, je suis Énée," "the audience, like the orchestra, catches its breath: at that moment he *is* Aeneas," wrote the Berlioz authority David Cairns in his definitive essay on Vickers. "The idea of the hero, in all its austerity and intoxication, its mixture of stoicism and obsession, comes alive when he sings the last act of the opera."[25]

Vickers said he thought he would be most remembered for this role, and in that he erred; Peter Grimes has become his historical signature. This is because the hugely complicated Berlioz work is performed infrequently, and because Énée, although conflicted, is a more static character and must share the spotlight with two strong women. But the part had, dramatically, all the features that drew the best from Vickers. This was a hero on a journey of destiny, torn between patriotic duty and the love of a noble woman. He loved, but even better, he suffered. With Vickers, it was exceptionally clear that duty would always win; thus resonated the teachings that had driven him since childhood. He surely sympathized with Berlioz's struggles to preserve the integrity of his beloved work. Berlioz could only have admired Vickers's intensely committed portrayal of Énée.

The tenor believed that vocally this was his most difficult role, although Énée's singing runs less than forty minutes in the course of the opera's more than three and a half hours. Fifteen years later, as he assumed the role for the Met's first production (with some cuts) in 1973, he told CBC Radio: "I don't think Berlioz understood the various tenor categories. . . . The first entrance of Énée is written for a pure Italian spinto . . . the second . . . for lyric baritone, not written for tenor at all . . . the third entrance, that's pure heroic, real big dramatic tenor. Otello stuff." For the exquisite love duet with Didon, "it's absolutely very lyric tenor, Beniamino Gigli kind of tenor." That changeability "constitutes the difficulty of Aeneas. Somehow you have to make a compromise with [a] basically dramatic tenor, and preserve your resources. As a dramatic tenor, if you let it go too much, you will find trouble in the next lyric scene. If you stifle the lyricism, you'll cramp yourself up so you won't be able to let go in the big ones." And "the position in the voice is very ungrateful sometimes."[26]

The American mezzo-soprano Blanche Thebom, who sang Didon at Covent Garden, recalled, "I had been told I would work with this very young and exciting new tenor from western, rural Canada." Vickers was perfect for Énée: "His voice was always a wonderfully masculine sound, as opposed to any kind of tenor, really. There was a depth of virility that you'd expect more in a dramatic baritone, a tremendously virile sound." And his face "was marvelous for that part—those great broad cheekbones, generous mouth. In costume, he was just like an ancient Roman statue, he's just such a handsome man." Vickers wasn't tall. "But you were not aware of that. He just came across as a tremendous person up there on stage." She recalled how director Sir John Gielgud arranged the love scene for the couple, as they sang of a night of love's infinite ecstasy. "It's a repetitious piece of music, not climactic. To build up the suspense, he had us look as though we were going to embrace maybe six times prior to the kiss that took place. By this time, the audience was in such a state of anticipation, at the time of the kiss, when the curtain fell, for every performance they cried out with excitement. It was such a relief to finally have it happen."[27]

The production generated massive publicity, from stories on Thebom's extremely long hair to talk of cots being set up in the Bow Street underground station across from the house for people who might collapse from the strain of the long performance. The cast kept an eye on two thick-furred Irish wolfhounds used in the Royal Hunt and Storm scene and housed in an air-conditioned trailer.

The press attention was welcomed by Webster, who was battling financial problems, as usual. He needed a big success, and this would be one not only for him but also for Rafael Kubelik, in his second season as music director (he would soon depart). Kubelik had done the second part of *Trojans* in 1940 in Brno and was enthusiastic about the Covent Garden plans. He said later that this lengthy opera is rarely performed because myth and allegory are always difficult to stage and because, before the advent of modern stage apparatus, the set changes for its ten different scenes would have made it impossibly lengthy.[28]

Rehearsals were not without problems. Haltrecht wrote that Vickers went to Webster to complain that the opera was being directed as though it wasn't centered on the hero, who was being used merely as a prop for the two heroic ladies. Webster let Vickers see him in a quiet chat with Gielgud, after which rehearsals progressed satisfactorily.[29] Vickers observed that knowing the music didn't seem essential for directors at Covent Garden. Gielgud had him kissing the queen's hand in the middle of a prayer. But he later learned that hand-kissing was a specialty of Gielgud's.[30]

Vickers further discussed the dramatic factors when preparing for the Met's 1973 production, having by then the experience of two productions at the Royal Opera House and one in San Francisco:

> Some may feel that the drama is not of consequence, preferring the epic quality. But I have a thing about the stage, about having something to say. The forces required are so overpowering that they present a problem for the three principals to hold their own. Add the free imagination of a great designer and the problem is accentuated. The lead roles deal with a legendary demi-god atmosphere, and if you go too far in that direction the work loses its grip on humanity.

Stage pictures alone "get boring," he added. He saw Berlioz at his greatest in "scenes of great personal tenderness—when Aeneas says good-bye to his son, and in the love duet, which is incomparable." Those are two of the most intimate scenes, in which the audience should not be able to help focusing on the performers, not on stage pictures.[31]

Ande Anderson recalled Gielgud's directing Vickers's first entrance, in Troy in the first act. Énée rushes in to report that two sea serpents have devoured the priest who warned of ambush from a giant wooden horse. Gielgud had Vickers coming right from the wings, but Vickers said he wanted to come from the sea. Gielgud said, "I'm giving you the best entrance in the business, right down the middle!" Eventually, said Anderson, Vickers agreed to enter in the middle. Gielgud said later that since the opera hadn't been fully staged before, he generally could do what he wanted with no argument, as no tradition existed.[32]

Vickers threw a scare into the house about two weeks before opening night when he told Webster that one of his children had the measles. Vickers had never had the contagious illness. Two other tenors each learned one-half of *Trojans*, but their services weren't needed.

In 1957 Covent Garden did five performances, June 16 and 19, and July 10, 17, and 19, in English. "The most exciting heroic tenor to come forward since Mario Del Monaco, and he has the virile presence of the ideal operatic hero," wrote the French critic Jacques Bourgeois of Vickers. The *Scotsman* hailed him as an "infinitely persuasive, great bull of a curly-headed hero, with something of the appearance of a larger-than-life—and more congenial—James Cagney."[33]

Among VIPs attending the performances was the new Canadian prime minister, John Diefenbaker, the longtime friend of the Vickers family. He and his wife, Olive, sat in the Royal Box on June 29 and visited backstage, where photos were taken. Vickers used the occasion to correct stories that the childless Diefenbakers had wanted to adopt him during depression days in Prince Albert. He said it was only an informal offer for a long visit, and that his family, who declined, "was never really hard up." That, of course, was not strictly true. The tenor also said that Diefenbaker had never loaned him any money, as also rumored. And he wanted no part of any "ballyhoo" about the prime minister's London visit to exploit the friendship.[34]

Victor Feldbrill, a conductor who had worked with Vickers in Toronto, recalled going backstage after one of the performances. "Jon said, 'Gosh, good to see you.' It was as if he'd just seen me the day before. He said, 'Let's go have a bite to eat,' and as we walked out, a funny transformation took place. It was almost as if he had donned a bowler hat. He looked British, as if he were waving a cane: 'Get us a cab, my good man.' Words like that never came out of his mouth before. And I thought, Oh, God, he's become a tenor. . . . He was the rage of London within a year."[35]

Vickers, who soon did don a homburg, also was the rage of the opera world, and offers poured in. In his businesslike way, he was poised to make the most of them. And in the 1960s the age of jet travel would take off, on the one hand giving singers, conductors, and directors unparalleled opportunities, but on the other, causing irreparable damage to many voices from doing too much too fast. The air age transformed opera-house scheduling, a situation of which Vickers took full advantage, especially to make time for his family.

Les Troyens, which had the attention of the entire world of music because of its rarity, generated huge interest in Vickers. Later he was fond of repeating that he made seven important debuts within three years and two months: Covent Garden, Vienna, Bayreuth, San Francisco, Buenos Aires, the Met, and La Scala. The correct figure of three years and eight months—La Scala came in December 1960—is still an impressive beginning for any singer's international career.

Herbert von Karajan apparently had not seen *Troyens* himself, although some of his scouts must have done so. Vickers flew to Salzburg in August 1957 to audition for the conductor, who was at the height of his power, with posts in Vienna, Salzburg, Berlin, and London and at La Scala. After less than half of the Lamento di Federico from Cilea's *L'Arlesiana,* including the first top A, Karajan called, "Thank you, Mr. Vickers," and the tenor thought, "Well, I sure impressed him!" But the conductor called Vickers offstage into the auditorium. He was working on a production and was in his jeans, a sweater thrown over his shoulders. Vickers recalled that Karajan "said, 'Let's do a new production of *Tristan und Isolde* next year.' And I said, 'You are crazy!' He looked at me—I don't think anybody had ever said such a thing to him before. He was serious, but I said no, because I was much too young." Vickers would have no problem doing it with him, Karajan said, but the thirty-year-old stood firm. He wasn't ready.[36]

"Then he wanted me to make my debut with him in Vienna that September—this was August!—in *Carmen.*" After an immediate order to his secretary to call Vienna and arrange for Vickers's appearance, Karajan "slapped me on the knee and said, 'One day you will be my Tristan.'"[37]

Later Vickers would praise "the ear of the man," able to tell so much of a singer's capabilities. Karajan, of course, was persuasive with countless artists, usually young, lighter voices, so that Helen Donath would sing Eva for him in the studio but not on the stage till much later. "One day you will be my ———" was a Karajan mantra, and those he favored could expect plum engagements and recordings. Many also felt he had destroyed certain voices by pressing them to sing unsuitable roles.

In fact, Vickers told Geiger-Torel that he had only postponed the *Tristan* offer for eighteen months or two years.[38] He also turned down Chicago's request for four *Tristan* performances. But those two years turned into fourteen before he took on this role, which became one of his great achievements.

In the summer of 1957 Vickers auditioned in Bayreuth for Wieland Wagner, the grandson of Richard Wagner. Wieland (he is generally referred to in the music world by his first name to differentiate among his grandfather and his elder brother, Wolfgang, with whom he recreated the Bayreuth Festival beginning in 1950) apparently could come to no conclusion at first. He had Vickers sing again, this time the Prize Song from *Die Meistersinger,* "Hochstes Vertraun" and the Gralerzahlung from *Lohengrin,* two *Walküre* excerpts, Max's aria from *Der Freischütz,* and Don José's Flower Song. Wieland asked him to sing *Lohengrin* the next year at the Festival, but Vickers balked, since he had never performed the role and thought it would be dangerous for his debut there. "I just felt it would have been suicide, and Wieland was very angry."[39] Vickers proposed *Walküre* and *Parsifal,* which were agreed upon for the following summer. Another youthful tenor, Fritz Wunderlich, then twenty-eight, also would turn down the role of the Swan Knight the next year, for much the same reason.

Ramón Vinay, who heard Vickers's audition, threw his arm around the Canadian's shoulder afterward and told him he must sing Otello, a proposition that Vickers at first pooh-poohed, saying he would consider the role in four or five years. Vinay, the renowned Otello who would revert to baritone roles in 1962, said that if Vickers waited five, he would like to sing Iago with him.[40]

Despite Wieland Wagner's high estimation of his new tenor, the Bayreuth contract would prove to be, at least temporarily, a casualty of a serious difficulty that arose in September 1957 between Vickers and BBC-TV. With trademark tenacity, Vickers would cling to the issue for twenty-four years. The dispute involved money; the businessman in Vickers rivaled the artist in righteous fervor. He was always painfully aware that providing for his family hinged on his vocal cords, just as he was, increasingly as his career took flight, cognizant of the rarity and value of his gifts. As was often the case, the Vickers view of the incident wasn't the same as that of the other parties.

A former BBC executive who asked not to be named said they were the ones who refused ever to work with Vickers again, because of what was seen as his unprofessional behavior.

All in all, the episode is a telling one, as it reveals Vickers's methods of dealing with administrators and his readiness to seek legal redress. It also shows that he got himself into deep waters as his career began, and that the situation probably taught him much about making future decisions.

In a nutshell, Vickers agreed to sing Herod, in English, in a live BBC telecast of *Salome*. At rehearsal, as he told the story, he found he was expected not to "mark" (as singers call the customary practice of undersinging at rehearsal to preserve the voice) but to sing out, far more than he had expected or thought good for him. He lost his voice, and a doctor ordered him not to speak for several weeks. According to Vickers, he thus missed out not only on the telecast but also on other engagements. He placed a value on them and vowed never to sing again for BBC-TV until it settled up for fourteen thousand U.S. dollars (later he even spoke of interest due). The BBC, after a frantic search, had to bring in a German tenor who didn't know the role in English and ended up singing it in German, but for a few key English phrases, while the rest of the cast sang in English.

The dispute made the London papers, and Vickers was infuriated by what he saw as duplicitous statements by the BBC about the situation (even a dozen years later, in 1969, he called them "a bare-faced lie").[41] The reports said he had nodules on his vocal cords, a serious matter, but apparently untrue. Nonetheless, the young singer, newly in demand, was facing a vocal crisis that for all he knew could have ended his recently launched career.

Someone who saw the incident in a different light was Fred Weidner, a tenor who was at the *Salome* rehearsals because his wife, the German soprano Helga Pilarczyk, was singing Salome. According to Weidner, it rapidly became clear at the first rehearsal on September 6 that Vickers didn't know his part, although all the other cast members were fully prepared. When the respected conductor Walter Goehr suggested that he rehearse Vickers separately that afternoon, the tenor declined rudely, saying he had no need of Goehr and would use his own coach.[42]

Lionel Salter, then the BBC's head of music and television, recalled, "We were staggered when [Vickers] turned up not knowing his part." Salter, who was vehement three decades later about it all, insisted Vickers did not know a single note of his part. "In those days, TV went out live, so there was no safety net." Vickers missed the first rehearsal and "bluffed it out. He said in that arrogant way of his, 'The part I can't learn in a week doesn't exist.' We were even more shaken. This arrogance doesn't go down well at all. You can't get Herod under your belt in a week."

A day or two later Salter got a call that Vickers was unwell and not able to take the part. Salter demanded a doctor's certificate, which was not forthcoming. Vickers had at his home the only copy of the score with Herod's text marked in English, and Salter drove over to pick it up. He parked a few doors away and heard the sounds of a party, with Vickers's voice audible. "When I knocked at the door, he was very taken aback."

Soon after, Salter planned a press announcement that Vickers had "troubled vocal cords" and would not sing in the telecast. "It got round to him and he flew into a rage. He said, 'If you print that I will sue.'" He just wanted it said that he was indisposed.[43]

On September 22, 1957, Vickers handwrote a twelve-page letter to Webster from his Kenton home, relating his version of the *Salome* tale, expressing his anger with BBC-TV and apologizing for causing Webster concern. Vickers hadn't wanted to sing Herod because he felt he needed a holiday. He had thought to price himself out of it, asking 400 pounds. The BBC had rejected that; meanwhile, William Stein, in New York, advised Vickers not to touch the role. But a few weeks later, the BBC had called to offer 225 guineas, with a guarantee of a second airing at half that, which would have given Vickers about 354 pounds. Pressured to accept the role, he had reluctantly taken it on, beginning rehearsals after a bout of Asian flu that had forced the cancellation of a *Carmen* in Vienna. To his shock, the first rehearsal he had attended was a run-through onstage; he was never offered a single music rehearsal. Chastised for not having the role under his belt, Vickers found the tension on the set unbearable. By his own admission, he had picked a fight with Goehr, an impeccable musician, over the length of a bar. Goehr asked Vickers if he wanted to teach him to conduct, so Vickers backed down. (In future years, Vickers would on several occasions ask other conductors if indeed he had to teach them to conduct.) Under continual emotional and physical stress, Vickers's voice gave out ultimately from overuse and repetition. On September 18 when he got home after seven and a half hours of rehearsal, it was gone. He phoned the BBC to cancel.[44]

After the *Times* ran a story that the BBC doctor said Vickers had vocal nodules, all hell broke loose. Vickers's London agent, John Coast, called the BBC to ask for a retraction, but could get no one to admit putting out the nodule story. Years later, Salter said he had told the BBC press office only that Vickers was indisposed.[45] When no retraction appeared, Vickers, still under orders not to speak, had Hetti call Salter's office. Vickers, listening on an extension, heard Salter's assistant try to intimidate Hetti by suggesting he had inside information about Vickers's condition. Furious, Vickers broke in and told the assistant that both doctors had denied the nodules diagnosis and that Vickers would seek legal advice unless a retraction appeared. Coast then got a call from the BBC saying that Vickers had been abusive, threatened to sue, and therefore no retraction would be put out. The BBC also was calling in the lawyers.[46]

On November 5 Webster wrote Stein that Vickers had sung *Carmen* the previous Thursday and Saturday "and is very nearly his old self." Stein had taken umbrage that Webster held him in some way responsible for the *Salome* fiasco. On October 30 Stein had written Webster that he was shocked at Webster's accusation. "Nobody, but Vickers himself, can tell you how carefully I'm trying to steer him." Webster wrote in the November 5 missive that "Vickers told me you had strongly advised against the Herod so you are absolved of responsibility."[47] Clearly, Webster was on guard to protect his investment in Vickers, a key player in the future of the new Covent Garden.

The BBC-TV issue would arise again and again through Vickers's career, although he did not avoid doing BBC radio broadcasts. It would come up again during his first few months at the Metropolitan Opera. And the aftershocks were felt more than two decades later by the Dallas-based critic John Ardoin, who could not have written more glowingly of Vickers over the years, but who also felt the cold wind of the tenor's chilly side, his Otello-like suspicion, and his enduring stubbornness. The major chronicler of Callas, Ardoin wanted Vickers to take part in a 1978 documentary on his *Médée* partner. Vickers first agreed, then backed out angrily when he discovered that BBC-TV was coproducer with WNET, New York. Ardoin was totally unaware of Vickers's BBC problems. "Jon blamed me, as if I had kept it from him. Too bad, because the idea had been to follow him offstage from *Tristan* [which he was singing at Covent Garden] and talk with him as he took off his makeup about Callas and the demands of being an opera singer." Vickers was "like ice" when Ardoin saw him at the Royal Opera House. Vickers finally agreed to be filmed if he would appear only in the American version, not on the BBC. But it was too late, because he canceled part of a *Tristan* performance and flew home to Bermuda next morning.

Such Vickers frostiness often was merely a response to a professional situation. But in this case "Jon made it personal. It made me very sad. I admire him so much," Ardoin said firmly. "We had been close. I asked him to sing at Larry Kelly's funeral [the Dallas Opera chief died September 16, 1974]. He was supposed to be rehearsing *Grimes* in Chicago. He came and sang 'Total eclipse.' Then I had a big Irish wake at my house, and Jon came. And he stayed. [Chicago Lyric chief] Carol Fox called and wanted to know where is he! He kept missing planes he was supposed to get on. Finally he flew back on the same plane that took Kelly's body to Chicago to be buried."[48]

In September 1978 mention of a BBC-TV telecast of *La Fanciulla del West* had to be deleted from Vickers's contract as the dispute continued. (He had to cancel the performance owing to illness, as it turned out.) He would not agree to a telecast, Coast told the Royal Opera House, although he had no quarrel with BBC radio relay and Italian radio.

For some years a *Grimes* telecast had also been foiled by the disagreement. Coast said Vickers should get a fifteen-thousand-dollar fee and in addition another fifteen thousand "for the old [BBC-TV] compensation dispute." In December, Coast wrote, "various attempts have been made in the past to settle this dispute. None has succeeded."[49] Vickers and the BBC finally settled completely and amicably in 1981, because all parties urgently wanted a video made of the Covent Garden *Peter Grimes*. This was recorded on June 30, and Vickers signed the agreement in his dressing room the night of the run's first performance, June 23, a not-unusual occurrence for singers making TV contracts.[50] The video, issued by Thorn-EMI, is a wonderful document of the spare and moving production, the only one released to date of Vickers's Grimes onstage. Unavailable for some years, it has recently been reissued by Castle Opera in the U.S.

A canceled Bayreuth contract arrived for Vickers after those news stories about his supposed vocal problems, but it was reinstated after a scout checked out Vickers again in London. The tenor had written to Wieland Wagner refusing to sing yet another audition for him personally to confirm his vocal health.[51]

The BBC story also threw a scare into Kurt Herbert Adler in San Francisco. He wrote Stein that he wanted Vickers for exposed roles, and therefore it would be imperative that nothing be wrong with his vocal cords, "as it would be impossible to replace him at the last minute. The news is regrettable and alarming; so would you please let us know what the *true* facts are and your honest evaluation of the situation."[52] No wonder Vickers was furious about the episode. He also had to quit Covent Garden's *Aida* because of his throat problem after *Salome* (Albert Da Costa stepped in, unsatisfactorily).

That October in New York, Stein brought Vickers to Rudolf Bing's attention as a dramatic tenor.[53] And that month, Vickers returned a favor to Regina Resnik. As she had recommended him for *The Rape of Lucretia* at Stratford in 1956, he recommended her to Webster and Kubelik for *Carmen* at Covent Garden. She was a striking, sultry gypsy, and she thanked Webster for making the role her European calling card as a mezzo. Joan Sutherland was the Micaela, standing up to Kubelik in a fashion Vickers must have admired, insisting she would sing the recitative, rather than speak the dialogue.[54] (She and Vickers did not perform together.)

In November 1957 Vickers was in Rome, singing Elgar's difficult *The Dream of Gerontius*, with Sir John Barbirolli (also a radio broadcast). This profoundly Christian text, about death and the journey of the soul to God's throne, resonated deeply with him. Although he hoped to perform it again, the opportunity never arose in his career.

It had been a year of triumph and trauma for Vickers, but his name was now known internationally. He had made the breakthrough for which he hardly had dared hope on leaving Canada.

6

A Don Carlos *Triumph and Bayreuth Debut*

VICKERS HAD A MAJOR YEAR AHEAD WITH THE EXTRAORDINARY *Don Carlos* in May 1958 at Covent Garden and his Bayreuth debut that summer. The year began with his first collaboration of many with the conductor Colin Davis.

A wistful Vickers wish was to sing Don Ottavio in *Don Giovanni.* He put its tenor-testing "Il mio tesoro" on display in a January 14 concert led by Davis, whose star also was rising (he was a year younger than Vickers). John Coast presented the event at London's Royal Festival Hall; it included the German pianist Hans Richter-Hasse, another member of Coast's roster. Karajan had been at the hall two days before, leading the Philharmonia Orchestra, and later that week Peter Pears sang in *Messiah,* with "original accompaniments."

Vickers knew that his type of voice and heartier conception wouldn't be accepted critically for Mozart, but he also realized that this showpiece aria would display his versatility and excellent breath control. "He sang the music as lustily as if it had been Wagner, revealing yet again how fortunate we are to have in our midst a real heroic tenor by way of a change from the lyric kind more usually produced by English-speaking countries," said the *Times* of London. "Nevertheless Mozart needs a suaver lyricism and a much smoother line than Mr. Vickers can yet produce, not to mention those countless small subtleties of phrasing that help to impart a period flavor." Davis said later that Vickers "wanted to prove he could sing" the aria, and that "considering the immensity of the voice," he was "frightfully good."[1]

In February 1958 Vickers turned down a *Tristan* offer from Lyric Opera of Chicago and looked ahead enthusiastically to a new production of Handel's *Samson* in the fall, first at Leeds, then at Covent Garden. Lord Harewood kept a close eye on Covent Garden's golden boy. He visited Wieland Wagner in February 1958 to make "concrete" Vickers's Siegmund contract and iron out scheduling between the German house and the tenor's summer Covent Garden dates. He had five *Troyens* that June and July.[2] But Vickers sang only Siegmund at Bayreuth in 1958, not the *Parsifal* Wieland had wanted. As Vickers explained it, he received his contract just four weeks before the festival began, so "nothing came of the Parsifal."[3]

The 1958 *Don Carlos* staged by Luchino Visconti was a centennial celebration for Covent Garden and a risk for Webster, since it was not a familiar work and had never really been successful. Smetana's *Dalibor* also was considered; Vickers always wished he had had a chance to sing the Czech knight whose story is similar to that of *Fidelio* but ends unhappily. But that never transpired anywhere for him. Webster and Harewood chose *Carlos*, and Webster decided on the Italian translation of the French for which Verdi had composed. He knew he needed a topflight ensemble, with Vickers, of course, to star. Webster's closeness to Callas led to the collaboration with two men who had worked with her at La Scala, Visconti and Carlo Maria Giulini. Webster snared Tito Gobbi for Rodrigo and Boris Christoff for King Philip, chose Gré Brouwenstijn over Amy Shuard for Elisabetta, and cast Fedora Barbieri, more of a contralto than mezzo, as Eboli. Vickers was the sole company member in the ensemble. Giulini attended every stage rehearsal, the tenor recalled of those days before jets changed opera's time sense. And there were four and a half weeks of rehearsal before the eight performances beginning May 9.[4]

Vickers made "a most fascinating neurotic of a Carlos," Haltrecht wrote, suggesting that Webster was aware that Vickers's heroic aspect "was leavened by the 'little-boy' element," as with *Ballo*. The second-act duet, with Carlo and the wife of his father, agonizingly projected "the ambiguous lover-mistress, mother-son, queen-subject relationship."[5] Harold Rosenthal wrote, "I doubt whether Carlos has ever been sung so well since Martinelli did it in New York in the '20s."[6] The opera was another smash success for the house, boosting its prestige and enabling Webster to bring in more top-ranked conductors and directors. It also was Visconti's first big success outside Italy.

Vickers sang the role infrequently (a scheduled Met *Carlos* never came to pass) and never recorded it. But fortunately a private recording exists from the 1958 performances, and his first great lines, "Fontainebleau, foreste immensa e solitaria," echo unforgettably through time. Here it is clear that the timbre of the Vickers voice, so utterly distinctive, was of superlative importance in setting him apart. There is literally no other tenor who sounds or ever sounded remotely like him. This uniqueness would be etched more deeply as age roughened the sound, making it only the more poignantly expressive. Classic beauty alone is never the point of singing like his.

In the summer of this busy year, Vickers fitted in two performances of the Verdi Requiem, always a favorite of his. On June 6 Regina Resnik also was among soloists in the Requiem at Royal Festival Hall, with the London Symphony Orchestra under Sir Eugene Goossens. On June 10 Vickers and Thebom sang the *Troyens* love duet (in English) at the Covent Garden Centennary Gala, with Queen Elizabeth and the Duke of Edinburgh in attendance. Callas was on the program, in the mad scene from Bellini's *I Puritani*.

Beginning June 16 Vickers did a run of five performances of *Les Troyens* at the Royal Opera House under Kubelik. The American tenor William Lewis, then twenty-six, who would have many associations with Vickers, was in the house for all the performances. He recalled the production as much better than the future Met *Troyens* (in which Lewis also would sing). Vickers was excellent, bouncing around on rubber-soled shoes, but he took the optional A-flat, not the high C in his big final-act aria, "Inutiles regrets."[7]

And this was the summer of Vickers's Bayreuth debut, and the development of what had already begun as a complicated relationship with the younger of Richard Wagner's two grandsons. Wieland Wagner could be a difficult man—"not once you got on the stage with him," said Vickers; then "he was fine. But to try and deal with him in negotiations as far as what to do and what not to do—he was absolutely impossible. He would just thump with his fist [and say], 'You will do what I want you to do.'"[8]

Of course, Vickers could be just as intransigent when it came to his own views. But he was hardly the only one to classify Wieland as difficult. The author Frederic Spotts, for example, said Wieland could be "irascible, quixotic, and ruthless," banning singers such as Dietrich Fischer-Dieskau for small annoyances.[9] It is perhaps a measure of Wieland's admiration for Vickers that he pursued him for several years after the tenor declined to fit in with Bayreuth plans. Vickers would be Bayreuth's first British Siegmund and Parsifal.

Although Vickers had proposed both roles at his audition for Wieland, he later backed off from singing Parsifal at his first Bayreuth Festival, feeling that he could not learn it as well as he wanted to in six months.[10] After settling on Siegmund for his debut, the two artists wrangled over first the issue of Vickers's real or imaginary vocal problems, then the complications of the singer's summer schedule—just the day before rehearsals began, Vickers sent word he would not arrive in time.[11]

Vickers coached for Siegmund with Reginald Goodall, for whom he had the highest admiration, as did many singers who made their way up to Valhalla, as Goodall's studio high under the Covent Garden roof was known. Goodall was English but had studied in the Toronto area and had sung in the great oratorios that were part of Vickers's schooling; he had worked in the Toronto churches so familiar to Vickers. Unlike Vickers,

Goodall had been introduced as a boy to a love of Wagner. The tenor also worked with him on *Parsifal* and *Tristan*, on *Fidelio*, and on *Peter Grimes* for his Met appearance. Goodall was close to Britten for a time, had conducted the *Grimes* premiere in 1945 at Sadler's Wells, and had worked on the *Grimes* recording with Peter Pears.

Vickers's Bayreuth debut as Siegmund was another triumph, following *Les Troyens* and *Don Carlos*. The doomed Volsung would become a signature role, suiting him ideally both vocally and temperamentally. Régine Crespin, a frequent Sieglinde, said Vickers was a very masculine Siegmund "and at the same time very sweet and vulnerable." Strong enough to pull the sword from the tree, he was yet a man to be pitied, and these twin facets both showed in his voice.[12] Siegmund, said Vickers, calls for the most heroic singing in all of Wagner, though it lies too low for a dramatic tenor, rising only to an A. It could be sung by a good lyric baritone, but he said the Germans didn't want that because they would miss the gleam on the voice.[13]

He sang those two Siegmunds in two Bayreuth *Ring* cycles with Hans Knappertsbusch, whom he adored. A visiting Goodall was also in the pit to observe. The stellar casts included Astrid Varnay and Martha Mödl as Brünnhilde, Leonie Rysanek as Sieglinde, Hans Hotter as Wotan, Josef Greindl as Hunding, Wolfgang Windgassen as Siegfried, and Rita Gorr as Fricka and Grimgerde.

Vickers later described how the concertmaster stopped him on the street to congratulate him on his success, but told him he had sung too slowly in the first-act "Winterstürme." "I said, 'No, it was Knappertsbusch.' He said, 'No, it was you.' I said, 'But I tried so hard to do exactly what [the conductor] wanted!' And he said, 'Yes, and he tried so hard to do exactly what you wanted, and it got slower and slower!'" Vickers smiled as he recalled this, but tempi would be a continuing issue between Vickers and many other conductors throughout his career.

The concertmaster continued, "Didn't you hear what he said to the orchestra when you finished? 'The young boy sings it slow, but let him sing it slow while he's still young!'"

Taken aback, Vickers was trembling when he went to face Knappertsbusch. He asked if he might sing the "Winterstürme" a little faster. Then, "I started to sing, and out loud he said, 'So!' Then he sat back, put down his baton and listened to me, smiling up at me—didn't conduct at all. There's a place in the 'Winterstürme' where the tempo changes; he picked up his baton, threw me a kiss, and we went on! . . . What a wonderful man!"[14]

"The greatest personal success . . . an ideal Siegmund," wrote Ralf Steyer of those *Walküres*. "Many harked back to Lauritz Melchior's time with the hope that in [Vickers] we have again won for Bayreuth a really great heldentenor."[15]

"This Siegmund was an event and the ovations after the first act were the best proof of it," wrote the *Wiesbaden Courier*. "Wieland Wagner had a very lucky hand when he engaged Vickers, whose acting knows no self-consciousness."[16]

Vickers called his first festival a two-pronged affair, magnificent on one hand, a nightmare on the other. After he arrived in Bayreuth, he waited days for a rehearsal. He finally got an orchestra rehearsal, but without Knappertsbusch, and it was outdoors. After continual requests, he said to Wieland's secretary: "You can tell Mr. Wagner something for me. And I never bluff. I'm going to be working on the stage with him personally on Siegmund tomorrow morning at ten o'clock or you're going to find another tenor." The next morning Wieland was there. "And he was marvelous . . . really an absolute genius . . . because then nothing mattered except the production. . . . He wasn't dictatorial, he wasn't shoving you into a mold, he was exploring your mind, exploring your talent, giving you as much as he could possibly pour into you of his gigantic talent." But Vickers said his greatest joy in Bayreuth was working with Knappertsbusch, whom he called the best Wagner conductor of his experience.[17]

On August 14, the day of Vickers's second performance, the festival asked him to return in 1959 as Siegmund, Parsifal, or Erik (in *Der fliegende Holländer*) but did not specify which. He was being welcomed into the Wagner festival family, with a great Wagnerian career ahead.[18]

But Wieland himself shortly wired to offer only Erik and nothing else. Vickers wrote in September that he could not accept that single ungrateful role. Later he gritted his teeth as he told of the negotiation. "Wieland got in his typical—this was just *typical* of him! If you didn't want to do what he wanted to do, when he wanted to do it, from the standpoint of his planning for his house, he was impossible. And he said, 'Oh, now you've got a fat head. Just because you've had a success as Siegmund, you think you can tell us what you're going to sing in the Bayreuth Festival!' And I said, 'No, that isn't my point at all, Mr. Wagner, I'm just telling you what I'm *not* going to sing in this festival!'"[19]

That October, Vickers offered to return if Wieland would give him another role in addition to Erik, which, he argued, wasn't the best follow-up to his *Walküre* success. By February 1959 Vickers was slated for *Parsifal* and *Der fliegende Holländer*. But it turned out that the *Holländer* coincided with Callas's *Médée* at the Royal Opera House in June. Vickers angered Wieland by pulling out to join Callas. Nevertheless, by May, Wieland's artistic director, Gerhard Hellwig, had invited Vickers for 1960 and asked about Tristan and

Siegfried.[20] Vickers declined the Tristan, as he had with Karajan. This back-and-forth would continue for six more years, until Wieland's death at age forty-nine, from the rare, tumor-causing Boeck's disease.

Vickers might have gone to Bayreuth for *Parsifal* in 1961, but that July he was to record *Aida* and RCA would not release him. His offer to be there for two performances in August was not acceptable. For 1962 he was offered *Tristan,* and for 1963 *Rienzi.* Neither was to his liking at the time. Vickers's only other Bayreuth appearance would be four performances of *Parsifal* in 1964, also under Knappertsbusch. He was invited for the 1965 new *Ring* under Karl Böhm, but this never came to pass.[21]

Hans Hotter believed Wieland was not the best judge of singers on a purely vocal basis. But he also told the author that Vickers was "by nature a little distrusting . . . he looks at people, [wondering,] 'What [do] you want now,' suspicious."[22]

Having been told that Wolfgang Wagner, when asked in 1974 about Vickers's absence from the festival, had said the tenor was "financially not reachable," Vickers responded, "We have never talked about the amount of honorarium. I wanted merely to get enough so that I could have a vacation in Bayreuth with my family."[23]

He later sounded bitter about his Bayreuth experiences and his failure to return. He would recount the story of rooming in 1964 with a rich woman who told him she missed the good old days when the Führer was there and who blamed Germany's defeat on the Jews. He had found the performances "like a black Mass. All those people walking up the hill to the shrine, homosexuals, men with other men's wives. I hated it. I was revolted by it."[24]

All of that may well have been true for him. But Vickers, typically, would make those stories sound as if his disgust was the sole reason he never returned, when in fact he clearly would have if he and the Wagners could have agreed upon his roles.

In August 1958 Vickers interrupted his Bayreuth stay to fly to Vancouver after his first Siegmund to sing two performances of the Verdi Requiem. In later years he described this as a "dumb" thing to do, but at the time the Vancouver festival was an important event for him in Canada.[25] He sang his first Covent Garden Siegmunds, just two, on September 24 and October 7, under Rudolf Kempe, with Varnay and Hotter in the cast. Andrew Porter reported that Vickers sang well indeed "but could not project his music as vividly as, after his Bayreuth success, we might have hoped."[26] (In the rest of the *Ring* that season at Covent Garden, Windgassen was excellent singing both Siegfrieds.)

Vickers faced a possible turning point in the late 1950s when he was offered the role of King Arthur in the 1960 Broadway musical *Camelot*, the followup by Lerner and Loewe to *My Fair Lady*. He considered it seriously but declined, later estimating he gave up about $750,000 in doing so.[27] Apart from the singer's own reminiscences, however, no records survive of any such offer, and Stone Widney, the production supervisor and casting director for the original Broadway staging, told the author he had no recollection of an offer. Richard Burton was director Moss Hart's choice from the beginning, he said, although Vickers's name might have been bandied about early on.[28] Burton rejuvenated his career with the part, and Vickers's conservatory schoolmate Robert Goulet shot to fame as Lancelot.

Vickers would never move into popular or what is now called crossover repertory. His future New York performances would be not on Broadway but at the Metropolitan Opera, and then only after years of protracted negotiations with Rudolf Bing, the Met's general manager. On June 1, 1957, Joan Ingpen had written from her artists agency to Bing in Paris that Vickers could not audition for him in Glyndebourne on June 30. That would be the day after a *Troyens* performance, and Vickers, Ingpen wrote, "does not feel that he will be in any shape to come down . . . for such an important audition the next day. . . . He is a very nice person and is deservedly having a real success here," she added. "His performance would benefit from having a little more polish but he has not yet had a great deal of experience."[29] Ingpen was not representing Vickers, she recalled, just helping him out.[30]

By 1958 talks were still ongoing, with Webster advising Vickers, who sensed that Bing "was liable to despise people if he could get his way with them by flattery or subterfuge."[31] When Bing asked the tenor to sing his first Tristan in a new production with Birgit Nilsson in 1959, he declined, saying he believed that new roles should not be tried out at the Met.[32] It was the first of a number of times he would disappoint Nilsson. He could have tried out the role at Chicago, San Francisco, or Bayreuth but declined those offers as well. A January 1959 clip from the *Dallas Times Herald* has Vickers scheduled to sing *Tristan* at the Met on January 6, 1960, with the soprano Aase Nordmo-Lövberg. This never transpired.

In March 1958 a major change had begun in Vickers's relationship with Covent Garden. His eighteen-month contract would be up in June. William Stein, his agent in New York, told Webster that Vickers wanted to change from a weekly contract (then at one hundred pounds a week) to a performance-based contract and asked him to consider what fee might be offered.[33]

That summer, even before he had made his Bayreuth debut, an increasingly confident Vickers entered into a game of financial hardball with

Webster, abetted by his London agent, John Coast. Vickers's agent for virtually all of his career, Coast had an unusual history. Taken prisoner in World War II by the Japanese in the battle of Singapore, he was held for three years and during that time began a long interest in Balinese dance and music. In the 1950s he toured with a Balinese troupe, including a visit to the United States with the Dancers of Bali, promoted by the legendary American impresario Sol Hurok. Coast then became a talent scout in Europe for Columbia Artists before opening his own agency. He looked like the actor Ronald Colman, elegant with a pencil mustache, and always in jacket and tie or cravat. His Javanese wife, Supianti (known as Luce), became involved in the agency, which would represent some of the biggest names in opera.

A letter from Coast to Webster dated July 19 and hand-delivered by Coast made clear that Vickers "would rather not sign a contract with Covent Garden" for less than 175 pounds per performance but instead would "take a chance on making real money in America and hooking offers after Bayreuth in Germany." The operas asked for by Covent Garden—*Lohengrin, Parsifal, Peter Grimes, Fidelio,* Smetana's *Dalibor,* and *Aida*—"are not only taxing, but should you be forced to bring in an outsider to sing them well, you would have to pay at least or more than 175 [pounds]." Vienna, Coast noted, would be paying Vickers for his 1959 debut nearly twice what Covent Garden had paid for his London debut only eighteen months earlier. Moreover, Vickers could get 200 pounds per performance "right now" in Canada and in America, and 700 pounds for one, in *Onegin,* "by picking up the phone this very moment." Coast added, "He now says that Mr. Stein and I should know him well enough by now to realize he is not a bluffer."[34]

Whatever his possible feelings that Vickers was being disloyal, Webster replied to Coast, "You know as well as I do I have to give in to his demands."[35] Days later, by July 22, he had agreed to the 175 pounds. Vickers did make amends by singing four *Samson*s at the Leeds Festival for 350 pounds, the price of two under his new pact with the man who had given him his big break.

Coast also had nonfinancial demands from the tenor: "Vickers wants to sing only twice a week. In order to ensure this he says he will sing only three times in seven days if he is paid a double fee for the third performance. If he is required to sing three times in a week, for example, on Monday, Wednesday and Saturday, he does not want to sing again the following Monday." He also insisted on working not more than 180 days in the U.K., for tax reasons.[36]

Vickers visited Webster's office after they reached the agreement and said, "I'm very sorry that I felt I had to have a showdown." The courtly, generally imperturbable Webster said, apparently approving, "If you'll fight with me, then you'll fight with anyone." And Webster continued as Vickers's mentor.[37]

Vickers enjoyed jousting with Webster. They had a common background in retailing in that the Dundee-born Webster once ran a large store in Liverpool. Webster's homosexuality (the "homosexual haberdasher" was one sobriquet for him by some denigrators) wouldn't have been mentioned publicly in those far more discreet days (although Webster had a longtime and public male companion). This was just as well, given Vickers's dim view of homosexuals in general. "He hates them," Ingpen said bluntly, adding that this was why Vickers would never sing Captain Vere in *Billy Budd*. He was convinced that Vere, like John Claggart, harbored desires for young Billy.[38] It remained a paradox that some of the most important people in Vickers's career, from Webster to Britten to Zeffirelli, were gay, yet Vickers never approved of that aspect of their lives. This may be laid in part to the tenor's strict, Bible-based upbringing.

In November 1958 a svelte Maria Callas sang her only *Médée*s in America, with the Dallas Civic Opera. Her Jason was Vickers, who had sung the role in the 1956 Philadelphia concert performance with Eileen Farrell. This was his American opera house debut, and the beginning of a mutual admiration between the Greek-American and the Canadian, whose collaboration extended only to that single opera. But Vickers became Callas's tenor of choice for Jason.

He had a vivid memory of receiving the Dallas offer from his agent. A telegram came when he was singing in *Aida* and two *Carmen*s in Manchester on the ROH tour in March 1958. He shaves with a straight razor and was stropping the blade; in his excitement, he threw the blade across the room and split open a finger.[39]

That Dallas day when Vickers met Callas, he began by metaphorically strapping on his sword. Bliss Hebert, assistant to the music director Nicola Rescigno, as well as to directors working there, had the job of driving Vickers to rehearsal. He knew the tenor a little from having stage-managed the New York concert *Fidelio* Vickers had sung in 1956. On the half-hour ride, "he was mutter, mutter, mutter. 'I've heard about her, her reputation, I won't let her get away with anything with me.'"

By that time Callas had had a lot of bad press, since the scandal of the January 2 *Norma*, the so-called Rome Walkout, when she quit after the first act, suffering a throat inflammation. Vickers also had heard she was instrumental in having a baritone, Enzo Sordello, fired from the Met in 1956.

Hebert, who was prompting in Dallas as well that season, and had done the Zeffirelli *Traviata* there with Callas, said she was "the most serious, professional artist I've ever met. Her behavior was beyond reproach."

So it was most unusual that she was late that day. Vickers and Hebert had been about ten minutes early. The tenor went into a corner and pulled out a paperback book. At rehearsal time, Callas wasn't there. "He's steaming in the corner. I can see he expects this willful prima donna," said Hebert, who was at the door when Callas finally arrived. She had been picked up late by an opera board member, and she was frantic.

"She said to me, 'This is terrible, my first rehearsal with Jon and I'm late. I feel terrible about this. Where is he?'" Hebert pointed to the corner. Callas, ever receptive to moods (Ardoin called her *strega*, witch, like Medea), could tell Vickers was in one. She asked to be introduced. "I took her over and I can remember almost verbatim, she said, 'Mr. Vickers, I can't tell you how sorry I am, but I had no control over arriving here. I've been waiting . . . and so looking forward to working with you. I've done this with several tenors and you're the first that has the voice that is appropriate and wonderful.'

"He looked up at her and melted. Absolutely melted. I think every other time she did Medea, it was always with him [it was]. And in years after, Jon had only the most wonderful things to say about her." She was five feet seven and thin, "and he being built like a bull, it felt like he towered over her," said Hebert.[40] In fact, he was about Callas's height, but Vickers fondly called her "the little Maria."

Vickers recalled about Dallas that Callas had begun "giving me orders as if to test what mettle I was made of: 'Don't do that; . . . don't look at me that way.' I stopped, looked straight at her and said, 'Madame Callas, [director] Alexis Minotis has already put me through the production. You show me what you are going to do.' We never had another problem working together. Her dedication was quite extraordinary. . . . She never tried to steal the limelight or upstage anyone."

Of their work in *Médée,* Vickers noted "the almost masochistic way she'll drive herself into her part. She won't let the little Maria show through." In 1960 he said of her: "A more cooperative artist it is impossible to meet."[41]

Vickers, whom Hebert recalled as looking like a wrestler with his huge biceps, was very supportive of Callas in the crisis during her Dallas stay. The afternoon of the *Médée* opening night, November 6, Rudolf Bing sent his infamous telegram dismissing her from the Met's 1958–59 season. He also put out a nasty statement to the press. At the time Vickers was himself in protracted negotiations with Bing for his Met debut (he would sign his contract the following February). He sympathized, because Callas's motive in having wanted to change some Met performances was only concern for her voice. He certainly had had enough such concerns himself. "Is this art?" Callas said, about her lack of Met rehearsals, her unknown partners. He would only agree. And he could only have been shocked as were so many that Bing chose the *Médée* opening for his bombshell. "Pray for me tonight!" Callas told the press.

But she had Vickers in her corner, although their characters were opposed in the opera. Their rapport helped them to throw off sparks onstage as Jason abandoned the mother of his children. Her fury that night was directed as much at Bing as at Jason.[42]

Vickers also defended Callas staunchly after an incident at a rehearsal that had begun at 5 P.M. the day before the performance and lasted nine hours, with Callas there the whole time. She became angry when one of the big pillars almost fell on her. Vickers recalled: "I heard one of the stagehands say, 'Ho, ho! This is the Callas we came to see.' And I said, 'I'm going to tell you something. If that pillar had nearly fallen on me, I'd have given you a lot rougher time than Maria Callas did.'"[43] In fact, he would do so in incidents in opera houses around the world.

The production, also given November 8, was world-class, directed by Minotis of the Greek National Theater, the cast including Teresa Berganza as Neris and Nicola Zaccaria as Creon, all in costumes of fabric woven in Greece. Vickers, far from a known quantity in the U.S., was greeted by *Dallas Morning News* critic John Rosenfield as "a broth of a lad with some young tenor woodenness of movement, [who] was a vocal treat, nevertheless, with a heroic and warmly colored voice."[44]

When the curtain came down after the first act on opening night, Vickers recalled to Tom Sutcliffe that Callas "flew across the stage and threw her arms around me . . . and said, 'At last a tenor who can act!' And the curtain went up again on Maria embracing me."[45]

The Dallas *Médée* production traveled to Covent Garden, where Callas, Vickers, and Zaccaria, with Rescigno, did five performances beginning June 17. Vickers had given up Bayreuth that summer to do it. Callas captured the city. Even Aristotle Onassis had to seek tickets on the black market, and he and his wife, Tina, threw a huge opening-night party at the Dorchester Hotel. Vickers, in short tunic and elevated lace-up sandals, sang magnificently, "and his struggle to remain settled in his resolves in spite of Medea's dark enchantment is effectively suggested," wrote Geoffrey Tarran.[46] The *Musical Times* made an important point about the versatility that Vickers would continue to offer through the decades: "We hear this singer so often and in such a variety of roles that there is a danger of his quality being underestimated; where else is there a heroic tenor who could equal him in Verdi and Wagner, let alone Handel and Cherubini?"[47]

Dallas saw the pair again in the *Médée* of November 19 and 21. Callas was at this time in the final throes of ending her marriage to Giovanni Battista Meneghini, still claiming Onassis was only a friend. This must have disturbed Vickers; such problems among friends upset him at other times, but he never let it affect his onstage professionalism.

Their last *Médée*s came in 1961 and 1962. On August 6 and 13, 1961, the site was Epidaurus, the fourth-century B.C. amphitheater, in the Greek National Opera Company presentation, Rescigno conducting. Vickers had no problem projecting for the sold-out audience (he said twenty-two thousand spectators were jammed into a space for sixteen thousand). On December 11, 14, and 20 they were at La Scala, under Thomas Schippers, with Giulietta Simionato and Nicolai Ghiaurov, as they were on May 29 and June 3 the next year.

Callas was one of the few artists who seem to have influenced Vickers, and many regretted that the pair never collaborated on anything else. But her bel canto repertoire was not his meat; he never sang in her specialties like *Lucia, La Traviata,* or *Tosca.* She had sung Isolde, Brünnhilde, and Kundry, in Italian, in the late 1940s and early 1950s, but she was three years older than he, and her voice had begun to deteriorate by the early 1960s, when his career was in full first flight. Theirs was a meeting of artistic minds, though the blending of those great voices was brief.

Vickers thought of her for Didon in the 1969 *Troyens* in London, but it was not to be. And he balked at singing one other role he might have had, Pollione to her Norma, one of her great parts. In his 1985 play *The Lisbon Traviata,* Terrence McNally goes so far as to have the Callas fanatic, Mendy, comment that this was the "tragedy" of both Vickers's and Callas's careers.

"The problem was, he was terrified because of the tradition in the first act for a high C. He didn't have a high C," asserted Callas authority John Ardoin. "I said to him, 'You should do Pollione,' and he said, 'I'll have the critics all over me'" if he sang it as written, minus the C. Ardoin didn't know whether Callas had asked Vickers to do the part, "but Pollione had been in his mind, because he knew about the C."[48] Vickers did sing the role to Montserrat Caballé's Norma in 1974 at the Orange Festival, successfully, albeit minus that C. (A video survives of that performance.)

All through his life Vickers would invoke the name of Callas as one of the few, with Wieland Wagner, who had changed the face of opera in their time. In his stagings, Wieland had delved into "the profound depths of the psychological meanings." Callas had taken works of art that many sopranos had used simply as demonstrations of vocal technique (always scorned by Vickers) and "translated them into real, living characters [with] great messages."[49]

Others grouped Vickers along with those two. Callas said, "Our duty is not to serve ourselves. We serve art and we serve the composers who were geniuses. We are not geniuses."[50] Vickers would often repeat the same sentiment.

7

New Roles, New Houses

VICKERS TOOK ON AN IMPORTANT NEW ROLE IN OCTOBER 1958, singing his first Samson at the Handel Festival in Leeds for four performances under Raymond Leppard. Covent Garden's production was said to be the first time this oratorio had been fully staged as an opera. On October 17 Queen Elizabeth and the Duke of Edinburgh attended, visiting the singers backstage.

Opera's review noted with relief that this tenor, whose successes to date had included Verdi and Wagner, was perfectly competent in a style that required cantabile lines and florid runs. Vickers was noble and moving all through, and sang his difficult final aria, "Thus when the sun," "with a finely controlled mezza voice [*sic*]."[1] This towering biblical figure, like the Saint-Saëns Samson he would sing five years later, was typical of the tortured hero at which Vickers excelled, and the story's scriptural origin was particularly to his liking.

Vickers was, as always, conscious of his physical appearance. He wore white shin pads for some reason, possibly having to do with his bowlegs. Those legs would never be a major hindrance; even Laurence Olivier worked to camouflage and expand with exercise his skinny shanks. "He has a few little weaknesses," said baritone Peter Glossop. "If he can show his physical strength, he does."[2] For months beforehand, Vickers worked out extensively so his body would be in top shape in his skimpy loincloth. Already muscular, he wanted more definition so his Samson would look like a bodybuilder who could bring down a temple (although that event is unseen in Handel's work).[3] In an interview with the *Yorkshire News*, "a dressing-room dissertation," the reporter called it, Vickers noted that nowhere in the story is there any evidence that Samson was a big man. His strength, said Vickers, was spiritual, not physical. "I sound like a preacher, don't I?" he added, laughing.[4]

The tenor's schedule was already heavy as his career expanded. He planned to travel overnight from the Leeds Festival and catch a plane for

Chicago to sing Beethoven's Ninth. Then he would wing to Montreal for a concert, then travel to Texas for *Médée* with Callas, then return to London before his Vienna appearances in January. He sang more Royal Festival Hall concerts in November 1958: On November 27 it was "Total eclipse" and Haydn's "And God created man" from *The Creation*, with the Royal Philharmonic, and on November 30 and December 4 he joined in Beethoven's Ninth Symphony, with Paul Hindemith leading the Philharmonia Orchestra.

On the eve of his Vienna State Opera debut as Siegmund, under Karajan, on January 8, 1959, Vickers wrote another warm note to Webster, who, he said, by treating his opinions with respect, laughing with him, chiding him, and fighting with him, had made Vickers grow up. Vickers said that before growing up too much, he wanted to express his thanks with youthful enthusiasm.[5]

He had a hectic schedule at the Staatsoper, but little rehearsal. From January 8 to 28 he sang *Die Walküre, Un Ballo in Maschera, Aida,* another *Walküre,* and then *Don Carlos,* with Sena Jurinac. In February he repeated *Walküre, Carlos,* and *Aida.* In March it was two *Pagliaccis* (his "Vesti la giubba" brought down the house), *Aida* with Birgit Nilsson—his first time singing with her—and on March 30 another *Walküre,* with Nilsson as Brünnhilde. (He also honored a commitment to the ROH tour in Manchester and flew in twice from Vienna to sing Samson, on March 16 and 27.)

In *Die Walküre* he rehearsed with one soprano, only to be confronted onstage with a Sieglinde he had never seen, Hilde Konetzni. But both gave great performances, record executive Christopher Raeburn recalled.[6] In Vickers's first phrases in Act 1, when he enters as the exhausted Siegmund, his voice showed he was at the end of his strength, recalled Richard Bletschacher, who was Karajan's assistant at the time. The tenor didn't try to display his voice, he merely wanted to show that Siegmund was almost in extremis.[7]

Karajan arranged the extremely moving "Todesverkundegung" scene of Act 2, in which Brünnhilde (Martha Mödl) tells Siegmund of his approaching death, so that Vickers sat, without moving, with Sieglinde on his lap. This, reminded Bletschacher, is called for in Wagner's stage directions: Siegmund leans over and gently kisses his bride/sister on the brow as he talks with Brünnhilde. But in many productions Sieglinde is left sleeping elsewhere onstage or is not even visible. Here Vickers made his biggest impression simply by sitting. "The main thing was his face. You didn't look anywhere but on his face, a man who was going to die, with the woman he loves on his knees."

Karajan knew that Vickers was one of the last tenors—perhaps the very last—who had the heroic and deeply human expression of the great singers of German roles before him, such as Max Lorenz and Melchior. "Jon's voice was not so big as those voices," said Bletschacher, "but his soul was as great as needed for this part." Moreover, his German was good; Vickers, Bletschacher said idiomatically, "had teeth in his mouth when he sang."[8]

"His Siegmund was justly acclaimed by the local critics as a revelation," wrote Joseph Wechsberg in *Opera*, "and hosannahs about a new Wagnerian tenor filled the air. Vickers has 18-carat gold in his throat, and he handles this wealth intelligently; his careful diction and disciplined movements betrayed the hand of Wieland Wagner. . . . As Don José and Radames, Vickers seemed to be less at ease, often forced his high notes, and generally gave the impression that these are not really his parts, not yet."[9] Later, Wechsberg wrote:

> I suppose one would have to go back to the young Lorenz or the young Melchior for comparisons, but since I didn't hear them when they were young, I can only say that Vickers that night was the best Siegmund I've heard in my busy operatic life. It was one of those moments that come every 20 years or so in the theatre. Vickers has grown astonishingly in the past two years and is now, with Miss Nilsson, the managers' answer to their Wagnerian prayers. He sings Wagner with Italian cantilene . . . and although he walks around with casual gestures, he has a deep feeling for the music and complete honesty about everything he does. When he sang, "Si ehe der lenz . . ." a shiver ran down the collective spine of the breathless audience. The love duet [with Konetzni] was sheer magic. Afterwards the audience got up and applauded throughout the entire intermission.[10]

Praised by this sophisticated music capital, Vickers must have felt, as at Bayreuth, great relief and justification for his deep belief in what he had to offer. Whatever his future insecurities, this triumph would stand. He later recalled twenty-three curtain calls after the *Walküre* debut and scores of curtain calls after the first night of the *Pagliacci*. After the latter, "the press the next day poured such lavish praise that I was swimming in a sea of unreality for weeks, if not for years."[11]

But he would not sing as often as he might have in Vienna, as problems arose with claques that booed and some less enthusiastic critics, as well as the changing fortunes of Herbert von Karajan, to whom Vickers remained loyal.

Vickers was in Vienna when he received his first Met contract, signed by Bing and dated February 2, 1959. The tenor agreed to eight performances from January 4 to March 18, 1960, at $750 per performance, with $1,000 for travel and expenses. He agreed to sing in *Aida, Pagliacci, Carmen, Fidelio,* and *Die Walküre,* "provided," according to a note in his own hand, "that neither Radames or Florestan shall constitute my Metropolitan Opera debut."[12]

He had rebuffed earlier feelers from Bing: "I told him that as long as he felt it was necessary for me to audition for him, I knew I wasn't ready for the Met."[13] Of course, he had auditioned for Bing in 1953, and the Met's George Schick had been at the Webster audition in Toronto. Vickers's Met invitation, he said later that year, was a direct result of his Covent Garden association.[14] But the fact is that younger dramatic tenors were in demand. Tristan was beyond Vinay's powers by 1959, and Del Monaco's Otello was a shadow of what it had been.

On February 5, 1959, Vickers wrote from Vienna with excitement to his mentor Geiger-Torel in Toronto about his Met signing. He hoped his debut would be in *Die Walküre,* he wrote, because he felt he could sing the part with complete ease and confidence thanks to what he had learned from Wieland. He thanked Geiger-Torel for giving him an excellent grounding in the role and in general stage deportment. When Vickers worked with Wieland, Geiger-Torel was often in his thoughts. He wrote happily that he could now use his hands without feeling self-conscious. He recalled how foolish he had felt trying a gesture Geiger-Torel had wanted in his *Gianni Schicchi* aria in Toronto, and how Geiger-Torel had gone over it with him. Now, such a movement came with ease.

He complained strongly about Vienna, though; it would never be a favorite place to sing. There was far too much intrigue, and the quality of the Staatsoper performances was extremely uneven, with grossly inadequate rehearsal time undermining even the best performers. Nevertheless, Vickers wrote of how much he enjoyed the broader Vienna experience—the beautiful house, excellent orchestra, knowledgeable audiences. Hetti and the children were with him, in a pleasant apartment at 73 Wahringerstrasse.[15]

Frankfurt-born Geiger-Torel wrote back to Vickers in mid-February, commiserating about the underrehearsed performances but saying that the city was ever thus. He recalled a saying, "Wiener Schlamperei," meaning, he wrote, "Viennese sloppiness with a cosy undertone!" Vickers would find this unevenness in many European houses, Geiger-Torel warned, and would meet few directors like Wieland with definite ideas, "who ask their casts to be precise and clear-cut in their actions and reactions." Fortunately, Vickers's training had prepared him to "stand on your own if you are abandoned by lazy or incompetent directors."[16]

A memorable *Parsifal* and a significant *Pagliacci* awaited Vickers in 1959, as well as an important debut in San Francisco. And he was contemplating a *Tristan* recording with Knappertsbusch for the following year.

His first performances as Parsifal came on May 28 and June 1, 1959, at the Royal Opera House, in a new production with Rudolf Kempe conducting. Karl Liebl had sung the opening performances, but when Vickers took over as the pure fool, "a magical change" was noted by critic Evan Senior. He sang with complete sincerity and a thorough understanding, evidenced by his careful differentiation of Parsifal's three repeats of "Das weiss Ich nicht" (I do not know) in Act 1. Gerda Lammers was Kundry.[17]

With the May 28 *Parsifal* Vickers savored what opera can be at its peak for performers and audience. "We transcended every sort of limitation that night," he recalled. "It wasn't illusion anymore, it was reality—a human experience. Many in the audience were crying, and on the stage we knew they were crying and we were crying too. All of us then, I think, were sharing a common feeling of being involved in suffering and in victory through suffering."[18] Vickers said much later that this had been the most thrilling night of his career, knowing that he had moved an audience so deeply.[19] When the curtain fell after Parsifal had opened the Grail shrine, there was dead silence in the hall. The curtain remained down. Stella Chitty, the stage manager, told Vickers backstage that the house manager had called her to say that under no circumstances should the curtain be raised again. So many people were weeping that it would have embarrassed them all. Not a hand clapped. The lights in the hall were kept down, and the crowd filed out in silence.[20]

That to Vickers was what opera should be—a revealing, transforming experience, not a mere entertainment, a pejorative word for him when it came to his art. (Later, he wanted to direct *Parsifal* at Covent Garden, but this never came to pass.)

Canadian talent was on display elsewhere in London as Glenn Gould performed in July with the LSO under Krips. On the tenor front, London-born Charles Craig made his Covent Garden debut in 1959 as Pinkerton and became a generally admired singer at the house. He would sing Otello, notably at the English National Opera, but never rose to Vickers's level of fame.

In the summer of 1959 Vickers took part in RCA's expensive London recording of Handel's *Messiah*, led by Sir Thomas Beecham, who viewed it as a work in the grand manner. "I never think about the purists," said the feisty Englishman. "They are a breed that has sprung up recently. If Handel and many other composers were left to the purists, with their parsimonious handfuls of strings and oboes, you would never hear any of them. The thing to remember is that no man knows how these works were performed originally."[21] Vickers perhaps should have taken note for the future, when Handel performance would become a major issue for him.

He and the ebullient conductor hit it off; Vickers described him as one with a mind concentrated and serious, and possessing an ear of great acuity. When John Coast called Vickers to say Beecham wanted him, Vickers couldn't believe it. But Coast said the conductor had heard the Handel *Samson* and, as Vickers later told it, said, "You were the only one who understood Handel style." Beecham asked for no rehearsal, and at the first session, the tenor was extremely nervous. They met, colliding in a doorway; Vickers told the conductor he was worried, and Beecham said he himself was worried about working with Vickers. Vickers then warned Beecham, "I don't possess what's considered to be the typical English oratorio tenor voice." Replied Beecham, "Thank God for that!"[22]

Vickers always enjoyed telling how he had to repeat the aria "Ev'ry valley shall be exalted." "Finally Sir Thomas laid down his baton and said, 'No, Mr. Vickers, it isn't *val-lee*, it's *val-leh*.' So I replied, 'You'll have to forgive my Canadian accent, but in Canada, a valley is a *val-lee*, and a *val-leh* is a man who dresses me.'" Of course, the only valets Vickers had had, or would ever have, were in the theater.

The "Comfort ye" is an extremely difficult arioso with, as Vickers noted, "a long run over a top A natural, which needs a good breath. As I went over the top, he [Beecham] said, 'You're damn good, Vickers!'" and told the technicians, "We'll take that one." Vickers joked to the engineer, "I'll give you half my fee if you put that out on the record!"[23]

Vickers's first appearance in San Francisco came on September 11, 1959, the season's opening night, as Radames, with Leontyne Price as Aida and Irene Dalis as Amneris, and Francesco Molinari-Pradelli in the pit. He had already sung a *Pagliacci* with the company, in Portland on September 5, and two *Carmens*.

He could have observed Mario Del Monaco, who was singing *Otello* and *Andrea Chénier*, and who took on an added third *Aida*, with Lucine Amara. And he might have seen Sebastian Feiersinger both as Walther in *Die Meistersinger* and in *Die Frau ohne Schatten*, the Emperor being a role later talked of for Vickers but too high and not his meat anyway.

In *Aida* Vickers showed "a darkish tenor of heroic quality, which rings out with great thrust and beauty," Arthur Bloomfield wrote. "Obviously a 'personality,' Mr. Vickers had his own ideas about interpretation—some good, some not so good. In the first scene he played Radames as a rather troubled and introverted fellow." For "Celeste Aida," this was a refreshing change from the usual stand-and-belt-it-out, the writer said. "Mr. Vickers showed that he can sing a phrase as if he really means what the words say," but his "impassioned lyricism sometimes found him lagging a fraction behind the beat."[24] One performance with Price was considered by Vickers to be among the rare peaks of his career, notably in the final tomb scene as she rested her head on his shoulder and her pianissimo faded ethereally.

Vickers was back in London for *Aida, Carmen* and *Pagliacci* in November and December. In November he also appeared in two performances of Beethoven's Ninth, conducted by Otto Klemperer, the finale of an eight-night Beethoven Festival at Royal Festival Hall. This apparently was the only time he sang onstage with Joan Sutherland (Ursula Böse and Gottlob Frick were the other soloists).

On December 16, 1959, came Vickers's Covent Garden debut in *Pagliacci*, which he had sung in Vienna the previous spring and had first sung in Toronto for the CBC. It was paired with *Cavalleria Rusticana*, both operas in a new production by Franco Zeffirelli. The Italian director spent most of his time on the Mascagni opera, with Charles Craig and Amy Shuard, rather than on the Leoncavallo, in which Joan Carlyle and Geraint Evans also sang. Although this lack of attention may not have endeared him to Vickers, there is no question that Zeffirelli, who vigorously acted all the characters in rehearsal, hurling chairs offstage in the finale, was invaluable to Vickers's development of a part that would become one of the tenor's signature roles.

This Canio had a dramatic entrance, throwing back the cover of the troupe's caravan to reveal himself. After "Vesti la giubba," Vickers bent down to pick up his clown's costume, clasping it for a moment as if, one reviewer suggested, it were his faithless wife, then dragging it as he walked away to stand, tormented, silhouetted against the sunset sky.[25] The dragging was in part to conceal his legs, but it was striking. He would play the moment in the same way, in a Zeffirelli production, in his final *Pagliacci*s at the Met in 1985.

But Zeffirelli's ideas sometimes diverged from Vickers's. The villagers, in jolly mood anticipating the entertainment, were opening bags of peanuts and munching as Vickers launched into "Un tal giaco." The director thought that was fun, but the tenor said, "Either I sing or they eat!" The eating was stopped.[26]

Vickers said later of that experience and Zeffirelli, "He expressed straight across the boards, 'In my productions the principals are of least importance.' If that kind of directing continues in opera it will kill it, because what Verdi and Shakespeare and Boito are . . . is so much bigger than any silly ass who thinks his singing or conducting or production or designing is more important than what the work is trying to say."[27] This would be a continual Vickers theme.

Critics noted Vickers's restraint and subtlety, the control of his volcanic rage. In the Covent Garden production Tonio got the last line, as in Leoncavallo's original: "La commedia è finita." But when Vickers sang it as Canio elsewhere, quietly and brokenly, he meant to show that Canio's entire life is over:

> The comedy, not only of [Canio's] relationship with Nedda but the empty, useless, insecure comedy, that farce that was his life, is done. He hung on to that *commedia,* he hung on to that ridiculous, ludicrous, pathetic position he held as a clown, as the reason for his existence. But the fact that he slipped from unreality to reality in the *commedia* showed how small and how unstable was the anchor of his life, which was nothing but this image, and he hung onto an image. He didn't have a core.[28]

Unlike Canio, Vickers took pains to keep his public and private lives separate. His dislike of interviews was already settled before he had reached wide fame. In July 1959 he had told a Prince Albert newspaperwoman visiting London: "I do not usually care to give private interviews, for I believe that an artist should be judged and interpreted by his performance alone and that his private life should be a thing apart."[29]

On one later occasion, John Coast hosted a supper party in a Soho restaurant, the group including a journalist and a Covent Garden publicist along with Vickers, Carlo Bergonzi, and Luciano Pavarotti. The idea was to promote Coast's stable of tenors. "Jon Vickers was furious! Furious!" recalled the publicist, Sheila Porter. "It was the idea of his being used as a publicity gimmick." Vickers never would do interviews that Porter wanted to arrange with the eight newspapers of the time in London. But she pinpointed a Vickers paradox, echoing Lord Harewood's view: "This person of enormous integrity, and refusal to compromise, at the same time was enormously concerned that he be given a big enough fee and enough respect and honor."[30]

Ande Anderson's view was that Vickers was often misunderstood: "He was not an opera singer, he was a huge operatic animal—he was born that way." Anderson added, "Unfortunately for a lot of people, he was fundamentally honest—he saw through artifice. He didn't suffer fools at all, let alone badly. . . . People thought it was a huge personality being itself, but they actually were looking at the truth."[31]

The Vickers persona was firmly formed by the end of 1959, three years after his arrival in London, which had signaled his entry into the international opera world. Even having found success in great houses beyond what he might have hoped for, he was determined to remain his own man in a complex world.

PART
3

THE 1960s

Ascendancy

Very often he wondered whether
he was going to have that great voice,
which was rather like a wild horse,
under control or not.
—*Sir Colin Davis*

8

The Met

MERLE HUBBARD WAS A REHEARSAL ASSISTANT WHEN VICKERS MADE his Metropolitan Opera debut in *Pagliacci* on January 17, 1960. "He was always volatile, always interesting, always honest, and always told you exactly what he thought," Hubbard, then with the Herbert Breslin agency, recalled in 1992. "There came a point in his years at the Met when he hated everybody to do with [the Met]. He liked me and he liked Bing. We were the only two people he would talk to." Vickers didn't always trust Bing. "But in the early days, he thought [Bing] was honest, and he didn't trust anybody else."

In those days at the Met, "They were afraid of [Vickers]," said Hubbard. "I think Jon even created a lot of that, because he wished to be removed. I don't think he wanted to deal with that crap on a daily basis. So this rather sweet little man, farmer from Canada, you know, would arrive, impeccably dressed, with impeccable clothes, and that bowler and the umbrella. . . . He was truly a prima donna. And I mean this in the best sense of the word."

Hubbard recalled an incident during a dress rehearsal for *Die Walküre* in the early 1960s. "He threw a fit for some reason. I don't know why." And he disappeared after Act 1. "The call came up to the rehearsal department, 'Where is Mr. Vickers?' . . . He's gone, he's cleared out, he's dressed and he's left. My boss said to me, 'Do you know anything about this?'" Hubbard didn't but thought he could find the tenor. He knew where Vickers liked to have lunch every day near the old Met.

> I found him a block away at a little greasy-spoon coffee shop, sitting on a stool, having a hamburger. He liked hamburgers. I walked in and I didn't say a word. I sat down on the next stool and I ordered a hamburger. He didn't say a word; he didn't acknowledge I was there. He took a bite on his hamburger and he said, "I'm not going back."
>
> And I said something like, "Who asked you? I didn't ask you to go back. You want to talk?" He said no. And I don't even know what it

was, I don't even know if *he* knows what it was that got him so angry. But after twenty minutes—we ate our hamburgers—he said, "I guess I should go back to rehearsal, shouldn't I?" I said, "Yup." That was part of the fun of working with Vickers.

And the moral was that even then you had to deal with him on some kind of terms that you understood with him. Because he would refuse to have played by the rules that existed. They simply didn't apply to him. If I had said to him, "Come on, Jon, come back," he would have told me what to do with myself. Well, he wouldn't have said it to *me*, because he liked me, [but he would have stubbornly refused].[1]

Walter Taussig, a conductor and coach at the Met from 1949, was among those in awe of the Vickers physique. Word went round, he recalled, that the tenor had been a woodchopper or lumberjack in Canada. "He was colossal," said Taussig. He agreed with Hubbard: "Everybody was afraid to incite his ire." True to form, whenever Vickers met Taussig's tall wife, Lore, he picked her up in those muscled arms. Taussig recalled that Vickers coached privately with Leo Taubman and always came to the Met perfectly prepared for his roles.[2]

The conductor Richard Woitach, who joined the Met in 1959 and often accompanied Vickers in recital, also remembered those early years. His impression was always that Vickers's voice approximated the cinematic technique of "surround sound." Nilsson's voice, for example, was a laser beam that hit you right in the face. But "Jon's voice would not hit as much as it would sort of come around you and then envelop you in this vibrating kind of a ring—no pun intended!"[3]

Both Vickers and the critics were lacking in total enthusiasm for his Met debut; it seems the conductor, Kurt Adler, had dragged the tempos. The tenor came offstage and said that it hadn't been good. Part of the trouble was that he had had neither a complete stage rehearsal nor a rehearsal with orchestra.[4]

There was a full house for that Sunday-evening performance, which was a benefit for the West Side Institutional Synagogue; the *Cavalleria Rusticana* sharing the evening featured Richard Tucker and Nell Rankin. The *Pagliacci* cast included Cornell MacNeil and Charles Anthony, with Maria Nache as a vocally limited Nedda. Regina Resnik was in the audience, as was Hetti Vickers, who made a rare appearance in news photos afterward.

Robert Sabin wrote of the debut that "we were spared excessive sobbings and rantings, and shown genuine heartbreak, instead. Mr. Vickers strained a bit on top tones, but this may well have been debut nerves. At all times his singing was well phrased and dramatically alive." The *New York Times'* John Briggs agreed, adding, "Mr. Vickers is a handsome young man who moves well on the stage. His Canio is a well-thought out, convincing portrayal that wins the sympathy of listeners." Vickers always remembered a review that said in his first "Vesti la giubba" he turned his voice "to the color of tears," a phrase that recalls Herbert Breslin's description of Vickers's voice as "an iron column that weeps tears.[5]

An equivocal note came from the exigent Irving Kolodin: "It is not likely that he will make his American career in such roles as Canio in *Pagliacci,* in which he introduced himself; he sings it with sure control, musical intelligence, and dramatic persuasion, but with neither the vocal style nor the richness of sound favored in this part." At a later date, Kolodin opined that Vickers's decision to make his debut as Canio was "quixotic," because it was "a style of singing for which he was . . . unsuited."[6]

Quixotic or not, Vickers had a distinct Met triumph in a new production of *Fidelio* a week and a half later, on January 28, led by Karl Böhm, with Aase Nordmo-Lövberg. James Levine, then a student of sixteen, was there, hearing Vickers live for the first time. "It was the most awesome thing I ever heard in my life, the first note of the part. I just fell out of my seat. I can still hear it," he recalled thirty-eight years later of that "Gott."[7]

Howard Taubman wrote of Vickers's "manly, resonant instrument" and said he had no trouble with the high As and B-flats of the aria. He gave excitement, and with care, he could become a "notable heroic tenor."[8]

After two performances, on February 9, the day he was to sing his first Met Siegmund, Vickers typed a hasty thank-you note to the Met baritone Theodor Uppman and his wife, Jean, who had sent him copies of a New York review. Touched by the gesture, he noted that it was the first time another artist had done such a thing for him.[9]

Vickers's first Met Siegmund, with Nilsson as Brünnhilde, Nordmo-Lövberg as Sieglinde, and Jerome Hines as Wotan, remained vivid to Speight Jenkins, who later became head of the Seattle Opera. With a background of opera attendance since age seven, Jenkins recalled the beauty of Vickers's voice and his thrilling power in the "Wälse! Wälse!"[10] Vickers got some nine curtain calls after the first act. There were shouts of "Birgit's Tristan," because Nilsson then was seeking her true partner. She loved singing with Wolfgang Windgassen, but his voice was small and his fee was large for the Met and he sang there only in early 1957, a few performances of both Siegfrieds and of Siegmund. She had made her Met debut in December as Isolde, with the less than heroic Karl Liebl as Tristan.

Other critics hearing Vickers's Siegmund on February 9, 1960, recorded some of the loudest and longest cheers heard at the Met that season. *Time* offered the statistics that the tenor weighed 215 pounds, with a forty-seven-inch chest, and gave his height as five feet nine inches, which was generous by at least an inch.[11] Vickers was "an unanticipated revelation," wrote Howard Taubman. "The Canadian tenor sang the role better than anyone has at the Met since the days of Lauritz Melchior, and he played it with more credibility than his memorable predecessor."[12] The second performance, February 20, was a broadcast matinee. Vickers continued into March, alternating Siegmund and Florestan, and Nilsson was his Leonore for the February 13 broadcast.

But behind the scenes there was tension of the peculiarly Vickers kind. He was brooding over the impresario Sol Hurok's public statement that his career would be finished in three years. And there was a further BBC-TV incident, of Vickers's making. Bing had just received the Order of the British Empire, and the BBC went to the Met to film his work there, with Humphrey Burton as producer. No doubt unknowingly, they set up to film a *Walküre* rehearsal with Vickers. Afterward, Vickers inquired about the cameras, and when he found they belonged to his nemesis, he called his Canadian lawyer (probably his brother-in-law, Ian Outerbridge, who handled other matters for him). He then sent a letter to Bing and his minions stating that until the BBC reimbursed him for the *Salome* episode, he would never agree to be filmed by them.[13]

Family matters also were a cause of distress. Ian and Hetti's father, the Reverend Leonard Outerbridge, died in Toronto on April 12, 1960, of the debilitating effects of a 1958 car accident in New Brunswick. His funeral was on that Good Friday, April 15, in Ripley, Ontario. Hetti had been living there temporarily, with their son and daughter, and was pregnant with their third child.

But the first part of the year had seen Vickers well launched at the Met, and he looked ahead to his *Otello* recording that summer.

In May 1960 John Coast wrote to Webster that in early December Vickers would be in London to do an arias album and then would be working on Lohengrin, perhaps for 1962. The album didn't come to pass for a couple of years. Vickers never sang Lohengrin, though he considered it early in his career and knew that Bayreuth wanted it. For the 1961–62 season (houses as yet did not plan too far ahead) Vickers was interested in a Covent Garden *Otello*, since he would record it in summer of 1960. But he did not want Joan Sutherland as Desdemona; his preference was Sena Jurinac. "I would be glad to explain why verbally!" Coast wrote.[14] One possibility is that the tall Sutherland would have towered over Vickers.

Coast told Webster that Vickers wanted not only to reassert his desire to sing heavy works like *Troyens, Parsifal,* and *Aida;* he also enjoyed the dramatic tenor roles in *Ballo* and *Carmen.* Vickers also suggested *Tosca* and *La Bohème* for Covent Garden, provided he had time to work on them (he had sung the first act of *Tosca* as a student in Toronto). He suggested his Canadian colleague Lois Marshall for *Bohème,* noting she had sung it a number of times for the NBC Opera. Marshall limped from polio, but this was not such a handicap for the ill Mimi. And he wondered if Webster would consider mounting *Andrea Chénier* for him. He liked the work very much; indeed, the *Chénier* arias on that solo album, which came out in 1964, are superb, although he would not often sing the role onstage.[15]

In 1959 Vickers had signed a three-year contract with RCA Red Seal, for two LPs each year. He got the standard Red Seal royalty rate of 10 percent (6 percent for material not in the public domain). Orchestral costs were to be charged against his royalties, but he got an advance of $1,500 for each LP. Alan Kayes, then Red Seal repertoire manager, recalled that despite Vickers's Covent Garden, Bayreuth, and Vienna successes, record companies weren't falling over themselves to sign Vickers, although he was certainly seen as a solid talent.[16] His first royalty payment came on May 1, 1960, for $1,772, another in November for $1,413; assuming he got $3,000 as personal advances for recording two LPs, his first year's recording earnings came to $6,185.

Vickers's first Red Seal recording, *Otello,* was under the baton of Tullio Serafin, described by Richard Mohr, who produced the recording, as a lovely old man at age eighty-one. The recording was made between July 18 and about August 8, 1960, at the Rome Opera House.[17] It was not a pleasant experience for Vickers, who would not sing *Otello* onstage for another three years. He later broke his RCA contract, calling it a mistake. He didn't like the Rome orchestra, or the schedule, and complained later that on the first day he had to record Otello's death five times, and on the second day had to sing Otello's first-act entrance, the "Esultate," four times. He and Tito Gobbi did their "Si, piel ciel" duet seven times one day, twice the next. The quartet was done fourteen times, and Vickers stopped counting after the seventeenth take of the third-act finale. "A human voice cannot take that kind of punishment, and all of it was for an orchestra to play the right notes," he told John Ardoin.[18]

Mohr recalled that Vickers was so unhappy with that "Esultate" that he objected when RCA wanted to reissue it. Vickers had learned those few important entrance lines as written. It didn't come up in rehearsal, but at that particular recording session, after Serafin heard the playback of the first take, he asked Vickers to do the traditional turn in the last line, "Dopo l'armi lo vinse l'urgano." Still, Mohr believed that the first act of this Otello is the best on record. "After that, Serafin's energies began to run right down the hill." He had to contend with Vickers's being new to this major role. And Desdemona wasn't really a role for Leonie Rysanek, although Serafin loved the beauty of her soft voice.[19]

Mohr recalled it was the habit of artists who recorded with the Rome orchestra to gather for dinner each evening, often at a certain restaurant on the Via Veneto. But Vickers never joined those meals. Nor did he stay in central Rome, as many singers did, but outside the city. "I don't know whether it was because he was being economical or antisocial, or just didn't want to be disturbed. When singers get together, they talk nonsense," Mohr noted in his dry fashion. "He may have had lunch with Gobbi on off days, but never [with] a group. He was a loner."[20]

When the record came out, reviews noted that Vickers was singing without the benefit of any stage performance of the role. And he did not display a ringing top like that of Mario Del Monaco. But Harold Rosenthal said that this was an Otello voice, one that suffers and brings a lump to the throat, as it had with Florestan and Don José's final anguish.[21] And Vickers's vocal acting ability is notable in the "Dio! mi potevi." But some would suggest he did the Serafin *Otello* too early and Karajan's, in 1974, too late.

When Vickers first began to record, he found it to be a nightmare: "It terrified me beyond words." He learned to enjoy it by going to a recording session in the same frame of mind as he had gone to voice lessons. He found the process far more cerebral than stage work, as vocal technical adjustments were made after playbacks.[22]

Terry McEwen recalled that Vickers had been signed by Decca's John Culshaw for a 1960 *Tristan* with Nilsson, who had moved from EMI to Decca with the purpose of recording complete operas. This record is Solti's only *Tristan* disk. McEwen said that Vickers backed out very late, leaving Decca with a month to find another Tristan. Vickers said his reason in part was that he decided it would be harmful to his voice, McEwen said. Decca got Fritz Uhl, Culshaw being "obstinately not a fan of Windgassen," Nilsson's favorite tenor of the time.[23] (Resnik was the Brangäne.) This action by Vickers could have been a background note to his future problems with Solti.

McEwen, who died in 1998, manipulated many projects behind the scenes at Decca. He came to dislike Vickers and recalled an unattractive story about the tenor. Vickers met Culshaw on a plane and Culshaw asked him about Resnik for a planned *Carmen*, with Del Monaco. "You'd think after all Regina had done for Jon he'd be anxious to put in a good word for her." But Vickers told Culshaw to be careful of her, that she wasn't as good as Culshaw thought. This scared Culshaw, who, McEwen said, had little faith in singers anyway. McEwen finally got Del Monaco to call Culshaw and say he wanted Resnik to record, which they did in 1963.

Why would Vickers do such a thing? "Because Jon was an s.o.b.," said McEwen. "He resented Regina because she helped him. No one was allowed to help him. He would have hated me if I had [made] that *Tristan* happen."[24] Resnik confirmed that she knew what Vickers had done, and it began a series of icy periods for their relationship, as Vickers continued to be distrustful of many people in his life.[25]

After the *Otello* recording, Vickers appeared at the Canadian National Exhibition in Toronto, and the critical reviews set in concrete an almost career-long battle between the tenor and Canadian critics. This had begun before he left Toronto for London, when he chafed because he felt taken for granted. Now it would escalate.

At the CNE he did a one-week stand beginning August 26, sharing headline billing with the comedian Phil Silvers, TV's beloved Sergeant Bilko. Vickers offered light fare including "Wunderbar" and "So in Love," as well as "Vesti la giubba," and joined in duets of "Vienna, City of My Dreams" and "You Will Remember Vienna" with the soprano Barbara Franklin. But the main program failed to list him, although it carried his photo and bio. Other performers were trained zebras, a vaudeville duo, and the Canadettes, a precision dance lineup.

This was Vickers's first Toronto appearance since his international success had been launched three years previously. Some critics said he was squandering his talent on largely inappropriate music in an inappropriate setting.[26] But it seems obvious that in that particular venue he could not have attempted anything much more serious than what he sang and still have held the audience's attention. He received a five-figure payment but must have had many second thoughts about doing the show, although he defended the presenters for doing the best they could with the stage they had.

Typically, the lack of billing stuck in his mind. In a 1964 Toronto interview he recalled being made to wait more than eight hours at a CNE rehearsal, doing nothing. Wasted rehearsal time was always a Vickers bête noire. "To add insult to injury, my name did not appear in the Grandstand program. I was a success with the audiences and Phil Silvers was a resounding flop. But who got all the play in the press? Phil Silvers. I tell you, it could only happen here."[27] He told the *Toronto Star* that he had used the CNE appearance "as an experiment, to find out if the Canadian press would accept me as anything else but 'a guy who's done pretty good—for a Canadian.' I am sorry to say they didn't." He formalized his view that he was an artist without honor in his own land.[28]

A major family event occurred on September 26, 1960, when Hetti gave birth to a third child: their second son, Jonathan Ian, named after her husband and brother.

Vickers had only two performances at the Met in the 1960–61 season, singing two *Carmen*s on October 29 and November 3 (Teresa Stratas, also a Met beginner, was the Frasquita). In November 1960 it appeared that Vickers, for his third season at the Met, would open that season in fall 1961 with Leontyne Price in *Aida,* at his request, although the Met had wanted him for a new *Lohengrin.* But as it turned out, the opener would be *La Fanciulla del West,* with Price and Tucker.

Another debut came that late fall of 1960, at Lyric Opera of Chicago, where Vickers would become a major audience favorite, in *Die Walküre* on November 16, 18, and 21. The cast was a by-now-familiar one for him: Gré Brouwenstijn as Sieglinde, Nilsson as Brünnhilde, Christa Ludwig as Fricka, plus Hans Hotter and William Wildermann. Carol Fox was then Lyric general manager, but Ardis Krainik also was there, and Vickers and Krainik would become fast friends over the years. She would become general director in 1981, replacing the seriously ill Fox.

This *Walküre* brought major cheers, with Vickers dubbed "this generation's Melchior" by Don (later Donal) Henahan, who said he was "brawny, blond and an actor (though a bit florid at times for Wagner) [with] a true heldentenor voice with the gleam and thrust of Wotan's sword."[29] Vickers also was seen as a Melchior replacement by the *Tribune*'s formidable Claudia Cassidy.[30]

Vickers closed the year with his debut at La Scala, where Callas had opened the season in a revival of Donizetti's *Poliuto,* with Franco Corelli. On December 17 Vickers began a run of five *Fidelio*s under Karajan. The cast included Nilsson as Leonore, Gottlob Frick as Rocco, and Hotter as Don Pizarro. The sets were modernistically ugly, in the view of Harold Rosenthal, and Karajan made what the critic saw as arbitrary cuts. But Rosenthal praised Nilsson and Vickers, noting the very real compassion in Florestan's dungeon aria.[31] Vickers had a Christmas break of just eleven days to spend with his family and new son before his Florestans resumed in January.

In February 1961 Covent Garden mounted a new *Fidelio,* with the irascible Otto Klemperer lured back to opera by Webster and Lord Harewood. The conductor also was in charge of the production. The radiant Sena Jurinac was making her debut as Leonore, having sung at the house since 1947. But at a rehearsal, Klemperer kept badgering her. Reg Suter, then a stage technician, recalled that after this went on for some time, "Jon walked to the center of the stage, looked down at Klemperer and said words to this effect: 'Miss Jurinac is making her debut in this role and she needs help from you, not bullying. If you do not stop, I shall walk off!'" Suter said the situation had been such that if Vickers had not spoken up, Jurinac might have been forced to cancel her performances. "He hated this kind of bullying."[32]

As it turned out, both Vickers, in his house debut as Florestan, and Jurinac had a great success, with the Queen Mother in attendance on February 24. He was in splendid form, wrote Rosenthal. His Florestan "was sung with burning intensity and generous tone. His voice is now certainly heavier and more dramatic than when we first heard him, but is always used to serve the ends of music." Jurinac was not relaxed at first but was little short of magnificent in Act 2, womanly, noble, moving.[33] Hotter, John Dobson, and Frick were also in the cast.

When Vickers returned as Florestan in September, Andrew Porter's review was prescient in noting qualities that would endure and strengthen through his career: "The timbre he brings to this part is by no means a conventional, smooth, clear tenor. There is a sense of strain in it. It is eloquent of suffering, fortitude, hardships nobly borne. When hope floods in, a kind of radiance suffuses the tones. His enunciation of the words is thrilling. He gives full value to every phrase, daring a greater expressive freedom than is customary today."[34]

Walter Legge, then with Angel, was quick to spot that all seven performances in February and March had sold out within twenty-four hours of the box office opening. He suggested that this meant EMI should reconsider recording the opera with Klemperer. By March 8 he had already asked Vickers when he could be free; Vickers suggested the last two weeks in August, but Legge feared that Klemperer and Nilsson, his choice for Leonore, wouldn't want to record then. The first fortnight in February 1962 was Vickers's other choice, and in fact the sessions took place that February and March.

Legge had said with typical bombast that if he got the cast he wanted, "we cannot fail to make one of the supreme recordings in the whole history of the industry."[35] He got Vickers, and Frick as Rocco, but in the end it was Ludwig instead of Nilsson; Ingeborg Hallstein instead of Anneliese Rothenberger or Elisabeth Söderstrom; instead of Gedda, Gerhard Unger; Franz Crass, not Prey, was Don Fernando; and Walter Berry, instead of Crass, was Don Pizarro.

The *Fidelio*s of Wilhelm Furtwängler (1950 Salzburg) and Bruno Walter (1941 Met) towered, but this one also joined the top rank. Alan Blyth, reconsidering it in 1992, called Vickers's Florestan anguished, soulful, "with his heart, at times, just too near his sleeve."[36] The role would remain one of the most memorable for Vickers admirers.

That winter and spring Vickers worked in Vienna with Karajan in several *Aida*s and *Walküre*s. In July 1961 he recorded *Aida* with Leontyne Price, Rita Gorr, Robert Merrill, and Giorgio Tozzi, under Solti at the Rome Opera House. (Price had made her Met debut in January, on the same night as Franco Corelli, in *Il Trovatore*.) At the end, when there were congratulations all round, Vickers said to Price, "We are finally finished." The soprano responded, "Yes, Jon, in spite of you," or "No thanks to you," producer Mohr recalled. "She had to do a lot of things over and over again" for reasons that had to do with Vickers. "Of course, Leontyne was always mistress of the *pianissimo*, and so was Jon, but a lot of the times it was not mezza voce, it was a falsetto that he was doing. He carried that on too long, being a tenor." Reminded that Vickers always denied using falsetto, Mohr said calmly, "All tenors do."[37]

No one in Rome could have guessed that Vickers had but one more opera ahead with Solti, and that after 1961 the two would never again work together.

9

The Solti Debacle

Those two, like two stags absolutely clashing in the jungle—one hadn't seen anything like it.
—John Copley, director

I N SEPTEMBER 1961 GEORG SOLTI TOOK OVER AS COVENT GARDEN music director, two years after Rafael Kubelik departed, during which period David Webster felt for a time that he might like to go it alone without a music chief. This was impractical, and Lord Drogheda, the Covent Garden chairman, invited Solti, who, after a tiff with his Los Angeles orchestra, finally accepted the job.

The Hungarian's stormy standoff with the house's star tenor during *Die Walküre* that September shook the house, said John Tooley, then assistant general administrator, at a time when Solti already had problems trying to gain public acceptance in England. In 1962 the conductor also would gain the first of his thirty-two Grammy Awards (for *Aida*); by 1968 he would be an honorary Commander of the British Empire, and in 1972 he would be knighted and become a British citizen. But Vickers, not among those bestowing accolades, vowed never to sing with Solti again. Years later, with his active memory for slights, he would refer to Solti as conducting "pure fascism," whatever that might mean.[1]

Tooley summed up the situation with a half-smile: "Jon, without putting too fine a point on it, thought Solti was a butcher. And Jon, aware in his own mind that his voice was God-given, [that] made him even more careful about it than might otherwise have been the case. And therefore any conductor who caused him to in his view strain his voice, was in fact acting against his Maker. And therefore, Jon fought back. Jon said, 'Look, this man's ruining me. I can't sing with him, so let's forget it.' That was the end of it."[2]

In the beginning of his tenure, Solti had many problems unrelated to Vickers. He was trying to fit into an English opera house, as a Hungarian of domineering charm who came from the houses of Munich and Frankfurt and was viewed as having a very Prussian way of working. "The paprika factor" is how his second wife, Valerie, would describe it.[3] He found Covent Garden amateurish in many ways, with its orchestra's limited repertoire and lack of rehearsal time, its unpolished chorus. The house was a far less formal place than he was used to. And he found the British press far more critical than he was used to; he even accused them of anti-Semitism. Before he left in 1971 he would help lead the house to glory, but the beginnings were painful for all.

The falling-out between Solti and Vickers "was a terrible sadness. We thought they were both fantastic. They were our idols. They should have worked together," said John Copley, now a well-regarded director.[4] He was a green twenty-eight-year-old stage-managing the new production of *Die Walküre* when Solti and Vickers came together for the second and final time. Sadness was the feeling of many concerned with this episode, from which ripples spread through Vickers's career in terms of opportunities lost. And Vickers's decision never to sing again with Solti was a body blow to Webster in particular as he fought to move the house forward.

In November 1960, as Solti began his plans for Covent Garden, he had written Vickers a cordial note (from the luxurious Beverly Hills Hotel in Los Angeles to Vickers's modest Hotel Esplanade, in Manhattan near the Met). The conductor said he had been sorry not to see the tenor on his previous visit to London and looked forward to their collaborations. He noted the scheduled *Walküre* and said he hoped Vickers would sing Otello in February 1962, in Italian. And Solti, anxious to present *Tristan und Isolde* in 1961–62, wondered if Vickers would be ready for the role of Tristan by July of that season.[5]

A hint of trouble arose in January 1961 when John Coast wrote to Covent Garden about a problem with the coming season, in which Vickers was to sing *Fidelio* and the new *Walküre* in the fall, and *Ballo* in February and March. (Vickers already had told the house he wanted "equal billing" with Victoria de los Angeles for a June 8, 1961, gala inaugurating the Royal Opera House Benevolent Fund.) Vickers had expected to open the season with the new music director and Nilsson in *Fidelio,* and was not happy that *Walküre* had been scheduled. Vickers also made it clear that he knew his roles and expected an absolute minimum of rehearsal.[6] He was already making Solti aware of how he expected to be treated.

In July, Vickers had recorded the *Aida* with Solti in Rome. No particular signs of conflict between tenor and conductor were evident as the recording sessions began, recalled producer Richard Mohr. Vickers downed his by now usual large batch of oranges. "He was a mass of nerves, but he covered it up. I think he was worried about that short top [range] of his. It was such a muscular production. I think he gave it 110 percent and hoped to get 100 percent out of it." Vickers's difficulties with the part demanded many re-takes, said Mohr, but the tenor complained later to John Ardoin that Solti "actually told us in a number of places not to bother singing because he intended to drown us out anyway."[7]

(The tenor made another recording, in September in London: *Die Walküre* for RCA's Red Seal, with Nilsson, Brouwenstijn, Gorr, George London, and David Ward, with Erich Leinsdorf leading the LSO. Rita Gorr, who had lately come to prominence, replaced the originally agreed-upon Grace Hoffman, a Cleveland native who had sung in Germany and London with Vickers. Vickers, London, and others weren't happy about this change, which they saw as dishonorable to Hoffman.)

The Covent Garden *Walküre* would open September 29. Vickers already had grown into the role of Siegmund, having sung it in several major houses. During rehearsals he felt he was being bullied, while Solti found the tenor uncooperative and obstructive. The problems lay in Act 1, although it's not clear whether the conflict was about where Vickers was to stand or Solti's view of the music.[8] At one point Solti asked him to sing the melody of "Winterstürme," Siegmund's lovely first-act aria, and forget about the words. "He wanted me to reduce Siegmund from a live human being on the stage, with all his youth and wildness, his weakness and passion, to a vocal line in the orchestra construction." Vickers said this in late 1961, when his wounds were fresh, to *Opera News*. The magazine did not mention Solti by name but ironically used a photo of Vickers and Solti with the article.[9]

Copley recalled, "It was Solti's first season. He had to be the boss. But Jon was not going to give up his way of doing things. They clashed really terribly. . . . When Jon pulled the sword out of the tree, he looked fairly dangerous. He did it with fantastic force. A real sort of rage was going on. It was scary."[10]

Hans Hotter, who directed the *Walküre* and sang the Wotan, said that Solti conducted well for singers, and Hotter got along with him. But "Solti is a dictator, a very hard-boiled egg. . . . It was hard for him to find mutual understanding." He recalled that Vickers "was swearing onstage, when we stood next to him. . . . He was not a flexible person, never has been." Hotter often heard Vickers complaining angrily about directors and conductors; the tenor said of one (not named by Hotter) at Covent Garden, "This man should be horsewhipped." Hotter saw Vickers as sensitive to criticism and very straightforward, but a good-hearted person.[11]

Webster tried to smooth matters between the two, but to no avail. "To be fair to Jon," said Tooley, his and Solti's approaches to music making were "poles apart."[12]

Solti's letter afterward to Vickers laid out his view: "I feel very strongly that each individual vocal part must fit in to the whole scheme in order to make a homogeneous performance. Don't misunderstand me—I don't want to enforce my own ideas, but to have the opportunity of exploring the singers' potentialities and to understand their conception." True, they had lacked rehearsal time, but "I felt that I met with a rejection of almost every suggestion. . . . Mr. Hotter, who has sung his part with me many times in Munich, found himself also presented with new ideas and we succeeded in making adjustments." Solti referred to plans for *Otello* in 1962, urging "the mutual desire to make a fine performance not only of the part but of the whole opera."[13]

Joan Ingpen also noted that in his refusal to work with Solti, Vickers did a major disservice to David Webster, the man who had made his career. "There was no question of [Solti's] not wanting him to sing at Covent Garden," said Ingpen. She could offer no specifics about the clash but laughed in her wry manner as she said, "Jon would stand at the stage door telling his fans that he wouldn't come back while that bastard was there! I knew exactly that he wasn't coming back the following season because his income tax was in a mess and he wouldn't pay it, and he'd been told he better stay out of the country for a year." But she admitted she thought Vickers was convinced "that Solti had slighted him in some way, which I never found out how or what. It was true for Jon, that's all one can say. Whether Solti meant it or not, I don't think he did, but Jon felt" he had been slighted.[14]

Ande Anderson, the stage manager who saw a great deal of Vickers's career, recalled that when Vickers disagreed with a conductor or director, "he became like a huge crab. He turned inside himself and shut himself off."[15] Lord Harewood felt Vickers was in the wrong. "He was incredibly stubborn, and after a bit it becomes a fault."[16] And there were those who felt Vickers's stubbornness often derived from insecurity, vocal or otherwise.

The problems between Solti and Vickers darkened the situation at Covent Garden in 1962. Solti tried early in 1963 for a rapprochement, asking him to sing Siegmund in a new *Walküre*, part of a *Ring* cycle to be designed by Gunther Schneider-Siemssen, with Hotter directing. But Vickers, typically, was not to be swayed from his decision, although even some critics begged for them to make up.

Later Vickers refused to go into detail on his differences with Solti on a CBC program. "But there is little question in my mind," he said, "that Mr. Solti is the kind of a man who feels that the conductor is absolute authority." Vickers said he himself knew more about Siegmund "than any conductor in the world, because I have sung it with more conductors than Georg Solti has ever conducted performances. More than that, I've ate [*sic*], slept, dreamt, everything else—Siegmund. I have sung it with, I don't know, twenty-five or thirty different Sieglindes. So I think that I've come up against far more personality facets of Sieglindes and Siegmunds than any conductor who stands on the podium." By 1961 Vickers had sung Siegmund in 1958 at Bayreuth, his role debut, then twice in fall of 1958 at Covent Garden, in Vienna with Karajan, under Böhm at the Met in spring 1960, with Erich Leinsdorf at the Met in winter 1960, and in Chicago. Vickers added:

> If a man is inflexible, I don't care whether it's Georg Solti or Herbert von Karajan, I don't care who it is, if they are inflexible I say they are imposing themselves on the work, instead of putting the work first and allowing each of us, Mr. von Karajan or Mr. Solti, whoever it is, and my meager talents, [to] combine them to project before the public a whole, a work. . . . That has been my whole desire throughout the whole of my career. I do *not* want to superimpose Jon Vickers's personality, I want to bring whatever my talents are, whether they're minor or great, vocally, mentally, histrionically, physically. . . .
>
> When I decided not to sing more roles with Mr. Solti, I was accused of being inflexible. That's the most nonsensical thing I've ever heard. I've sung Siegmund with Knappertsbusch, with von Karajan, with Kempe, Leinsdorf, Rosengarten, Böhm, ad nauseum you can go on and name them. But the thing that's wonderful about it is that each one of these men, they have this genius that's far greater than mine, and the wonderful thing is that we can work together. We polish and improve.

But he admitted of his view of Siegmund, "I think the basic core of the man I am incapable of changing. . . . Maybe that's a weakness on my part, but there are all kinds of little facets" that can be polished.[17]

An odd footnote came at the memorial service on July 2, 1971, for Sir David Webster (who had died May 9) in the Church of the Holy Sepulchre in High Holborn, London. It coincided with Solti's final Royal Opera House appearances, two *Tristans*. Dame Ninette de Valois, the Royal Ballet founder, and John Tooley read, and Geraint Evans gave the address. Birgit Nilsson asked to be excused from the "Liebestod" because she had to sing Isolde the following day. So she taught it to Heather Harper, who had never sung it; she was conducted by Solti. Vickers was the only other soloist, conducted by Colin Davis in "Total eclipse," from Handel's *Samson*, of which he had once given Webster a dress rehearsal and four performances for the price of two.

The finale of the service was the "Wach auf" and final chorus from *Die Meistersinger*, with ROH principals joining the ROH chorus. "Heather Harper, Gwyneth Jones, they all stood up. One person stayed seated and didn't join in," recalled Sheila Porter, then head of Covent Garden publicity. "It looked so strange." She thought, and others said to her, that it was simply because Solti was conducting the chorus.[18] Vickers had sung his bit, and even in that crowded church he still refused to come under the Solti baton for Sir David.

The soprano Roberta Knie recalled, however, that in the mid-1970s Vickers considered singing Tristan in Paris with Solti, in February and March 1979. Knie would have been Isolde, although Ingpen had wanted Gwyneth Jones, but Vickers wouldn't do the opera with Jones until she had sung it first elsewhere. But as Knie recalled it, Vickers upset Solti in some way, and they never did work together again.[19]

Solti declined to speak about Vickers for this book, and in his memoirs, completed just before his death at eighty-five in September 1997, the conductor said nothing negative about the tenor. "For some reason," he wrote, "Vickers and I had never got on well, which was a pity, since he had an excellent tenor voice; we could have done some very good work together."[20]

Valerie Solti spoke of her husband after his death in terms that could apply equally to Vickers. Solti, she said, had been called dictatorial and arrogant, but he wasn't like that at all. "He was a man who drove himself. He had great standards, he never compromised, and therefore he would say or do things which perhaps people didn't understand, because he knew how it should be. This wasn't arrogance. He respected every single one of his musicians and colleagues." She noted that Solti had written that conductors are interpreters, serving the composers. "That was his motivation."[21]

Perhaps the conductor and the tenor were simply too much alike.

When Vickers's fourth child and third son, Kenneth Evan, was born October 28, 1961, in London, Vickers was in Chicago doing three performances of *Andrea Chénier.* He would be back in London for a November run of *Fidelio,* but not before singing an *Aida* at the Met on November 6. Webster cabled him there with congratulations on the birth of the child, who would grow up to be a strong family conservator of his father's operatic legacy.

For the *Chénier*s, which were not wholly successful, Vickers was partnered by a merely serviceable Maddalena, Shakeh Vartenissian, a onetime Met comprimaria. The tenor nevertheless showed off his "elegant Italian, with instinctive taste and much musical finesse," said *Opera,* and Claudia Cassidy wrote in the *Chicago Tribune* that "Jon Vickers must have had aficionados fighting between acts as to whether he should stick with his formidable career as a heldentenor or toss it overboard for . . . the Italian roles," though his "Improvviso di Chénier," she felt, lacked fire. Donal Henahan thought "his singing was almost too refined and without the Italianate thrust," but Roger Dettmer suggested that while maintaining his Wagnerian supremacy, Vickers was taking over the domain of Del Monaco, a prediction that would not prove true.[22] Vickers, who liked this poetic, principled character, would say that it was unfortunate that the audience always strongly applauded the first act, which included the impassioned "Improvviso." They should have wept instead, he felt.

At the time of the birth of their fourth child, the Vickerses' eldest, Allison, was seven, Billy was five, and Jonathan was one year old. Hetti, at home in Harrow after the birth of Kenneth, told London's *Evening Standard* of October 31 in a rare press comment that "she really does not know when her husband will be able to get home to see his new son." This situation, and perhaps stress over the *Chéniers*, must have contributed to Vickers's quarrel with Galina Vishnevskaya at their one rehearsal for two Met *Aidas* (after the London *Fidelios* he would return to New York for the second performance, on November 25). The volatile Russian soprano was making her debut amid much turmoil, as she was unfamiliar with the workings of the house.

While rehearsing the Nile Scene, Vishnevskaya wrote in her autobiography, "I noticed that [Vickers] was getting into an increasingly bad mood; it was plain that he didn't want to rehearse. We went on like that until just before the final duet, and then he got ready to leave. 'At this point, everything is clear: we stand up and sing,' he said." Vishnevskaya made a reasonable request: "If you don't want to do what I suggest, then I'll do as you wish, but we can't stand in one spot throughout a long duet. This is a show, not a concert."

Vickers said, "But I'm telling you, I have no more time. I have to leave." The soprano said, "Shame on you! How rude. I'm a woman . . . I'm a guest here." To which Vickers replied accurately, "We're all guests here." Vishnevskaya didn't understand the Met setup and "took his answer to be boorishness." What did he mean, all? Vickers responded, "Like I said, 'all'! Okay? Good-bye, girl!' And he left."

This was only Vickers's fourteenth performance at the Met, and his debut there in *Aida*, which he was never to sing again there after those two performances. He sang forty-four performances of Radames at Covent Garden, the last in June 1969, but with its daunting B-flat in "Celeste Aida," it was always a part that put Vickers on edge. The director (an unnamed man overseeing the Margaret Webster staging) told Vishnevskaya that Vickers was "very nervous" because his wife had given birth to a daughter instead of a son, "or perhaps the other way around."

The night of the first *Aida*, Vishnevskaya also was upset because a male union member had to apply her body makeup. She refused to look at

Vickers during their first scene. "Vickers saw that no loving gaze would bring me out of my foul mood. . . . So during the first intermission, right there on the stage, he strode over, picked me up and tossed me into the air several times. With that, peace was concluded."[23]

Vickers apparently didn't damage Vishnevskaya with this by now frequent ploy. But she wrote later, not specifically about Vickers: "Many male opera singers, especially those who do the dramatic, 'bloody' roles, have a great need to impress the audiences with their masculinity. . . . If such a singer has not left several healthy bruises on his victim's body, he feels he hasn't given his all to the performance."[24]

In November 1961 Coast was negotiating for two more operas with EMI, now Vickers's label. The tenor had developed the habit of going over his contracts carefully, often causing delays; as Coast explained, "He has an excellent contract brain and rather enjoys them." Coast urged that the royalty agreement be laid out as RCA had had it with Vickers.[25]

The proffered contract called for the tenor to record, at the end of 1962, a complete *Lohengrin* and the third act of *Die Meistersinger*. Vickers would get two thousand dollars for the first and fifteen hundred dollars for the second, plus royalties. (Neither would ever come to pass.) Already under contract were sessions in fall 1962 for *Samson et Dalila*, with an overall royalty of 4 percent, 2 percent to be calculated against an advance of two thousand dollars, and 2 percent retained against Vickers's share of the production costs (also shared by other artists).[26]

Among other offers at the time, Giulini wanted to do a *Trovatore* with Vickers, and Klemperer asked him for *Lohengrin*, neither of which occurred.[27]

Vickers had an unpleasant experience in Vienna that November, appearing in a new production of *Fidelio*. He recalled being booed during the performance and heavily booed at the end. Alluding to "political reasons," he quoted a Vienna paper as writing, "It is the tragedy of our year that this once great operatic voice is lost forever to the world."[28] This apparently had to do with his loyalties to Karajan, not universally popular there.

Vickers was back at the Met on December 23, 1961, unusually close to Christmas, since he always tried to keep his holiday schedule free to be with his family. But this was a broadcast matinee of *Die Walküre*, led by Leinsdorf, with Nilsson as Brünnhilde. Gladys Kuchta was Sieglinde. He was back for more on December 29, also with Nilsson, and January 10 and 23.

The force of personality that Vickers exerted on the opera world was clear in a January 1962 interview with the *Toronto Star*. The first impression of the tenor is "his almost brutal strength of will. He is blunt, vehement, forceful, dogmatic, dominant," wrote Blaik Kirby. "You hardly dare to argue, for you half fear that Jon's reply might be a right to the jaw—and he has a shirt-popping set of wrestler's muscles. Yet he is not unpleasant; he's courteous . . . perhaps even friendly but underneath it a suppressed, disciplined fury seems to be boiling steadily." Vickers had boiled over the day before when a previous interview, he said, distorted his ideas and made him look "egotistical, self-centred and a fool about my profession." He declared to Kirby that this was his last interview, a threat he occasionally made but never held for long.[29]

By 1962 Vickers was a known quantity in opera houses, but he was viewed as an upstart by Mario Del Monaco, who was demanding from the Met's Bing a fee of twenty-five hundred dollars tax-free for a future Otello and an opening night. Bing said he'd stick with James McCracken and Vickers. The Italian tenor lost his temper and said he'd skip the Met if another Italian, Franco Corelli, opened the season. And he called Vickers and McCracken "comprimarios."[30]

A fallow period was in store for Vickers at Covent Garden because of his tax problems with the British, as well as his difficulties with Solti. After a 1967 *Die Walküre* at Salzburg's Easter Festival, Andrew Porter would write in London, "How sadly we have missed his intensity, his poetry these years."[31] Vickers did not appear at the house in the 1962–63 season or the 1964–65 season. In winter 1964 he sang a run of six *Aida*s and six *Fidelio*s, and on the spring tour, three *Aida*s and three *Otello*s. In 1965–66 he sang six *Parsifal*s and six *Ballo*s, and in 1966–67 just eight *Carmen*s. If not for his refusal to work with Solti, Vickers might have sung his first Otello at the ROH in the 1961–62 season. That slot was filled by Del Monaco.

By 1962 Vickers was having serious problems with England's tax collectors, the Inland Revenue. They considered him a United Kingdom resident, subject to taxes because he spent so much time there, and they were delving into his past earnings. Coast informed Webster on April 7 that the situation had "temporarily shattered both Jon and all his plans." Some of his earnings had been frozen "and he had to get a 50 percent loan from his bank manager for current expenses. Until he has distabished [*sic*] his residence in this country, he literally cannot afford to sing here and has asked me to cancel everything." Vickers was "terribly distressed," Coast reported. An April 16 letter noted that Vickers "doesn't want to sign *Lohengrin* contracts until he has something in black and white" from Inland on the tax situation for 1959–60 and 1961–62.[32]

The issue was the length of his stays in England. Into 1963 Vickers fretted that if he brought his family for two months while he sang at the Royal

Opera House, Inland would again say he was setting up a home as a resident. That summer Coast told Ingpen that because of the tax problems, Vickers was giving notice that he would not do *Lohengrin* the following spring. There were too many imponderables, Coast wrote; Vickers may also have been coming to the conclusion that he would never sing the role. If Covent Garden wanted him for *Don Carlos* or some other role, and his income tax was settled, that would be fine with Vickers.[33]

In February and March 1962 Vickers recorded *Fidelio* for EMI with Klemperer and Christa Ludwig at London's Kingsway Hall. Release was delayed because Vickers wanted a much higher fee.[34] In May he sang *Fidelio* at La Fenice in Venice; he and Gré Brouwenstijn sang in German, the rest of the cast in Italian, led by Böhm.

While problems with Solti and taxes were the dark side of 1962, a happy personal event was Vickers's settling on a farm near Orangeville, Ontario, an hour's drive from Toronto. This land was to be a focal point for his family life and a nourishment for his artistic life for the rest of his career.

Jon and Hetti had planned to leave London for Switzerland, no doubt for tax reasons, and had bought property there. But Hetti convinced her husband that because all he needed was proximity to an airport, he could return to the Canadian countryside he loved.[35] They spent hours driving around Ontario, seeking the right place, and sold the Swiss property without having ever set up residence there. There seems to have been a family connection to the property they settled on, as land records show that in 1926 it was listed to Margaret Vickers, possibly the Margaret who was Vickers's grandmother. On January 30, 1963, the property was sold to Hetti Vickers for $36,000; in fact, it was never in the name of Jon Vickers. Spruce Winds, in Alton, Caledon Township, is a setting of idyllic peace, with hills, glades, a large pond, and a working farm. Vickers would own several other pieces of Canadian land and do very well with those investments, in his money-savvy way.

He enlisted the help of his old friend John Diefenbaker in smoothing the way financially for his return to Canada. On January 21, 1963, he wrote the prime minister in Ottawa from the Alden Hotel, where he often stayed in New York when at the Met, to say that he and his wife had decided they wanted to bring up their children in Canada. But he feared a Canadian residence would cause an income tax problem, and he asked Diefenbaker if he, Vickers, could discuss the issue with someone in government. He wanted assurance that his tax returns would be handled by someone who understood the problems of a person who worked in several countries with different tax setups.

Diefenbaker wrote back warmly on January 27, saying he was glad of

Vickers's return and that he would bring Vickers's letter to the attention of the minister of finance. Vickers was indeed referred to various high-up internal revenue officials. He thanked Diefenbaker in a February 19 letter devoted chiefly to sympathizing with Diefenbaker's stand against what Vickers (among many Canadians) saw as American attempts to dominate Canada in economic affairs and nuclear-arms policy.[36]

Thus reassured, Vickers now could return to the days he recalled so fondly, his young years working on the White farm in Saskatchewan. Kirkton, his father's birthplace, was perhaps an hour to the southwest of the farm. Nearby was Eaton Hall, the home of Lady Eaton, daughter-in-law of Timothy Eaton, the founder of the department store chain, for whom the church was named in which Jon and Hetti had wed.

Typically, Vickers had his own vision for the redbrick, peaked-roof Victorian farmhouse. He personally drew up the plans, oversaw construction, and found a German workman in the area to restore the house's white-painted gingerbread decoration. New railings carefully copied existing ironwork.[37] He and Hetti scoured the area for old houses from which to use bricks for an extension, a double-size living room. They bought an old Mennonite schoolhouse and were delighted to discover imprinted upon each brick, "God Is Love. Love God." The addition integrated perfectly with the old section, distinguished by smaller windows; the home eventually was about six thousand square feet. From the living room picture windows the pond and rolling land can be seen. "Jon has an unusually high emotional reaction to nature," Hetti said.[38]

The elder Vickers children were enrolled in Canadian schools, and the farm became the tenor's base. He would always return to it between engagements, even for just a few days, and tried to spend six months of the year there. He would study for roles in the large library of which he was so proud. And he recharged himself with labor on the earth—castrating bulls, riding a tractor to plow fields. He developed a herd of three hundred beef cattle and had a black labrador named Cassius. He dug in all the fence poles, and with their own hands he and Hetti planted a thousand trees on the property. Vickers, once a tool salesman, became a skilled woodworker over the years, with a basement workshop. He made much furniture, including bunk beds for his three sons.

Colin Davis was among those who visited the house and marveled at Vickers's work. The conductor found him "a great paterfamilias . . . a big, hearty host."[39] And for Vickers, the work of his hands always seemed more fundamental to life than any reality he created onstage. He enjoyed having his neighbors know him simply as another farmer driving his truck, although often absent in foreign lands (and driving Cadillacs as well). He sang in a local church and donated an organ. He always loved animals and reminisced about helping with the births of calves. Once, on a visit to his in-laws' summer cottage, he swam well out into a lake trying to retrieve an injured seagull. Hetti was quite upset.[40]

But he was a realist about nature. Richard Woitach recalled breakfasting with the tenor at the farm, looking out on the greenery:

> All of a sudden Jon excused himself and walked over to the broom closet, pulled a shotgun out, opened the window, and fired the shotgun. I saw this body fly up in the air and then flop. It was a groundhog. He didn't even break stride, he just shot this thing, put back the [gun], like John Wayne . . . and went on with the conversation. I didn't say anything. That's the way he operates.[41]

Vickers's residence in Canada was not to mean he would perform there more frequently. The Canadian Opera Company was still having growing pains. He had begun to earn the top fees that he would always demand, but Canada was still young culturally, lacking the proper settings for an artist of Vickers's stature. The novelist Margaret Atwood would later describe the perception of Canada in the early 1960s, when one year saw the publication of only five Canadian novels, as "a kind of hopeless cultural backwater."[42]

Vickers said in a Toronto interview in July 1963, when he was singing at the Stratford Festival with the National Youth Orchestra: "I'm not a deeply emotional or sentimental man. So I've often turned down Canadian offers from people who thought they could get me back here for a bucket of sentiment and half my fee." But he was glad to blend his talents with those of the new Youth Orchestra, enjoying the idealism he found in the young players.[43]

10

Lonely Hotels

VICKERS WAS TRAVELING IN EARNEST BY THE EARLY 1960S. WHILE he took his family with him when he could, often it was not possible. The writer David Cairns suggested that the Vickers temperament, combined with those lonely times, was a factor in his demeanor before and during performances:

> He used to very often be by himself, and he would be sitting in his hotel room reading. I mean he *reads*, and he would be building up this great head of steam inside, thinking about the role. And if it were a tormented character like Otello or Peter Grimes, he'd be building up all this sort of turbulence. He would be on his own all the time, not seeing people, and then he would arrive for rehearsals, and it's not surprising it forced its way out.[1]

Vickers sang Siegmund and Radames at Mexico's Opera de Bellas Artes in September 1962, notably with Régine Crespin as Sieglinde. A gastric infection he picked up there kept him homebound for several weeks on his return and forced him to cancel a COC *Die Walküre* (he was replaced by Karl Liebl). By September 23 he had recovered enough to sing for perhaps the only time directly alongside New York's hometown tenor star, Richard Tucker. The occasion was the opening of the New York Philharmonic's new hall, later named Avery Fisher Hall, at the new Lincoln Center complex in Manhattan. First Lady Jacqueline Kennedy was present as Leonard Bernstein did his podium dance.

Vickers sang in the opening Gloria from Beethoven's *Missa Solemnis*, bouncing a bit on his toes. He could be heard above Eileen Farrell, as well as Shirley Verrett (then Verrett-Carter) and Donald Bell. Then in Vaughan Williams's *Serenade to Music* for solo voices and orchestra, Vickers and Tucker stood shoulder to shoulder, giving a good view of two strong sets of tenoral cheekbones and chins. Vickers sat out the program-closing Mahler Eighth, in which Tucker did tenor duties.[2]

That fall, *Samson et Dalila* by Camille Saint-Saëns was recorded for EMI in Paris, with Georges Prêtre conducting Vickers, Rita Gorr, the French baritone Ernest Blanc as the High Priest of Dagon, and the National Opera Theater Orchestra. The notes with the LP record (only now in the CD age do we treasure those luxuriously large booklets filled with photos) include a daily "diary" by the French journalist Sylvie de Nussac. She notes that the stage in the Salle Wagram was built for an EMI recording of *Boris Godunov;* singers like the vast platform, a meter high, because their voices rise well over the orchestra in front of them; it's somewhat like being in a theater. On September 26 Vickers, Gorr, and Blanc greet each other for the first time and "fall into each other's arms." They are old friends, all having made Bayreuth Festival debuts in 1958 (Vickers as Siegmund, Gorr as Fricka in *Das Rheingold*, Blanc as Telramund in *Lohengrin*). Vickers already has a major reputation in France, and he receives enthusiastic applause from the orchestra. He is a little pale, having just arrived from New York, with only two hours' sleep. He doesn't speak a word of French "but sings it with impeccable pronunciation, which arouses general admiration." (Charles Dutoit, for one, would later disagree about Vickers's French.)

He's absent the next day, because he asked not to record on consecutive days so as not to tire his voice. On September 28 Vickers records the Act 3 "Vois ma misère, hélas," of the imprisoned Samson. Blanc arrives early, saying, "I came to hear Vickers. It's not every day that you hear fine voices. And there are not many Samsons like him." In the final scene, Vickers cracks on the B-flat in the midst of his climactic line. "Very politely but very firmly, he tucks his score under his arm and announces, 'I don't sing any more today, please.'" It's time to wrap anyway.

A week later, October 8, Vickers is ill (perhaps a recurrence of his Mexico problem). He has gone to London for the weekend on business and is unable to return. But he's back on Wednesday and sings magnificently during the whole session (scenes 1 and 2 of Act 1). Afterward he says, "The doctor told me—if you can sing for an hour, you'll be lucky!"[3]

After spending some time at the end of the year at his new Canadian property, Vickers was at the Met with two of his best partners in January 1963. He sang the January 26 broadcast *Fidelio* with Birgit Nilsson, led by Böhm, and did five more, two with Nilsson. On January 31 he and Teresa Stratas teamed for one *Pagliacci*, led by Kurt Adler.

A recital billed as Vickers's first in the United States was advertised for Sunday, February 24, at Academic Hall in Dwight Morrow High School,

Englewood, New Jersey. It was to be presented by John Harms Concerts, which listed March and April recitals by Anna Moffo and Birgit Nilsson. But the New York–area newspaper unions were on strike, so no records are available as to whether Vickers's concert took place.

In April he was in Berlin for an *Aida* under Böhm, directed by Wieland Wagner. The cast included Gloria Davy, Christa Ludwig, and Walter Berry. Vickers was listed as a guest artist from Covent Garden. All the while, he was looking ahead to a major role debut that spring. His first appearance in Verdi's *Otello* at one point was going to be in Zurich. But it came on May 17, 1963, at the Teatro Colón in Buenos Aires. It was his first appearance in the stately hall of more than four thousand seats and excellent acoustics, dating from 1908. The Colón used to be much more of a major stop on the world opera circuit than it is in the 1990s; Caruso, Ruffo, Chaliapin, Melchior—they all sang there.

The theater booked Vickers heavily. After four *Otello*s he had little rest before beginning six *Carmen*s on June 2, and beginning June 28, he sang four Saint-Saëns *Samson*s, also his first onstage. (It was at this time that another young tenor, Luciano Pavarotti, singing in *Rigoletto* in Dublin, was spotted by Joan Ingpen of Covent Garden; four months later his career took off.)

Vickers prepared for *Otello* by reading many of Shakespeare's plays, not just *Othello,* plus five commentaries on that play. His voice was affected somewhat by the climate in Buenos Aires, both humid and cold, which often troubled singers from other countries. Nevertheless, *Opera* saw him as a "fiery but not exaggerated Otello."[4] The conductor was Berislav Klobucar, with Raina Kabaivanska as Desdemona and Quilico as Iago. (Vickers's conception of the Moor is discussed in a later chapter.) For the *Carmen*s he had recovered vocally and was in splendid form. *Opera* described his Samson as "stripped to the waist and brimming over with vitality in voice and acting."[5]

Vickers enjoyed the Colón experience, although he had never worked so hard, with fourteen performances and fifteen orchestral rehearsals in fifty days. "I guess I was lucky there was no revolution," he told a Toronto reporter afterward, noting tense times with Argentina's election the day after his last performance. He also talked of having established a regular circuit of the world's most prestigious houses: the Met, Chicago, San Francisco, Covent Garden, Vienna, and La Scala. But he had troubles in those last two houses. He spoke of preparing to sing the Emperor in a new *Die Frau ohne Schatten* at the June 1964 Vienna Festival, but never did sing that demanding part.[6] And he was always wary of the claques and politics of La Scala.

In September 1963 Vickers lashed out at Canadian critics once again, in an interview in his hometown paper. Those critics "are responsible for Canada's cultural starvation," he declared, by failing to educate the public about opera. Canadians should be exposed to good music "and must be induced to see the value of such pleasure in their lives." He singled out the Toronto writer Nathan Cohen, who reportedly had said that Canadians wanted quality, not quantity, in their music. The insinuation, as Vickers interpreted it, was that Canadians "would prefer to hear one internationally famous singer than a dozen talented Canadian performers. How else are Canadian artists to gain experience and international acclaim unless they are given a hearing in their own country?"

Still stung by the indignities of his 1960 appearance at the Canadian National Exhibition, he complained that "an artist is without honor in his own country," whereas in Europe "he is almost reverenced, not because he is a star, but because of the talent with which he was born."[7] He must not yet have known that on November 23 he would be honored in his home province with a doctorate from the University of Saskatchewan.

But first Vickers would take his Siegmund to San Francisco for performances on October 10 and 15, 1963. The Iranian-born Lotfi Mansouri directed him for the first time, with the Swedish soprano Siw Ericsdotter as Sieglinde and Amy Shuard as Brünnhilde, Leopold Ludwig conducting. Other tenors in town for the season were Sandor Konya as Radames and James McCracken in *Pique Dame* and *La Forza del Destino*.

Mansouri recalled that Vickers was well settled in his role by then. The director would come to avoid halting the tenor for any detail, for fear that a lengthy Vickers lecture would follow. Ericsdotter, making her North American debut in her role, was very nervous. At the dress rehearsal she became flustered and made a mistake. Vickers, angered, went down to the footlights and asked Mansouri why, if the soprano couldn't remember her part, did he himself bother to show up to rehearse. "But on opening night, typically he gave the curtain call to this lady after the first act, the way he did—he would lead them forward and take a step back behind them," something not all tenors would do. Mansouri saw this behavior toward the soprano as an example of two very different sides of Vickers, which Mansouri would experience further.[8]

In October Vickers sang only two *Fidelio* performances at Chicago Lyric (Sebastian Feiersinger took the other two), with Régine Crespin and Boris Christoff, so he would be perfectly ready for his first Otello in that city. Tito Gobbi was Iago and Sena Jurinac was Desdemona on November 2, 8, and 13 (the Bulgarian Dimiter Uzunov was Otello on November 4). The critic Claudia Cassidy proclaimed Vickers "no great Otello" on her first hearing. "He has the look of the role, dark, stalwart, with a hint of nobility in torture, and a flair for costume once he learns to handle capes. He has the sound of it—heldentenor with the Verdi mirror of moods—once he got past the love duet . . . which neither he nor Miss Jurinac could handle. He needs more fire, more stature, more splendor, but much of the time they seemed within his reach."[9] Those were the only Otellos he would ever sing in his eighty-eight opera performances with Lyric.

He was then in Philadelphia for *Die Walküre* in November with Régine Crespin and Mignon Dunn. The season in that city offered a wealth of tenors, with Mario Del Monaco in *Otello,* Franco Corelli in *Il Trovatore* and *Tosca,* and Jan Peerce in *Rigoletto.*

Vickers had begun to carve out his repertoire, with Siegmund and Otello but not Manrico or Cavaradossi, with Parsifal but not Lohengrin or Walther. There was room for many tenors of many kinds, and Vickers would create a unique gallery for himself.

In January 1964 William Stein wrote to Francis Robinson, Met assistant manager, a sentence that seems quaint in the promotion-soaked world of three decades later. Regretting he had only a press biography of Vickers to send Robinson, he said: "Vickers himself does not believe in publicity; since he does not sing anything but opera, he does not need it."[10] This was a view that Vickers would hold throughout his career, angered by the attention given those singers who had no qualms about using any marketing tools at their disposal.

In January 1964 Vickers received at his farm a telegram from Wieland Wagner asking whether he could sing *Tannhäuser* that summer, with Giulini conducting, instead of *Parsifal*. Vickers cabled next day that his *Parsifal* contract had been signed and mailed, and no, he could not accept *Tannhäuser*.[11] He then was off to Geneva for a Saint-Saëns *Samson,* under Jean Fournet, with the same cast as on his recording.

In April Wieland wrote again to invite him for the 1965 Festival, to sing Siegmund in two cycles of a new *Ring,* under Böhm. Wieland also asked for four *Parsifal*s, but said if Vickers wanted only one role, he hoped it would be Siegmund.[12] But Vickers declined. Coast explained that he had a heavy Met season, staying there till the end of the tour in mid-June. Then he planned a period of holiday and study before the next season, feeling that such a break would add to his vocal longevity. But he did hope to do his first Tristan in Bayreuth in 1967.[13] Wieland clearly wanted Vickers to sing at the festival in the years beyond 1964, yet those performances were not to be.

In May 1964 Vickers was in a feisty mood talking of Canada. He was to make his first appearance that fall at the O'Keefe Centre in Toronto, in *Carmen* for the Canadian Opera Company. This hall was to be denigrated continually by many performers and observers over the years for its unwieldy size, too-wide stage, and poor acoustics. Vickers also blasted it, although as yet he had been only in the audience.

The O'Keefe, he told the *Star*'s Hugh Thomson, "is nothing: neither operatic, legitimate, concert or vaudeville house. As long as Canadians allow beer interests [O'Keefe is a brewing company] to build their performing-arts centres, they will get places built to make money, and let true performing art be damned.

"Much has been made lately of the Canadian Opera Company going into the red by $48,000 this past season. This is nothing," he added. "The Vienna State Opera mounted a new *Turandot* this past season which cost $125,000; and bear in mind Vienna has six opera companies. When will Canadians realize that opera is culture and that it is not going to pay for itself?" This was a high-handed comparison, given opera's long history in Vienna compared to its brief existence in Canada.

He had refused a request to cut his fee for a recital that August 30 in Charlottetown, Prince Edward Island, as part of its centennial celebration: "If Canada cannot pay my fee after 100 years, when can it?" And he felt insulted to be asked to take half his fee for his upcoming fall *Carmen*s with the COC. "If I did, what would the poor kids at the Royal Conservatory get for their part in the shows?" (Nobody seemed to be suggesting that their fees be cut.)

Vickers touched again on the theme of his being an honored artist abroad who gained little respect in Canada. After the small inconvenience of having to wait a half hour at a Vienna State Opera Rehearsal the previous season, he had received an apology from Karajan himself the next day. He contrasted this to what he felt had been his shabby treatment at the 1960 Canadian National Exhibition, in another example of his inability to let go of slights, however far behind him.[14]

The tenor was busy in Manchester that June on the Covent Garden spring tour, singing three performances as Radames, followed by three Otellos, his debut in that role with the company. David Cairns heard that debut and later wrote, "Vickers is the only modern Otello who commands both the notes and the moral grandeur of the part."[15] (Callas was then at the Paris Opéra for *Norma;* available records don't show Vickers being asked to sing with her.)

In a 1974 Canadian TV documentary, Vickers could be seen making up for *Otello* and saying: "Sometimes as I'm putting the muck on my face, I think, 'What a perfectly ridiculous way to make a living.' But I suppose everyone has unpleasant aspects to their jobs; makeup is one of mine. However, I feel this way only at the outset, because gradually the makeup process involves me and becomes quite absorbing."[16]

Vickers always did his makeup himself, Covent Garden's Ron Freeman recalled, with some help on Otello's dark body makeup and Florestan's long hair and grimy dungeon appearance. While preparing, he would bring to life the character he was about to portray. "Some artists are quite happy just to sit there and be made up, and let you create the character, and then they'll go out and sing, which is very typical, shall we say, of some of the German artists. But Jon, the moment he comes in the theater, he's developing a character. I'm sure he starts the moment he leaves his front door."

Vickers was always at the Royal Opera House in plenty of time for this process. He would be certain all "his bits and pieces" for makeup and costume were ready—as well as the oranges he would consume. Though he didn't sing much in the dressing room, as many artists do, "you'd see him, his mind changing as he was putting the makeup on . . . so a character developed," said Freeman. "You could read it in his face."[17]

Vickers's August 13 performance at Bayreuth that summer, preserved on a Melodram recording, was not only Knappertsbusch's fifty-fifth and final *Parsifal* at the Festspielhaus (he had first conducted it in 1914 in Elberfeld) but also the conductor's final appearance of his career. Of this *Parsifal*, Peter Diggins wrote, "At certain phrases—'*Auch deine Träne wird zum Segenstaue; du weinest . . .*' during the Good Friday spell, members of the audience gasped at the sheer beauty of the Canadian's voice. And this in staid Bayreuth!"[18]

That Vickers's second visit to the Festspielhaus should be his last performances there baffled many. It was in part because of Wieland's premature death in 1966; although they fought over roles, Wieland surely recognized Vickers's worth. Vickers called his Bayreuth experience one of "the somewhat sad aspects of my career to date," though it gave him great "inner satisfaction" that "I was allowed to be Knappertsbusch's last Parsifal."[19]

Asked in a 1975 Salzburg interview whether he had purposely avoided singing in German houses, Vickers said of course he had not, but that he had had few invitations. He noted that he had sung in Hamburg, Berlin, and Mainz, "but so far this has been all. I have never understood why the many great stages in Germany have never engaged me for a Wagner production. I thought to myself that something like chauvinism could have a part in it . . . to protect one's own people."[20] It is true that, despite his being one of the finest interpreters of his time of three major Wagner roles, his German career was not large. (Vickers's name appeared in programs of some German-language houses as Wickers because in German Vickers, with the V pronounced as F, has the same meaning as the coarse Anglo-Saxon word for sexual intercourse.)

For very different reasons, Vickers also sang little with the Canadian Opera Company, a sore point that became inflamed over the years. The company may have been too small in the 1960s to present Vickers properly, but in 1976 Lotfi Mansouri took over and enlarged it artistically and financially. He had worked with Vickers several times elsewhere but could never get him to accept an invitation to the COC. Every year the director would send invitations to Coast for any role Vickers cared to sing, and Coast would reply that "Mr. Vickers said Toronto wasn't ready for him." Fees apparently weren't the issue—negotiations never even got to the point of discussing them, and Mansouri was paying the same or higher fees as the Met at that time for top singers such as McCracken and Sutherland.[21]

But in fall of 1964, long before those stalemates of the 1970s, there was a happy collaboration between Vickers and the COC. On September 14 he had opened there in *Carmen*, with mezzo Mignon Dunn. (He picked her up at one point, as he so often did with his stage women, but because Dunn is a tall woman, he almost decapitated several choristers.) Richard Cassilly, then with New York City Opera, was to sing Radames on September 26 but had a throat problem. Herman Geiger-Torel, the COC chief, called Vickers at his farm to ask him to step in. Tenor Ian Garratt recalled:

> Jon came right down. There was no rehearsal, he just stood onstage and chatted about a half hour before the production began. We got under way about 10 P.M. . . . Jon did the role to perfection. You'd think he had rehearsed with the company for a couple of weeks. He paced himself throughout the singing. I can still see Geiger-Torel pacing backstage, puffing his cigar and saying, "This is magnificent! I can't believe it! What a performance." I thought he'd burst a blood vessel with ecstasy. But Jon took it all in stride. It was just a piece of cake to him.[22]

Marilyn Horne sang Amneris, and the record executive Terry McEwen recalled going to see her afterward. "Jon sang a gorgeous performance. He was dressed in his Aeneas costume from *The Trojans* at Covent Garden." (Apparently he had kept it at home.) McEwen had disliked Vickers personally since their recording differences, but he approached him backstage. "I said to Jon that it was a magnificent performance, really beautiful, and he snarled at me, 'You're surprised, aren't you! Big surprise for you.' He was charming," McEwen said sarcastically.[23]

On February 11, 1965, the Vickerses' fifth and last child, Wendy Patricia, was born in Toronto. Shortly thereafter, Vickers was at the Met for *Walküres* with Nilsson and Rysanek, beginning February 22, and his first of only three career performances of Erik in *Der fliegende Holländer*. Böhm conducted the *Holländer* at the Met on March 1, and house conductor Joseph Rosenstock took the April 13 student matinee and the May 22 tour performance in Minneapolis, which also featured Rysanek as Senta and George London as the Dutchman. Erik was a relatively small meal for Vickers, but Martin Bernheimer found him "little short of spectacular. . . . The huge voice [was] tastefully scaled down whenever Wagner's special brand of Wagnerian bel canto demanded."[24]

After two performances of *Otello* in Mexico that summer, Vickers was in New York for the final, hectic months at the old Met, which was soon to move to Manhattan's newly constructed Lincoln Center. On September 28, the night after Gedda opened the season in *Faust*, Vickers began a run of seven performances in a new, heavily cut Met production of Tchaikovsky's *Queen of Spades*, in an English translation by Boris Goldovsky, under Thomas Schippers. With Stratas as Lisa and Resnik as the Countess, the production also had five spring performances on the Met tour. Vickers would sing five more in the second half of the 1967 Met season. McCracken took a few around Christmas, when Vickers preferred to be at home with his family.

John Ardoin noted that much of the role of Herman lies around the tricky upper middle range of the tenor voice. "But Mr. Vickers seemed not to give it a thought. His singing was full, beautifully controlled and rich in color."[25] Franz Kraemer recalled that Vickers didn't like the character of the gambling-obsessed soldier because "he was mean to the girl." But it fitted Vickers in that Herman is an outsider and misunderstood, as is Peter Grimes.[26]

Wieland Wagner wrote Vickers in September 1965, in what must have been one of his last letters to the tenor, expressing regret that Vickers had declined to sing at the festival that summer. He said Vickers belonged to Bayreuth as a major Wagnerian, and inquired about parts he might sing for 1967. Did Vickers plan to study Siegfried in time for 1967, 1968, or 1969, he asked, presumably referring to the younger Siegfried. He also noted Vickers's previous suggestion of doing Tristan there about that time.[27]

The Toronto Symphony disliked Karl Böhm for his record with the Nazis. (He had conducted first the Dresden and then the Vienna State operas throughout the war, and though he was afterward cleared of all charges of party involvement, the rumors of his Nazi ties were slow to disappear.) For his part, he didn't much like the Toronto Symphony either, feeling the lack of acceptance and respect. But on October 10, 1965, the CBC televised live a symphony concert led by Böhm, with Vickers singing Florestan's "Gott, welch Dunkel hier," and, from *Die Walküre,* "Winterstürme" and "Ein schwert." Franz Kraemer, who had first wooed Böhm for an earlier Beethoven concert, directed the telecast, and for dramatic interest he put Vickers on the gallery above the orchestra in Massey Hall. This showcased the tenor's enormous voice, and balance with the orchestra wasn't a problem because there were TV mikes and audio control, Kraemer said.

Despite Vickers's admiration for Böhm, two incidents stood out in which the tenor opposed the conductor. "For Jon to sing these things was nothing. He could do it in his sleep." As usual everywhere he went, he was chary of his rehearsal time. After a dry run two days before, with no cameras, Kraemer asked Vickers to come for a rehearsal the morning of the concert. "He already had his place here [the farm], and he said, 'Why, why, why do I have to come? It's no good! I should not come!' He felt anybody could stand in for him on the gallery. Böhm said, 'You must come! This orchestra isn't used to Wagner!'" The Viennese Kraemer, who had been present when Toscanini threw out a singer who declined to rehearse in Salzburg, got his way. "The concert was a triumph. He was wonderful. I said, 'Thank you, Jon.' He said, 'It would have been better if I hadn't come to the rehearsal!'"

Vickers was being a perfectionist about his vocalism. But Kraemer said his dislike of the rehearsal "to me was a little unprofessional. By that time he should have known enough about television to know cameramen have to know what's going on."

The issue of when Vickers would sing Tristan arose during that rehearsal discussion. "Böhm said, 'This fool will not sing Tristan with me.' Vickers said, 'It's too early, Maestro. I cannot do it. It's bad for me.' They fought to the bitter end about it. Böhm said, 'I'll be dead by the time you sing Tristan.'"[28] Vickers was not being entirely truthful, as he had been in talks at various times previously about Tristan. He knew Karajan was waiting for him, and he must have enjoyed having those two great musicians, and others as well, begging for his services.

On October 24, 1965, Vickers took part in a United Nations Day concert at the U.N. in Manhattan, with Leonard Bernstein leading the finale of the Beethoven Ninth. Then he was off to Chicago for four Lyric performances of *Samson et Dalila,* with Bumbry, Jean Fournet conducting. He might have watched rehearsals for *Wozzeck,* with his Covent Garden compatriot Geraint Evans in the title role. It was a part that would be suggested for him both by Karajan and by Chicago's Bruno Bartoletti.

In January 1966 Vickers sang two performances of the first act of *Die Walküre* in Montreal with Zubin Mehta, who was then just thirty years old. The conductor recalled learning from the tenor: "As a young person, loving music as I did, I would indulge myself too much. And Jon said to me, 'Stop milking every phrase, for God's sake.' He meant it so sincerely, he was never arrogant about it." Over the years, Mehta would note that Vickers was always 100 percent involved in a work from the first rehearsal. "When singers mark [do not sing full voice] at rehearsals, they act 'markingly,' but Jon's intensity never subsided. He would mark occasionally but he was always 100 percent."[29]

In his earlier years of stardom, Vickers also made lasting impressions on some of his female colleagues. British mezzo Yvonne Minton recalled her first brush with Vickers when she was a Flower Maiden in *Parsifal* in February and March 1966. She had just joined Covent Garden. The maidens "were all doing our little bits . . . and he turned to me and he lifted me off the ground, as only Jon could do, and said, 'You've got the most beautiful voice, my dear!' or words to that effect." Far from being flattered, the pretty blonde singer thought "it was quite the wrong thing to say in front of all my colleagues," with whom she had just begun to work. It was "so embarrassing, and I was dreadfully shy."[30]

The shabby but beloved old Met, at Broadway and 39th Street, closed the doors on its glorious echoes after a farewell gala on April 16, 1966. Vickers sang the "Winterstürme," conducted by George Schick. Tenors among the honored guests were Richard Crooks, Frederick Jagel, and Giovanni Martinelli, and performers included James McCracken (in Otello's "Si pel ciel"), Jan Peerce, Franco Corelli, Sandor Konya, and Kurt Baum.

On May 1, 1966, Vickers made his recital debut at Philharmonic Hall (later Avery Fisher Hall); it had been postponed from February 1, and was part of a Great Performances series presented by the agent Herbert Barrett. Vickers was accompanied by Leo Taubman. He told the audience, "Against better advice, I chose my own program. I *like* these songs." He would continue to talk to audiences through his recital career. The recital showed his "extraordinary interpretive powers," wrote Allen Hughes, who saw the tenor as "a barrel-chested man with the easy stride and affable manner of a football coach." Saying that Vickers was wasted on trifles like Irish ballads, Hughes praised his projection of mood and image in Purcell songs and Beethoven's cycle *An die ferne Geliebte.* "Winterstürme" was the last encore. But George Movshon noted Vickers's "spectacular control of dynamics" and the surpassing beauty of the voice. He said the hit of the show was "Total eclipse" from Handel's *Samson,* with Vickers giving it "full emotional intensity plus wonderful architecture for the long phrases."[31]

That July and August, at Vickers's Salzburg Festival debut, he was historically paired in *Carmen* with the Escamillo of Ramón Vinay. The fifty-three-year-old Chilean was now back to baritone roles, but contrary to his prediction back in 1957, he and Vickers never did sing *Otello* together. (Also in August, the Spanish tenor Plácido Domingo made his first Met appearance, outdoors at Lewisohn Stadium.)

On the 1966–67 Met roster, in the new house, Vickers's name was listed above that of Fritz Wunderlich, whom Vickers had met and admired, and who was to have made his debut as Don Ottavio in *Don Giovanni*. But that golden-voiced German tenor's career was cut short tragically when he died in a fall on September 17, 1966, at age thirty-six.

It is generally assumed that Vickers always hoped to sing his first Tristan with Karajan, when he felt ready. However, in a testy letter to Gerhard Hellwig, artistic director for Wieland Wagner at Bayreuth, in September 1966, Coast wrote that Vickers wanted to sing it first with Kempe, in the next two to three years, and was looking for the right venue. Apparently, Coast had heard little from Bayreuth in the previous two years; he tartly noted that Hellwig's letter had been sent to an address he had left two years before. He also acerbically corrected Bayreuth's spelling of Vickers's name.[32]

On October 17, 1966, Wieland Wagner died in Munich at the age of forty-nine, leaving his brother, Wolfgang, the sole artistic director at Bayreuth, where Vickers would never sing again. Vickers was in San Francisco, where he would sing Don Carlos at the San Francisco Opera, with Claire Watson as Elisabetta and Horne singing her first Eboli, Glossop as a strong Rodrigo, and Tozzi as King Philip, with Molinari-Pradelli conducting. The tenor might have strained himself during the three performances, for he canceled two performances of Lyric Opera of Chicago's *Otello*, returning to his farm (or possibly to Vienna) to recuperate from an acute inflammation of the vocal cords. He sang October 14 and 22 with Gobbi's Iago and Kabaivanska's Desdemona; Charles Craig stepped in as the Moor October 16 and 19.

He had more hard work back in San Francisco, where beginning November 4 he sang in the first professionally staged U.S. production of *Les Troyens*, with Régine Crespin as Cassandre and Didon. He also did four *Carmen*s with Grace Bumbry. While in San Francisco Vickers might have seen Vinay singing his first U.S. Falstaff.

The *Troyens* was presented in three hours, with cuts including the early scene between Énée and the ghost of Hector, and giving Crespin prominence. At a press conference, Vickers said that the opera is really Énée's story, but with the cuts it became mostly Didon's. "Of course I'm very jealous, but I couldn't think of a nicer soprano to get the advantage." He offered a stalwart characterization, Arthur Bloomfield reported, although his costume was a cross between a Santa Claus and a Superman suit. His soft singing tended to be softer than the Crespin *pianissimo,* and their blend may have been less than ideal, but the total result was nothing to quibble about.[33] Kenneth Dean Wallace found that Vickers "handles French heroic opera with the same intelligence and dramatic forthrightness he brings to Wagner and the moderns. In other words, he knows instinctively when a whisper will produce a far greater effect than a shout."[34]

Vickers later gave some insight into his softer singing, for which he was criticized on occasion, apropos a recording he made that November of *Die Walküre,* with Karajan leading the Berlin Philharmonic. Joining him in a church outside the city were Gundula Janowitz, Crespin as Brünnhilde, Josephine Veasey as Fricka, Thomas Stewart as Wotan, and Martti Talvela as Hunding. Karajan's approach to Wagner was "at once thrilling and fraught with vocal danger," Vickers wrote in *Opera Canada.* There was no fear of being swamped by the orchestra, but the singers faced the problem of a great deal of *piano* and *mezza voce* singing while carrying a vocal line of quality and vitality. "Von Karajan's handling of the score minimizes excessive wear and tear on the voice, but the singing of it is infinitely more difficult and exacting." While listening to a rehearsal tape in which the tenor was singing the "Winterstürme" *mezza voce* to preserve his voice, Karajan suddenly said to Vickers, "But that's exactly what I want!" As a result, Vickers from then on sang the aria in that soft way, not because it was easier—on the contrary, he found it much more difficult to do—but because he respected the conductor's musical judgment and sense of interpretation, though his decision would lead to charges of mannerism by those who disagreed with the Karajan style.[35]

The year 1967—a strenuous one for Vickers, with some major role debuts— began with the death on January 8 of his much-loved mother at age sixty- eight, in Prince Albert. He spoke about her on a 1968 London radio show, *Desert Island Discs,* on which guests chose favorite recordings. His selections for that program included Bach's "Sheep May Safely Graze." He explained that his mother's death had been "a really remarkable personal experience . . . for me. . . . Certainly it was not a sad experience—sad only in that I was saying good-bye. . . . Here was a woman who with complete happiness, complete contentment, no resentments, no bitterness, no fears, faced her death. And I feel that the mood of 'Sheep May Safely Graze' is that—an expression of one's complete faith in eternity."

The impact of the loss followed him onstage. He said later, "I sang my first *Peter Grimes* seven days after I buried my mother. That was very difficult. When I described the death of the boy—'Picture what that day was like, that evil day'—it was difficult to keep myself emotionally removed."[36]

There was much concern at the Met as to whether Vickers would be able to sing. But he told colleagues that it was what his mother would have wanted, that he should fulfill his duty.[37]

11

Peter Grimes

This is whatever day I say it is!
— Peter Grimes

THE LONELY FISHERMAN PETER GRIMES, A ROLE THAT BENJAMIN Britten wrote for a totally different type of tenor, was Vickers's greatest achievement, and the role for which he will be best remembered. It cemented him into the century's exclusive gallery of great portrayals, with the Boris of Chaliapin, the Canio of Caruso, the Don Giovanni of Siepi, the Violetta and Norma of Callas, the Empress of Rysanek.

He was a riveting Tristan and Otello, and as of this writing the only really successful Énée since Georges Thill. He himself felt *Les Troyens* was his finest accomplishment, vocally speaking. But his Grimes was a mighty amalgam, a collision, as Leighton Kerner called it, of a role with a particular voice and stage persona.[1] The result, as so often is the case with the greatest of music, seems inevitable, destined. "If he sang Otello from his gut up, he sang Grimes from his bootlaces," said Gwynne Howell, who appeared in both operas with Vickers (and whose comment recalls the nineteenth-century tenor Jean De Reszke, who said one should sing from the ankles).[2]

In the Covent Garden video's haunting final scene, for which Vickers disliked the term "mad," when Vickers as the hunted Grimes repeats his name, on his knees, his arms outstretched, it is as if the fisherman holds his soul in his huge hands, to display its agony, to say farewell to life. Such moments as this distill the pain and passion Vickers poured into his portrayal, unforgettable to all who witnessed it, from his first lines, "I swear by Almighty God, that the evidence I shall give, shall be the truth, the whole truth and nothing but the truth!" God and truth were abiding concerns, absolutes, as he called them, throughout Vickers's own life. And those who saw him as drawn to Christ-like, masochistic parts would find much confirmation in his embrace of this opera and its cruelties.

But his mastery of the role was not without ironies, notably that he was never comfortable with, and even hostile to, the homosexuality that is intrinsically linked by many with *Grimes* and its composer. And the vocal line allows full play for the falsetto and crooning for which many criticized

Vickers. In addition, Vickers's credo was always that the composer came first, that singers served him. But Britten walked out of at least two performances of *Grimes* with Vickers and never came to appreciate the Canadian's vision of the role, which certainly was not Britten's lyrical concept. "He didn't like me," Vickers said bluntly.[3]

Vickers's idea of and performance in the title role of this multilayered masterpiece were far from Britten's view, even as Britten's realization of Grimes was wholly different from the monster fisherman in George Crabbe's 1810 poem, *The Borough,* that forms the basis of the opera. "Britten was a composer who did not like being 'interpreted,' and so I suppose he thought that Jon was too free with the score," said the conductor Sir Charles Mackerras, a Britten friend.[4]

None of that matters in the final tally. Vickers onstage wrenched the opera into a universality of theme—the agony of the outsider—even as he himself became in many ways more and more an outsider to the world of opera as his career progressed, and with it his scorn for many directors and conductors. This universality has made *Peter Grimes* a classic of the twentieth-century operatic repertoire, and Vickers is now even more identified with it than is its creator, Peter Pears, although Pears's shadow hung over Vickers for many years in England. As the director Elijah Moshinsky says, at times a composer may not realize what he has wrought; it takes the interpretation of others to spread fully the wings of his creation.[5]

One odd matter discovered in the research for this book: There is a startling lack of any record of or commentary upon Britten's view of Vickers's Grimes portrayal. Several important books dealing with Britten, including the massive 1992 Humphrey Carpenter biography, make no mention of Vickers. The Britten Archive at Aldeburgh has yet to unearth any written or other record of the composer's view, or of anything he may have discussed with Sir Tyrone Guthrie about text changes used by Vickers for the Met's *Grimes* production and for his recording. I do not know whether it is by chance or purpose that this gap exists on a major interpreter of the opera that ranks with Britten's finest work. But Vickers's suspicious mind would find a reason. He noted in 1984 that "the whole Britten mystique is very, very powerful, the groups surrounding Ben and Aldeburgh and everything else."[6]

Two years before his 1967 Met Grimes, Vickers had taken on Herman in *The Queen of Spades,* another breakout role, and another example of his bending the voice to his will. He said later: "I made my career on the basis of refusing to be classified. I have fought that tooth and claw. I find it amusing when people say, 'Oh, Siegmund is absolutely for you.' Then they turn around and say, 'Peter Grimes is just built for you.' This is nonsense.

Siegmund is the other end of the spectrum from Grimes. So when people say these parts were built for me, it is not true. I have made myself conquer these parts."[7]

What he had done more or less was to create a *Fach* (a German classification of vocal roles) for his unique voice. He cannily gauged both his strengths—the control he had learned for his big sound, his dramatic stage persona, and the passion he could pour forth—and his weaknesses—lack of security above the B-flat, lack of agility as the voice aged (probably his basic difficulty with Tannhäuser). He also knew he had no patience for roles that lacked meaning and were simply romantic tenor showcases. Even had he been able to do Calaf's high-wire act, it would not have interested him. James Levine believed Vickers related very strongly to the kind of role that wasn't part of any sort of general style, and was a singular challenge.[8]

Like *Fidelio*, *Grimes* was to Vickers an ideal opera, filled with major human themes and with challenging music that he mastered so intelligently. He believed it to be the most significant opera of the twentieth century. And it can be said that Grimes is a creature as private and conflicted as Vickers himself. Vickers as the Parsifal-like innocent fool for his art saw himself as persecuted by the mob of commerce in the opera world, as continually misunderstood as to his motives as poor Grimes.

Of the vocal demands, Vickers said that no other work he had sung required such absolute technical ability. "You are always exposed as a dramatic tenor, as in the Pub soliloquy where he says 'Now the Great Bear and Pleiades' all on E-natural, mezza voce, at an incredibly slow speed, with crescendos and diminuendos, right in the passaggio of the voice. Then in the Hut Scene, you have this very pliant sort of coloratura on E, F, G, A and even B-natural, a high tessitura that is extremely controlled."[9]

The baritone Theodor Uppman was the creator of Britten's Billy Budd in 1951 and covered the role of Captain Balstrode in the 1967 Met production of *Grimes*. He was amused as he recalled Vickers's discussing phrases with him and saying words to the effect of, "If only Britten had known *me*, he would have written it [differently]."[10]

Some felt Vickers's effort to modulate his voice for the soft high passages, especially in the Pub Scene, resulted in a croon, or even a whine that was off-putting. Others thought the result succeeded, and that, as with *Les Troyens*, Vickers's very effortfulness enhanced his portrayal. Vickers explained in 1984 that he used "one kind of voice for the inner Grimes, and another for the outer Grimes," a technique that he said few critics recognized. He used "a veiled quality in the *mezza voce* for a very distinct dramatic purpose; it's something contained . . . there's confusion, there's an injury. You use a technique for a purpose. And I believe that the writing was designed really so that the extrovert and the introvert are very clearly defined in the vocal line."[11]

Levine, who never conducted the tenor in this role, noted that Vickers found a way "to produce this phenomenal intensity without breaking himself," as a Shakespearean Lear or Othello must learn to do. This fascinated the conductor, who had had a similar experience with *Wozzeck* and found a way to "go home and eat dinner" after it, having, he hoped, given the audience a wrenching experience. But Levine said that Grimes wasn't as taxing of Vickers's resources as Otello, Tristan, or Énée.[12]

Peter Grimes had premiered to great success on June 7, 1945, at Sadler's Wells in London. Pears hinted at the time about the homosexual allegory aspect of the work, says the scholar Philip Brett,[13] but in the 1940s any explicit public discussion was chilled by British laws against sodomy. (It was not until 1967 that sex between men was partly decriminalized.) The opera "just fails to make explicit enough . . . its . . . 'hidden' theme of its hero's divided nature . . . which is finally the sole claim on dramatic interest," said Philip Hope-Wallace.[14] This issue has occasioned continued discussion over five decades. In 1971 Andrew Porter wrote, "It has often been suggested (though seldom in print) that Grimes's inner struggle (like Claggart's, and perhaps Captain Vere's) is against a homosexuality that neither he nor, for that matter, his creator is consciously aware of."[15]

In November 1947 Covent Garden opened a new *Grimes* production with Pears, directed by Tyrone Guthrie, who apparently cut some of the music. As Philip Brett observed, theater people like Guthrie have a far more cavalier attitude toward cuts.[16]

Vickers may well have heard the March 1948 broadcast of the Met's first *Grimes*. He became better acquainted with the work when he sang in the chorus of a 1952 CBC production in Toronto. And he seems to have had it in mind from his beginnings at Covent Garden, where other singers said he was always looking at the score.

He learned the role in part with Reginald Goodall, who had led the Sadler's Wells premiere. In discussing the Pub Scene, Goodall told Vickers, "You know, Jon, Britten wrote this for Peter, and Peter only had one good note, and it was E-natural!" Met wig mistress Nina Lawson recalled him returning excitedly to his dressing room after leading Grimes's new apprentice from the pub at the end of Act 1. "He plunked a note on the piano and said that Peter Pears only had one good note" and he, Vickers, "had it too."[17]

Vickers, as with all his roles, researched Grimes thoroughly, immersing himself in not only the Crabbe poem but also Crabbe's other works and a biography by his son. He also visited Aldeburgh. Nothing about the Grimes in the poem related to the Grimes in the opera, he found; Crabbe was rejected because he was an aesthete, not a tough fisherman. Vickers saw the use of the sea, with Britten's haunting music, as representing the inner turmoil in Grimes. The message of the opera, he said, was that other people's points of view must be recognized, and that the community can help them. He felt enough attention wasn't paid by audiences and critics to the sufferings of characters in the opera other than Grimes, like Mrs. Sedley, the laudanum addict: "It depressed me terribly that there is such super-concentration on the role of Grimes."[18] This comment would raise the eyebrows of those who knew that Vickers usually insisted on being the dominant character; indeed, he could not help himself from being so in many works, even when not the title character (as in *The Bartered Bride*).

He met with the director, Guthrie, before accepting the 1967 Met *Grimes*, his debut in the role. Guthrie, who at six feet four inches towered over the tenor, was low-voiced and patient. Vickers told him: "I will not play this opera from the standpoint that Grimes is a homosexual; to limit it to that would be to deny the greatness of the work. Peter Grimes is a study in the entire human psychology of human rejection. It may have been written by a homosexual for a homosexual, but this work is timeless and universal and it's wrong to think that homosexuals are the only ones who ever felt rejected." Guthrie absolutely agreed, Vickers said, "and he, Colin Davis and I revolutionized the work."[19]

His idea: "I want the audience to come away taking a serious look at themselves and their relationship to their fellow man," Vickers told William Albright. "I want to suck the public into being sympathetic with the crowd in its condemnation of Grimes so they too reject him—and then show them another side of Grimes and show them how wrong they were."[20]

Vickers was very definite on the topic of what he saw as the homosexual subtext of the opera. Britten "wrote it to win compassion for the homosexual," he said. "Every time I saw the opera with Peter Pears, that is what I saw." But in later years he said he had liked Pears in it, calling his performance "beautiful, very moving." Vickers believed that Britten "learned to hate *Grimes* because he had revealed too much of himself in it."[21]

Mackerras told the author it was widely believed that Vickers was "violently antihomosexual." He noted it was known that Vickers had deeply offended several gay directors, such as Zeffirelli and Visconti, by saying publicly that a homosexual could not appreciate "normal" love and sex and therefore should not direct such operas as *Carmen, Aida, Samson et Dalila, Die Walküre,* and *Don Carlos,* where heterosexual love is a dominant factor.[22]

In 1981, when the Philips *Peter Grimes* recording came out, the issue of the small text changes that Vickers used arose anew. In July of that year he told

David Cairns that at least some of the changes stemmed from a visit by Guthrie to Britten before the 1967 Met production. (Guthrie had directed the heavily cut version at Covent Garden in 1947.) But no available record from the Britten and Guthrie archives supports Vickers's story, and Dr. Donald Mitchell, chairman of the Britten Estate, doubted very much if Britten had been asked. "I'm sure he would have politely said that really Vickers should stick to the published form." Still, Britten was a practical man of the theater. If the changes had been presented as a way to make the words more communicable in the United States, the composer might have consented. But as for "other substitutions, peculiar to Vickers himself," such as in the Hut Scene, the answer, Mitchell believed, would have been no.[23]

In Act 2, when Grimes is questioned by Ellen as to how his new apprentice got an ugly bruise, the Montagu Slater text has Grimes's reply as "Out of the hurly-burly." Vickers sings that line on the recording, but at the Met and later at Covent Garden he sang the blander "How should I know?" Guthrie and Britten, he said, had decided that "hurly-burly" was an expression foreign to the American ear. "How should I know" was "perhaps not so poetical and, as some have suggested, does not have that delightful degree of ambiguity about it," Vickers told Cairns.[24]

But he did not mention that he changes "her breast is harbor too" to "her heart is harbor too," or that he made a number of changes in the Hut Scene text. The "heart" may simply have offered an easier vowel to sing and more intelligibility, suggested the Canadian tenor Ben Heppner, a 1990s Grimes. But Richard Woitach thought that Vickers indeed might have been uncomfortable to think someone in the audience could have laughed inappropriately on hearing him sing "breast."[25]

In the Hut Scene, the lines "Telling stories! That's no way to make things better than they were!" was substituted for "Here's your sea boots! Take those bright and fancy buckles off your feet!" In this case, the changes make sense if it's true that Guthrie's goal was to make the words more understandable for Americans. But in his rage in the hut, Vickers didn't sing to his apprentice, "I'll tear the collar off your neck." He substituted, "I'll teach you not to lie to her." That might have been more of Vickers's own idea, as revealed when, for the Met's 1973 revival, Vickers said he changed a number of points on which he had disagreed with Guthrie's original staging. "I thought he had me treat Grimes' young apprentice too harshly in the original," he told John Ardoin.

> I wouldn't handle my own son that way, although I'd be rough and tough with him when necessary. There have been times when I have come home in a bad mood because of something that had nothing to

do with my son, and I've seen a frightened child; he could feel my anger. I applied this in *Grimes*.

When Grimes returns to his hut in a flaming temper, it is because he is angry that Ellen has deserted him and because he had let his temper rule him and had slapped her. Grimes, however, is not angry with the boy, but the boy is terrified because of Grimes' temper. When the lad starts to sob, he gets through to Grimes, and in that moment, I try in a clumsy way to comfort him. This is all mine, not Sir Tyrone's.[26]

Vickers on occasion refused to work with certain boys in *Grimes* when he felt they would suffer psychologically.

Asked about Vickers's retention of the text changes in later productions, Colin Davis said, "Well, he liked it. He was a very obstinate man. He preferred it, he stuck with it. 'This is whatever day I say it is!'" The conductor was quoting from *Grimes*, Act 2, and laughed at how apropos the quote was for Vickers.[27]

The text issue remained so bothersome to Vickers that he dragged it out yet again in a brief commentary that he, among others, was invited to write for the July 1996 program of Tanglewood's fiftieth anniversary of the first U.S. performance of *Grimes*, which had been commissioned by Serge Koussevitzky. He repeated the story of the 1967 changes and asserted that they were left in place for the 1981 Covent Garden production and video "out of respect for Britten's apparent wishes," though why a British production would retain changes made for a U.S. audience is not apparent. The tenor also referred to speculation and confusion about the origin of the changes, noting "there are those who have been unjustly vindictive, believing that members of the cast took it upon themselves to alter the text. Nothing could be further from the truth."[28] Yet no cast member other than Vickers was ever accused of making changes (though some made minor accidental slips that can be heard on that record and are noted in the libretto). He was the only one who could have been an instigator.

If the archival evidence for Britten's reaction to the 1967 changes is slim, the anecdotal evidence presents a clear picture of the composer's displeasure with the changes and with other aspects of Vickers's portrayal. In summer 1967, for instance, Britten and the English Opera Group were at Expo 67 in Montreal. The critic William Littler recalled a woman's going up to Britten after a press conference to say that she had just seen Vickers at the Met in *Grimes*, in a magnificent performance. "I could see Britten almost stiffen, because Peter Pears also was at the press conference. And Britten's answer to the woman about Vickers was, 'I'm sure it must have been fine if he followed the score.'"[29]

That was a mild public response. Privately, Britten was "absolutely incensed" about Vickers's portrayal when he saw it in the 1975 Royal Opera House production, said Colin Graham, a director and Britten friend. Graham "got the full blast" from Britten the day after that *Grimes* dress rehearsal. "He was really, really angry. Jon had been so inaccurate and cavalier with the score, changing words and notes as it suited him. . . . Jon said [of the 'hurly-burly' phrase], 'Nobody understands this, I'm not going to sing it.'" Although Britten felt that Vickers's fisherman was "too mad" for too much of the piece, so that the character lacked development, it was the musical changes that chiefly upset the composer. A lot of those alterations can be heard on a BBC broadcast tape. But the nonconfrontational Britten never told Vickers of his views.[30]

The score was not the only issue with Britten. He said in the 1940s, "I've always inclined to the clear and the clean—the 'slender' sound of say, Mozart or Verdi or Mahler," and that liking was characteristic of all his work.[31] Small wonder that the Vickers robustness made the composer turn his head away in disgust. (He also disliked Richard Cassilly's portrayal.)

The Welsh tenor Robert Tear was another who frowned darkly at Vickers's Grimes, although he called Vickers a great artist. Tear, who also sang the role, had a solid basis for complaint: He was close to Britten and Pears and, with both gone, billed himself as one of the remaining defenders of Britten authenticity. He and Pears, he said, felt obligated to sing Grimes the way Britten wanted it, which, Tear said, was "exactly the way Pears sang it at the first performance." Vickers, however, "plowed through" the work, driven by what Tear called his "huge ego," disregarding Britten's lyrical concept. "Ben walked out of two performances by Vickers," Tear recalled. "Couldn't bear it." Tear reaffirmed that after the first performance by Pears, Britten "wasn't interested, because thereafter *his* concept of it was gone. The way he cast it the first time was the way he wanted it."[32]

One journalist, who preferred not to be named, recalled that Britten and Pears had gone to the first rehearsal of Vickers as Grimes in 1969 and walked out because it was so different from Pears's portrayal, so very physical. They saw Vickers pick up the boy and hated what his actions seemed to say about Grimes's relationship with the child.

John Tooley also laid out the composer's dislike of Vickers's portrayal. "The last time Ben came, he actually came with me [probably in July 1975 for the new production]. But he was very ill [he died December 4, 1976] and he only came for the second act, particularly for the Hut Scene, which appalled him. Because he said, 'Jon sentimentalizes this ballad ["In dreams

I've built myself some kindlier home"], and it's not to be sentimentalized.'"
Britten "never believed that Jon in his characterization had enough of the
visionary in it . . . and thought that the whole thing was too manic. Manic
from the first bar." In contrast to Tear's view, Tooley said that Britten "could
see a number of interpretations to his works. They weren't confined to a
view which was established by Pears. But he just didn't like Jon's, which is
fair enough. Jon and Colin Davis between them I think produced a very
valid interpretation of *Grimes*. And that's Colin as much as Jon. It's not solely
Jon."[33]

Davis told the author he never spoke to Britten on the issue, but he knew
"Ben wasn't very happy with me either. He didn't approve of what we did."
Vickers "put a lot of Crabbe back" and employed his ferocious temperament. "You could imagine him beating up boys . . . [but it was] difficult to
imagine him being attracted to them." And Davis believed that Vickers had
strengthened the opera. "It's a very unpleasant piece, you know, very violent,
angry. . . . I think between us, we managed to bring out more of the violence
of the piece, without the cloying sweetness."[34] This, however, would seem at
odds with Britten's view of the Hut Scene as expressed to Tooley.

In July 1975 Covent Garden mounted a new production to replace the
1947 *Grimes*, and the spare, non-picturebook look was ideally suited to the
strength of Vickers's portrayal, far more so than the Met's realistically
detailed production. Director Elijah Moshinsky recalled plunging directly
into rehearsal of the final so-called Mad Scene with Vickers. "I'd worked out
a set that was very, very stark and very strong. I just brought him onto that
set and said, you have the whole set to play with. I said one other thing, that
he was chasing his own shadow, that the moonlight would be behind him,
and in front of him would be the shadow of Grimes. I wanted to see if he
could chase the shadow and make his hallucinations clear. And he just took
that idea and went with it. And what I loved about him, but was also very
difficult, was that he committed himself every moment to what he performed. That's very unusual in opera singers."[35]

But it was Richard Cassilly, not Vickers, who would sing Grimes at
Covent Garden on March 24, 1977, the seventieth performance of the
opera in the house, given in memory of Britten, who had died less than four
months earlier. Vickers doesn't appear in the program among those commenting on Britten. He's not identified in a large photo and is listed only,
seemingly unavoidably, in mention of other *Grimes* productions. Tooley said
that Cassilly was always scheduled for the performance and that certainly
no Britten interests had blackballed Vickers (Tooley himself later would be
a trustee of the Britten Estate).[36] But this absence does seem odd.

Cassilly, who died in February 1998, was a creditable Grimes. One story goes that when he was rehearsing at the Met, he was told he was singing some wrong notes. When the score was checked, it was found that Cassilly was right, but they were not the notes that Vickers had sung and that Met listeners were used to hearing.[36]

James Levine appreciated the long-lasting impact of Vickers's success with the role. Domingo decided to leave it to Vickers, but today, such artists as Ben Heppner and Anthony Dean Griffey are singing Grimes, "and most of those people discovered the theatrical viability of the piece through Jon's performances."[36] Griffey, an American, confirmed that Vickers had an impact on him. He first sang the role in Tanglewood's production for the fiftieth anniversary of the opera, when he was twenty-eight, and later at the Met.

He had seen Vickers's Covent Garden video (as well as Anthony Rolfe-Johnson at the Met, and a Philip Langridge *Grimes* tape). In general, Griffey felt that for Vickers, singing "was not about, listen to my beautiful high C, but his notes mean something. . . . If I had a tenor I molded myself after, it would be Mr. Vickers." He saw the Canadian as a compelling actor and individualistic artist. "It's important to develop your own style. That's what I learned most from him." He met Vickers after the Tanglewood performance, and was "in awe." He was happy that Vickers "didn't say, 'When I sang Peter Grimes I did it this way.' He was very complimentary and open."[37]

12

A Prophet in His Own Country

INGLED WITH THE *PETER GRIMES* PRODUCTION, WHICH OPENED
January 20, 1967, Vickers sang five performances of *The Queen of
Spades,* again with Stratas, a strenuous pairing of roles at the Met.

His first appearance at Karajan's Easter Festival, which had begun in
1966 in Salzburg, came in March 1967; he sang two performances of *Die
Walküre,* Ticho Parly a third. His Sieglinde was Gundula Janowitz;
Brünnhilde was Crespin. A similar cast would return the following Easter.
In 1969 Karajan would do *Siegfried,* with Jess Thomas; Vickers never did
sing that title role, and never seriously considered it.

Vickers's first *Otello* at the Met (he had sung it on tour two years previously) came on April 3, 1967, with just two performances conducted by
Mehta, with Gabriella Tucci and Gabriel Bacquier, plus an August 25 date
in Newport, Rhode Island, with Kurt Adler, Renata Tebaldi, and Peter
Glossop. Peter G. Davis found the Vickers Otello "a trifle detached—a noble
figure but one who never became terribly upset" and seemed "incapable of
murder. Yet is there anyone who sings the role more beautifully?" Davis
admitted that Vickers "lacks the *squillante* quality which some may feel is
absolutely essential," but found plenty of excitement. He noted that the
monologue "Dio! mi potevi scagliar," sung from "a crouching position as if
some giant fist had pressed him to the ground, made an overwhelming effect
through the tenor's ravishing tone and superbly arched phrases."[1]

Allen Hughes suggested, however, that "his particular vocal mannerisms
do not lend themselves especially well to the creation of a universally tragic
character. These mannerisms, which may take the form of sudden, sometimes almost explosive, crescendos of tones, or, on the contrary, quick diminuendos or switches from full voice to half-voice, create at times a
quasi-crooning style that is not unattractive but which is too personal for
unrestricted general use."[2]

The next year, John Ardoin offered a timely contrast of the Otellos of
Vickers and McCracken when the Canadian played the Moor in November

1968 with the Dallas Civic Opera. *Otello* in America had meant mostly McCracken in the years when Vickers was breaking out. The American tenor was "a great bull of a man, thundering his betrayal in open, wounded outcries." Vickers's Otello, in contrast, suffered inwardly, and when his torment surfaced in Act 4 without his subduing it as in Acts 2 and 3, "it leads with crushing inevitability to Desdemona's death." McCracken was more of a doubter, but with Vickers, "you feel a monumental tug of war and nerves between Otello and Iago," until Otello hears Iago and Cassio talking in Act 2. Ardoin saw Vickers "at the summit of his powers" at this time, although great things were still in store for Dallas. "He commands a stage with a wisdom seated in knowing how to make each movement and gesture count." Vickers always studied each role seriously, and Ardoin took note of his "intimate knowledge . . . [he] applies vocal color and stress proportionately to the color and stress of a word, a phrase. He is more than a tenor; he is a creative, aware musician."[3]

Less enthusiastic was Olin Chism of the *Dallas Times Herald*, who dubbed Vickers's physical portrayal "a little overdrawn."[4]

On April 30, 1967, Vickers sang his second and last Carnegie Hall recital, accompanied by Richard Woitach, then a Met assistant conductor. Leo Taubman, Vickers's longtime vocal coach, had died recently, and Woitach had worked in Taubman's studio with his singers. Vickers opened the 6 P.M. Sunday concert by noting that Woitach's name had been left off the program. He first sang four sections from Handel's *Messiah,* followed by five Scarlatti songs. Then came Purcell songs in lighter, romantic vein. In "Man is for the woman made," avoiding an unattractive word he sang "princess or harridan," instead of "queen, slut or harridan." After Purcell's "Sweeter than roses," in which the tenor's huge voice rollicked up and down the staff as the aftermath of an embrace was described, Vickers quipped to the delight of the audience, "Must have been some kiss!" (The quip, audible on a private tape, was excised from the VAI release.)

The second half was Schumann's *Dichterliebe,* exquisitely sung. For an encore, Vickers promised the audience only one, but they got all of Dvořák's Four Gypsy Songs. The concert sponsor in this seventy-fifth jubilee season of Carnegie was the Canadian Educational Foundation.

In July 1967 Vickers had a Canadian triumph with a highly praised *Otello* as part of Expo 67 in Montreal. This six-month festival presented artists and companies (including La Scala and the Vienna Staatsoper) from around the world, in celebration of Canada's centennial. Birgit Nilsson was there in *Elektra,* Ingmar Bergman directed *The Rake's Progress,* and the Bolshoi presented Prokofiev's massive *War and Peace.* The Montreal Symphony Orchestra staged *Otello* with Vickers, Stratas as Desdemona, and Quilico as Iago, with Mehta in the pit. The production was sumptuous, with a fountain and enormous black marble columns in the castle's great hall. Vickers "was a tower of strength," wrote Eric McLean. "He has made the part his own."[5]

Mehta was not exempt from Vickers's exigent demands. It's not clear at which *Otello* this occurred, possibly at the Met, but at one rehearsal Mehta cracked open his score and was sight-reading. This was obvious to Vickers, who said, "Son of a bitch, you haven't studied it, have you!" Mehta pleaded a hectic schedule in Israel and Toronto. Incensed, Vickers told him to go back to his hotel and study. Vickers was going home. "Call me when you learn the score."[6]

Vickers went into one of his rages when Princess Grace of Monaco attended the *Otello*. There was massive security backstage, and cast and audience were prevented from moving about until the royal party had left. Vickers, still in blackface, was seen shouting loudly that he, who had sung for the queen of England, was being held in bondage by what he called a "common movie star."[7]

In May and June 1967 he sang in eight *Carmen*s at the Royal Opera House, and was Don José again in Salzburg in July and August. He was at the Vienna Staatsoper for his only *Parsifal* there, on November 1. One review found him involved and impressive, although it suggested he looked more like a solidly built backwoodsman than the youth of noble birth that Parsifal was. His "large and beautifully controlled tenor" was praised, and his portrayal was "spiritually fulfilling in a way that one has hardly ever heard from a Parsifal." In Act 3, however, his hushed *pianissimo* was inaudible at times.[8]

Herbert von Karajan added a notch to his steely sword with a new *Die Walküre* that he conducted and directed as his debut with the Metropolitan Opera, opening November 21, 1967. Vickers sang with Janowitz as Sieglinde, Nilsson as Brünnhilde, Ludwig as Fricka, Thomas Stewart as Wotan, and Karl Ridderbusch as Hunding. The Gunther Schneider-Siemssen production was spare, as was the restrained orchestra and singing. The lighting was in Karajan grays and blacks, but a blinding beam of light silhouetted Siegmund's battle with Hunding.

Vickers recalled that Karajan had been worried about working with the heavily Jewish Met orchestra. "He confessed to me that wearing a Nazi uniform had been a mistake, and he asked me how I thought the orchestra would behave. I told him that they were musicians first, Jews second. As I predicted, in ten minutes he had them eating out of his hand."[9] That comment was typical of Vickers's bluntness, sometimes viewed by others as insensitivity.

Met assistant conductor Walter Taussig, who had been an academy student in Vienna with Karajan (Kurt Herbert Adler and Nicholas Goldschmidt, he said, were in the same class), was among many who noted the Karajan effect on Vickers, who, he said, "almost crooned" the "Winterstürme."[10]

A new Covent Garden production of *Aida* opened January 24, 1968, with Vickers partnering Gwyneth Jones, singing her first Ethiopian maiden, with soft high notes in the Nile Scene. Grace Bumbry was a sensuous Amneris; John Shaw sang Amonasro. Vickers was a virile Radames and a tender lover as well. In *Opera* Horst Kogler wrote: "Nor have I ever experienced such a sexy Radames as Jon Vickers, even if he looked more like Marcus Aurelius than the Egyptian warrior; and if one could at first complain of his lack of portamento for *Celeste Aida* (especially around the break in his middle register whenever he has to leap from C to F), he certainly improved from act to act. His burning intensity and passionate singing in the Nile scene, in his last encounter with Amneris, in the tomb, are still vividly reverberating in my ear."[11]

It's not clear in which *Aida* run this took place, but Vickers told a funny story on himself in a CBC interview. Everyone else in the cast wore a hat or helmet, but Vickers appeared simply with a black wig. That, he admitted, was not the costume designer's plan. "I honestly and truthfully felt I could not sing 'Celeste Aida' in that absurd-looking hat. I thought people would laugh, and I'm sure they would have." He talked to the director, who rationalized: "Well, it's perfectly obvious, Jon. You are having an unofficial conversation with Ramfis and all of a sudden the generals—this formalized meeting with the king was sprung upon you and you never had a chance to get your hat!" Laughter all round.[12]

In February and March he was back at the Met for more Siegmunds, with Rysanek and Janowitz as Sieglinde, Nilsson and Crespin as Brünnhilde.

In the summer of 1968 Vickers was in Buenos Aires again, to sing *Pagliacci* and *Carmen*. Bruno Bartoletti, who conducted the *Pagliacci*s and who came to know Vickers well in Chicago, was deeply impressed by the tenor's Canio. Years later he recalled how, during the postlude to "Vesti la giubba," Vickers would move very slowly to the back of the stage, a man destroyed by pain, never staying for applause, indeed not desiring it. Vickers had not gotten along with the director, and Bartoletti felt his stage movements were his own conception (though as previously noted, Zeffirelli may deserve some credit).[13] Richard Woitach of the Met later said that Vickers's goal was always to prevent applause at the end of "Vesti," so that the beautiful postlude wouldn't be drowned out, and the full impact of Canio's wretchedness would be clear.[14] When first-night critics said that Vickers probably couldn't sing the traditional interpolated B-flat in the first scene, the tenor then took it every night thereafter to show that he could.

During the Buenos Aires *Carmen*s, Robert Merrill, who sang Escamillo, recalled that after one performance, Vickers "blew up and broke all the furniture in his dressing room. Next day, there was nothing in the room. I had to lend him a chair." Merrill didn't recall the cause, but it could have had to do with his Carmen, Grace Bumbry, said by some to be a singer who failed to meet Vickers's particular standards of professionalism.

Merrill expanded: "Something happens to him onstage." Of a Met *Carmen*, the baritone recalled, "He kicked me over. I thought I broke my back. I said, 'Jon take it easy, it's only a performance!'" But Vickers brushed off this suggestion. Merrill concurred with others about Vickers's physicality with female singers, and demonstrated by grabbing the author's arm to show how Vickers did his damage.[15]

In Buenos Aires in July, Vickers had an opportunity to sing Rata-Sen in *Padmâvatî*, the 1923 ballet-opera by Albert Roussel. This was a work Vickers had been eager to take on, as it offered a theme similar to the loyalty seen in *Fidelio*.

Vickers continued to try to spend time each summer with his family. Around this time, he later recalled, he was upset when a hockey scout called to offer his son Kenneth, eight, a summer hockey school scholarship. Many parents would have welcomed this, but Vickers saw

> the brutality, the crass greed that would rob a little boy of his summer holidays in the sun, playing as the spirit might move him, which is the divine right of every little boy . . . [that would] cramp him and warp his tender personality by imposing on him the regimen and the discipline of a hockey school . . . where he would be taught that the only thing that matters is to win . . . not that the thing that matters is not whether you win or lose, but how you play the game.
>
> The latter produces men, the former produces merchandise to be bartered in the flesh markets of big business masking under the name of sport.

He would say this in a 1973 speech in Montreal, and his words foreshadowed an unstoppable trend in the world of athletics as well as the world of music.[16]

The fine Welsh bass Gwynne Howell joined Covent Garden in 1968 and would sing King Marke to Vickers's Tristan there in 1978 and 1980. He recalled Vickers's standard daytime "working clothes" as either gray trousers and a blazer, usually navy, or brown pants and a black or red polo shirt. "He was a short, strong, squat man, but he always looked about eight foot, six inches." Howell also vividly remembered Vickers's working personality.

> He would not tolerate anything less than professional. He always spoke out. And because of his strength, everybody always said, "Absolutely, Jon, definitely right."
>
> When Jon was in full flood, everybody shrunk away, but it was like a storm, he had to blow himself out. He had to get this thing off his chest. And he'd come back and say, let's get on with it. But while he was rolling, it was a delight, really. . . . He livened up the most boring kind of rehearsal.

In 1969 Howell was in *Peter Grimes* at the Royal Opera House.

> There's one line Grimes sings, "I must have help." Now, Jon was big enough to pick up the whole set, the boat, and everything else. He'd pick up the boy as if he was a lollipop. But with the dimension he got into his character, everybody was saying, "Yes, yes, give Jon as much help as he needs!"
>
> He was so committed. He was not just performing an opera onstage for an audience, he sucked everybody around into these things. For the time he was there, it was alive. His Otello was like that too.

Howell well remembered how physical Vickers was onstage. The bass always enjoyed singing of Marke's betrayal in Act 2 of *Tristan*. "At the end of the act, Jon would come up and say, 'That's great!' and shake my hand. I wore several kinds of Celtic rings, and twenty-four to thirty-six hours later, the marks of the rings were on my fingers!"

Recalling some Desdemonas left breathless by Vickers's Moor, Howell mentioned another physical singer, Boris Christoff, as Boris Godunov, kicking the tenor Shuisky. "I don't think Jon was like that. He pushed his own limits, but his limits were more extreme than the limits of his colleagues."[17]

Vickers's 1968 Met season began September 21, in four *Carmen*s, with Shirley Verrett, under Mehta. He then did two *Walküre*s with Karajan, the October 31 performance with Nilsson as Brünnhilde and Crespin as Sieglinde.

La Scala was never a favorite house for Vickers, but he sang there in two more seasons. On December 12, 1968, he began a run of six performances of *Die Walküre* (with Charles Craig filling in), with Georges Prêtre conducting. The Sieglinde was Božena Ruk-Focič, with Shuard as Brünnhilde, Veasey as Fricka, David Ward as Wotan, Talvela as Hunding.

Vickers sang two more *Carmen*s at the Met, with Bumbry, in January 1969, then two more *Walküre*s with Karajan, the second, on March 1, the matinee broadcast. Then came his second Met *Grimes* run with Colin Davis, beginning March 13; Phyllis Curtin stepped in for one Ellen, and Lucine Amara sang the rest. He would also sing the role for the first time at the Royal Opera House, in five performances in May and June that year.

Amara later noted that the difficult places for the soprano are the unaccompanied duet with Grimes at the end of the Prologue and the quartet with the Nieces and Auntie:

> Jon Vickers always had a bit of pitch trouble in that duet and would go just a bit flat. I learned in rehearsal that the thing for me to do was always to sing just a bit sharp there, deliberately, and it would pull him up just enough, and we would end up in key when the orchestra came in again. "Thank you for that," he would say, every time, because he would be terribly upset if we would end up under pitch at the orchestra's entrance at the end of that scene.

Amara praised his *pianissimo* in the Pleiades monologue and called him heartbreaking in the final scene.[18]

Vickers was highly honored and, in his view, deeply injured by his homeland in 1969.

The tenor did not fit into the Canadian mold in many ways. He was Canadian in the Scots money sense, in his love of his homes and land and the outdoors, in his geniality in greeting admirers and old friends. Although he could be very emotional about how much he identified with his homeland, he nevertheless could not understand or deal with his country's unenthusiastic reaction to his success.

Canadians, many observers agree, generally have not been single-minded strivers for success in a chosen field; they are accommodating, polite, even gentle. And the country has no tradition of high culture; Canadians define culture broadly, to include their much-loved ice hockey masks, for example. In general, they deplore the showiness, what they see as the vulgarity, of those who do succeed.

None of this fitted Vickers very well. He never could have reached the pinnacle of his art without being single-minded; he never could have survived in the cutthroat world of international opera by being accommodating. And although his disparagement and avoidance of publicity seems a Canadian trait peeking out, it confounded him that his countrymen took his stardom so coolly. A popular Canadian figure, a well-known Canadian name—that was never Jon Vickers.

Yet in 1969 he did receive Canada's highest recognition, the Companion of the Order of Canada, created by the queen, for his international contributions to the arts. The award was announced on December 20, 1968, by the governor general; the Companions are limited to 15 persons annually and to 165 living Companions at any time. The insignia was presented on April 8, 1969, at Ottawa's Rideau Hall, residence of the governor general. Others in the group were the composer Jean Papineau-Couture, the producer Norman McLaren, a medical researcher, public officials, a doctor, and an architect. Vickers had just returned from a run of *Pagliacci* that had begun on March 24 at La Scala with Nino Verchi conducting, and a cast including Peter Glossop as Tonio and Raina Kabaivanska as Nedda.

For dressy occasions Vickers often would wear his Order badge—a stylized snowflake bearing the crown, a maple leaf, and a Latin motto—and its ribbons. The motto bore a weight of irony, considering the tenor's long and outspoken dissatisfaction with his country's artistic standards. "They desire a better country" (*desiderantes meliorem patriam*), the award proclaims.

This Olivier of opera would never receive a British knighthood. Canadian citizens were barred from accepting honorary titles by the Canadian parliament's 1919 Nickle Resolution. Such titles were seen as patronage and vestiges of colonialism. The resolution was later rescinded, but it still was not the policy for Canada to recommend its citizens for those honors.

Then, less than a month after the honor, came the review that sent him into a fury. On May 1 Vickers, recovering from flu, sang at his longtime friend Nicholas Goldschmidt's Guelph Spring Festival in War Memorial Hall, Guelph, Ontario. It was a restrained and religiously sober program, the most dramatic piece being "Total eclipse," which replaced "Vois ma misère" from *Samson et Dalila*. The "Winterstürme" was a ringing encore for the packed house. In opening comments, Vickers praised the festival as part of "the growing cultural life of our country."

A Vickers recital, with Leo Barkin, aired later on the CBC, included several works that had been on the Guelph program, with the tenor presumably in better voice. A radio tape is available, so one can say that those pieces wonderfully displayed the expressive colors of Vickers's voice: Stradella's "Pietà signore," Purcell's Three Divine Hymns, Beethoven's Gellert Lieder, four songs from Vaughan Williams's *Pilgrim's Progress*, Brahms's Four Serious Songs. They were a canvas for Vickers's own serious sensibilities, marked out by the beauty of the works and his own musicality. It is a great pity this program is not more readily available.

"Now, now that the sun has veiled its light, and bid the world goodnight, to the soft bed my body I dispose, but where, where shall my soul repose? Dear, dear God, even in thine arms," sang Vickers in the Purcell, his inimitable timbre making the words ineffably moving.

It sounds wonderful on tape. But after the Guelph Spring Festival recital, the *Toronto Star*'s William Littler wrote that without operatic makeup and costumes, the tenor appeared on the concert stage "like just another heavy-set middle-aged tenor, suffering the vanity blow of thinning hair. And he sounds even less like the Jon Vickers who belts out grand opera at Covent Garden and the Met."[19] Littler was exercising his right of fair comment; the appearance of an artist is fair game. He had certainly heard a great deal of the tenor's singing for comparison. But Vickers was outraged. It seems his youngest son, Ken, was teased about those words, and Vickers was always fiercely protective of his family. The episode must have grated on him particularly since he had so recently received that highest honor and might have felt wounds healing with Canada.

It was so distressing that Vickers reportedly backed out of discussions for a 1970 Toronto *Fidelio*. "I'm not bitter. I'm hurt," he told the *Globe and Mail* in March 1971, still stung by that review.

> This is my home, and I don't like to have my kids ridiculed in the schoolyard because of personal attacks like that. They can say what they like about my performance, but they're not going to insult me personally.
>
> I'm an international artist, but I'm an ordinary man and I have ordinary sensitivities. I'm not going to have the period of time that I have allocated to being in my home made unpleasant by things like that.

He also spoke of that time, and how he enjoyed the way the people of Orangeville, three miles from his home, thought of him as a local farmer. "I like that. And more than that, I do farm. I breed beef cattle, Aberdeen Angus and Herefords. I ride a tractor and mulch out barns, and plow and haul hay, every chance I get. It's my sanity, on the farm. I've shunned publicity like the plague."[20]

Tristan und Isolde was planned the next year for Vickers, who had decided upon San Francisco for his debut in the role. In summer 1969 Kurt Herbert Adler sought to have Rudolf Kempe conduct, telling him Vickers also very much wanted him. In fact, Adler had to ask Vickers for Kempe's address.[21]

A bit of a schedule problem arose because the Met had planned more

*Walküre*s led by Karajan in November 1970, and the orchestra rehearsal conflicted with the last performance of the *Tristan*. John Coast put his finger on the nub of the issue: "Karajan does not want Jon to sing his first Tristans with anyone but him. It would therefore be deeply embarrassing for everyone if you ask Karajan if Jon could arrive later for rehearsals at the Metropolitan, and he finds out that Jon has been singing *Tristan* with you. *We* want to inform Karajan about your *Tristans* in a correct and straight-forward manner if and when the contract matures."[22]

In fact, those *Walküre*s never transpired, and Karajan never again conducted at the Met. The house's 1969 strike had been such a disruption that many schedules had to be changed. Karajan apparently was trying to renegotiate his contract with Bing, and matters collapsed. In addition, Karajan had wanted Helga Dernesch for the *Ring,* but Bing had insisted on Nilsson.[23] Whether Vickers himself at some point told Karajan about San Francisco isn't known. It seems he would have wanted to be straightforward with the conductor he so admired. Coast was asking five thousand dollars per performance for the *Tristan* for Vickers, who was then getting four thousand dollars at the Met. And of course Vickers wanted his usual first-class airfare.

In early December 1969 it looked like Erich Kleiber to lead the *Tristan,* but he pleaded a November *Wozzeck* in Munich. Meanwhile, Coast passed on a request by Vickers: he wanted no solo curtain calls after each scene of *Tristan*. The tenor felt that group calls at the end of acts and solo bows at the performance end should be enough. His concern was the risk of spoiling the mood of the opera.[24] This seems odd, since *Tristan* has no breaks between scenes. But Coast also mentions the *Aida* in which Vickers had just sung in San Francisco; the tenor must have objected to bows after scenes then. Perhaps Coast was not totally familiar with *Tristan,* but he was ever mindful of his client's desires.

On September 17, 1969, one hundred years after the death of Hector Berlioz, the Royal Opera House opened a new production of *Les Troyens.* Led by Colin Davis, it was directed by Minos Volanakis, who designed it with Nicholas Georgiadis. The cast for eight performances included Vickers and Ronald Dowd as Énée, Josephine Veasey and Janet Baker as Didon, and Anja Silja as Cassandre. The first complete recording of the work, part of Davis's Berlioz cycle for Philips, began two days after the opening and was spread over the next five weeks at Walthamstow Town Hall in London.

It was a very difficult situation, a strain on all concerned as six more Covent Garden performances continued (through October 10). And the hall's small stage was hardly suited to the large structures, both auditory and visual, of this epic (five acts and nine tableaux), which needed to have appropriate musical perspective even though unseen. Nevertheless, the effort produced a magnificent recording that thirty years later has yet to be superseded. It was another triumph for Vickers, and is a cornerstone of his great legacy.

"It was a mad thing to do," said the English writer David Cairns, then employed by Philips.[25] The *Troyens* project was last-minute: Philips first had refused to do it, but had a change of heart when it was discovered that Davis might defy his contract and do the record with EMI. He had led several concerts of each part separately and an excellent Proms performance of the entire work. Berlioz is a composer with whom Davis had deep empathy and with whom he is today strongly identified.

EMI had actually set up the recording sessions for 1969 at Walthamstow. Philips took over the plans, but the hall was available only during the run at the Royal Opera House, when all concerned would be fatigued. Still, the producer, Erik Smith, told Alan Blyth that the pros and cons were about equally balanced. "There's no doubt that the involvement and tautness Colin and the cast achieved throughout was made possible only because he could return to the opera as a whole every few days."[26] But "everybody was very fraught," said Cairns. When the octet in Act 1 was being recorded and the producer wanted to do it again, "I remember Vickers standing there saying, 'I am not going to leave my voice on the studio floor!'" He kept saying it, then finally called for his car and left, ending the session.

Vickers made a small change to his final "Italie!," shortening the note. And sometimes the tenor said certain passages should be sung *forte*, when they were marked *piano*. He justified those changes by saying Énée was "this great hero," which is what Smith always called Vickers after that, recalled Cairns.[27]

Peter Glossop, who sang Chorèbe, recalled another Vickers dustup. Lyric mezzo Anne Howells sang Ascagne, son of Énée, and when Vickers heard a playback of their scene, he began thumping the table. Engineering can make many differences, and Howells sounded as if she had the big voice of a Fiorenza Cossotto, while Vickers's sound was that of a lyric tenor. "He said, 'This is stupid, my voice is ten times the size of hers! I'm not having that!'" And the section had to be reengineered.[28]

Blyth felt of the finished product that Davis "allowed Vickers' sometimes rough singing to pass," and that for all his commitment, the tenor "too often sounds uncomfortable and strained."[29] But if one follows Cairns's view, that very strain only adds to Vickers's noble, romantic, and heart-rending portrayal. Notable is his final singing, "Inutiles regrets" (futile regrets), as Énée decides he must leave Didon to fulfill his destiny of founding Rome, though he knows his departure will destroy her.

As Cairns has said of him in general: "It is as though he were the embodiment of some ancient prophetic cry, with a power to move feelings touched by few in this or any age."[30]

THE 1970s

Gaining
the Heights

A great performance by Vickers is like giant
sculpture on which the hammer-blows are still
visible. Struggle is native to it; a more polished
style would be incongruous. His is a voice
predestined, like Aeneas and his men, to toil.
—*David Cairns*

13

A Unique Tenor Repertoire and a Tristan Debut

IN THE 1970S VICKERS ADDED AN ENORMOUS GERMAN ROLE, TRISTAN, to his repertory. He refined his portrayals of Otello, Peter Grimes, Parsifal, and Énée, while Florestan, Siegmund, and Canio remained staples. He also took on successfully some unusual roles including Laca, Herod, Pollione, and Benvenuto Cellini. The argument can be made that no other tenor in at least the second half of the twentieth century mastered such simultaneous peaks in varied repertory, and that Vickers has not received the recognition due such an achievement.

He became the reigning Tristan, and at this writing no worthy successor has appeared in the fifteen years since Vickers last sang the role. The Canadian tenor Ben Heppner, who also sang Grimes, had a major success as Tristan in Seattle in 1998 but has yet to refine his portrayal. Domingo promised it for years but at this point, 1998, may only ever record it. He also promised Grimes but has dropped those plans. Vickers, McCracken, and the somewhat overlooked Vladimir Atlantov were the Otellos of choice; Domingo then succeeded in the role. But the Spaniard never sang Énée again after his shaky 1983–84 performances at the Met.

Pavarotti has his own shining place in the Italian sun, but his Otello was never to be sung onstage, only in strained concerts, and no one would imagine him as Tristan or Grimes. José Carreras lacked staying power and, finally, real gravitas, although his Saint-Saëns Samson was praised. Nicolai Gedda and Alfredo Kraus were specialists.

Moving backward, Franco Corelli and Carlo Bergonzi again were the brilliant Italian and French interpreters. But Corelli could only regret he never essayed Otello, and German roles were never the goal of either tenor. Richard Tucker had many proponents, but acting of any subtlety was never his strong suit. Mario Del Monaco and Giuseppe di Stefano were bulls of tenors, with gorgeous sound and dramatic stage presence, but again one would not think of them as Tristan or Grimes or Parsifal, or as Handelians. But the noble Vickers sang all those as well as major Italian parts. Wolfgang

Windgassen was a lighter-voiced Wagnerian and did not stray far from German roles. And Lauritz Melchior's list of roles was overwhelmingly German, although he did sing Otello thirty-one times and wished that the Met had offered it to him.

One must go back at least as far as Giovanni Martinelli to come close to Vickers's achievement. But that glorious Otello and Radames in his lengthy career sang Tristan only once (in Chicago in 1939, with Kirsten Flagstad).

Vickers began 1970 with his first appearance with the Boston Symphony Orchestra, in early January. Maureen Forrester joined him for three performances of Mahler's *Das Lied von der Erde,* led by William Steinberg. Vickers's program listing proudly included his "second career as a cattle farmer." His easy power and delicate touches in the difficult songs were noted by critics.

Then came two Canadian concerts, the first on February 21 in Winnipeg, with Teresa Stratas and the Winnipeg Symphony Orchestra. Together they did the duet from *Carmen* for Don José and Micaela, the bedchamber scene from *Otello,* and the finale of *Pagliacci,* and took nine curtain calls.

On February 24, he was in Montreal for another concert, with Franz-Paul Decker conducting. Besides Otello's death scene and Dvořák's Gypsy Songs, he sang the aria from Halévy's *La Juive* "Rachel, quand du Seigneur." The role of Eléazar, another religious man in a quandary, was one in which many could imagine him, but he never performed it.

He admired Caruso's recording of that aria, made shortly before the Italian's death. Vickers, with two daughters, of whom he was very protective, felt certain Caruso's own daughter was much in his thoughts when Eléazar sang about picking his child up from the cradle and promising God that no harm would come to her. Then she would suffer, because of him. Vickers related to this strongly.[1]

In March and April he was at La Scala for *Pagliacci,* with Raina Kabai-vanska. He had a great success, with audiences shouting his name.[2] He flew to his Canadian home, then spent a week out west, visiting his father in Regina, Saskatchewan. After a concert *Fidelio* at the Casals Festival in Puerto Rico came about three weeks visiting his wife's mother, who still lived in Ripley, Ontario; then it was on to London for the June 30, 1970, Royal Opera House farewell gala for the departing Sir David Webster. Vickers sang the *Troyens* love duet, with Josephine Veasey, and Peter Grimes in the Pub Scene.

In July Vickers decided on a new structure for his payments, switching from Artistes Internationaux, which had subleased his services for the United States, to Beacon Concerts Ltd. of London.

At the August 1970 Salzburg Festival, Karajan's new *Otello* production found Vickers in top form. His Otello, "taking a frame out of Laurence Olivier's film, was one of the great performances of his career, a Moor gently civilized on the surface but given to sudden and terrifying storms of temper," wrote James Helme Sutcliffe. Karajan's staging had the dying Otello fall backward onto an enormous bed, then painfully drag himself across the bed to kiss his wife (Mirella Freni) for the last time. "His actions were so truthfully portrayed by Vickers as to bring a lump to the throat of the most hard-boiled operagoer."[3]

Vickers discussed future roles with Karajan, and in 1970 or 1971, the tenor recalled, they talked about *Götterdämmerung*. Vickers never wanted to sing the young Siegfried, agreeing with Anna Russell that he was a "L'il Abner," although the part may have been unattractive to Vickers also because it lies high. But he found the Siegfried of *Götterdämmerung* an interesting role and offered to do it for Karajan and for Covent Garden as well.

He also told Karajan he was ready for *Tristan* and would not want to postpone that to do *Götterdämmerung*. Karajan had wanted Vickers's Tristan since he first heard the Canadian sing, so the conductor put *Tristan* on his schedule instead, and that Siegfried never came to pass.[4] In 1976 Jean Cox was singing the elder Siegfried at Covent Garden. Unfortunately for Wagnerians, Vickers never sang it there or anywhere else.

But other negotiations had been burning up the wires for what was planned to be Vickers's first Tristan, in October 1970 at the San Francisco Opera. Kurt Herbert Adler was eager to tout him as the third tenor to sing his first Tristan there, following Ramón Vinay and Jess Thomas. His measurements had been sent for costumes in April, listing the tenor with a 47-inch chest, 39-inch waist, 46 inches at the hips, 17½-inch neck, a size 9 shoe, and a 7½-inch hat size.[5]

On June 19 John Coast wrote to chastise the company's public relations department for a Vickers reference in its season brochure "which I know will give him offence." One can be sure Coast was accurately reflecting Vickers's own sensitivities. The complaint: Birgit Nilsson was referred to as "the world's leading Wagnerian soprano . . . partnered with a great Canadian tenor." This, wrote Coast, "is nonsense. Mr. Vickers is one of the two or three ranking world tenors, as Mr. Adler will be the first to admit, and which gentlemen of the stature of von Karajan, Klemperer, and others, prove by engaging him over and over again." Canada "in fact rejected him consistently for years in his early career, and what pleases Mr. Vickers more than anything else is the completely international reputation he now has, plus the fact that he is not limited to either the German or the Italian repertoire."[6]

This comment reinforces the idea of Vickers's unique repertoire, and lets slip a hint of the bitterness that the tenor felt toward his native land.

As his San Francisco contracts were in a final flurry, Vickers was in a car crash on August 16, 1970. He was driving a minibus in the Salzburg area, with his wife and five children as passengers, when the bus collided with a car. He was hit in the head, and daughter Allison had to scramble over the front seat to brake the bus. No one was injured seriously, but Vickers suffered a concussion, and Hetti needed stitches in one ear. The tenor had stitches in his forehead and was hospitalized for several days. He could recall nothing of the crash. But he was able to sing the final *Otello*s on August 25, five days after he left the hospital, and August 29. He had sung on August 10 and 13 and missed an August 18 performance.

Adler, keeping tabs on his Tristan, sent a telegram of wishes for a speedy recovery. Richard Woitach, who worked with Vickers on Tristan, recalled that the tenor told San Francisco he was having memory problems after the crash.[7] Peter Glossop, who was singing Iago in Salzburg, said that Hetti stayed with her husband in the hospital. The Vickerses asked Glossop and his then wife, the mezzo Joyce Blackham, to move into the lovely villa they had taken outside Salzburg to care for the children. "They still talk about it," said Glossop. "Jon can be quite strong with his children, but with me, they did anything they liked."[8]

Another accident occurred on September 25, this time a collision with a rope. Vickers was at his Ontario farm when he went out that night to chase a howling dog on the property. In the dark he ran into a rope supporting a tree in an area where structural work was being done on the house. The rope caught the tenor right across the larynx but caused only soreness—no hoarseness—apart from the shock.[9] Vickers was able to sing a September 29 concert *Fidelio* in Montreal, under Franz-Paul Decker.

An anecdote about a Vickers neck injury (whether this or a later one is not clear) shows how his remarkable musculature stood him in good stead. He told colleagues he had once walked into a clothesline; his neck had hurt for a few days, but he had thought nothing of it. Several months later, pain and headaches sent him to a doctor, who took X rays. Vickers was shown a black spot on the film, and the doctor told him he had actually broken his neck. But the muscles around the break were so strong that they held the neck in place and it had healed.[10]

To Adler's dismay, Vickers arrived for the *Tristan* rehearsals in October with a different throat problem looming. On October 21 Dr. Shirley Baron, the company's doctor, had Vickers in his office when Adler called and was told no medicine could help the tenor in time. Adler asked if switching to

Fidelio would mean Vickers could appear (this would give him less to sing and far less pressure). But Vickers departed that day for Toronto.[11] Adler got Windgassen, upon whom Nilsson insisted, to sub as Tristan (for forty-five hundred dollars), his first in the United States.[12] Windgassen was fifty-six and had retired from Bayreuth in summer 1970, though he continued to sing elsewhere. By 1965 he had sung Tristan 179 times.

Richard Rodzinski later said he thought Vickers had looked forward to the *Tristan* and had gone to San Francisco despite the developing throat problem, in hopes it might improve. Rodzinski added, "Adler was a tremendously gutsy, fearless person in negotiations, but he was always a little shy of Vickers. There was no rapport as Adler had with so many other artists."[13]

The writer Arthur Bloomfield said Vickers had complained to Adler that the five full orchestra rehearsals he wanted for *Tristan* weren't available, but Adler reminded him that the agreement had been for four. Bloomfield suggested a cold-feet theory, noting that three weeks after the *Tristan* opened, James McCracken lost his voice during an *Otello* series; Vickers was called and agreed to sub (although McCracken recovered).[14]

In December 1970 Vickers contracted with the Gramophone Company (later EMI) to record *Fidelio* for a ten-thousand-dollar advance and a proportionate 10 percent royalty. There had been some dustups about it, with Vickers seeking his advance before the tapes had been approved, contrary to the company's standard practice.[15] On December 16 he opened in a new Met production of the same opera, conducted by Karl Böhm and directed by Otto Schenk, with Leonie Rysanek, Walter Berry, Giorgio Tozzi, and as Jaquino, the Scot Murray Dickie, who became a good friend of Vickers's. The production marked the bicentenary of Beethoven's birth, and Vickers sang ten performances.

This was the only time that Schenk, himself an actor, worked with Vickers, but he recalled it as a quintessential experience. At rehearsal "I kept stopping him and telling him what to do with his hands. And Vickers said to me, 'Why do you stop me so often? My hands are famous!' I said to him, 'Your acting is famous and you are famous, but I never heard that your hands are famous.' We were both furious." Then Bing appeared.

> He had a way, he was always there at just the right time. And he put us both together and he said, "I had one wish. You are a fool"—to Vickers—"and you, Mr. Schenk, are a fool, and my wish was to get these two fools together." And so we listened, and I stopped telling [Vickers] anything, and after a while, Vickers stopped and said, "Why don't you stop me anymore and tell me things? I was silly."

> And then in the "Namenlose freude" [duet], I showed him how to
> put his hands to caress her [Leonie Rysanek as Leonore], and when
> they did it, it was one of the greatest moments . . . it was the tension,
> we were all so excited!

But Schenk emphasizes that "they did it themselves." He does not take credit for that moment, and he recalls that it stayed to the end of the run. "I loved him, I appreciated him, and he me, after Bing came in," says Schenk.[16]

The rest of Vickers's Met schedule into 1971 comprised only seven *Carmens*, including two with Resnik in March. He sang three *Fidelios* in April 1971 at the Salzburg Easter Festival, and nipped back to London for *Parsifal*, beginning April 21 at the Royal Opera House, with Goodall finally in the spotlight. He conducted at a majestic pace, and Kiri Te Kanawa made her ROH debut, as the leading Flower Maiden. The twenty-seven-year-old New Zealand soprano said of Vickers, "He terrified me—I had such respect for him." Afterward Vickers told her, "You should have been more seductive. All I saw were your frightened eyes."[17]

The man to whom Vickers so largely owed his career died May 9, 1971, in London. Vickers attended the funeral for Sir David Webster and sang at the July memorial service.

Coast wrote the ROH's Tooley that he had discussed repertoire with Vickers in the car on the way to the airport. The tenor would love to do Handel's *Samson* again; he had sung it in 1958–59. And "if only he were younger and had better legs, he said, he would love to sing Gluck's *Orfeo*." He also wished to sing the Male Chorus in Britten's *Rape of Lucretia,* as he had in Canada; he probably would do Kurt Weill's *Rise and Fall of the City of Mahagonny* at San Francisco in 1972, and he thought it was "time he put Herod into his voice again."[18]

Beginning July 1, Vickers was at Covent Garden for four *Grimes* performances. And on July 18, at the Stratford (Ontario) Festival, he sang Leoš Janáček's *Diary of One Who Vanished,* using an English translation obtained from Peter Pears. Richard Woitach, who accompanied him, recalled that Vickers had relearned it after doing it some years earlier.[19]

But the main event of 1971 was Vickers's debut as Tristan, a role upon which he would place his indelible stamp, joining the ranks of the few great Tristans of the century.

Richard Wagner's *Tristan und Isolde* is the peak of operatic sexuality, its lengthy second-act duet a virtual coupling and recoupling of the lovers throughout the night, till rude discovery by a betrayed king. Stagings of this timeless story rarely show the pair making love, but this is hardly necessary, for the vivid aural sensations bring inescapable pictures to most minds. Although Vickers by the early 1970s had mastered Siegmund and Parsifal, his other two major Wagner roles, he always expressed a deeply ambivalent view of the composer, speaking bluntly about Wagner's connection with the anti-Christian Nietzsche and flatly opposing Wagner's views of morality as Vickers saw them.

Wagner, after all, was an adulterer. Siegmund took up with his twin sister, Vickers often reminded his concert audiences. *Parsifal* could be "blasphemous" if the staging made him Christ-like. Tristan betrayed his king and sought love in death, a concept the disapproving Vickers found "very, very strange." Wagner seduced us all with his magnificent music, Vickers said, disapproving also of that feat. He himself tried to resist, because in his plainspoken view Tristan is "a thoroughly despicable human being." He has no redeeming feature, yet "he's made to get away with it, he's made to look the marvelous hero, dying heroically for having betrayed his uncle, who gave him everything." Isolde was just as bad, alike a faithless betrayer. Their sin was that "their love was more important than anything . . . the love between you and your sweetheart, your husbands and wives, is not supreme over every other aspect of life." For Vickers, duty, loyalty, and concern for the larger society also counted heavily.[20]

Still, he knew he had to sing Tristan. How could he criticize the composer, he often said, if he hadn't sung this work? People would say that he simply could not do it. Moreover, the role fitted well in his gallery of outcasts, of the misunderstood, the lonely heroes. And it gave him a great deal of time onstage, including a protracted death scene that in Vickers's hands was a stunning tour de force. Vocally, Tristan's second act lies high, with a number of A naturals, but the relatively short singing in the first act and the punishing final act both lay well for Vickers's voice. Some observers, however, felt that at age forty-four he had waited too long to take on this role.

In March 1971 Vickers had expressed a reservation in a Toronto interview: "Tristan is a dangerous part, mainly because of its length and its emotional intensity. I think the German language affords you an opportunity to sacrifice a lyric line. Once you find yourself making that compromise, sacrificing something vocally for the sake of self-preservation in a long opera, it may creep into your other work."[21]

Although he never wanted to be labeled a Wagnerian, from a career standpoint it was a logical step. Vickers knew that if the part worked well for him, he would have offers from around the globe. He could ask fees for it as high or higher than for Otello, always assuming that companies could find an Isolde for him. He knew that Karajan waited like a bridegroom for a dowry of rare treasure. Windgassen retired in 1972; tenors singing Tristan in the 1970s included Jess Thomas and Helge Brilioth, but none has been marked down as truly matching the role's greatness.

Mastering Tristan would lift him to a sparsely inhabited operatic peak. As with Otello, however, the emotional as well as vocal demands made Tristan a role Vickers would ration, scheduling it perhaps six times a year, along with six Otellos.

Vickers often seemed to stress the conflicted torture of most of his characters, not their romantic joy and sexual pleasures, often given them but fleetingly by their creators. His Otello, Don Carlos, Riccardo, and Don José writhed not in sexual ecstasy but chiefly in jealousy, rage, thwarted longing; in the case of Parsifal and Samson, it was horror at the power of passion. But as Elijah Moshinsky saw, Vickers always offered a subtext, and that sexuality was always there, the underside, waiting in darkness to be revealed. The writer Harold Brodkey had a trenchant comment in a 1994 *New Yorker* piece about his illness with AIDS, in which he mused on sexuality in the arts of the twentieth century. Popular art, he said, "is not as sexual as Jon Vickers's singing, for instance. He caused embarrassment in American audiences as Sinatra never did. He caused embarrassment in the way Billie Holiday did, in night clubs, from the sheer authenticity of the sexual-emotional event."[22]

Richard Woitach coached Vickers for Tristan, particularly the third act, spending time with him at the farm. "It was very leisurely, a luxury, we were able to keep repeating. He already had a pretty strong idea, he knew what it all meant . . . it was just a case of being able to do it with another person." The conductor recalled that a favorite line of Vickers's came in the first act, when Tristan reluctantly responds to Isolde's request that he speak with her shortly before the ship is to arrive in Cornwall. "War Morold dir so werth, nun wieder nimm des Schwert": "If Morold was our lord, Take up again my sword (And drive it surely and fast, Take your vengeance for all that's past)." Woitach marveled at "the way he would caress that line, and it's one of the most beautiful lines. I never quite figured out why that was such a favorite of his. Because he's saying, 'You loved this other man so much, take the sword, kill me.'"[23]

Ernest Newman writes that three times Tristan seeks death as a gateway to purer happiness, finally succeeding, as he tears off his bandages, to die in Isolde's arms. Vickers, however, in one of his many quarrels with Wagner's ideas, summarily rejected the idea that death can be a door to bliss.[24] But those who found a masochistic side to Vickers would see those lines about asking for a sword's blow as fitting in nicely.

Vickers chose Teatro Colón in Buenos Aires, the site of his first Otello in 1963, as a less pressured setting than a Tristan under the demanding gaze of Karajan, the perfectionist he so admired. "So that I'd feel more confident with Karajan," he admitted.[25] Birgit Nilsson had first sung Isolde at Colón in 1955, in a run interrupted by the overthrow of Juan Perón. The stage and hall are enormous, she recalled, and gestures had to be enlarged. But the acoustics are magnificent, and singing requires no more effort than in a much smaller theater because voices carry with such amazing ease.[26]

The first *Tristan* finally came on September 25, 1971, with Horst Stein conducting, and with Nilsson, Grace Hoffman as Brangäne, Norman Mittelmann as Kurwenal, Franz Crass as King Marke, and Ricardo Yost as Melot. Ernst Poettgen directed. It was repeated September 30 and October 3, 6, 10, and 14. Oscar Figueroa reported: "Those who watched him had the feeling that they were seeing the incarnation of Wagner's hero, something which had not been felt since the golden days of Max Lorenz and Lauritz Melchior. . . . After many years this opera finally had two stars."[27]

Most who saw any Vickers Tristan performance recalled it as among their most remarkable experiences with opera. It is another Vickers paradox that he could speak so ill of a character and composer and yet create a blazingly unforgettable portrait with all the resources of his voice and physicality. Elijah Moshinsky recalled that Vickers was a sensation in his first London *Tristan*, in May 1978. Moshinsky, who directed, concurred with the writer Peter Conrad when he said Vickers gave "a sense of a critique of the opera as he was performing it. . . . He somehow delved in it so hard that he was able to extract something sort of subterranean out of it. Now, whenever I've done *Tristan* since with anyone, they can barely sing it, let alone extract anything from it. He was able to phrase it as sort of a dramatic poem of suffering . . . [that] through suffering you can achieve some kind of transcendance, which was this Wagnerian philosophy."[28]

In 1980, when Vickers sang six *Tristans* in May and June at Covent Garden, Max Loppert wrote of the tenor's face that "a melancholy knightly intelligence [is] incised on every crack and cranny." Vickers

> does not merely relax the classical rules of Wagnerian singing, he moves far outside their realm, emitting great shouts of despair like boulders from a mighty sling, whispers of love and croons of anguish, and (at times) a variety of parlando inflexions uncomfortably ap-

proaching the Schoenbergian *Sprechgesang.* Step outside Vickers' third act for a single moment and you may find yourself blinking incredulously at [the] quality of the acting, dangerously close to ham. The genius of the performance lies not least in its willingness to live dangerously.[29]

The great English baritone Thomas Allen recalled a 1978 ROH *Tristan* in which, early in his career, he sang Melot. He was in a second-floor dressing room with Paul Crook, the Shepherd, when "we heard this animal screaming" over the speaker. Allen had a gut instinct that something special was occurring; "the only other time [like it] was [Alfredo] Kraus in *Faust*—it caused your mouth to drop open." They went down and stood directly behind the battered stage door to watch Vickers, as only other singers can appreciate a performance. "This man was just glowing. He had transcended normal performance. We stood there, astonished at what we heard. He was totally unleashed; he took all risks and let rip completely. It took superhuman strength to do what he was doing. . . . Some would say it was foolhardy or whatever. I would not agree with that. He didn't stint himself, what he gave that day."[30]

David Cairns, who thought Tristan may have ranked as Vickers's best role, saw a spontaneous element in the performances. He recalled a detail in Act 3 in that same run of ROH *Tristan*s in May and June 1978. "When he heard the pipe, a new tune that shows the ship is coming, he did the most wonderful mime. It was absolutely pitiful, the joy. I can't describe it in detail, but I remember it was one of the most moving things I've ever seen on the stage, because his whole being sort of radiated the joy." But when Cairns returned a few days later, "he didn't do it. Obviously he was inspired that night."[31]

Tristan was vocally difficult for Vickers, as it is for any tenor attempting it. The New Zealand bass-baritone Sir Donald McIntyre, who sang Kurwenal at Covent Garden in several runs with Vickers, recalled that "as [each] run went on in *Tristan*, [Vickers would find] it more difficult each time, and usually by the time he got to the end, he'd cancel the last one or two [performances]. The first night he was in very good voice . . . when it got too much, he disappeared." Vickers's voice "was superb when it was *pianissimo,* superb when it was *forte.* He found the difficulty up higher in his voice. In the higher tessituras he found it very difficult if not impossible at times. . . . In the middle of the voice he could do it quite easily." He could sing the higher notes in *Peter Grimes* "in a sort of a head type of voice, not exactly a falsetto. . . . But somehow he couldn't do it on the *mezzo-fortes.*" In general, McIntyre was impressed with the "incredible amount of decibels"

Vickers had, shown off by beginning some phrases in *pianissimo*, crescendoing "into a treble *forte*, so the sheer presence of the voice was quite overwhelming at times." McIntyre added, "The tremendous tension he had in his body, this was the main thing that made him work. I don't think he was a particularly great actor."[32]

In December 1971 and January 1972 Vickers recorded *Tristan und Isolde* with Karajan and the Berlin Philharmonic, in Berlin. The lovely blonde Austrian Helga Dernesch, a Karajan favorite, was the Irish princess, with Christa Ludwig as Brangäne, Karl Ridderbusch as King Marke, Walter Berry as Kurwenal, Bernd Weikl as Melot, and Peter Schreier as the Young Sailor and the Shepherd. This recording contains the celebrated twenty-seven-minute, unrehearsed take of a large section of the Act 2 love duet. Karajan, ever the sly psychologist, said it was just a runthrough, and Dernesch and Vickers soared through the exceedingly difficult section incorporating "O sink' hernieder, Nacht." When they finished, the orchestra gave the singers and Karajan an ovation, the tenor recalled, "because they knew we hadn't even run through it before together. I was just electrified. We never spliced a note."[33] Karajan said it could not be more perfect, although some critics would disagree.

Dernesch recalled a funny moment elsewhere in the duet. She could not pinpoint the phrase, but it was a higher note that should be very soft, after which Tristan comes in immediately. Karajan urged her to do less and less on the note and she finally managed a *pianissimo* so extraordinary that Vickers quite forgot to sing. "He really liked what I did. He watched me. It was a miracle." After Vickers's flub, she cried to Karajan that she couldn't possibly do it that way again. The conductor said he would splice it in.

Dernesch sang with Vickers in *Tristan* at the Vienna Staatsoper the following year, and in *Fidelio* in Dallas. But she did not feel a special relationship with him, as she had with partners such as Jess Thomas and James King. Karajan had told her that for *Fidelio* she and Vickers would be "a quite wonderful match," she recalled. "Actually, we were not." The chemistry was not there. In their entire time in Dallas, they never had a meal together. During the *Tristan* recording, they had only one or two meals together with Karajan. This is unusual because recording casts often become close, if they are not already, and socialize to ease tension.

But Dernesch found that Vickers took off for his home every free day he had, so there was never a time for this Tristan and Isolde to get to know each other better, and Dernesch never met Hetti Vickers. Of course, in the early 1970s the Vickers children were still in their teens, and he wanted to spend as much time as possible with them. "He's very kind," said Dernesch, "and I think a little bit shy."[34]

The perceptive American conductor James Conlon, now head of the Paris Opéra, recalled being invited by Karajan to sit in on three weeks of *Tristan* rehearsals in Salzburg, he thought in 1973:

> I sat in the dark theater and watched, and one thing struck me that didn't correspond to my image of either man. It must have been the first day they saw each other; I think it was the beginning of the third act. Karajan always came in at the last minute. You would sort of feel the earth trembling—here he comes. He walked in and straight to Vickers and threw his arms around Vickers, their arms were around each other. One always thought of Karajan as being so cool, withdrawn, and Vickers so frightening, so unapproachable. I don't know their relationship, but I had a feeling of warmth.[35]

And 1973 was the last time that Vickers would sing with Karajan. In 1989 Karajan told the author Richard Osborne of Vickers:

> I have long been fascinated by his work. He is a very complex man; he thinks deeply about every role and you must talk to him in great detail. But his presence on stage—above all, his delivery—is so good.
>
> In the great roles—his Tristan, his Otello—it seems to me he brings to the part a unique sense of musical phrasing. The phrasing may be very individual but he will lift it and project it. With so many singers the music simply goes in one particular way; with him it is always individual and special.
>
> Later in his career, when the top of the voice started to disappear, I tried to persuade him to do *Wozzeck* with me. He would have made a marvellous Wozzeck.

Osborne noted that Karajan also had directed Vinay as Tristan at Bayreuth. Said Karajan, "Yes, but Vickers was much better."[36]

Jon Vickers, age ten, center, astride a snow camel, an appropriate steed for a future Egyptian warrior in *Aida*. At the King George School, Prince Albert, early 1937. Photograph by Grace Kernaghan, courtesy of Robert Motherwell. ▨

Vickers as Frederic, with Cecelia Allen as Mabel, in *The Pirates of Penzance*, Flin Flon Glee Club, 1947. Photograph courtesy of Dorothy Young Liss. ▨

Vickers in 1973 at the house in Prince Albert where he was born in 1926; it has since been torn down. Photograph by Richard Bocking. ▨

Jon Vickers and his father, William Vickers, with Jon's sons, William, Kenneth, and Jonathan, at Christopher Lake, Saskatchewan, August 1963. Photograph courtesy of the Prince Albert Historical Society and *Prince Albert Herald.*

Hetti Vickers, Jon's wife, right, with Frances Myrle Vickers, his mother, and Allison Vickers, oldest of Jon and Hetti's five children, at Christopher Lake, Saskatchewan, August 1963. Photograph courtesy of the Prince Albert Historical Society and *Prince Albert Herald.*

Vickers with Eva Likova in *Pagliacci*,
CBC-TV, 1955. Photograph by Henri
Paul, courtesy of Eva Likova.

Vickers and the
Canadettes at the Cana-
dian National Exhibi-
tion, 1960. Photograph
courtesy of CNE
Archives, Alexandra
Photo Studio Lands.

Vickers as Siegmund in
Die Walküre, Bayreuth,
1958. Bayreuthes Fest-
spiele GMBH/Siegfried
Lauterwasser.

Vickers as Parsifal with Hans Hotter
as Gurnemanz at the Bayreuth Festival, 1964. Bayreuthes Festspiele
GMBH/Wilhelm Rauh.

Vickers with Colin
Davis at 1969
recording of *Les
Troyens*. Baritone Peter
Glossop is at left.
Photograph copyright
by Zoë Dominic.

Vickers rehearsing
Die Walküre with
Herbert von Karajan
in Salzburg, 1967.
Photograph copy-
right by Siegfried
Lauterwasser.

Sir David Webster receives a farewell gift from Canadian singers on his retirement from the Royal Opera House in July 1970. André Turp is at left, Vickers at right. Photograph by Donald Southern, courtesy of the Archives of the Royal Opera House. ▨

Vickers as Énée in *Les Troyens* at the Royal Opera House, Covent Garden, 1960. Photograph by Donald Southern, courtesy of the Archives of the Royal Opera House. ▨

Vickers with Maria Callas in *Médée* in Dallas, 1958. Photograph by Jane Purse, courtesy of the Dallas Opera. ▨

Vickers as Pollione in *Norma*, Chorégies
d'Orange, July 1974. Photograph copyright
by Studio Bernateau.

Vickers with Leonie Rysanek and chorus members in *Fidelio* at the Metropolitan Opera, 1970. Photograph by Dan McCoy, courtesy of the Metropolitan Opera Archives. 𝓦

Vickers with Birgit Nilsson during rehearsal at the Roman theater in the Provençal town of Orange, France, where they were performing in *Tristan und Isolde* in 1973. Photograph by Winnifred Bocking. 𝓦

Vickers as Peter Grimes at the Royal Opera House in 1975. Photograph by Donald Southern, courtesy of the Archives of the Royal Opera House.

Vickers as Vasek wearing the Act 3 bear suit in *The Bartered Bride* at the Metropolitan Opera, 1978. Photograph copyright by Winnie Klotz.

Vickers as Nerone, with Gwyneth Jones, in *L'Incoronazione de Poppea* in Paris, 1978. Photograph by Daniel Candé.

Vickers, with Siegmund
Nimsgern as Kurwenal, in
Act 3 of *Tristan und Isolde* at
the Lyric Opera of Chicago
in 1979. Tony Romano/Lyric
Opera of Chicago.

Vickers with Roberta Knie in *Tristan und Isolde*
at the Lyric Opera of Chicago, 1979. Tony
Romano/Lyric Opera of Chicago.

Director Rolf Liebermann showing Vickers how to deal with Kundry's kiss in *Parsifal*, Geneva, 1982. Photograph copyright by Odette Weil, Paris. ▨

Vickers in the title role of Handel's *Samson* at the Lyric Opera of Chicago, 1985. Tony Romano/Lyric Opera of Chicago. ▨

Vickers in his final *Otello* performances, Cape Town, South
Africa, in 1984. Photograph by Glynn Griffiths and Bee
Berman, courtesy of CAPAB.

Vickers with the Flower Maidens in a
Chicago Lyric Opera production of
Parsifal, 1986. Photograph by Karen
Engstrom, copyright 1996 by the
Chicago Tribune. ▨

Vickers in his final Met appearances in
March and April 1987 in *Samson et Dalila*,
with Marilyn Horne. Photograph by
Winnie Klotz, courtesy of the Metropolitan Opera Association. ▨

Jon, Hetti, and their daughter Wendy on a Royal Opera
House tour of South Korea and Japan in 1979. Photograph
copyright 1979 by Gillian Widdicombe.

Vickers and his second wife, Judy, whom he
married in 1993. Photograph copyright 1998
by Marbeth.

Billy and Peter: Theodor Uppman, who created the title role in Britten's *Billy Budd*, with Vickers, famous as Britten's Peter Grimes, at a New York Wagner Society program in 1998. Photograph copyright 1998 by Marbeth. 🎵

Vickers at a tribute to Maria Callas, December 1983, at the Lyric Opera of Chicago. Tony Romano/Lyric Opera of Chicago. 🎵

14

A Moor Does Battle, Énée and Tristan at the Met

SPRING 1972 SAW THE DEPARTURE OF SIR RUDOLF BING FROM THE Met after twenty-two years. Vickers, in white tie and his Canadian Companion medal and ribbons, sang the "Winterstürme" in the *Die Walküre* scene with Leonie Rysanek at the April 22 farewell gala. When an hour of the gala was telecast April 30 on CBS, Vickers's piece was cut out; he, like some other singers, was seen only briefly and not heard. "Life is funny," he noted a few weeks later. "The trouble with me is I don't hire public relations advertising [*sic*] to seek out the press. I believe Madison Avenue has no place in the arts. I believe a singer stands on a stage by virtue of his ability, not because of an inflated public image."[1]

Bing would die at ninety-five on September 2, 1997, after long years of suffering from Alzheimer's disease, during which he was visited often by Teresa Stratas. Vickers wrote in a roundup of comments in the November 1997 *Opera News* that Bing was a man

> of brilliance, nobility, dignity and great spiritual strength who did not suffer fools gladly.
>
> Each time Sir Rudolf decided to enter into negotiations with me, I learned to admire and respect him more and more. He was a magnificent general manager and a consummate showman when the situation required it. The sense of power that emanated from him and the driving force within were rooted in a deep and devoted love of music and of the operatic art form. . . .
>
> Sir Rudolf saw the nobility of purpose of opera and would not tolerate shoddiness or pretense. It is a source of great happiness that we became such close friends.

In the summer of 1972 the man chosen as Bing's successor, the Swedish director Goeran Gentele, died in a car crash. New Yorker Schuyler Chapin took over the house for the next three seasons, aided considerably by Rafael

Kubelik, a conductor long familiar to Vickers. In 1974 Chapin would find himself involved, with Vickers, in one of the Met's most famous rows.

In June 1972 Vickers sang his first Covent Garden Otello (having done the opera with the company on tour in Manchester in 1964). Joan Carlyle was Desdemona, with Kiri Te Kanawa covering the part, though she did not perform. The conductor was Colin Davis, doing his first *Otellos*. A deeply serious musician but often ready to enjoy absurdity, Davis recalled Vickers stifling Desdemona in a wild fashion. At one performance, "in the scrum they rolled off on the wrong side of the bed and completely disappeared from view. I think they were in a state of helpless laughter. It was very funny!"[2]

Vickers planned to commute to Canada between the penultimate and final *Otello* performances. It was examination time for his children, he explained. "It would be psychologically bad for them if I were not there. Somehow my presence there might help them."[3]

He told Alan Blyth that he believed his interpretation of the Moor was "less fussy than it used to be," but thought his basic approach had changed little. He downplayed Otello's blackness as a factor in his fear of Desdemona's supposed infidelity (despite his singing of his dusky face). "It's perhaps because he's getting a little old, or perhaps it's a waning of his sexual drive, and only in the last resort, perhaps his color."[4] He was to change this view late in his career.

He got some mixed reviews, several commenting on mannerisms, fussy or not. Tom Sutcliffe disliked everything about this Otello, writing that Vickers was "obsessed with the idea of infatuation." He made "great sweeps across the stage, arms wide like the mating display of some exotic bird, with the menace not of a victorious general but of a horror-film tyrant or vampire— before an imaginary mirror."[5] The *Musical Times* said Vickers seemed not to relate to anyone else onstage, a comment echoed by a number of observers over the years.[6]

Andrew Porter wrote that Vickers's first London Otello was "noble" and expanded upon his Met Moor in December 1972 as

> superb: more controlled, more dignified, less constantly close to madness, no less passionate and intense in voice as in demeanor. Like Tamagno, who created the role, he declaims it with heroic vigor; not just each syllable but of a word like "Gloria!" each single letter makes its effect. . . . The love duet was charged to an unusual degree with sensuality. Miss [Teresa] Zylis-Gara and Mr. Vickers sang and acted it with smoldering inner passion, and the sound of the solo cellos rose around them like musk.[7]

Gerald Fitzgerald found that Met Otello "a civilized intellectual given to introspection and quiet brooding; barbaric fury erupted to the full only during the murder scene, and then it was terrifying. Careful phrasing and clarion power characterized the tenor's singing, which was beautiful to a fault."[8]

In November 1972 Vickers was back in Dallas for an unusual double bill of Purcell's *Dido and Aeneas* and *Pagliacci*, at the opening of the season and the renovated Music Hall. He and the American mezzo soprano Tatiana Troyanos were taking the Purcell roles for the first time. Both were "superbly attuned to the opera" and expressed "a deep, communicative melancholy," wrote John Ardoin. He admitted Dido has the advantage of her moving lament, but "I can never again think of Aeneas as a secondary to Dido after Vickers' performance." The critic again reached into his bag of superlatives: "Too rarely have I experienced such nobility of phrase and meaning as Vickers brought to the scene following Aeneas' encounter with Mercury. It was one of those beacons of truth which shine infrequently from the operatic stage today."

And for *Pagliacci*, with Raina Kabaivanska also led by Nicola Rescigno, Ardoin said Vickers "is the major Canio of the day, an intensely human portrayal." His Canio, like his Otello, "broods inwardly rather than makes a show of surface anguish, and by building the storm of the part from the inside out, his characterization is all-of-a-piece rather than a series of big moments." His singing "is complete in every sense, as moving for sheer sound as it is for how that sound is put to the service of the text and the music." He drew fine lines between the nature of the tragedies of Canio and of Aeneas, a contrast speaking volumes "for his awareness of the human spirit and the depths of his artistry."[9]

That December the Met's *Otello* had twenty-nine-year-old James Levine in the pit in his third Met season. This was the new Zeffirelli production that had premiered the previous March, with James McCracken in the title role, Teresa Zylis-Gara, and Sherrill Milnes. As with other Zeffirelli efforts at the Met—notably his *Bohème, Tosca, Turandot*, and more recent *La Traviata*—the scenery took a large role and tended to dwarf the singers. When Otello first appeared on the stern of his ship, he was high above the stage and well back. Vickers hated the cables he had to negotiate and believed his positioning lessened the power and effectiveness of the entrance. It also meant the tenor had to project his ringing "Esultate!" much farther toward the audience. Volume was never a Vickers difficulty, but still, the Met is big enough as it is.

Vickers recalled of the production: "They wanted to stamp me out like a cookie and make me exactly what Zeffirelli had made the previous Otello.

And I just said, 'Get lost.' I created a bit of a sensation: I just said, 'I'm going to be seen, and I'm going to be heard, or I'm going to be fired. And that decision is going to be made now!'"[10]

There was some difficulty casting the Iago, and then Vickers had a rehearsal shouting match with Met director Fabrizio Melano, filling in for Zeffirelli, which deeply embarrassed Melano. This was remembered by many at the Met as adding to Vickers's fearsome reputation. Tito Gobbi had bowed out two days before rehearsals began, and after several other baritones were found to be busy, Louis Quilico was asked by Chapin to take the role. Then Chapin called to ask if Quilico had had a problem with Vickers, because Vickers said the baritone would not want to sing with him. This was news to Quilico, who had learned, as he said, "If Vickers walks in the room and says, 'The room is white,' and the room is black, I say the room is white! I never contradict Mr. Vickers!" He theorized Vickers had told Chapin that simply because he wanted another baritone who would also stand up against the Zeffirelli production. But Quilico was already under Met contract, and Chapin asked him to appear. Vickers was cordial at rehearsal, but Quilico felt he must walk on eggs.

Then came the day when Vickers had a major confrontation with Melano. "He was screaming 'stupid!' and calling Mr. Zeffirelli [in absentia] all kinds of names," said Quilico. "All of a sudden they were really screaming at each other." The baritone then boomed, "Shut up!" to both men, saying they were wasting everybody's time with their tantrums. "Jon," Quilico said in his earthy fashion, "we know you're going to do what you want. Do me a favor—do it! And that's all! Shut up! And you, Melano, you know he's going to do it. Do me a favor—let him do it, okay!"[11]

Melano wouldn't discuss his different recollections, but said the incident was "a big thing." He and Vickers "made our peace" and worked well subsequently. Chapin, then acting general manager, recalled Vickers threatened to quit several times and was none too pleasant with Levine.[12]

After the first performance on December 5, Vickers got a prized shower of torn-up programs. But backstage he grabbed Quilico's wife and begged to know, "Lina, was I good?" Vickers was always that way, said Quilico: "He had to be the star." But the baritone admitted that after the second act's rousing "Si pel ciel" duet, with those two huge-voiced singers, "The reception Vickers and I got, I never saw that again, ever."[13]

Zeffirelli said later that Vickers had been right about the stage design. "McCracken did what I wanted, but it wasn't right. . . . It was too far away for the 'Esultate.' I don't consider it my best production at the Met. . . . When I saw [Vickers], I said, you are absolutely correct, calm down. I don't remember if it was during those performances, but I know that I apologized and it was corrected."[14]

Chapin recalled that the day after the *Otello* opening, Vickers came to say he had too much to do and must drop the forthcoming *Pique Dame* production, for which rehearsals were just beginning. Fortunately, Nicolai Gedda also was scheduled for it, with William Lewis as his cover.[15] Vickers always prepared well, but one wonders if he had been entirely ready for the Russian part (it was the first time the Met had done a Russian opera in that language).

Vickers was especially intense when he was singing the Moor, Met makeup chief Victor Callegari recalled. At one *Otello* intermission, when the tenor was getting a touch-up, he was so full of adrenalin that "everything he touched would either break or be thrown against a wall," not purposefully but inevitably. "I always felt in the room the intensity of this man. He was really getting ready for battle," which Callegari compared to a movie with General George Patton dressing to face the Nazis. But Vickers, like the many greats of the 1960s with whom Callegari practiced his art, including Corelli, Bergonzi, and Tucker, was a no-nonsense man who liked a joke and with whom "it was a pleasure to work."[16]

Vickers's involvement with the role of Otello would grow and change in years to come. He found its infinite variety ever-challenging, each performance a different one for him and, he hoped, the audience.

Unfavorable changes in the tax code of Canada finally caused Vickers to move his home base to Bermuda, although the Ontario farm was kept in the family. Edgar Benson's White Paper on Taxation changed his attitude about spending the rest of his life in Canada. The tenor spoke with the first finance minister of Canada and told him the new laws "caught me at the worst possible spot." He was told the net had been set for much bigger fish, but Vickers also was caught. He was prevented from averaging out over many years some of his highest income periods. "It just wasn't economically feasible for me to continue a world career and remain in Canada."[17]

On March 16, 1973, he took title to Blue Horizons, a 4.75-acre estate in Tucker's Town, the poshest end of Bermuda, adjoining the Mid-Ocean Club, the island's most exclusive golf club. The enormous house is on one of the island's highest elevations, overlooking the airport. Many well-to-do Americans and Britishers lived in this island enclave; in recent years, those names have included pop star David Bowie, CBS-TV's Morley Safer, businessman and would-be U.S. president Ross Perot, and producer Robert

Stigwood. It was a good place for a person who craved privacy. Bermuda also had the benefit of being two hours by air from New York City. This proximity meant the Met became even more of a favorite house for Vickers, as his agent often reminded its administrators.

He got a good deal on the house, under $2 million, possibly around $1 million, from Stavros Spyros Niarchos, the fabled Greek shipping tycoon. (Rival Aristotle Onassis's liaison with Maria Callas had faded, and Onassis's son had died in a plane crash in January.) Niarchos had added sections to the house but had let the property run down. There was much scope for Vickers's fix-up hobbies in this, one of the island's biggest houses, and he and all the family pitched in. Although Vickers must have seen it as a real estate investment, it was certainly a lavish abode for a man of modest family background.

Niarchos had had a habit of backing out of contracts. With his lifelong penchant for legal action, Vickers hired a savvy lawyer who got an injunction for Niarchos to execute the contract in Bermuda. The tycoon failed to do so, and Vickers got the property. He wanted something big, saying many of the small island houses made him claustrophobic, and he was flush with his success in the opera world. "He talked big," said J. J. Outerbridge, a first cousin of Hetti's who dealt with the sale.[18]

Vickers and his wife would make their home there for the next fourteen years, returning to the Ontario farm for frequent visits, especially in summer. The younger Vickers children went to school in Bermuda. Kenneth and Jonathan attended the Saltus Grammar School in Pembroke; Wendy went to Bermuda High School, a private girls' school, then to Saltus for its grade twelve combined with the private school. The China-born Hetti gained Bermuda citizenship. But the island is very restrictive about the number of persons allowed that privilege each year, and it was difficult even with her family background there. She had to enlist legal help.

Vickers was a church elder and sang with other parishioners at the Scots Presbyterian Christ Church in Warwick. Though often asked to take part in the Bermuda arts festival, he would decline, preferring not to perform where he made his home. They had a very small circle of close friends there and mingled with Hetti's relatives at various family events, including at an annual gathering of the Outerbridge clan each Boxing Day. Some residents said others were somewhat in awe of Vickers and hesitated to approach him. His wife didn't travel with him when the children were in school, and since he was away so much, his Bermuda roots weren't deep.

Sometimes vocal coaches from the United States, including Richard Woitach and William Fred Scott, then in Boston, would fly to Bermuda to coach him on roles. He worked on *Die Winterreise* at Blue Horizons with the aid of a Bermuda pianist/organist and teacher, William Duncan. They did about five sessions and Duncan recalled that Vickers would tell him, "Play louder!" He liked to have the sound envelop him. Duncan only played; he did not coach: "I learned from him. He knew all about the poetry, the meanings, the symbolism."[19]

In April and May 1973, Vickers was in Berlin to record *Otello* with Karajan, for which he received twenty thousand dollars from EMI, plus royalties. The sessions were in the Philharmonic Hall, with Freni, Glossop as Iago, Michel Sénéchal as Roderigo, and José Van Dam as Lodovico. This was his second *Otello* on disk (the Serafin had been in 1960).

On the Canadian front, Vickers took part in a tribute to former Met manager Edward Johnson, a Guelph native who had died in 1959, at the close of the sixth Guelph Spring Festival. Vickers apparently contributed his fee to a new Johnson scholarship endowment fund and was thanked for his generosity in the program. On May 14, 1973, accompanied by Richard Woitach, Vickers did his usual excerpts from *Die Walküre* and Handel's *Samson*, along with the *Grimes* final scene. And he sang both Aeneas's Lament from Purcell's *Dido and Aeneas* and the wrenching aria from *Les Troyens*, "Inutiles regrets." The novelist Robertson Davies, master of Massey College at the University of Toronto, recalled a lesson taught by Johnson: "There is only one instant that matters to the artist and his audience, and that instant is now, the moment of the performance." This aptly applied to the work of the soloist of the evening, Vickers, as critic John Kraglund noted.[20]

Vickers and Nilsson were Tristan and Isolde in July at the Orange festival, with Böhm leading what was dubbed "the *Tristan* of the century." Vickers held the crowd spellbound in his forty-minute final scene.

Later that year, Vickers talked about retiring at age fifty and said in a two-hour CBC radio special that he might turn to conducting. He was considering a return to the Royal Conservatory for two or three years, "not with the idea of a major career," he said on *Jon Vickers: A Life in Music*, which aired October 23. His goals would be modest; he said some Canadian provinces, maybe a city like Winnipeg, might find he had something to give.

For the Met's 1973–74 season, Vickers sang three huge roles, and two were marked by crisis. The house premiere of *Les Troyens* was October 22, with seven more performances, and then a leap to a March broadcast, all led by Rafael Kubelik. In January and February Vickers had two *Tristans* and five *Otellos*, each production with news-making situations involving the sopranos.

The Met's *Troyens* was performed uncut but for about eight minutes for Didon before her final big scene. Kubelik made use of an excellent cast. Alan Rich wrote that Vickers's Énée was

> the work of a supreme musical artist, a singer with more command than anyone I know of dramatic vocal color, a man whose every musical gesture means something vital to the situation in which he is involved.
>
> While not perfectly endowed by nature to suggest either the hero-ism or the ardor of Aeneas—and his Gorgeous-George blond wig really ought to be reconsidered—Vickers is one of those exceptional singers whose command of the art of singing dwarfs any and all other considerations.[21]

Levine considered that Vickers's performances were better than those he had done at Covent Garden, at least as preserved on record. "It was a good time for him, he was in excellent form."[22]

The versatile American tenor William Lewis sang Helenus, son of Priam, in all the performances, and covered for Vickers. He also sang Énée in the two nonbroadcast March performances (and sang it twice in 1983). A member of the small club of those who have sung Énée in the past four decades, Lewis also sang or covered a number of roles sung by Vickers (including Grimes), as well as many by Domingo, the Met's Énée of 1983, and is an experienced, educated analyst. He describes Énée as "a French dramatic tenor role, a little bit different from the heldentenor, and different from the Italian dramatic [roles] because it is high, with several high Bs and a high C in strategic places." And it's full of contradictions: The love duet must be soft, but "you have been yelling all evening, until all of a sudden you have to sing a very sustained lyric tenor love duet on high B-flats and high Bs." When Énée arrives and greets Didon, he must sing heroically. "Then all of a sudden when he gets in the boudoir, he's singing like a Werther—not even Werther, like someone who would sing *Manon*, something light. It's almost impossible for the human voice to change that fast, unless you use falsetto, and in the Met, a falsetto is not heard. If you have to use a mixed voice, sometimes you get it and sometimes you don't. It's very difficult . . . first you've got to be a Vickers-type tenor, then you've got to be a Gedda-type tenor." Lewis is convinced that "Berlioz read it in a book that a lyric tenor can sing this high, and a dramatic tenor can sing this high. He knew everything about orchestration, but he didn't know one God-blessed thing about the human voice."

So Lewis is sympathetic, but he says that in 1973 Vickers "never sang the high C [in the big aria 'Inutiles regrets']. He sang the optional A-flat. [Levine confirmed this.] He fought the high B [in the love duet], just like he fought the high B in *Pique Dame*. Sometimes he would get it, but most times he would not. And as we went offstage, he would say, 'I overblew,' whatever that means. It means he missed the note." Of the opening aria of the first section, *La Prise de Troie*, Lewis says, "You just have to sail on the stage and sing this thing that is very fast and very high, in the lyric tenor range. It's above the staff all the time, ending on a high B. It was terrible for Vickers, and Plácido had to transpose down." Dramatically, Énée is what Lewis calls "a posing role," especially in the Met's lavish staging. The costumes were so cumbersome that realistic love scenes were impossible.[23]

Vickers had enormous stamina: After *Les Troyens*, he was in Dallas in November for three performances of *Andrea Chénier*, in a new production by Peter Hall. It would be Vickers's final Chénier, a role he felt had inspirational qualities but not the depth of his major parts. Nicola Rescigno conducted on November 30 and December 4 and 8, with Ilva Ligabue as Maddalena Coigny, Lili Chookasian as Madelon, and Silvano Carroli as Gérard.

John Ardoin noted that Vickers "brings a dignity and melancholy to the poet no other has unearthed. . . . [In the third act] the quiet release of emotion from Vickers is of so human a dimension, one is drawn closer to Chénier as a dramatic figure than ever before. As for his singing, Vickers combines nobility and musicality as do few others and without sacrificing excitement. What enormous phrases he drew within the first-act *Improvviso* and how superbly shaded was his singing throughout."[24]

On December 13, 1973, Vickers was in Montreal for a benefit concert, under Decker, at which he sang the "Winterstürme" and "Vesti la giubba." He was about to plunge into weeks of turmoil at the Met, with the *Tristan* that he awaited eagerly. It would bring him rare New York headlines and a large measure of disappointment, as well as one night of triumph.

Remarkably, Vickers sang Tristan only twice at the Met, and only once there with Birgit Nilsson. That performance, of which the private tape is a classic of that stolen art, came on January 30, 1974, after weeks of tumult chiefly surrounding the casting of other Isoldes. The Swedish soprano Catarina Ligendza had canceled two days before rehearsals began. Vickers put his foot down at the substitute, Klara Barlow, an unknown commodity as Isolde, and refused to sing the opening performance with her. He did take the January 26 broadcast with her.

Vickers, who never made a habit of speaking to the press in crisis, said of his withdrawal in a January 5 *New York Post* interview with Speight Jenkins: "In no way do I want my action to be taken as a criticism of Klara Barlow, or the management [of the Met]. The whole production has been under-rehearsed, from my standpoint, and I do not want to make my debut as Tristan at the Metropolitan under such conditions of pressure." He had called the Met from Bermuda to say he wasn't well, however, and arrived in New York six days after rehearsals had begun. He said what he was doing "can in no way be called leaving in a huff." He claimed no desire "to hurt Klara, whom I respect, and secondly, I don't want to take a crack at the Met. They need all the help they can get and I believe my decision makes for the best Tristan for both Miss Barlow and me."

Schuyler Chapin, the Met's acting general manager, was furious. A day later, after Erich Leinsdorf also vented in the press, about amateurs at the Met, Chapin called Nilsson to apprise her of the situation. A couple of days later, Vickers worked on Act 1 with Barlow and Leinsdorf to familiarize himself with the production, but the tension onstage, Chapin said, was almost visible. The director, August Everding, also pleaded that Chapin cancel the performance.[25] On January 11 Chapin told the *New York Times*, sounding grumpy, "There is too much passion over singers, rather than over the work."

Kubelik, in his first season as Met music director, missed the fireworks. He was in Munich, not due back until February 9, but he had advised Chapin to drop *Tristan* and substitute *Tosca*. However, Chapin was under pressure to balance the Met budget, and the switch could have cost one hundred thousand dollars, so Kubelik agreed they should gamble on *Tristan*. A number of Met productions lacked enough rehearsal, Chapin admitted, because of financial concerns.[26] Observing all this *Sturm* was James Levine, at age thirty Kubelik's right-hand man.

A back story to this crisis may explain why all concerned were so angry. It began with Goeran Gentele, according to some sources. Before his death, he had planned for his first Met season the *Tristan* that, with Nilsson, had been hugely successful in Bing's final year. He asked Ligendza, however, and told Leinsdorf that Nilsson wasn't available for the initial performances. Leinsdorf warned Gentele that Ligendza was unreliable. But it seems Nilsson could indeed have made herself available. One can only speculate whether Gentele may have been jealous of his fellow Swede's fame. When Ligendza canceled, Leinsdorf was angry, since he had warned of this. Gentele had told Nilsson he was asking Ligendza, and Nilsson, never one to insult a colleague, didn't protest. But she was a diva not disposed to step in when she had not been the first choice.

Jess Thomas showed up on time as the alternate Tristan, and soprano Doris Jung was on hand, because Leinsdorf had insisted on her as a cover in case of a problem with Ligendza. But Leinsdorf was further upset, Chapin wrote in his memoir, because an agent sent in an unprepared soprano as a possible sub, and the conductor almost quit at that point. Meanwhile, Barlow got wind of the situation and wired Charlie Riecker at the Met, where she had sung Donna Anna and in *Fidelio,* that she had just finished more than forty Isoldes in Europe. Two days later, after the Met checked out her Isolde with European houses, she was sent a ticket to come and audition for Leinsdorf. Richard Woitach played for her. Leinsdorf was not happy with this (no one on the music staff auditioned her first), but Chapin said Barlow sounded splendid and told her so. Leinsdorf then appeared in Chapin's office, with his wife, and asked to be released from his contract. Vickers was next, telling Chapin he had nothing against Barlow but would not sing until Nilsson arrived. Chapin sensed that some of Vickers's feeling must have come from Leinsdorf, but did not bring that up.[27]

Barlow, who remained hurt and bitter about the episode years later, said that Leinsdorf wanted name singers and, she believed, had joined forces with Vickers against her. But she never had an opportunity to speak with Vickers about the situation. She said Leinsdorf had been unkind and selfish.[28]

It was the afternoon after that when the *New York Post* broke the story that Vickers was withdrawing because of the tensions brought on by Ligendza's canceling. Chapin lined up another conductor in the house, Leif Segerstam, in case Leinsdorf should actually depart. Next day, however, Leinsdorf did go in and work on the first act with Barlow and Vickers. The Met manager recalled feeling he would go to any lengths to save the scheduled Nilsson-Vickers performances. He told Leinsdorf as much.[29]

The mezzo Mignon Dunn, who sang Brangäne in six performances (Michèle Vilma sang January 30 and February 4), recalled of the traumatic time: "Everyone tried to be very good colleagues to Klara. She did some of it just beautifully. It was a big thing to hand her, but she had sung it before." However, "she was probably not [Vickers's] idea of what it should be at the Metropolitan Opera. And I think Erich was just going along with things and doing the best he could. But Jon felt this was not a right thing and he wasn't going to do it. And that's what I say about Jon, that you have to respect that he has always the courage of his convictions."[30]

On January 8 Vickers took part in the dress rehearsal, wanting to work with Everding while he was still in the house, Chapin wrote. (This conflicts with the *Times,* which said the director had slipped on the ice, cracking two ribs, and had to leave before the dress.)[31] Doris Jung subbed for Barlow, who felt she needed to rest for the first night. During the third act, Chapin recalled, Vickers noticed an aide whispering to Leinsdorf. "'What is this, a union meeting?' he shouted from his Tristan rugs. 'If so, I'm walking out of here right now.'" He began to rise, but the conductor shouted his apologies and asked to begin at the top of the scene.[32]

In the January 11 opening performance, Barlow was vocally a warm and pliant Irish princess, Speight Jenkins wrote, but lacked the power Isolde needs in the lower register, so it was not necessarily Leinsdorf's fault that she was somewhat overwhelmed by the orchestra. Thomas seemed vocally unsure, but sang an extraordinary first act. Tristan's music, the most difficult dramatically and vocally in the repertoire, "needs a tenor with steel vocal cords and a Phi Beta Kappa brain." Thomas certainly had the latter.[33]

Leinsdorf told Jenkins later that he was overwhelmed by the cheers when he entered the pit that Friday night, and that his hands were shaking so that he had to pause before beginning. Of Vickers he said, "I very much hope he lives up to his commitment. He sang a magnificent dress rehearsal." And he praised the graciousness of Thomas; a bitter Barlow described it differently, saying Thomas "was kicked around."[34]

Vickers must have been enraged by Harold Schonberg's review of the first night. The critic wrote that Barlow had held her own as a svelte, feminine, sensitive princess, and the Met came through. But he wrote that Vickers had given "a confusing variety of reasons" for bowing out. "He has a history of canceling Tristan performances. Several seasons back he left a Tristan cast in the lurch in San Francisco. He has not sung the role in this country, and one might guess that he is afraid of it." In fact, doctors had told Vickers not to sing in San Francisco.[35]

Barlow sang three performances, then was quite ill with a sinus infection for the January 26 Saturday matinee broadcast. She had cortisone injections and hot towels on her throat; she couldn't talk but could sing. She wanted to drop out, but there simply was no one else to sing Isolde. Vickers minded his own business backstage during that broadcast, and so did Barlow. "I was too sick to give a damn" about the tensions, she recalled.[36]

Vickers seemed to be saving his best for Nilsson. Much of the time, Jenkins noted, he "dropped his voice to that strange soft croon so beloved of Herbert von Karajan, and so disappointing for an audience. The whole wakeup scene needed at least a slight boost of volume to be heard, and the opening of the mad scene had to be taken on faith." In all, there were "too few bursts of his glorious voice in all its power."[37]

The *Times'* Raymond Ericson said Vickers gave "an extraordinarily beautiful performance." Always intense, "even in his first appearance, with his abrupt phrases as he confronted Isolde on the ship, his presence dominated the action. In the long, difficult third act, his anguished, feverish longing for Isolde was projected with a depth and power not seen here by this reviewer." But he also noted a problem: "The tenor has a vocal mannerism that is sometimes disturbing, a swelling in and out of tone, which seems to break the vocal line. But his singing of Tristan's music, for the most part, had a sensitively molded flow. It was a supremely lyrical performance, rising to an eloquent climax in Tristan's mortal delirium."[38]

Barlow also sang January 15 and 19 performances with Thomas. Nilsson came in on January 30, with Vickers. Thomas sang it with Nilsson on February 4, because Vickers had *Otello* opening February 9. Nilsson sang the final *Tristan* February 14 with Thomas.

For that memorable night of January 30, Donal Henahan reported that "snowstorms of confetti" fell for both artists, and said that Vickers "met Miss Nilsson on her own lofty terms." George Movshon said the soprano at last had found a tenor with "the metal, the manliness, the dramatic insight and the musicality to do justice to this music. Vickers is such a man. There was valour where it was called for, passion in the love duet—and the long-breathed mezza voce lines ran with hallowed gleam through the orchestral web."[39]

That was Vickers's second and last Met *Tristan*. He and Nilsson went to Chapin shortly thereafter and volunteered to sing the opera again the next season. The unimaginative Chapin told them no *Tristan*s were scheduled that year.[40]

Another crisis awaited. The Met's Saturday broadcast matinee on February 9 opened the *Otello* run, conducted by Levine. Stratas was scheduled, but at ten that morning the cover, Kiri Te Kanawa, received a call that Stratas had canceled. Stratas had been ill the previous day and had missed one rehearsal. But on Friday night Te Kanawa had been told Stratas would go on. So the New Zealand soprano was startled and rushed.

She had never had a stage rehearsal to learn the complexities of Zeffirelli's big production. Vickers, who had met Flower Maiden Kiri in London, said later, "We did conspire a bit before Kiri came in." When she arrived more than an hour later, he, Levine, and Met stage director Melano were on hand to walk her through the sets.

Vickers told a London interviewer, "The Met debut is a very frightening experience. The first time you come in everybody says, 'Who is this?' . . . I tried to make a bit of a fuss of her to let her know she was among friends." Te Kanawa added, "Jon was marvellous: he got me through it." Terrified, she had got through on pure concentration. Vickers whispered to her during the performance that she was doing beautifully.[41]

Chapin had feared the tenor would be angry at the substitution, but his reaction was quite the contrary. Te Kanawa got an ovation, and on the second curtain call Vickers put his arms around her, moved her forward, and left the stage to her. In the wings, he joined forcefully in the applause.[42]

Stratas sang the other four performances with Vickers. Te Kanawa returned in March with McCracken as Vickers awaited the March 16 *Troyens* broadcast.

On February 27, the night Vickers sang his eighteenth Met Moor, his father, William, died in Regina, Saskatchewan. The funeral was on Tuesday, March 5, at St. Paul's Presbyterian in Prince Albert. Vickers did not attend; had his mother still been alive, he undoubtedly would have gone. His next Met performance was March 16, 1974, the broadcast of *Troyens*, with William Lewis taking over the March 11 and 20 Énées. McCracken did the rest of the *Otello*s.

Back home at Blue Horizons in Bermuda, Vickers fired off a four-page letter to Chapin, laying out his deep disappointment about the *Tristan* episode and distress about the previous season and future Met plans. Dated April 24, 1974, the letter was pure Vickers—citing his own high standards, detailing injuries done to him, ending with a warning that he would now proceed solely on a business basis with the Met. This last echoed what he had told David Webster some sixteen years before.

Who else could be expected to sing Énée, Otello, and Tristan in the same season, and why was he not given special respect for that feat, he wondered. He spoke of striving for an artistic level that would fulfill his obligations to God, his art, his employer, and himself. He felt his standards had been ignored and that he was wrongly called arrogant or fearful when he tried to uphold them. The Met, he charged, had not prepared properly for the *Tristan* he had so much anticipated. He called Leinsdorf a liar about Vickers's being so late to rehearsal (he said he was two days late, not six). He complained that Chapin had no-commented, failing to support him, so that Vickers appeared the villain in the press. He complained of a supposed arrangement for Barlow to be reviewed on the front page of the *New York Times*, and of Chapin's supposedly taking Barlow as his guest to a Met Guild dinner. He had the biggest responsibility in the *Tristan*, but his reviews, he felt, were perfunctory. He further complained that his load of eight *Troyens* in twenty-three days was extremely taxing, because, he said, Énée carries the load of that opera. He was upset that plans to open the 1975–76 season with *Jenůfa* had been dropped, as had plans for a new *Forza*. And he brought up financial issues of his contract.[43]

On May 13, Chapin wrote back to apologize, but said he was baffled about many of Vickers's comments. (He said Barlow had merely been present at the Guild dinner and they had just shaken hands.)[44] However, a number of observers felt Vickers was justified in his criticisms of Chapin's handling of the Met's operations in general. Around the time of the *Otellos*, Kubelik had cabled Chapin he was quitting as Met musical director, citing administrative issues. He left after that season.

By September Vickers had thought better of his outburst and phoned Chapin, who returned a warm note to Bermuda on September 27.[45] Vickers wanted to continue singing at the Met, at least for the time being. But he had endured an extremely frustrating season, and as he neared age fifty, in 1976, thoughts of retirement grew stronger.

15

A Man and His Music

IN MAY 1974 VICKERS APPEARED IN THREE PERFORMANCES OF A revival of Britten's *The Rape of Lucretia* at his friend Nicholas Gold-schmidt's Guelph Spring Festival. He had sung the Male Chorus in the 1956 Stratford Festival production, his only other career appearance in the part. Colin Graham, now with St. Louis Opera Theatre, directed. Vickers told him he had only accepted the part because "the critics tore my heart out in Toronto and I will never sing there again." Guelph seemed to be a safe spot from which to snub the Toronto press, said Graham.

Vickers arrived for the last three days of the three weeks of rehearsal. At his first staging rehearsal, he handed his score to Graham and asked to have it bound to look like an ancient tome. Graham asked if he meant to sing the whole role from the book, and when Vickers said yes, Graham pointed out that while some of the part consists of historical quotation, most is the Chorus's personal observation and could not be sung from a book.

The tenor began to argue, but "our redoubtable répétiteur," Mary-Nan Dutka, slammed the piano lid and said fearlessly, "Mr. Vickers, we have been working very happily for three weeks—are you now going to ruin all that work in the last three days?"

Vickers turned purple and other colors, Graham recalled, then said, "You are quite right. May we turn this rehearsal into a music call, and I guarantee to have the part by heart by tomorrow morning." He was as good as his word and behaved "like a lamb" from then onward, said Graham, giving a stunning performance.[1]

One critic raised again a key issue with Vickers, his tendency to be so strong that he unbalanced the rest of the production, to the detriment, however unintentional, of the other singers. "He was like a sun on that small stage," wrote Eric McLean, "and he had the effect of diminishing the light produced by the lesser stars around him." This was in no way a failure of Vickers's colleagues, McLean noted.[2]

The American soprano Roberta Knie first sang with Vickers on May 21, 1974, at the Vienna Staatsoper, on the occasion of Vickers's first appearance there since he had departed in support of Karajan. The opera was *Fidelio*, conducted by Leopold Hager. Knie said she was asked to sing "because they said I had good nerves. They expected Jon to be booed, and Jon expected to be booed. There were Karajan enemies as well as Karajan lovers, you know. Sometimes when you take a stand like that, it can backfire." But instead, "they screamed and stomped and roared the whole evening, and I must say we all sang well."

The cast included Theo Adam as Pizarro, and Adam's unavoidable absence at a runthrough the night before gave Knie a trial by fire in her first dealings with Vickers. Adam's Mercedes was damaged badly in an accident as he drove from East Germany, although he was unhurt. This was explained to Vickers, but Knie says he didn't quite understand, although his German was good at the time. "He got in this god-awful rage and started pacing back and forth: 'Why should I have to be here, why isn't Theo here,' and on and on and on."

Knie, in awe of Vickers but feeling herself in her role as the loyal Fidelio, felt she should try to save the situation. Though she had never met Vickers before that day, "I just patted him on the arm" and explained again about the accident. "Jon calmed down, we had a wonderful rehearsal and a fabulous performance the next day. So that was my real introduction to Vickers the artist.

"I wasn't ever afraid of Jon. I know people have said they've been afraid of him, but I simply wasn't. . . . If I had been a Tosca, I might have reacted totally differently, but I was Fidelio!"

And the two voices blended well: "After the 'Namenlose freude,' [the orchestra] had to wait a long time because we had such wonderful applause."[3]

As if 1974 had not been strenuous enough already, Vickers took on two new roles opening a week apart with the Chorégies d'Orange in France. Both were successes, even amid the mistral that gusted excessively over the outdoor amphitheater for much of the festival.

On July 13 he was Herod to Leonie Rysanek's Salome, with Ruth Hesse as his wife and Thomas Stewart as Jochanaan, Rudolf Kempe conducting. "Tottering in a heavy, shell-like costume that made him seem a glowing scarab, he sang his lines, never barking. Pitiful, evil, he lusted hysterically during Salome's dance," wrote *Opera News*.[4] Charles Pitt saw this Herod as a heady, tipsy figure, and massively virile. Vickers wore a royal oriental costume, "which he treated with royal disrespect, spilling wine over it, wiping his hands on it." His performance was so good that he unbalanced the work, wrote Pitt in an echo of that view.[5] Vickers, however, seems not to have been entirely happy with his efforts.

On July 20, resplendent in armor, he essayed the Pollione that he never sang with Callas. His Norma was Montserrat Caballé, and both spun out long legato phrases. A video of this remarkable collaboration survives.

Vickers gloried in, even gained some kind of release from, the few parts that allowed him to give vent to degenerate lust spiced with huge anger. These would be Herod and his Nerone four years later. He also did well with the slimy Sergei of Shostakovich's *Lady Macbeth of Mtsensk*. Such roles were in sharp contrast to the heroes and victims for which he was best known. But he never sang either Herod or Pollione again. As with some other roles, this in part may be laid to a lack of imagination at some opera houses.

Also that summer, Vickers agreed to do the first and only film documentary on his life, *A Man and His Music*, for CBC-TV. The producer was Richard Bocking, his old friend from Port Arthur and Winnipeg days, then working in Vancouver. The tenor was not trusting of people he met after becoming famous and had turned down other requests. "He'll never do it, Dick," Hetti warned Bocking when he visited the Ontario farm. But Vickers finally said yes, with the proviso that his family not be shown, which they were not. Bocking regretted that Hetti's warmth and loveliness were not recorded for posterity. But Vickers was always perhaps overprotective of his family, guarding them as zealously as a Rigoletto. He even worried about the possible kidnapping of his children.

The ninety-minute documentary aired on October 30, the day after Vickers's forty-eighth birthday. It included clips from *Pagliacci*, *Otello*, *Fidelio*, and the *Tristan* with Nilsson in Orange, plus a *Grimes* scene in a bare rehearsal room. His farm was shown, but there was no mention of his recent move to Bermuda. Vickers was seen visiting old friends in Prince Albert, and the house where he was born, since torn down, was documented.

Bocking recalled witnessing Vickers's power as a singing actor in the *Grimes* climax, photographed in one take with two cameras. "When it ended, with Jon prone on the floor, there was total silence. The large crew surrounding him seemed almost incapable of breathing. I couldn't even utter the customary 'cut.' Jon waited, then raised his head, looked about, realized the spell he had cast and broke it with a mighty burst of laughter."[6]

In 1974 Vickers recorded an album of Canadian music, with Richard Woitach at the piano, for CBC Radio Canada. The sessions took place in St. Anne's Anglican Church in Toronto, and the selections included Jean

Coulthard's Six Medieval Love Songs, romantic and erotic English translations of Latin texts. Vickers would sing them again on his 1985 Canadian album. Two others were poems by Kenneth Patchen, set by Srul Irving Glick and dedicated to Vickers.

Vickers sang *Peter Grimes* in the autumn of 1974 for five performances in a new Lyric Opera of Chicago production, staged by Geraint Evans and Ande Anderson, with design by Carl Toms and costumes from the Met. Bruno Bartoletti conducted, the Polish soprano Teresa Kubiak was Ellen Orford, and Evans was Balstrode. Bartoletti found Vickers's performance had such impact that the conductor never was happy doing the opera with anyone else.[7]

On November 18, 1974, Vickers was involved in another collision of his hopes for bringing world-class opera to Canada with the realities of box office and audience response in that country. He and Don Martyn, a cousin of Hetti Vickers who had a new firm called International Cultural Events, planned a major Toronto concert. Vickers would be joined by Birgit Nilsson and bass William Wildermann, a Canadian Opera Company veteran, with Zubin Mehta leading the Toronto Symphony. Vickers's hope was to present a couple of programs each year, including one with Joan Sutherland and Luciano Pavarotti.

Two performances, with a ninety-minute break, were planned for one evening in Massey Hall, which seats about 2,750. The organizers needed to sell 5,000 seats to break even. Some observers thought the two concerts in a single night would be confusing, and each performance sold only about half the seats (news stories had said the tickets were gone before they went on sale). The symphony had to be paid for two concerts, even though both were the same night (for a cost of twenty-one thousand dollars). Vickers sang for one fee, around eight thousand dollars; Nilsson got about the same and took only 30 percent for the second concert. Reviews were good, especially for Mehta, who conducted the *Meistersinger* Prelude and Act 1 of *Die Walküre*. But Vickers's group lost fifty-two thousand dollars. The tenor simply wasn't used to losing money, and of course his blame fell in part on the press.

While in Chicago, before that ill-starred concert, Vickers had been working on Leoš Janáček's *Jenůfa*, for the Met's new production by Schneider-Siemssen, directed by Gunther Rennert, opening November 15. His last *Grimes* in the run was October 15, and he was at the Met in time to see Britten's *Death in Venice*, given its U.S. premiere with Peter Pears as Aschenbach. It was the ROH production, and Colin Graham directed. Graham said that Vickers, after his huge success with Grimes, was considering all the Pears roles generally. But Graham was witness to an incident that revealed Vickers's dislike of matters relating to homosexuals.

He and Graham were in the wings for a performance of the Britten work, in which an aging man is obsessed with a beautiful young boy. With no preamble, said Graham, Vickers "seized me by the lapels, lifted me off the floor, and pronounced into my face, 'If anyone ever asks me to perform this role in this perverted opera I will kill him!' He dropped me and walked out of the theater." Graham, unaware of Vickers's animosity toward homosexuals, was stunned.[8]

For the *Jenůfa*, Teresa Kubiak took the title role, alternating with Margaret Tynes, and William Lewis and Sandor Konya sang Števa, with Astrid Varnay as Kostelnička. It was sung in English translation, with John Nelson conducting.

The role of the tormented Laca was another outsider for the Vickers gallery of portraits. He said in notes for the December 21 radio broadcast that he felt the frustrated Laca "has always gotten the short end of the stick. Števa, his playboy half-brother, gets the mill, gets everything because he belongs to the Buryja family. Laca was brought into the family by a second marriage and is treated like a common laborer." He suggested that when Laca inflicts a cut on Jenůfa's cheek, the knife is symbolic. Števa drops the scarred beauty, but Laca is a changed man, "just hopelessly in love with Jenůfa." He also noted that the slashing is the only time Laca loses control of himself, control being very much an issue with Vickers himself.[9]

David Cairns was deeply impressed by Vickers in the 1977 ROH *Jenůfa*. "It makes me want to cry just to think of it." What was so marvelous to him was that Vickers managed the transition of Laca, who begins as an ugly, uncouth character, making nasty remarks in the background and then slashing Jenůfa. And when she's in trouble, he comes to inquire for her.

> Gradually, he turns into the hero of the opera. And Vickers *thought* about this. At the end when she says, "You must see I'm not someone that you can ever live your life with" [after her dead child is discovered], the way he sort of turned towards her, it was just wonderful.
>
> He's the only Laca I've ever seen who really manages this growth of the character. He clearly thought deeply about it, about how to show the character evolving. It's wonderful, just awe-inspiring, and incredibly moving.

Cairns also recalled that Vickers had coached for the role with a Czech man in New York, discussing how a Czech would sing, even though the performance was in English.[10]

On January 8, 1975, another tenor from a poor, devout family, Richard Tucker, died unexpectedly in Michigan, at age sixty-one. His funeral was at the Met, and at a concert tribute February 6 at Carnegie Hall, Vickers joined singers including Leontyne Price, Horne, Bumbry, Bergonzi, Siepi, and Merrill. Vickers sang "Total eclipse" and, with Teresa Zylis-Gara, the *Otello* love duet.

The next week, Vickers began eight performances of Don Alvaro in the Met's *La Forza del Destino,* widely spaced from January 17 to March 26. It was the only time he would sing the role. He liked the character of Don Alvaro, another man pursued by the fates in a work with religious aspects. James Levine recalled that Vickers had responded with *Forza* when the conductor asked if there were anything he wanted to sing at the Met for which he hadn't had an opportunity.[11]

The tenor did have continual difficulty with high notes. He tended to crack on the B-natural at the end of the second act, recalled the writer Bruce Burroughs, so he usually changed it to an A-natural. But on the March 22 broadcast, he decided on the B and negotiated it well, Burroughs recalled.

How he reacted to those vocal problems may have depended upon which night you caught him. One night when he cracked a lot, Burroughs was backstage to praise his performance. "He said he was a little off form, or some remark like that. I said nevertheless it was very moving, and he said, very defensively, I thought, 'Oh, I know what you guys are going to say years from now. You're going to laugh and say do you remember how it was when Vickers tried to sing this part.'"[12]

Vickers was booed for his cracking at the performance attended by the Toronto baritone Terence Shawn. Surely it was one of the few times Vickers had heard boos, and Shawn went to see him, thinking he would be depressed and wanting, like Burroughs, to tell him what emotion he had brought to the role. "There was a burst of laughter, and the double doors [backstage] burst open and Jon came out looking not like a famous tenor but like a famous banker" in his bowler hat, Shawn recalled. "He seemed on top of the world."[13]

Burroughs wrote: "So great an artist is Jon Vickers than an evening-long trauma with most notes above A did not materially diminish the strength of his performance. For once Alvaro emerged as the deeply tragic figure he is, palpably demonstrating the dignity and restraint of one possessed of royal Inca blood. (Surely the aria has never been more movingly sung.)"[14]

And Andrew Porter offered this insight: "The intensity [Vickers] brought to his aria almost tore it to tatters—but then he often begins by overexpressing a role and settles later into a more disciplined interpretation."[15]

As for more Verdi, Vickers still wanted to sing *Ballo* again, and in March 1975 Coast was asking the Met's Chapin for it in 1978–79. Vickers, he wrote, "regards Verdi as a masseur of the voice."[16]

Vickers made a wonderful departure into his second Berlioz role, the title character in the rarely performed but richly rewarding *Benvenuto Cellini*. It was the Boston Opera Company's grand revival in March 1975, the first professional staging of the opera in the United States. Vickers and the equally individualistic Sarah Caldwell, the company's director, who conducted the *Cellini*, made quite a team. This was the only time he portrayed the real-life Florentine goldsmith and sculptor. But the role, generally thought to be owned by Gedda, suited Vickers admirably in dramatic terms, if not always vocally. Cellini battled authority, esteemed his own talents (and was born a few days after Vickers's own birthday, about November 1, depending upon calendars, in 1500).

The high tessitura was a worry, and Caldwell asked John Ardoin, the critic and author, to urge Vickers to take on the part. Ardoin recalled that Vickers told him, "'Not in a pig's eye!' I said, 'What's the problem?' He said, 'Have you looked at the score? There's a top C-sharp. I can't do that bloody thing!'" The writer called Caldwell; the first-act trio does have a C. He could hear wheels turning in Caldwell's mind, and she said she thought "we're going to find Berlioz left an alternative version." That apparently isn't so, but Caldwell took the trio down a half step, said Ardoin.[17]

William Fred Scott, the company's artistic administrator and associate conductor, recalled a rocky road to the performances. First Vickers turned down the role, then said he didn't have time to learn the French but would do it in English. A translation was found at Covent Garden, and Caldwell arranged for a Juilliard School coach to go to Bermuda to help Vickers. He wasn't happy with her, and Scott was next to hop on a plane for Bermuda that February.

Scott had no sooner boarded than a phone call at the gate told him Vickers had called to say not to come. He got off the flight; Vickers called that afternoon, said he'd looked at the score again, and Scott got back on the same flight next day.

He spent a week with Vickers at Blue Horizons, and the tenor got the part down at great speed. "We worked twice a day intensively on the score. He was a very smart musician. . . . He got very proud of himself for having learned it. We went boating, and it was strange to be out in a boat with Peter Grimes," Scott recalled.

Vickers gave a wonderfully athletic performance. But that did not extend to high notes; Scott said Vickers sang no high Ds (although Vickers would say that he had). The final-act aria was omitted.[18]

But he fenced like Errol Flynn, threw a pie, and raced up a huge ladder to Cellini's melting pot. Porter wrote that Vickers "compasses the volatile inconsistency" of the firebrand who adores both Teresa and the statue he is creating. "Urgent, ardent, heroic, poetic, Mr. Vickers was a thrilling Cellini. His voice lacked suppleness for some of the tender music; the force and fire of his singing were ample compensation."[19] Vickers displayed an easy production, noted Paul Hume, "that gave him ravishing high soft notes and full-throated exclamations of immense power. Every word he sang, in the fine English translation used, came out impeccably clearly."[20]

The cast at Boston's Orpheum included Patricia Wells as Teresa, Cellini's beloved; John Reardon as Fieramosca, the papal sculptor; and Donald Gramm as Pope Clement VII.

Bolting up that ladder was a Vickers idea that startled all connected with the production. "It was an enormous, tall ladder," said Caldwell, "a specially designed metal ladder that looked like it was thin, a tall spindle, and he must have gone twenty-five, thirty feet in the air. It was just incredible, what a thriller!" It was an extraordinary act, but "it certainly grew out of the impulse of the character. It was something Cellini would have done, not just Vickers becoming a wild man." Vickers "was very careful about what he did, but he didn't become a sideshow. He held himself with great dignity. . . . There are many things one thinks of other performers doing that one couldn't imagine Jon doing," she said, referring nonjudgmentally to 1990s commercialism on the rise in the music world.

Although Vickers wasn't as widely known as Pavarotti and Domingo, Caldwell said, "I don't agree he didn't get respect he deserved. He is held in remarkably high regard, as an artist, as a musician, as a singer, actor, someone who cared very much about what was happening. He was not afraid to express himself when he did not approve. He was a very good colleague." And she saw him with an enormous following of his own. "He was a very, very sexy tenor. Very handsome man. Very virile. I think that our audience would have come to anything he did."[21]

Vickers sang *Fidelio* in 1976 with Caldwell, later declined the Roger Sessions *Montezuma* (he first thought it was the 1755 opera by Karl Graun), and canceled a 1988 *Médée* in Boston because his wife was ill. Caldwell also discussed *Stiffelio* with him.

In late April 1975 Vickers sang the difficult and erotic Janáček song cycle *Diary of One Who Vanished* at the War Memorial Hall in Guelph, Ontario. He had first sung it in the early 1960s, and again in 1971 at Stratford, Ontario;

now his old friend Nicholas Goldschmidt had encouraged him to do the piece again. The young mezzo soprano was Janet Stubbs, just finishing work at the University of Toronto opera school, and the accompanist was Rudolph Firkusny. The recital was broadcast on the CBC.

He made excellent use of his beautiful soft higher tones and his full dramatic voice for this story of a man infatuated with a sensuous gypsy woman, the first of Janáček's works inspired by the young married woman with whom he fell in love in his sixties. Stubbs recalled that Vickers told her, "What's a pretty little girl like you doing here with me?" He was forty-eight at the time.[22]

In October 1975 Coast told the Met that Vickers would get $6,500 at Covent Garden in 1976–77 and wanted $7,000 from the Met for 1977–78 and 1978–79. Richard Rodzinski, a Met artistic administrator, replied that that amount was out of the question. The Met had never paid more than $6,000 as top fee and would never do so, which of course did not prove to be the case.[23] About this time Vickers probably averaged at least $250,000 annually in fees, not including stipends for hotels and air fares.

Between May 15 and June 16, 1975, Vickers appeared in five performances of *Tristan* with L'Opéra de Montréal at Place des Arts in Montreal, led by Zubin Mehta. A video also was made, conducted by Franz-Paul Decker, released commercially in 1999 by VAI. Vickers had been asked to direct the opera, but he felt the added load would jeopardize his singing.[24] He did narrate the video, with English and French versions.

Roberta Knie was a warm, womanly Isolde with Vickers for the first time, and she recalled an erotic moment in rehearsal that didn't occur in performance. It sheds some light on Vickers's spontaneity in developing a role. Knie got the job after the Norwegian soprano Ingrid Bjoner was dropped (Vickers may have felt she was too tall, and she may have thought his voice too big), and Catarina Ligendza quit, Knie says, possibly because she feared the size of the hall, as she perhaps had with the 1974 Met *Tristan*. Knie had sung in *Fidelio* with Vickers in 1974, and had sung the finale of *Die Walküre* in an April concert in Montreal with Decker. Mehta had heard her as Salome in Vienna. She had just done her first ten Isoldes, in Bologna in a Wieland Wagner production from Stuttgart, and in Lyons.

Knie flew from a Strasbourg performance straight to the Montreal rehearsal. She dropped her bags at the hotel and went to rehearse, in jeans and T-shirt. Mehta was there to work on the second act. "My hair at the time was mid-thigh length, and it was up in pins and combs. Ernst Poettgen [the director] was telling us what to do, but my hair started coming down. And Jon, in the love duet, simply proceeded to take my hair down." Mehta, seeing the tenor handling hunks of his Isolde's red-blonde tresses, said, "O my God, that's the most beautiful thing I ever saw!" But the director was not similarly impressed. "Poettgen got very upset. He said, 'This is a symbolic love, this is not an erotic love. That is too erotic.' I don't know how much Jon understood of Ernst's ravings. . . . We were singing, we were getting to know one another. Poettgen said if we did anything like that in the performance, he was walking out. But I think Jon and I did a very erotic *Tristan*," even without the hair.

A story has been passed around that Vickers once said Isolde was "a bad girl." Knie had the facts: "Jon's exact words were 'Isolde is not a nice girl.'" She is certain his view came from Karajan, who, not to put too fine a point on it, she thinks "brainwashed" Vickers. It was probably already a view to which the tenor leaned.

Knie recalled that in one of the first Montreal discussions about the characters, with Mehta present, "Jon was telling about what an evil person Isolde was. Now, this had all been pumped into him by Karajan. . . . [Jon] said this is an evil love, Isolde is an evil woman, she seduces a wonderful man and causes a rift between him and his uncle, a noble king and a noble knight, putting the whole evil, as Jon called it, on Isolde." Knie had done much research on the part, reading in German and coaching with Astrid Varnay and Bayreuth coaches. She spoke up boldly to Vickers, but in a friendly manner. "I said this is not what Wagner wrote. . . . Whatever you wish to call the love potion, you can't call it evil. Brangäne deliberately did it to keep the two people from dying. You can believe in the symbolism of it, you can call the love potion what you will, but that is the legend. . . . So you cannot say these are two wonderful men who are torn apart by this horrible person!

"I said, Jon, the music is just too voluptuous, it's too wonderful to have to call this woman evil!" Her ideas challenged Vickers, she thinks. Mehta said "very gallantly and gently he had to agree with me from a musical and text standpoint." Later, he told Knie "he was scared to death when I did this," not knowing how Vickers would react. "I was an innocent. I didn't know Jon had a bad reputation," said Knie.

After the second performance on the big, raked disk of the single set, she stood on the side of the stage, with huge ovations going on. "Jon said something to the effect of, 'Is there anything you think we could do to make this better?' I said, 'I wish I had more personal contact with my Tristan onstage . . . these two people are very intimate, they're so attuned to one another, and I feel a wall sometimes.'" Mehta gasped again. "That had been ingrained by Karajan, is my thinking. So the third performance was dynamite!" The difference? "Jon was very warm, very close, there was specific eroticism that perhaps hadn't been there before. It's in the music. I think that's what won Jon over. You cannot deny the the eroticism, the closeness, the intertwining of these two souls."

After one performance, Knie recalled, Hetti Vickers told her, "I don't know exactly what you did to Jon; I know you've had a lot of conversations. But this is the Tristan I knew he always had in him and never did before." After another performance, Vickers and Knie left the stage arm in arm as usual, and an attractive, young blonde woman was standing backstage. "She was just sobbing, and Jon put his arms out to her." It was his elder daughter, Allison, then twenty. "The three of us walked off the stage, Allison between us. We were all sort of hugging. I said, 'Why are you crying?' and she said, 'That's the most beautiful thing I ever saw!'"

Knie said further on the Karajan theory that Vickers had told her the conductor was at odds with his second wife, Eliette, when they had done *Tristan* in 1972. Karajan chose an Isolde, Helga Dernesch, "who looked like Eliette, and made her wear her hair as Eliette had worn it, and [Karajan] said she was an evil person." Knie said Karajan made Dernesch do things antithetical to the music and damaging vocally to Dernesch, "to bring out this evil which is not there!"

Knie and Vickers were an erotic pair onstage, with much touching and real kisses. "He always tasted of oranges," she recalled, as Vickers continued to munch the fruit at performances. Indeed, some thought there was a romantic relationship there, an issue Knie would not discuss. But they had a close communion onstage. One night they were lying back, preparing for the second-act love duet. "Jon would always talk to me like this [through gritted teeth]," Knie recalled. "He said, 'Jesus, look at Zubin.' I looked down and there was Zubin, the orchestra playing and Zubin with his hands folded in front of him, not conducting, grinning from ear to ear." Tristan and Isolde sang "O sink' hernieder"; this went on for minutes, "just pure heaven," with the conductor enraptured, said Knie. When the music swelled ("Ewig nacht"), "Mehta picked up his baton. I will never forget that."[25]

The notorious "Dristan *Tristan*," in which Vickers spoke his mind from the stage, occurred on December 9, 1975, in Dallas. This was the first German opera offered by the company, and there was some nervousness about the box office. But all three performances sold out. It was the production from Montreal, with Decker conducting again, also with Knie, Josephine Veasey as Brangäne, Jef Vermeesch as Kurwenal, and Nicola Zaccaria as King Marke. A review pronounced Vickers's performance a "tour de force that left you limp from sympathetic exhaustion," and praised Knie's lyrical but gripping Isolde.[26] John Ardoin saw in Knie the warmth and commitment of Martha Mödl. Vickers's Tristan was "a man who loves completely and inwardly; how can one ever forget the long-lined ardor of his singing in the 'Liebesnacht' or accept less in the future from another?" In the final act, "Vickers took us beyond music, beyond theater, on to a wrenching plane of truth that was profoundly moving."[27]

At the second performance, a matinee, the house resounded with coughing like a tuberculosis ward, as can be heard on the private tape. As Act 3 began, Vickers, the wounded Tristan, lay on a pallet. Coughs marred the prelude, with its mournful English horn solo, and when the Shepherd sang his four lines, the first vocal entrance in the act, some were made almost inaudible by the hacking in the audience. Directly after the Shepherd sang his last line, "has he not waked?" Vickers chose his moment. He had been fuming on his pallet, and he suddenly said loudly, "Shut up with your damn coughing!"

The audience was "a little stunned," recalled company chief Nicola Rescigno.[28] It was a moment of fierce contradiction, because Vickers very much lives his roles. Vickers said he had never moved a muscle, had just spoken out.[29] Decker continued calmly, and shortly Kurwenal made his vocal entrance. The noise seemed to have abated for the rest of the final act.

Knie had the speaker on in her dressing room, as she prepared for Isolde's dramatic climax. "It scared the hell out of me," she said, because to break character was so contrary to theater protocol. But at the time she was focused on her role. She didn't talk with Vickers about it, but a visitor backstage recalled that the tenor was very pleased with himself. "He was rocking up and down on his wedgies. He said, 'How'd you like that!'" reported Roger Carroll, then active with the Dallas Opera Guild.[30]

Vickers told John Ardoin:

> Here was this fine orchestra and beautiful English horn player doing their utmost to establish an atmosphere of this dying, sick man, Tristan, preparing the mood in which I could sing; and members of the audience were simply not allowing them to set this mood. . . . People must understand that coughing and other racket destroys [*sic*] the very thing they had paid their money to enjoy. . . . If I can go on that stage for four-and-a-half hours without once clearing my throat, an audience can sit still and not cough.[31]

Such behavior is not without precedent, from a tenor stepping forward to offer a high C to a New York critic to Sir Thomas Beecham, who shouted "Shut up!" to a 1936 Glasgow audience that spoiled the final bars of *La Bohème* with applause.[32] Kurt Masur expressed displeasure with coughing by halting a New York Philharmonic performance at the end of 1998.

News stories about the incident (it even made *People* magazine) included a comment from Marilyn Horne, who was singing there and had been at the performance. She said the audience had been rude, and she backed Vickers's action, as did Knie.

Before the third performance, Rescigno went to Knie and asked a favor. She recalled, "He said, 'We've had some threats against Jon and we feel he's going to be booed. We don't want a solo curtain call. Do you have any objections?'" Isolde's is traditionally the final solo bow, but Knie had no problem agreeing to go out with Vickers for his last bow. Vickers was informed of this and refused. "He said, 'I did it and I will take what they think I deserve.'"

With that large set, the singers had to mount steps behind the stage and go forward for bows. "Jon said, 'Well, I'm going now,' and started up." But Knie slipped up behind him, took his hand, and they walked on to an ovation. "We will never know whether Jon was going to be booed or not." One can speculate that Vickers characteristically might have preferred to take his bow alone and, like so many of his stage heroes, suffer any punishment the crowd might have inflicted.

Knie added her own footnote at that third performance. She was nervous about the threats, and when the curtain went up, she heard a great amount of exaggerated coughing. Isolde's first words are, "Who dares mock me!" Knie was seated with her head down, but she stood up and addressed the audience, in character. "I deliberately did it, I exploded that line out into the house. If they didn't know what she said, they would have known what I meant! And there was no more coughing that evening."[33]

But it wasn't all *Sturm und Drang* in Dallas. The quartet got along so well that at the end of the run, the crew gave them an award as the nicest cast with the most friendly atmosphere ever at the Dallas Opera, Knie recalled.

The incident showed that Vickers and Solti could have had much in common. The conductor once was so disturbed by coughing at a Chicago Symphony subscription concert that he turned to the audience and said, "If you knew how long we worked on that *pianissimo* phrase, you would control your coughing." He was less crude than Vickers had been, but their idea was identical.

Vickers began 1976 with *Otello* at the Greater Miami Opera (now the Florida Grand Opera), Emerson Buckley conducting. Performances on January 17 and 24 were at the Dade County Auditorium, and the January 21 performance was at the new, 2,950-seat Miami Beach Theater for the Performing Arts. Old friend Peter Glossop was Iago, and Teresa Zylis-Gara was Desdemona for the Nathaniel Merrill staging and Nicola Benois design. It was Vickers's "ringing tenor at its thrilling best," reported *Musical America*.[34]

He wasn't at the Met for the 1975–76 season, but the New York audience gave him an extremely warm reception at his February 6 Carnegie Hall recital, his last at the famed hall. Richard Woitach accompanied him, and he made, as usual, several comments during his performance. "I really love this number," he prefaced Vaughan Williams's "Song of the Road." A male voice shouted from the balcony, "And we love you!" This stopped Vickers only briefly. He went on to call it a tune "that John Wayne would sing, if John Wayne could sing."[35]

The program included a gorgeous rendition of Beethoven's song cycle *An die ferne Geliebte*, as well as his frequently sung Scarlatti, Purcell, and Vaughan Williams songs. The critic John Rockwell complained that Vickers's singing "was afflicted with all manner of mannerisms. . . . Mr. Vickers weaved back and forth between full voice and crooning. He wobbled and yawed rhythmically. He swelled and faded long-held syllables and distorted vowel sounds with little regard for musical phrase or declamatory integrity."[36] This review would be typical of a growing number of critical complaints about Vickers's vocal mannerisms that would dog him for the rest of his career.

A more sanguine view came from Jack Diether in *The Westsider*: Vickers "breathes music as naturally as air, and he 'rolls' into it with his whole body at the first downbeat. His easy informality and apparent carelessness on this occasion annoyed some of the daily press, but enraptured his audience, who offered him a standing ovation and clamored for more than the four encores." Woitach was on Vickers's "wavelength," and thus "in their unusually free rendition of Beethoven's song cycle . . . highly subjective in its use of rubato, I have never heard the vexatious final speedup into Allegro molto e con brio sound more motivated and less mechanical." Diether compared Vickers to Paul Robeson: "The dominant impression was one of controlled power, with much more in reserve."[37]

In 1976 John Coast recorded in a letter to Richard Rodzinski at the Met that in San Francisco Vickers was getting $6,000 per performance, a net figure, plus his airfare. He was there seven and a half weeks to sing twelve performances, nearly two a week. His next Covent Garden contract would give him 17,000 Swiss francs, or $6,762, per performance, on which he would pay about 10.5 percent tax. Vickers had been asking Paris and La Scala for a $7,000 fee (in 1975 Coast said he was scheduled for *L'Incoronazione di Poppea* at Scala, but that he "hates" the house and would try to get out of it). Vickers was not happy with the financial situation in Vienna, where in 1975–76 his fee was $6,483, taxed at about 20.8 percent, so his net per performance was $5,135. Coast wanted Vickers to be guaranteed by the Met no less than $6,000 per performance.[38]

Discussions were ongoing about a *Troyens* possibly for 1978–79, and Coast told the Met that Vickers would be happy to sing four performances, but would not be willing to rehearse the Met production again. But this run never transpired.

Vickers didn't want to give up any of his Vašeks (in *The Bartered Bride*) because he "occasionally welcomes an easy sing," as Coast said.[39] And in 1976 he was looking ahead to a lot of heavy repertoire at the Met: *Peter Grimes, Otello,* and *Tannhäuser* in 1977.

In January 1976 the Met had been talking with Coast about *Lohengrin* for Vickers. Coast told Vickers that if James King sang the role, so could Vickers, but Vickers was hesitant. He asked for a couple of weeks to think about it.

In March 1976 the Covent Garden company toured to Italy, and Vickers sang four performances of *Grimes* at La Scala. He enjoyed the visit, although he didn't like La Scala's "warring claques and political influences," as he told Alan Blyth. The *Grimes* was so successful, Vickers said, "because for once the cognoscenti came to the house and the clowns stayed home."[40]

On the return to London, Vickers sang six *Carmen*s, followed by three *Fidelio*s at the Royal Opera House. Mackerras, who led the *Carmen*s, recalled that Vickers was "very aggressive" with the conductor and with Josephine Veasey, the reigning Carmen, at all the rehearsals. But as usual, Mackerras found the performances wonderful. "He portrayed the degeneration of Don José superbly, from nice, religious, small-town mummy's boy to dangerous, insane killer."[41]

Vickers was Parsifal four times in May at the Paris Opéra, with Horst Stein conducting and August Everding directing the original 1973 production. In the four previous runs, Parsifal had been sung by Helge Brilioth, René Kollo, and James King. Vickers had two Kundrys, Nadine Denize and Gisela Schroeter, and three Amfortases, Siegmund Nimsgern, Theo Adam, and Tom Krause, with Kurt Moll as Gurnemanz and Jacques Mars as Klingsor. The run began May 14, with a radio broadcast, apparently on delay, on May 19, not a performance day.

Vickers was in demand for Tristan. In June 1976 Coast wrote to Tooley, looking ahead to Covent Garden *Tristan*s in 1978 and 1980: "Jon is becoming more and more strongly of the opinion that this is the *only* Isolde who has never let him down and with whom he has complete rapport on the stage." He referred to Knie, who was doing all the Brünnhildes at Bayreuth that summer.[42] How this related to Nilsson isn't clear; some insiders would suggest that Vickers didn't like being in the shadow of such a big-voiced singer and strong personality as the Swedish soprano, and that he found Knie more malleable.

In 1976 Vickers received another Canadian honor, one of the Molson prizes for arts and humanities, with a cash award of twenty thousand dollars.

Another Vickers performance that stayed in the memory of all who saw it was a run of an English-text *Queen of Spades* in July 1976 at Festival Canada in Ottawa. It was only his second appearance in the role of Herman (the first at the Met in 1965), and his last. Maureen Forrester was the Countess; Teresa Kubiak was Lisa. Mario Bernardi led the National Arts Centre Orchestra for the striking production by director Vaclav Kaslik and designer Josef Svoboda that used slides, photos, and various projection techniques to great effect.

Franz Kraemer recalled that Vickers sang a Christ-like Herman. "He wasn't going to be the bad guy. That was always a problem for him."[43] This Herman was onstage from the opening curtain to the end, in an asylum where his obsessions had driven him. Through a scrim-wall of his room, flashbacks appeared in which he took part, with his hallucinations emphasized by howling winds, swirling waters, and playing cards of all sizes.

Vickers let out all the stops: "One moment soft and tender, the next ranting and raving: strutting like a Napoleon or cringing from his fantasies, like a child—matching his voice in a glorious wedding of sound and dramatic insight that is unique among artists before the public today," reported Ruby Mercer.[44] At one performance Vickers startled the audience by throwing a glass against a wall, smashing it. In the end, Herman killed himself by breaking a mirror to slit his wrist.

Robert Jacobson wrote that Vickers "dominated the stage from first to last. In ringing voice, the tenor created a tragic figure of terrifying strength and heart-rending poignancy, shaped with the full range of hues, from the arrogant military man to the whimpering creature on the floor of his cell."[45]

Bernardi, who had known Vickers since Toronto conservatory days, was responsible for bringing him to Ottawa. Then music director of the arts center, Bernardi said it was viewed as "a big splash, Vickers finally singing in Canada, which he did rarely." But a rocky time lay ahead. The rehearsal period was only three weeks. Bernardi hired a cover tenor, really just a stand-in who could merely sing the notes. That was just as well, because the day before he was expected, Vickers called from Bermuda to say he had a terrible cold and vocal problems. Discussions went on for several days, until Bernardi begged him to come because it was essential to work him into the unusual staging. Reluctantly, Vickers flew to Ottawa, where he, Hetti, and four of their children were put up in the lovely home of the center's director general, G. Hamilton Southam. Bernardi recalled: "He said to me, 'Look what you've done. You've got me traveling with a cold, it's bad for me.' And many times, he said, 'I think I better quit. I don't think I can do this.'"[46]

The other major problem was that Vickers had forgotten much of the role since his Met assumption (that translation was by Boris Goldovsky). So every day Bernardi had a coach working with him; as was typical, Vickers re-learned the role extremely rapidly. When orchestra rehearsals began, he was still gruff and congested and wanted everything played very fast. When he got involved in the stage rehearsals, the big turnaround came. "He realized this was tailor-made for his talent. He could be onstage from A to Z." The opera's title could well have been changed to *Herman* for this production, said Bernardi. The conductor thought the role, a half-crazed, tormented man, was in the category that best suited Vickers, like Grimes, and like Sergei in *Lady Macbeth of Mtsensk*. The real Vickers "was a very strict man with himself, terribly religious."

Tyrannical also was a word Bernardi felt applied. "He was not a very good colleague," to the conductor at least. But Vickers seemed to get along well enough with the other singers and with director Kaslik. By the opening date, "we were biting our nails. He was still not very comfortable vocally."

Bernardi's experience was a case study in the kind of tempo problems to which Vickers subjected conductors. The first performance had to go rather fast. "There were long phrases he couldn't cope with, and I had to rush through everything. As the performances went on, about the third one, everything was at the right speed. By the fifth, he had slowed everything down so much that I had to go to him and say, 'Jon, they can't play it so slow now.' All the bowings we had devised were either normal speed or his speed. The moment you start prolonging it, the winds have to take more breath, the strings have to change bowing more frequently." Vickers was totally unsympathetic to those problems. But by then, the production was a stunning success and Vickers was extremely pleased with it all. "The orchestra is the last thing people notice," Bernardi said wryly.

By the end of the run, Bernardi thought, Vickers's voice was "absolutely intact and beautiful," with no sign of any deterioration of age. "Of course, [what he sang] had no bearing on what poor Tchaikovsky had written. [We had to] add a beat to the bar for a big breath. It meant nothing to him, to have a 4/4 piece with a 5/4 bar. But he's not the only singer who does that. There are ways to make it look like it's still a 4/4 bar." Bernardi recalled that his friend Charles Mackerras had once been stopped by Vickers's addressing the pit, saying, "Charles, that has to go faster." Told it wasn't written that way, he said, "Oh, never mind. I want it faster, not slower."[47]

Those types of incidents make it appear that Vickers's often-expressed concern for the wishes of the composer could be somewhat situational.

The night after the opening, Vickers was in Montreal for an Olympics concert at the Place des Arts attended by Queen Elizabeth II. It was unusual for him to sing two nights in a row, but, as he said, "It's just the Beethoven Ninth."[48]

16

The Tannhäuser *Scandal*

Everybody said I lost my nerve. I assure you I didn't.
— Jon Vickers in 1991, on *Tannhäuser*

THE MINNESINGER TANNHÄUSER TARRIED IN THE LUSH REALM OF Venus and took a painful road to Rome. But Vickers was destined for neither journey, and the reason remains a major paradox of his career. He pulled out of a revival planned especially for him in early 1977 at Covent Garden, and at the same time canceled a run at the Met that would have led to the opening night he never had in the New York house.

Rarely does a singer make such a decision on the religious and moral grounds pleaded by Vickers (another religious singer, Jerome Hines, declined a *Faust* staging as pornographic). The way Vickers's decision was made and publicized, Covent Garden's response, the views of other singers, and Vickers's description of the situation in later years—all these factors give insight into the way his mind worked and how he was regarded by the opera world.

The bottom line is that many singers asked about the incident say flatly that Vickers quit because he found the role too difficult to sing. The first-act Venusberg scene requires high notes and agility in abundance. The second-act ensemble is if possible even tougher, with the tenor's vocal line lengthily in the passaggio, from E to A, some of it very exposed (with light orchestra or none at all). There's a *pianissimo* G entrance, a naked G-sharp. Roberta Knie, who knew Vickers's voice well because she sang Isolde with him many times, said it was definitely not an easy range for him. He told her the third-act Rome Narrative would have been no problem, but she doubted he could have gotten past the second act.[1]

But Vickers himself never deviated from his moral pronouncement, never mentioned vocal factors as being a concern.

Was the role in fact too tough for him? He never sang Walther in *Die Meistersinger,* and that part lies high. If difficulty was the problem, why did it take him so long to make his decision? Why did he allow Covent Garden to proceed so far? If his religious explanation is accepted, the same questions may be asked. The score is plain to see, the story plainer to most eyes. Why contract for it in the first place?

If, in fact, Vickers was perfectly accurate about his moral objections and how they grew upon him as he studied the part, this fact should reverberate in his other choices through the years. This is true of his rejections of Britten's *Billy Budd* and *The Rise and Fall of the City of Mahagonny*, the first because he suspected Captain Vere of homosexual desires for Billy, and the work by Weill and the anarchic Brecht because he found it communistic (though he discussed an English version with San Francisco in 1970). But others (including Hetti Vickers) wondered why he sang the evil Nerone and Herod.

Even more interesting is the question of whether Vickers could have deceived himself into believing that he disliked the role on religious or moral grounds alone, when in fact the tessitura was the problem. Known for speaking his mind, and for his insistence on honesty and his publicly voiced hatred of hypocrisy, how could Vickers have dealt emotionally with such a deception? Why might he have found it so difficult to admit there was a vocal problem, perhaps in addition to a moral one? Answers are not easy to come by.

Clearly he was not going to view the knightly singer in the tolerant fashion of the writer Ernest Newman, who noted that the Tannhäuser of legend began to figure as a symbol of moral license in the thirteenth century as a new bourgeois society took hold. The merchants and burghers may have been scandalized not merely by references to wine and women in his songs, said Newman, but also by his reckless pleasure in taking two baths a week.[2]

Perhaps Vickers would have concurred with Victor Gollancz, the music-loving English publisher who wrote in his memoir that the opera had "neither depth to the gravity nor inwardness to the excitement; under the noise there was an absence of genuine life that made the whole thing seem contrived." It was to him typical of a failing in much of Wagner's music: "Something hard, square, or literal. . . . there is no inside to such music: no heart, no spirit. *Tannhäuser* in particular is full of it."[3]

Tannhäuser was among several heroic roles long bruited about for Vickers but which he never took on: Wagner's Walther, Lohengrin, the younger and elder Siegfrieds, and the Emperor in Strauss's *Die Frau ohne Schatten*. All have in common a higher tessitura than Siegmund, which is notably low and which Vickers sang successfully for twenty-five years, or than Tristan and Parsifal. He sang the more lyrical Erik in *Der fliegende Holländer* a few times, but it was not a character to hold his interest.

In 1972 he already had reservations. He told Alan Blyth that he thought of Tannhäuser, Lohengrin, Siegfried, and Walther as German *spinto* parts, and he just did not think of himself as that sort of singer. He thought the elder Siegfried might suit him vocally.[4] But in later years he would say he was never asked for it, and apparently directors and intendants had the idea he wasn't interested—or else they didn't want a Siegfried who could not sing both his characters' *Ring* roles.

As early as September 1974 Vickers's agent, John Coast, sought solid confirmation that Covent Garden would plan *Tannhäuser* for Vickers. Zubin Mehta had said that he would be available in 1977, and the conductor was contracted for the production in January 1975. In December 1974 the Royal Opera House sent rehearsal schedules to Coast for Vickers, with work to begin February 7, 1977. John Tooley, ROH general administrator, said he was startled when Vickers actually signed a contract for the part.[5] And Vickers's Met contract dated July 9, 1976, specified eight *Tannhäuser* performances in 1977–78, as well as five of *Peter Grimes* and four of *Otello*. Vickers would be paid $5,000 for each performance, plus $17,000 in living expenses from November 14, 1977, to February 11, 1978.[6]

Vickers was "torturing over" Tannhäuser with Knie in September 1976, she recalled, when they were doing *Die Walküre* in San Francisco. She thought it odd that he was worried about Tannhäuser when Siegmund was, in Vickers's view, equally problematic morally.[7] Vickers recalled he had the role memorized but for the Rome Narrative and was studying it at home in Bermuda. As he put it in a 1988 lecture, "I learned Tristan in three months. I learned Peter Grimes in twelve days. But I choked on Tannhäuser for thirteen months. I have a profound Christian faith, and I don't apologize for it. . . . Wagner challenged the redemptive work of Jesus Christ. . . . Tannhäuser was despicable . . . brutal, abused Elisabeth . . . and at the end he gets a pat on the head from [the Almighty]."

He recalled: "My wife brought me a cup of tea and it sat there with scum on the top. I didn't touch it. Finally I got up and walked into the kitchen and said, 'Hetti, I hate it!' She said, 'Then you're a fool. People are constantly calling to offer you things you like. Why do this?'" Vickers portrayed this as the moment of decision. He said he immediately called John Tooley at Covent Garden and the Met and told them he would not do the role. "It was an awful blow for John."[8]

In fact, on November 18 he called not Tooley but Coast, whom he rarely if ever mentioned in public. Coast then had the nasty job of informing the two houses.[9] Coast told Tooley it would be the most difficult conversation they had ever had. Vickers had decided "that he cannot sing Tannhäuser on moral grounds." Tooley asked what those were, and Coast said he had best talk to the tenor, who had gone to Vienna. Coast called Richard Rodzinski at the Met the same day (ten minutes after Vickers had called Coast) and told him that Vickers "is a very strong, Old Testament Christian, and although he has the opera three-quarters memorized, he objects to it from a religious and philosophical aspect." Vickers found it "repulsive," called it "a sick opera," and could not accept the attitude toward Rome and the redemption of sins, Coast reported to Rodzinski.

Vickers asked Coast "to pass on to Jimmy [Levine] his sincerest apologies and his willingness to do whatever else Jimmy would want during that time period, be it *Tristan, Troyens,* or whatever else is in his repertoire. Coast added that [Vickers] no longer goes to Bayreuth because he finds that a sick place." Rodzinski asked if the tenor had any such attitude on Parsifal, but Coast said Vickers "found nothing objectionable" about that role, "although he did refuse the Wieland Wagner production, which to him was incompatible with his concepts."[10] In fact Vickers did that production in 1964 at Bayreuth but declined to follow certain of Wieland's stage directions, which may have had to do with the spear in the Good Friday scene.

Vickers shortly after stopped off in London and met with Tooley, who recalled: "Jon said, 'I have now looked at the text of *Tannhäuser* and I have decided that it is blasphemous, and that I, with my God-given voice, cannot utter blasphemy.'" Those were virtually his exact words—"I cannot utter blasphemous words." Tooley was wryly exasperated recalling the conversation in 1990, even amused. Tooley told Vickers that before he had signed the contract, he must have looked at the work.

> "Oh, yes," he said, "but it's only now that I've really come to terms with it."
>
> We then entered upon a discussion lasting an hour, an hour and a half, on all sorts of theological subjects concerning Tannhäuser. One of the things I said was that one interpretation was that Tannhäuser finds salvation through death. "No," said Jon, "remember the penultimate line." The penultimate line refers to Heilige [sainted] Elisabeth. He said, "I have nobody between myself and my Maker. I have no intermediaries." End of story.

The pure Elisabeth does intercede for Tannhäuser with God, and, as Wolfram von Eschenbach sings, Tannhäuser is thus redeemed.

Vickers also told Tooley, "As you know only too well, I've only ever taken on roles which have a moral message to them, or the character plays in a totally moral manner." Tooley said, "Well, look, what about Siegmund?" Vickers brushed that aside. "He said, 'Oh, well, in Siegmund, I've got to stand on the side.' I said, 'But Jon, you can't be serious! Look, you have a child by your sister. It's incestuous love! Are you telling me that this is not an immoral story?' 'Oh, no,' he said, 'I stand on the touchline.' And I said, 'Well, you produced a baby.' Silence [from Vickers]." Tooley laughed as he repeated that the conversation was still vivid in his memory. "He was totally convinced that he was right in rejecting it on moral, religious grounds," at least for himself.

Tooley didn't ask Vickers about the vocal difficulties. "No, no, there was no point. That's hurtful," he said. "One understands that quite often they can't actually say it to you—'I can't do it.' Jon couldn't, and I didn't press him on it. No point. It would hurt him." It seems clear that Tooley, who had great respect for the tenor, believed that Vickers found he could not sing the role.[11]

Neither the ROH nor the Met gave up easily, nor did Coast. Both Richard Cassilly and Spas Wenkoff turned out to be unavailable for the Covent Garden production, so the plan became to press Vickers. Coast's wife and partner, Luce, was to meet with Vickers on November 22 in Vienna, where he was singing Siegmund, Helga Schmidt of the ROH told Rodzinski that same day. "If that fails, Helga and John Tooley will call, and they ask that I call too," Rodzinski reported.[12]

Vickers was at the Bristol Hotel, and Schmidt reported the next day that Mrs. Coast found him "in a positive mood, willing to discuss the matter, not stubborn," with his cancelation "not definite." Vickers's "main reservation," reported via Mrs. Coast, "is that Tannhäuser did not really regret his sins and chooses to return to Venus, which [Vickers] feels make a mockery of the redemption of sin. He is a Protestant, but his main interest is the Old Testament."[13]

It was Rodzinski's turn; he called Vickers on November 24 and the tenor told him he was "totally determined not to do it. He said he had struggled as he was memorizing the role to identify with Tannhäuser but says he always hated it and . . . 'my conscience will not allow me to sing it.'" He said the opera is "anti-art" and "a personification of evil." He noted that on the other hand, *Peter Grimes* was important to him "in its commentary on social justice and other philosophical principles." Rodzinski said he respected Vickers's convictions and the Met would seek another opera for that period. Vickers suggested René Kollo be asked if the Met continued with *Tannhäuser* plans. He stated again that the Met was important to him financially as well as in allowing him to commute to Bermuda. He hoped he could substitute another opera and keep the opening of the 1978–79 season.[14]

The *Tannhäuser* would have been Mehta's Covent Garden debut, and he also worked on Vickers in December, as did Tooley. Coast had gone so far as to suggest that Tooley have a "religious and philosophical expert" present for his meeting with Vickers, "but Tooley thinks he can cope," Coast wrote Rodzinski on November 29.

Finally, on December 6, Schmidt called to say that Vickers had said

"100% no to Tannhäuser" and the ROH would cancel it. That announcement came in January, and on January 24, Vickers called Rodzinski to ask him not to announce his Met cancelation. Rodzinski told him his doing the role had never been announced in the first place.[15] But the plans came out anyway in the news stories.

Terry McEwen recalled that Mehta sent Vickers a telegram reading: "I understand your point of view. You are right. Tannhäuser is immorally high."[16] Mehta could not recall sending any such message.

The ROH announcement to the media on January 7 said Vickers was withdrawing from the opera in which he was scheduled to open February 28. A spokesman said the company was canceling the six *Tannhäuser* performances, and that Vickers would sing instead in March in *Otello*, a staple of his repertoire. Vickers, said the reports, had sent an apologetic telegram to Tooley. And it wasn't revealed that Vickers's appearances in *Tannhäuser* for fall 1977 at the ROH also were off.

Vickers's telegram, as released by the house, read:

> It is with profound regret that I must inform you that I wish to withdraw from the revival of *Tannhäuser*. This decision has not been made easily, any more than was the decision to accept the offer in the first place.
>
> As you know, it has always been essential for me to have a point of personal contact with the personality of each role I portray so that by my identification with the role I can bring the characters to life on stage.
>
> I failed completely to find any point from which to begin. I am therefore convinced of the impossibility for me to interpret *Tannhäuser*.
>
> This decision, I know, is late in arriving, due to the prolonged, intensive study and enormous effort on my part to come to grips with this work. I apologize for the difficulties that this will cause you, but thank you for your cooperation and understanding.[17]

Covent Garden probably would not have conceded so rapidly and, outwardly, as graciously for many singers. News stories referred to Vickers as one of the highest-paid tenors in the world, along with Pavarotti and Domingo, commanding up to seven thousand dollars a night. It is a measure of Vickers's tremendous importance to the house, and his long history there, that the situation was smoothed over so well.

John Cunningham suggested in the *Manchester Guardian* at the time that Vickers simply "bit off more than he cared to sing." He noted that even if there had been "panic and confusion backstage" at Covent Garden, there was a "smooth front," and there was never any question of getting another tenor for the part. Vickers's home base, Cunningham believed, was understanding about the situation—that a major star could have eleventh-hour doubts about a role. He called Vickers's decision "a quite courageous admission: better than a first-night indisposition."[18] If in fact it had been an honest admission, it could be agreed it was courageous.

The American tenor James McCracken took over the Met *Tannhäuser*s in 1977, very successfully, having both high notes and a solid middle range. He later told the author that Vickers "would be hard put to deny me straight in my eyes. . . . He didn't do it because it's the highest dramatic role that Wagner wrote." And Vickers didn't have those notes.[19]

McCracken's cover was Richard Cassilly, a hardworking American tenor the same age as Vickers who never reached the topmost tenor rung. He would take over the fall 1978 opening of *Tannhäuser* when McCracken quit in a dispute about the Met *Otello* telecasts, and he was also to have covered Vickers in the *Tannhäuser* at Covent Garden. Cassilly later expressed bafflement at Covent Garden's handling of Vickers's cancelation, with some bitterness.

He recalled that the chorus had been working on *Tannhäuser* and had to turn quickly to *Otello* just a few weeks before that opening. Vickers went to the first *Otello* rehearsals and the chorus didn't know the music. "He made a big speech [that] he would come back after the chorus learned the music. And he went home, back to Bermuda or wherever the hell he was living. After reading them out." Came the *Otello* opening February 28, "and John Tooley went out in front of the curtain and thanked Jon Vickers for saving the season!" Cassilly said with amusement in his voice. "Why? Please tell me why? He didn't save the season, he made it extremely difficult. And Tooley felt obligated to go out and pin another medal on Jon.

"He told everybody the rules by which he would play, and people have—done it," said Cassilly, laughing shortly.[20]

Cassilly was among the tenors who believed that Vickers found he just could not sing the tricky role; he called Vickers's excuses rubbish. The American sang it many times, with varying degrees of vocal success; he had a serious wobble later in his career. But as Tannhäuser, as in other roles, he was praised for his musicianship, intelligence, and dramatic instincts. He also was among the many singers who tapped the forehead when the Canadian's name came up, to indicate all was not right inside. Then again, Cassilly seems to have been somewhat jealous of Vickers's success.

The baritone Peter Glossop was very close to Vickers but, tellingly, would not discuss the *Tannhäuser*. "I wouldn't ever do something derogatory of a great personal friend," Glossop told the author. But he offered: "It was at a later stage in his career, and Tannhäuser [would have been] the toughest role in the career. . . . Leave it at that."[21]

The bass William Wildermann, a golfing buddy of Vickers's, said bluntly, "We all felt it was strictly beyond him vocally at the time. Tannhäuser is probably one of the most difficult tenor parts ever written, and after trying it for a while, he decided, and that was his excuse, that if he can't identify with something, then he would rather not do it." Wildermann noted that Vickers had said continually of many Wagner parts that he had to wait until he was vocally and physically ready.

Some felt that Vickers was hypocritical in using a moral excuse and blowing it up publicly. Wildermann noted, "He made a big thing out of . . . not being able to identify with the part, but that's his approach to everything . . . that everything he does is done with great thought. . . . Most of us, we just do it, and take a chance." He recalled that Jerome Hines ran into trouble doing his *Walküre* Wotan at Bayreuth. "He nearly died, and he said, 'I'm never going to sing that again.'"[22] Hines said he felt the role would cost him too much vocally in the long run (though he sang it eight times at the Met).

Wildermann sang Sarastro in *Die Zauberflöte* but then decided it was too low for him, and German audiences wouldn't want him in the role. Such singers simply accepted their vocal limitations. But Vickers, in declining various roles, spoke of disliking the characters (as the young Siegfried) or the style (some Italian roles), rather than simply saying they weren't vocally appropriate.

Hines sang Biterolf in a 1941 *Tannhäuser* in San Francisco with Lauritz Melchior, who was outstanding, and the bass recalled Ramón Vinay's postponing a *Tannhäuser* opening because he had such difficulty. "If [Vickers] thought it was a vocal problem, he would have said so. If he said not, then it wasn't. A lot of people don't want to believe [that others] take a stand on moral problems. I was cheering for him," said Hines. "Jon was careful not to bump his nose, like di Stefano doing Calaf, or Birgit, who bumped her nose on Lady Macbeth."[23]

It was only in later years that Vickers said he had rejected *Il Trovatore* and the Emperor in *Die Frau ohne Schatten* because he felt he simply lacked the vocal ability to sing them as they should be sung. "There's a certain self-preservation in all these things," he noted of those decisions.[24]

Recent situations similar to the *Tannhäuser* episode would include those involving Domingo and Pavarotti. When the Spanish tenor got cold feet just weeks before singing *Les Troyens* for the Met's centennial opening in 1983, he made no bones about that fact in the press. He made headlines and sent the

Met scrambling for possible replacements; in the end Domingo transposed a few sections downward.

In 1989 Pavarotti had been scheduled for months to sing *Werther* in Pittsburgh. The previous year he had lost almost one hundred pounds, in part so that he might cut a slimmer figure to portray the romantically suicidal twenty-three-year-old poet. A couple of months before, Pittsburgh suddenly switched its ads to *Tosca*. This may have had more to do with the tenor's not learning *Werther* than with his ability to sing it.

Along with Hines, Dorothy Kirsten supported Vickers's decision. She wrote in her autobiography that she respected him enormously for giving up the role. "When he realized it was not right for him, he had the courage to admit it and made it official."[25]

Longtime Met conductor Walter Taussig said Leo Slezak was the only tenor in his memory who could sing Tannhäuser, and Taussig backed Vickers's decision. "He should not have sung it. He would have ruined his voice! Tannhäuser is much worse than Tristan."[26]

Others remained mystified that one of their number could turn down a major role on moral grounds; morality simply doesn't enter into such decisions for most singers. To them, these are stories, fables, entertainment; to Vickers, opera was "lousy entertainment." To him, the goals of this art were far different.

The answer may lie in part where Franz Kraemer puts it, echoing the writer Peter Conrad. Vickers could never shake the feeling of guilt about being onstage. "He very often said, 'I'd rather be on a farm and use my hands [instead of doing] all this sham stuff.'" Added Kraemer, "And if you don't like being up there, then you want to be sure that the roles you do have real meaning."[27]

James Levine's job at the Met didn't include talking singers into roles, and he wouldn't have wanted to try. "Artists have great difficulty doing what they're not really convinced of," he said. As to whether Vickers's moral grounds were a cover, Levine's analysis was: "It could be. It's a murderous role. But Jon had found his way through a lot of murderous roles. Énée is a murderous role, Tristan is no piece of cake. Otello isn't. And Jon had a set of unique characteristics which would have made what he did with anything he sang fascinating and exciting in many respects, regardless of whatever minor liability there might have been."

But Tannhäuser is unique among the four toughest roles of the Wagner canon, Levine noted, the others being Tristan, the young Siegfried, and Walther von Stolzing. Tannhäuser is an intense fellow, "written at the extreme" almost all through. The first part is strenuous, the second scene is full of top As. The second act has three big scenes, and then in Act 3 comes a complex solo scene, with a low tessitura, just the opposite of the rest of the piece. "And I think it's possible that as Jon worked it, maybe he found some nut he wasn't able to crack. That wouldn't surprise me. But I never asked him. I just accepted that he wasn't going to do it, because he had come up with a basis where it wasn't possible to twist his arm."[28]

Along with Levine, Elijah Moshinky may have the solution closest to the truth of the Tannhäuser puzzle. Moshinsky had been assigned to direct; he and Mehta already had worked on it. Mehta told Moshinsky he foresaw no problem at all with Vickers's handling of the vocal demands, but this might have been wishful thinking because Mehta was eager for his own Covent Garden debut. Moshinsky told the author: "I personally believe the following: It wasn't a question of being able to sing it musically or not. Because he wasn't that sort of artist. I really do think that he couldn't find the psychological knob to hang his performance on. And I think it's the particular kind of contradictory sexuality, which is something he always used to portray brilliantly—no one could do that like he could, longing against . . . purity against danger." But with Tannhäuser, "There was something about the way Wagner wrote it which was indulgent and unpleasant, and it was the fake religiosity of the end that he couldn't do. And I do believe that to be the case."[29]

If one is to conclude that Vickers was not a hypocrite, then one must find substance in Moshinsky's argument. It is probably more rational to believe that both vocal and moral demands played into Vickers's unyielding decision. But the episode remains part of the Vickers legend, for better or worse.

Vickers was absent from the 1976–77 season at the Met. Scheduling there was growing more problematic for him, and more tax issues were threatening. His final San Francisco performances came in 1976, when he was on better terms with Adler after the 1970 *Tristan und Isolde* fiasco. He sang in *Die Walküre*, beginning September 11, and *Peter Grimes*, opening October 9. Roberta Knie was Brünnhilde, Leonie Rysanek Sieglinde; Heather Harper was Ellen and Geraint Evans Captain Balstrode.

On October 26, 1976, Vickers received an honorary doctor of music degree from Brandon University in Brandon, Manitoba, one of the towns he once lived in while working for Woolworth. The speech he gave was described later as an embarrassment by Dr. Lorne Watson, then music dean, who had invited him. Watson called it anti-intellectual, right-wing, and, not to put too fine a point on it, full of what Watson considered ridiculous remarks. "He even dragged in the castrati somehow."[30] This was an example of how Vickers startled audiences for his talks as he veered from music to politics to morality.

The Dallas Civic Opera opened its twentieth season in November 1976 with Vickers in Handel's *Samson,* receiving a fine reception. Vickers sang with strength and subtlety on the unit set that featured rough stone stairs under a brooding sky, with Lotfi Mansouri directing. But thunder also rolled behind the scenes. Conductor Nicola Rescigno wasn't familiar with the work, and, as Mansouri noted, "Handel cadenzas are very difficult and you really have to be with the artist there." Tension thus arose between Vickers and Rescigno.

Mansouri had his own difficulties; he knew by now that working with Vickers meant walking on eggshells because the tenor could be very defensive. Fortunately, diplomacy has been a Mansouri trademark. Issues arose with Vickers about the ballet and about the catafalque for the final scene where Samson lies dead. Vickers objected to the ballet postlude in the scene, choreographed by the Canadian Brian Macdonald. "He said, 'There shouldn't be that much dancing when I'm dead.' Brian walked out," recalled Mansouri.

As to the bier, Mansouri placed it center stage, and knowing that profile is difficult for most bodies, put it on a little rake with Vickers's head upstage, feet downstage. The tenor told the director that a woman friend sitting in the house had said the catafalque was at a bad angle for him. Mansouri suggested equally that the bier could be shifted, "and have your friend stay in the auditorium and tell me which angle she might like."

Patiently, Mansouri had the stagehands change the placement: "I put it sideways and, of course, his tummy showed. I put it on the other side; it was not good. I put it upstage with his feet going up; that was bad. I said, 'Jon, any way you're comfortable, I'll organize it.' Finally, when it just wasn't working, he got kind of upset and he said, 'Goddamn it, you do it the way you want!'" Mansouri went back to the first position, which he had known was right, "but if I had told him that, he wouldn't have bought it."

As to the woman, Mansouri believed it was a romantic interest, although someone else who was in Dallas said it was merely an aggressive Dallas socialite on Vickers's trail. But Mansouri said, "That's why sometimes I had trouble when he was starting to quote the Bible to me. If you believe in certain things, then carry it off in your life." Mansouri saw what he called "Dr. Jekyll and Mr. Hyde" in Vickers. "I felt there were two Jon Vickerses, the one that wanted to be worldly, attractive and dashing, [have] love affairs, [be] Don Giovanni. And the other one who would read the Bible to his kids before every meal." Mansouri believed that most who knew Vickers were aware of this dichotomy. He also felt that this conflictedness added to the tenor's strength as a performer.[31]

Vickers talked in later years about how he created his characters.

> I believe that in the human psyche there are all potentials for good and evil. And the thing that differentiates between the personality of individuals is the balance of those facets of personality. . . . I study the role in a very abstract, objective way, trying to analyze the facets of personality which are the predominant ones that must be brought forward to make the character live on the stage.
>
> Having done that, I turn to the music itself. I do it originally only through the text, then I turn to the music. And because music speaks to me—and it *really* speaks to me—I have to be very careful of my own emotions with music. I surrender my emotions to the music and observe my reactions and say, that's too much, that's too little, that has to be enhanced, that has to be hardened, that has to be softened. And I analyze the role in terms of finding the facets within my own personality that have to be enlarged or diminished, or hardened or softened, so that in a way, I myself sort of die.
>
> And by the time I go on the stage, as soon as the curtain's up, I'm not Jon Vickers. I don't mean that I'm not in control, don't misunderstand that. But the whole character is formed from the inside out. . . . It's probably because I build my characters from the inside out that they have this greater sense of commitment and intensity.[32]

He also talked with a CBC radio interviewer about his roles, saying, "If ever I find that I'm on the stage and for a minute I think I'm Jon Vickers, I'm embarrassed. . . . When I see other performers who go on the stage in one role after the other and they are simply Mr. or Miss X, then I am embarrassed for them too, and I don't want to see them."[33]

The director Elijah Moshinsky's view of Vickers's portrayals was that the tenor "has trained himself to make that entrance into the ego of the character very direct. And that gives a lot of his performances something very uncontrollable. . . . And that is, of course, great interpretation. . . . He also enters the violence of the character, so that you have lots of stories of people who've sung [*Pagliacci*] with him, or *Otello*, where they've said he's become dangerously violent. The point is that in order to be inside the part, he also opens himself up to the psychoses of the part, becomes psychotic with the character. And that's why I say he's a very complex kind of person. Sometimes he [comes] close to madness, because he's developed this ability for complete identification."

Vickers, along with the rest of the cast, had a stormy time with the *Otello* at the Paris Opéra, then led by Rolf Liebermann. Vickers sang five performances in April 1977; he was sandwiched between two runs of the Terry Hands production with Domingo, in 1976 and 1978. Joan Ingpen had a fancy title with the company, *controlleur technique de la programmation artistique:* "I did what I've always done, the plumbing," that dirty personnel work behind the scenes of every house.[34]

Solti was in the pit for Domingo in the first run, but not, of course, for Vickers. Nello Santi led the 1977 and 1978 runs. And Domingo got the TV presentation in July 1978. The American Sherrill Milnes was Iago, and Margaret Price, the highly regarded Welsh soprano, was the Desdemona all through.

As Milnes recalled it, Vickers reached to choke Price so realistically in the final-act rehearsals that she became too frightened of him to wish to continue. "She became more and more nervous with Jon kind of losing himself in the character." Price also had great affection for the Hands production and didn't brook criticism of it. The situation was not helped when, at a rehearsal break, Vickers made what was apparently a musical correction to Price that she felt was inappropriate. One source recalled it concerned the Act 1 love duet. They were standing in the house, with their coats in the seats, and the angry soprano grabbed her purse and swung it over her arm in the air, hitting Vickers in the shoulder, though certainly not hurting him.

Then there was the problem with the French chorus. Vickers got up on a chair and lectured them in English "like a preacher," Milnes recalled. "He said, 'When I do this, you should do that.' They were saying, 'Who is this guy?'" They didn't understand what Vickers was saying and wouldn't have cared about his views if they had.

Milnes had his own problems with Vickers. The tenor would grab the front of Milnes's costume, thereby gripping some of Milnes's chest hair. "I have a moderate amount of hair on my chest, and it would hurt!" Milnes would beg, "Jon, Jon, easy!"

Milnes took on the somewhat amazed look singers often got when talking about Vickers as he described another rehearsal incident. In the second act, Iago tries to soothe the brooding Otello: "I sing, 'Non pensateci piu' [Think no more of it], and I just reached out and [touched his shoulder]. And I don't know if it was Jon or Otello talking. But he said, 'Don't touch me! Don't touch me!' in English but in a rhythm, almost as if it were part of

Otello's lines."[35] Milnes illustrated in a harsh whisper. He seemed affronted that Vickers could not have made his point, to an experienced colleague, with less drama. However, Iago's line comes directly before Otello tells him to stand back and begone, and as Otello moves into the touching "Ora e per sempre addio, sante memorie" (Now and forever farewell, holy memories). Vickers might be excused for concentrating on this most important section.

Finally, Milnes recalled, Price came to the point of saying that it's easier to find a Desdemona than an Otello, and she would leave. As Ingpen recalled the episode, "Margaret came in, in tears, and said Jon had hit her or something. I think he'd got carried away . . . lost control of himself for a bit. She was really scared." Price was still in Ingpen's office at the Palais Garnier when "Jon barged straight in. My assistant outside was quite unable to stop him. Margaret sort of got behind me, and Jon was really playing Moses at that time." Ingpen pointed Price to another exit. "I said to her, get out there. And Jon did actually pick up a chair, ready to throw it at me." Ingpen wondered why nobody came in to rescue her. "I think that's the time I said to Jon, 'Stop behaving like an Old Testament prophet.' And you know, we ended up friends."

She was giving an example of how Vickers's rages tended to blow themselves out. But they could cause turmoil for a production. "He was being very difficult. I think it was really the young man who was staging the production, and Jon didn't like it. But this boy was stuck with being faithful to the one we'd done with Domingo, and with [the way] Jon saw it. So there was a bit of a flare-up. Nobody could quite get at what it was that was bothering Jon."[36]

At a meeting with Liebermann, Ingpen, and Milnes, Vickers sat stonily with his coat and bag at his side. He was ready to leave. "You know Humphrey Bogart in that scene in *The Caine Mutiny*?" said Milnes. "He sits there clicking those balls in his hand. It was like that [with Vickers]. I thought I was seeing a man being destroyed. And Vickers got very Canadian. You know, they have a way of saying 'eh,' and it got so that every other word he said was 'eh.'"[37]

Ingpen recalled, "Jon pointed at me and said, 'I thought this woman was my friend.' He was way out. But I thought afterward that he was unhappy with himself. The artist defense system starts to work. It's everybody else's fault, not their own. Liebermann said, 'Why don't you get away for forty-eight hours,' which was really rather sensible. Jon did, and came back not exactly as a model of easiness, but things calmed down." Price remained.

A group including Ingpen and the young director went for dinner after a performance, probably the last, and Ingpen recalled "on the pavement, about one o'clock in the morning, Jon's saying, 'Well, I'm sorry I was so difficult.' And we said, 'Think nothing of it!'" Herself the wife of an actor, Ingpen laughed at the memory, but added, "You see, you can't perform with the kind of intensity that Jon brings and expect to be quite normal in private life. I really think that's true. They're always more fragile in private life. And Jon sang with more intensity than anybody I know, [except] possibly Julius Patzak," an Austrian tenor who had been an outstanding Florestan at Covent Garden in the early 1960s. "He was quite a different person from Jon, but with the same sort of intensity.

"But Jon brought it to everything. I remember onstage after one of those *Otellos*, saying to Jon, 'You were fabulous,' which he was, you'd got caught up . . . and he said, 'I know I can't sing it like I used to.' But he'd been marvelous." She realized that he had been upset because he couldn't do the part as he wanted. One also might guess he felt Domingo on his heels by 1977.[38]

Insecurity dogged Vickers in a way that few admirers would have imagined. If he wasn't as excellent as he wished to be, he didn't deserve success. If in his own eyes he had failed, he would feel, as he had learned from his father, that he had let his profession down, let his talent down, let God down. As Teresa Stratas said, he always asked 500 percent of himself.

17

From Moose Jaw to Monteverdi

I N JUNE 1977 VICKERS SANG LACA IN JENŮFA AT COVENT GARDEN, DIRECTED by Ande Anderson and conducted by Charles Mackerras, who recalled him as being quite difficult. Vickers's attitude rankled because the conductor was known as an expert on the Czech composer, which Vickers certainly was not. But in the five performances, Vickers was "so marvelous that one could almost (almost!) forgive the outbursts and sulking at the rehearsals, after a very late arrival," Mackerras wrote to the author.[1] Also that June, Vickers was looking ahead to his twenty-fifth anniversary with Covent Garden, in spring 1982. He thought those would be his farewell performances there, and he hoped for a new production of *Samson et Dalila*.

In July Vickers returned to Israel, where he had sung *Samson et Dalila* in 1972, to perform the only two other works he would sing there: Beethoven's Ninth, with Giulini leading the Israel Philharmonic, and seven performances of *Fidelio,* with Mehta conducting. The *Fidelio* cast included Gundula Janowitz and the famed Jewish tenor Misha Raiztin. William Wildermann, who was Rocco the jailer, recalled a warm relationship with Vickers. "We went out golfing every morning at four A.M. because it was the only time you could go, it was so hot. He had his whole family with him there, all his kids." Vickers gave the bass some financial advice at one time, insisting that gold was the only thing to buy. Wildermann was impressed by his certainty, but then lost money on the strategy.

Like Mansouri and some other observers, Wildermann also thought he saw another side to Vickers's personal life. "I've always, through the years of travel, had a feeling that he was on the make for some gal or another or singer. And I always felt that he was a little clumsy about it [with] the women. It was not very smooth, or very suave or very elegant. . . . But I could still sense . . . he would make an effort occasionally." Wildermann never heard of anything coming of such advances, if advances they were.[2]

Vickers, who exuded a warm masculinity (and Dior's Eau Sauvage cologne), would have had as many opportunities with women as any of the big-name tenors whose romantic exploits became public fodder. But he was not interested in the social circuit, rarely going to post-performance parties, except sometimes on the Met tour. Those with whom he formed those deep friendships, which may or may not have been something more, were usually, though not always, colleagues, women who worked onstage or backstage with him. He did struggle with temptation, continually, but whatever transpired, there was never an end to his essential faithfulness to his much-cherished union with Hetti.

Artistically, Wildermann was struck by a Vickers innovation in the *Fidelio* dungeon scene, an action that Wildermann passed on to other tenors in the part. When Vickers had his vision of Leonore and rose in his chains, "He gets up [panting] and goes forward, reaching, reaching, and suddenly he's stopped by the chain, which just got me every time. And he just collapses. Suddenly the chain, the reality, stops him. Leave it to Vickers to think that one out." The trick was that Vickers would ask for the chain to be a length that would halt him just at the right moment in the aria.[3]

Another *Fidelio*, also with Janowitz and Mehta, took place on August 6, 1977 at Orange, France, with Mehta again leading the Israel Philharmonic. The performance was filmed by Pierre Jourdan, whose father was the actor Louis Jourdan. Vickers raised a ruckus during rehearsals, objecting to the staging of the finale, in which the released prisoners were going to lynch the prison guards, which is not in the brotherly and forgiving spirit of the work.[4]

Because of labor trouble at Covent Garden, Vickers was able to accept an offer to tour western Canada. The tour, organized by Margaret Galloway, opened on September 8, 1977, in Moose Jaw, Saskatchewan, a town of about thirty-five thousand some forty miles west of Regina (and where Hetti had once lived). Galloway did it up royally, with the mayor welcoming Vickers onstage. He had sung in these small towns often in the past, but some audiences on the tour weren't aware of their countryman's international career. The Moose Jaw reception, with a standing ovation, sent word circulating of what they might expect.[5]

Hetti didn't accompany her husband. Vickers, who never had an entourage of any kind, insisted he didn't need an aide, but Galloway provided him with one. They began by driving separate cars, but Vickers, who enjoyed being at the wheel as always, soon took over that duty for both.

He got approximately five thousand dollars for each performance, far less than his usual fee, although a few towns paid a little more. And the CBC aired some concerts, so Vickers picked up that fee as well. The dates, which included Regina and Saskatoon, where the local symphony orchestra also took part, were organized so that Vickers could fly back to New York and open the New York Philharmonic season with Act 2 of *Parsifal* under Leinsdorf.

On September 27 he wound up the tour by returning to his hometown for a concert and a tribute, the first major recognition by little Prince Albert of his global accomplishments (as described at the beginning of this book). At the September 28 concert in St. Paul's Presbyterian Church, Vickers wore his Order of Canada medal and was accompanied by the American pianist Peter Schaaf. He dropped Énée's big aria, "Inutiles regrets," from *Les Troyens* from the program, saying, "It's a monstrous thing to sing," and replaced it with the *arioso* from Purcell's *Dido and Aeneas.*

One news story noted that some years before, he had given two concerts in Prince Albert's Orpheum Theatre, and apparently had been so incensed with the quality of the auditorium and piano that he vowed never to return. Ending the tour there may have been a mutual "all is forgiven" signal, but if so, Vickers did not want to talk about it. "He summarily ended an interview without a word upon being asked a 'clear the air' question about his former feelings about his old home," reported a Saskatoon interviewer. "'I do not talk about things like that,' he said, closing his door with vehemence when asked for an explanation of his behavior."[6]

On September 16, 1977, Maria Callas died in Paris. The loss for Vickers was another stroke in the darkening opera picture.

That same month, while in Saskatchewan, Vickers turned down a Covent Garden *Grimes* for the following May because it conflicted with plans for a *Grimes* recording. He then planned four days at home in Bermuda before beginning a May and June 1978 *Tristan* run at the Royal Opera House. John Coast wrote to Covent Garden: "He does not have the type of voice that Windgassen used to have, which can cope with many performances in a week." Vickers therefore wanted to be at his best for the *Grimes* and the *Tristans.*[7]

Vickers did a run of *Peter Grimes* in Chicago in October 1977 with Teresa Kubiak as Ellen. The American soprano June Anderson made her Lyric Opera debut as the Second Niece. She was in her twenties and flattered when Vickers "adopted" her, as she had heard he did with young singers on occasion. They had dinners and talks, and during one full stage rehearsal, Vickers stopped everything and burst into "June Is Busting Out All Over." One night he hoisted the tall blonde Anderson and the First Niece, Winifred Brown, one under each arm, in his usual display of strength.

After the last performance, Vickers told Anderson in a dressing room chat that she was too sweet, not tough enough for a music career (as he seems to have told various women). But her role as Niece had not offered a chance to display the coloratura fireworks for which she would become known. Anderson recalled nothing romantic in Vickers's attentions, although she pleaded possible naiveté. When she sang with him in Chicago in 1985, she found no trace of his previous warmth.[8]

In 1977 the farm in Ontario, which underwent many legal transfers over the years, no doubt for tax purposes, was transferred from Hetti Vickers to her brother, Ian Outerbridge, who had become a prominent Toronto attorney, and his wife, Patricia. In May 1979 they would transfer it to a legal entity, Ontario Limited. But Jon and Hetti continued to spend time there, especially in summer, and the children also visited. Vickers kept some of his acreage that was purely farmland, with no residence, which was the tax issue.

And in the late 1970s Hetti Vickers learned she had breast cancer. Her battle for the next decade would have a profound impact upon her husband's final career choices.

An amazing *Pagliacci* sung by Vickers at the Met on January 2, 1978, became another of the performances upon which his legend is built. "I never heard anything like it before or since," recalled Speight Jenkins, who laid this special intensity to Vickers's still being so furious at McCracken's success with *Tannhäuser* in December.[9]

This Canio was "150 percent terrifying," from his warning in the first scene, "Un tal giaco." When, in the final scene, he began "No, pagliaccio non son," there was total silence in the hall. Vickers reduced his voice at one point, "singing softly while seeming to break down and cry at the agony of it all before he raised it again in a blazingly lyrical flight of rage," Jenkins wrote in his review.[10]

During this aria, Vickers took a swing at a small vase on the little stage used for the commedia scene, sending it flying into the orchestra pit, where it hit a cymbalist on the head and wound up on the bass drum. Later, he picked up a small table and threw it off the mock stage. After the murders, he almost shrieked, "La commedia è finita!" Jenkins recalled, "You saw a man literally turning himself inside out. When Silvio ran at him, I thought the man [Silvio] was dead. If I had been Silvio, I would not have run at him!"

The Nedda was Elena Mauti-Nunziata, who, wrote Jenkins, was full of spitfire intensity. Giuseppe Patanè conducted. "It was superhuman. The crowd went totally crazy," Jenkins added. Leonie Rysanek was there with her husband, and on the way out, Jenkins asked if she had ever heard anything like it. "She said, 'He won't sing any more this week. No one can sing like that and sing again.' He had literally oversung even himself."[11] Rysanek also told the author that Vickers had gone over the edge a little that night. "He was so emotional, so violent, so furious onstage, much too much. I told my husband, I bet he won't sing the next performance. And he didn't."[12] Ermanno Mauro took over on January 6 and 11.

This is the kind of performance that certainly can't be learned or planned. It displayed a risk-taking little seen on today's opera stages, possible only for the deeply individualistic artist Vickers exemplified.

One of Vickers's most remarkable departures from his usual repertoire was a delicious collaboration in March 1978 at the Paris Opéra, in Monteverdi's *L'Incoronazione di Poppea,* with Rolf Liebermann masterminding a sensuous production. Julius Rudel presided over the equally lush, though controversial, orchestration that Raymond Leppard had created in 1962 in Glyndebourne. Liebermann was fully aware of other and more "authentic" versions, but he "sacrificed musicology for dramatic expression," he wrote. How can one believe, he said, in the forceful desires, the brutality, the sheer excess of Nerone, if he is sung by a "hybrid being," a mezzo soprano or countertenor whose artificial range obscures the ruler's virility? Liebermann compared Nerone and Poppea to Tristan and Isolde, and he wanted a couple with heft, both vocally and in personality.[13]

"What a cast!" said Joan Ingpen, at the time on Liebermann's staff at the Paris Opéra. Gwyneth Jones, Vickers, and Christa Ludwig as Ottavia were joined by Jocelyne Taillon, Valerie Masterson, Nicolai Ghiaurov, and Michel Sénéchal.[14]

Nerone is the epitome of evil, an insane dictator who exiles his wife and commands his tutor's death to satisfy his lust for Poppea. But this was a moral tale to Vickers. He could not stomach Tannhäuser, whom he saw as spiritually rotten, but he had no qualms about giving us portraits of unredeemed evil. He could say of Nerone, as of Herod: Regard the abyss, and learn from the ruin that such behavior brings. Here, however, the paradoxical Vickers shows himself once again. Nerone is not punished for his sins; the end of the opera is a joyous celebration as Poppea joins her mate on the throne. This is difficult to square with Vickers's rejection of Tannhäuser. It is closer to his view of Siegmund, a role he sang despite often-expressed reservations about that hero's incestuous love.

Nerone was Vickers's most overtly sexual role, more so than Herod, who yearns for his wife's daughter. Nerone wallows in the fleshly delights of his future empress. Liebermann showed it all, and Vickers really let himself go. The love scenes with the alluring Jones, on view in the video version taped on April 22, are erotically beautiful. For once, Vickers is not a man flagellating himself for his desires or for his trafficking with a faithless lover. He is flat-out reveling in lust, and if anything Vickers adds too romantic a tinge to his duets with Jones.

As viewed on tape, his half-naked chest gleams with sweat. He rests his head on Jones's belly as she sings of the apples of her breasts, and he insists those breasts, "le mamme tue," deserve sweeter names. He had no problems with the sexual scenes, Jones said. "I had the feeling he quite enjoyed it. We both did." And "I never for one moment had any complaints from Jon, [nothing to suggest] he thought it was immoral. We were lying on a bear rug, and I had a little red chiffon over me and that's it. He has wonderful music, about caressing my apples, which he was doing, so sensual. This is what drove the Parisiennes out of their minds. I've never seen so many binoculars looking out" from the audience, she recalled.

Jones spoke highly of Vickers as a colleague: "He gave you such a feeling of security. He always came to my dressing room before a performance. He would say, 'Now, how is my leading lady, the most important thing for me is that you are feeling happy and comfortable.' You felt he loved you, and I loved him. It was such a warm relationship. Not any funny business, but he was just such a wonderful person."[15]

Rudel wanted to do the piece so badly that although he was constantly busy at New York City Opera, which he had run for twenty-one years (till 1979), he gave in to Liebermann's pleadings. The conductor made sixteen Atlantic crossings in three weeks to accomplish his task (he also did the 1979 run). "I will never forget the first rehearsal," he said. "Vickers and Sénéchal, who is no slouch, started the duet in the second act. And Vickers . . . sang rings around Sénéchal, who sat there getting greener and greener in the face as Vickers just ran through these coloraturas in an incredible fashion." Yes, Vickers was occasionally "a little cantankerous, as he tends to be. But he and I were able to get along very well."

Once when Rudel returned from one of his New York trips, Vickers had changed something in a recitative. Rudel mentioned it and Vickers "went into a tirade about, well, I wasn't here, and he decided with the stage director that he wanted to do it that way and now I'm going to have to accept it. And he went on about my absence, which had been agreed upon." Richard Stilwell, the Ottone, told Rudel that Vickers had said afterwards, "Do you think I was too rough on him?" This showed, Rudel felt, that Vickers sometimes had second thoughts about his outbursts.[16]

Poppea opened on March 17, 1978, for ten performances. The taped version aired on TV on July 6.

"Jon Vickers has the firm lower register that a tenor needs in this octave transposition and was a superbly authoritative Nero; massively masculine with his physical lust for Poppea very evident, by turns hysterical and imperious. Completely egocentric in his raging scene with Seneca and no more so than when in imposing Wagnerian voice, he orders [Seneca's] suicide. His bacchanalian revel with Lucan (Michel Sénéchal) to celebrate Seneca's liquidation found the two men intertwining their bodies and finally Nero carolling [*sic*] across the stage on stilts. It was certainly coarse," wrote an approving Charles Pitt.[17]

Vickers was "a mighty Nerone, a far cry from the 'high castrato' Monteverdi wrote for," noted an October 1988 *Opera News* article on the composer. "This version, with large orchestra and full-volumed singing, may displease early-music buffs, but it certainly communicates the excitement of the piece. Vickers's drunk scene is at once comic and terrifying, surely what the composer intended. The love duets sizzle, unlike some anemic 'authentic' performances."[18] Liebermann would certainly have agreed.

Peter Hall's *Tristan und Isolde* production was revived at Covent Garden in May and June of 1978 by Elijah Moshinsky, with Colin Davis conducting. Roberta Knie was Isolde, with Vickers, Josephine Veasey as Brangäne, Donald McIntyre as Kurwenal, and Gwynne Howell as King Marke. Vickers was in superb voice, wrote the critic Elizabeth Forbes. "He attacked the role with an intensity that in the last act reached the superhuman." Knie was "equally heroic."[19]

However, Vickers could not complete the opera in the fourth performance of June 7. He told Knie he had hay fever. Howell recalled the Vickers wasn't in good voice but told Davis he'd do his best. Intervals were lengthy, and after the second act it was decided that Vickers wouldn't sing the third act. "He said he had to preserve his voice for the next performance," Howell recalled. Everybody agreed, so strong was Vickers's persuasiveness; as Howell said, "Absolutely right, definitely, Jon!" Vickers left the theater and the third act proceeded, with an extra as the dying Tristan, but none of his music, the act simply beginning with Isolde's entrance.

Howell added, "The thing was, we discovered the next day or day after that Jon had gone straight to the airport and jumped on the plane to Bermuda, and somebody else [Spas Wenkoff] sang the last performance. 'Cause Jon had had it. Sometimes singers have had it. . . . But for me as a young singer, it was interesting to see what people could do and get away with, or manipulate to suit them and protect themselves."[20]

In June 1978 Vickers contracted for Puccini's *La Fanciulla del West* at Covent Garden in March 1980, but it never came to pass. That July, Paul

Garner, an aide to Plácido Domingo, called the Met to say the Spaniard was "terribly upset" that the Met would televise Vickers's *Otello* in the coming season. Domingo feared that his own Moor would not then be televised the following year. The Met's Richard Rodzinski soothed Garner, saying that in no way would the Vickers airing affect Domingo's.[21]

James McCracken had been the substitute choice for *Tannhäuser* to open the Met in fall 1978, but he was furious that he wasn't included in the season's four telecasts. He quit the *Tannhäuser* and all his twenty-eight scheduled season performances in that opera, *Carmen*, and *Aida*.

Vickers teamed with soprano Jessye Norman for the first time on August 12, 1978, at Tanglewood, for the first act of *Die Walküre*, with Seiji Ozawa leading the Boston Symphony Orchestra. Howell sang Hunding. Norman had sung Sieglinde earlier in the orchestra's winter season. It was Vickers's first summer performance with the BSO, and some Boston observers were skeptical that he was actually giving up some of his cherished summer for it. But the evening was a triumph, with a ten-minute ovation from the crowd of almost eight thousand for the BSO and for the two powerful voices that blended rapturously in their love duet.

The *Boston Globe*'s Richard Dyer noted that Vickers sounded rougher than in the past, "and he is not above resorting to pure showbiz." When he cried "Wälse," on that long sustained high note he rotated 180 degrees in his white jacket "to give everyone in the audience a piece of the action." This was true heroic singing, Dyer noted, "yet it was also singing of the greatest variety and emotional depth, and that is something equally rare and wonderful."[22] And that roughness simply added character to the tenor's uniquely expressive voice. This observation by Dyer became more and more true for admirers of the tenor in the final decade of his career.

That summer Vickers indulged his love of driving, taking his family on a cross-country tour in a motor home, from Mount Kisco, New York, to Vancouver Island. He had never before had a chance to show his children his native Canadian west.

In the fall of 1978, the Met was a stressful place for Vickers, as the house echoed with musical choices he had made. The September 18 opening night was *Tannhäuser*, with Cassilly replacing McCracken in the title role Vickers had rejected (Jess Thomas also sang some performances). *Billy Budd* went on the next night, with Peter Pears as Captain Vere, another role about which Vickers was conflicted. James King was singing *Fidelio*. Vickers's run of five *Otello*s began September 21, with Renata Scotto and Cornell Mac-Neil, under James Levine, with the live telecast September 25. His emotional investment was heavy as always. The challenger, Domingo, was in the house for *Werther;* the Spaniard's Moor had continued to grow in stature in the three years he had sung the part.

Around this time, Vickers had decided to retire from the stage. It was apparently in 1978 that he flew his family to New York to see what he thought would be his final Otellos. He was fifty-two and had always spoken firmly of singing no later than age fifty, or fifty-five at most. But three weeks later the family was at lunch in Bermuda and son Kenneth blurted out, "Dad, there's no way you're quitting." In the vernacular of his generation, he said, "It's a cop-out," meaning that Vickers would be turning his back on his still considerable resources. Vickers recalled: "Everything I had tried to teach the children about personal responsibility and the necessity of continuing to do your best in all circumstances had been so firmly implanted in them that I was getting it quoted back at me."[23]

Instead, he decided that 1983 would be his retirement year. He recognized the danger of outstaying one's vocal powers, a temptation to which many singers succumb. He felt that Melchior and Martinelli had made this mistake.[24] But Vickers never regretted staying on. He said later, "I'm very glad I did because probably the greatest reward of my career, in artistic terms, is that I went through a period when they said, 'Can he sing it? He's fifty now, fifty-two, how much longer are you going to last? Will he sell tickets if they hire him?' Then all of a sudden, oh, I was a living legend, I was the standard by which every tenor had to be judged." When that kind of talk began, he quipped, "I said, boy, now I know I'm finished!"[25]

As he sang his fall *Otello*s, the tenor was preparing for a most unusual role, that of the stuttering Vašek in the Met's new production of Smetana's *The Bartered Bride,* in English, with Gedda and the tiny, volatile Stratas, opening October 25, conducted by Levine. The live telecast was November 21. Vickers himself had mixed feelings about the role, but this was one of the few in which he had an opportunity to display humor. Audiences may not have appreciated this because they so identified him with the serious, heroic roles. Critics didn't seem to value it (one review of his Boston *Cellini* said he didn't have a light touch). His Nerone had moments of drunken comedy, but humor, like joy, was rare for him onstage. Florestan found joy, and Parsifal a spiritual ecstacy, but Vickers's stage persona largely was somber.

The Boston critic Richard Dyer suggested that Vickers sang Vašek just for fun. "There wasn't really anything for him in it, but it was enjoyable. It wasn't a character at all, but it was Jon Vickers having fun, which is why you went to see it."[26] But Vickers said of Vašek, "I'm going to make you weep for him," to bring out the young man's simple humanity.[27]

Opera summed up the performance:

> And what is one to say of the casting of Jon Vickers as the stuttering Vašek? Although he is far too mature, he is certainly impressive—to the point of dominating each scene in which he appears, and making Vašek into a focal presence, which he is not—and certainly that good-natured simplicity which is so much a part of Vickers' being, and which makes him the only believable Parsifal today, is perfectly in tune with the amiable oafishness of Vašek.
>
> But the very size of the voice, and the overwhelming strength of his stage presence, upsets the balance of the piece. About the only thing that can be said, apart from an expression of wonder, is that never again will we see a Grimes, a Tristan, Otello and Aeneas emerge from a bear costume.[28]

The conductor Julius Rudel had a thought on such roles concerning two other major tenors of the time. Pavarotti didn't mind playing the clown, as with his Nemorino, but Domingo never could, Rudel posited. "He's concerned about his image as the hero so much that he doesn't let himself really go. That gives him a little wall that is not quite breached."[29] It's certainly hard to imagine Domingo playing the Witch in *Hänsel und Gretel*, which Vickers wanted to do. Anthony Laciura, a wonderful character tenor at the Met and Santa Fe Opera, recalled that once in a chat Vickers said he'd enjoy doing Siegmund one night, the Witch the next. But Bing never agreed to this idea.[30]

In February 1979, seemingly stimulated by doing Vašek and Nerone, Vickers was "still in the mood to break new ground," Coast wrote to Ingpen at the Met. "His mind is still very wide open for a right new role." Coast noted the *Fanciulla* scheduling and said that *Idomeneo* was possible, "though I am quite sure he wouldn't want to follow any other tenor in *Idomeneo*."[31]

That January and February, Vickers sang another run of *Poppea* in Paris, with seven performances and basically the same cast as in 1978. Hetti was with him in Paris, and toward the end of the run they flew to London, where Vickers received the prestigious Evening Standard Opera Award. It was given for his Tristans of 1978. By this time Hetti had had several operations for her cancer and was hoping for the best.

Vickers fitted in three performances of *Samson et Dalila* in March at the then Greater Miami Opera, with Emerson Buckley conducting, occasionally lecturing the cast on the opera's story.[32]

Vickers sang his last Met *Otello*s on tour, in spring 1979, in Cleveland, Minneapolis, Detroit, Philadelphia, and finally the outdoor setting of Wolf Trap Farm Park in Vienna, Virginia. (He also did *Parsifal* and *The Bartered Bride* on the tour.) His final *Otello*s, outside the United States, were yet to come, in 1984. But Domingo would open the 1979–80 Met season as the Moor, on September 24. Vickers was at Covent Garden for a run of nine *Pagliacci*s that June and July.

At the 1979 Guelph Spring Festival, Vickers sang for the first time the challenging Schubert song cycle *Die Winterreise,* from the Schiller poem about a forlorn lover. The critics would have much to say about his idiosyncratic interpretation as he refined it into the next decade.

The New York pianist Peter Schaaf accompanied him at Guelph, and he was coached by Nicholas Goldschmidt, the festival's artistic director, who had urged him to take it up. "One wondered whether any other singer ever managed to get as much of the musical variety into an initial skirmish with the score," said John Kraglund.[33] Jacob Siskind found it "still in the formative stages" and criticized "Vickers' too careful planning of the interpretation that left me totally uninvolved."[34]

John Diefenbaker, the Canadian prime minister and Vickers's friend from Prince Albert, died on August 16, 1979. At the state funeral in Ottawa on August 19, Vickers donned a choir robe to sing "Then shall the righteous shine forth," from Mendelssohn's *Elijah.* He held the music well out in front of him, apparently having forgotten his glasses.

In September 1979 came a major Covent Garden tour of Korea and Japan, the company's first in the Far East, with Vickers singing *Peter Grimes* in seven performances. Hetti and daughter Wendy joined him. It was an enjoyable trip for all, and the *Grimes*es were often electric performances.

Vickers had made his first appearance at the Houston Grand Opera in 1964 in *Un Ballo in Maschera.* But the experience of David Gockley, the highly respected HGO general director from 1972, dates from Vickers's 1979 *Otello.* Gockley also hired Vickers for *Pagliacci* in 1982 and two *Grimes* runs, in 1977 and 1983. Vickers was signed for *The Queen of Spades* in 1982 but had to withdraw after the dress rehearsal because of illness.

"I think he was always very pleasant here, very professional, as long as everything revolved around his interpretation," said Gockley in a 1989 interview. "Both times with the *Peter Grimes,* we put him with somebody we knew was going to play ball with him, Ande Anderson," Vickers's longtime Royal Opera House associate.

"One had to play to his ego all the time," added Gockley, recalling the plans for *Pagliacci*. Gockley wanted Jean-Pierre Ponnelle to stage it, but Ponnelle expressed doubts about working with Vickers. "So I got them to meet in France, and they talked and everything was hunky-dory, and they came here and worked for two and a half weeks, seriously, and there was a tremendous mutual respect. I think Ponnelle knew where to give, where to take—and where to take advantage of [Vickers's] strong and dangerous personality. The result was one of the most vivid and theatrically awesome stagings that we ever offered."

Pressed about the Vickers temperament, Gockley said, "He basically had very strong opinions about the way things should be done, and he was fairly intolerant about most everybody else's opinion. And you were on good terms with him so long as you basically agreed with him—or feigned agreement. He has very strong political and religious, and social opinions, and he would preach if given half the opportunity at a party or a social occasion."

But Gockley believed Vickers's opinionated nature played favorably into his dramatic portrayals, "because they were such absolutely single-minded interpretations, passionate and believed-in. It's almost as though he stepped into a belief system of the character—or, and this is probably more correct, he bent the character into his belief system, and to the extent that he could do that, he gave absolutely unequaled portrayals."

Gockley wanted Vickers to sing Herod in *Salome* but felt he could not meet Vickers's price of fifteen thousand dollars per night. Despite his admiration for the tenor, Gockley said this singer was not a box office draw for HGO.[35]

Vickers took part in an October 14, 1979, gala at Chicago Lyric Opera, with Mirella Freni, Leontyne Price, Margaret Price, Tito Gobbi, Sherrill Milnes, José Carreras, Luciano Pavarotti, and Plácido Domingo among the stars. Pavarotti said later, "You know what I remember that night? It was Vickers. He sang so beautifully, it touched me. It moved me to cry."[36]

In November and December in Chicago, Vickers sang seven *Tristan*s, with Franz-Paul Decker conducting. Roberta Knie was Isolde, with Mignon Dunn as Brangäne, Hans Sotin as King Marke, and Siegmund Nimsgern as Kurwenal. The Melot was Richard Versalle, the tenor whose fate it would be to drop dead of a heart attack onstage at the beginning of a Met *Makropoulos Case* in 1996. He had studied Vickers's Grimes in Chicago.

In this period, Knie recalled yet another Vickers furor that blew itself out but upset all concerned. Ardis Krainik sent a car to Knie's hotel after calling to beg her help with Vickers, who was in a rage at an Act 3 rehearsal. Knie found him "yelling, pacing back and forth. He was just livid. They said he was angry that the rehearsal pianist couldn't play" the music. Knie walked up behind him, "put my hands on his shoulders, and said, 'Jon, Jon'—and he turned around and hit me in the belly! Fortunately I saw it coming. . . . It's the only time he ever hurt me physically. He didn't know who I was, he was just in a rage."

Knie held him and shook him and asked what the problem was. "He started on this tirade about the quality of the opera houses." Knie explained, as she'd been told, that the assigned pianist had mashed his hand in a car door and that another pianist was trying desperately to sight-read.

Vickers shouted, "Well, why didn't somebody tell me!" Of course, they had tried to. "He said, 'Let's go to lunch,' and that was the end of that."[37] It was another case of Vickers being so caught up in his own concerns that, almost literally, he could see nothing else.

The 1970s were ending for Vickers, but the next decade held much for the tenor and his listeners: the last master portraits of Otello, Tristan, Grimes, Parsifal, and a Handel *Samson* memorable in many ways. But there would be another frustrating situation in Canada.

PART

5

THE 1980s

Winding Down

Tonight I bought a cow.
—*Jon Vickers*

18

A Winter's Journey

A GROUP OF STARCHY WHITE HOUSE STAFFERS CHECKED OUT THE Metropolitan Opera house before an early 1980s visit by the American First Lady, Nancy Reagan. They ate in the Met cafeteria with Fred Plotkin, house manager, and Johanna Fiedler, press director. "A fellow in a lumberjack shirt, suspenders, jeans, and boots comes up to the table and pulls out a chair, saying, 'Is this taken?' He sat down with the startled White House people, who looked down their noses at this crude intruder," Plotkin recalled. He said, "Hello, honey," to Fiedler and told the others, "I'm Jon." Finally, one of the baffled visitors asked, "Do you work here?" "I help out," he said. Plotkin introduced Vickers as one of the world's greatest tenors. "Oh, not *one*," Vickers responded.[1]

But the big box office names were now a Spaniard and an Italian. Domingo continued to gobble up roles; he wanted to do *Pique Dame* at the Met in 1981; Vickers had sung it there in 1965–66 and in 1967. It seems he wasn't asked about 1981, although it was still in his repertoire. Levine, however, said, "It would surprise me if there was something Jon wanted that we weren't offering." They always had good communication on the matter of roles.[2] In any event, a union-management dispute at the Met killed the first three months of the season, and the Met determined that a new *Traviata* was a better choice for Domingo than the gloomy Russian piece.

Vickers might have done more *Aidas* (he had sung only two, in 1961), but the Met was hoping for a new Zeffirelli production, no doubt with Domingo. Said Joan Ingpen of Vickers's waning years at the Met: "One has to face the fact, if he's a tenor, that Pláci and Luciano were the two big draws in the Met, for gala evenings. I mean, Jon was ten times the artist that Luciano is, but not in the same popular repertoire."[3]

But in 1980 at the Met he did a run of *Fidelios*, under Leinsdorf and with Hildegard Behrens, in January and February. He was scheduled for Dick Johnson in *Fanciulla* at Covent Garden in April but canceled because of what the ROH listed as a "persistent throat infection." And so we missed seeing him striding in cowboy boots; he never did sing that role anywhere.

Vickers sang *Die Winterreise* at the 1980 Maggio Musicale in Florence, and that summer he appeared twice at Tanglewood, singing *Winterreise* with Gilbert Kalish on June 29, and in concert with the BSO on July 4. He arrived for the festival in a recreational vehicle with several family members. The night of the *Winterreise* was rainy, with occasional thunder rolls, and when Vickers arrived onstage he called the audience heroes for attending in the open-air concert shed.

Donal Henahan was critical of his Schubert effort: "He is not one of the day's great vocal technicians and these 24 stark and deceptively plain songs made the unevenness of his production more evident than it sometimes is in the opera house. The sudden barks and lapses into crooning, which have long disfigured his voice at stressful moments, often came at inappropriate times in the Schubert narrative. He was best in the slower, heavily treading pieces." But, Henahan noted, the challenge is more interpretative than vocal, and "Mr. Vickers, guided by his pianist's restraint and avoidance of sentimentality, had a plausible road map for this journey and followed it thoughtfully. Even when one could not completely respond to the singer's broadly anguished conception, his dignity could be appreciated. A little too often, even so, his theatrical instincts got the better of him and a harsh outburst of sound would result."[4]

Andrew Porter took the occasion for a longer and most interesting summation of the previous two decades of Vickers's career that began, "Jon Vickers is not a subtle interpreter." He also wrote of unevenness, adding, "That for this music Vickers would seek to restrain his natural violence of expression was predictable. That he restrained it to a point where much of the singing proved—well, dull is too hard a word, so let us say ordinary—that was disappointing. I didn't think Vickers could be ordinary. I am not sure that the narrator of Winterreise does have a dramatic personality with which a singer can 'identify.'" The suggestion is that if Vickers finds identification essential, this in part may have caused a lack of success with the cycle.[5]

For the July 4 Tanglewood concert, Vickers gave a rare performance of "Ah, si ben mio" from *Il Trovatore*, an opera he never sang in entirety, followed by "Niun mi tema," from Otello's death scene. This was followed by Verdi's *Hymn of the Nations*, with Vickers as soloist and the Tanglewood Festival Chorus.

Richard Dyer was disappointed that Vickers didn't do the cabaletta from the *Trovatore* aria, and while he admired the splendor of the tenor's tone, he could not admire "the way he pulled the rhythm around and bellowed his way past all the expressive graces noted in the score." Dyer felt "Di quella pira" should have suitably followed, although he must have known that Vickers never had essayed that high-C aria and was not about to begin in 1980. The *Otello* section was done with Vickers's usual power and tragic dignity, but as Dyer noted, this music doesn't make its full impact out of context. Since Vickers appeared so infrequently, Dyer felt "it is a crime that the BSO did not present him in something suitable that he alone is equipped to sing."[6] But the tenor did manage the *Hymn* solo with unrivaled fervency, although Dyer later recalled that it had to be transposed down for Vickers. Chorus conductor John Oliver could not confirm this.

Vickers was asked yet again to the Canadian Opera Company for fall 1980, to sing *Peter Grimes* in the staged Canadian premiere of the opera. He declined as usual, and William Neill sang the role (Neill was to become the teacher of the acclaimed Canadian tenor Ben Heppner). Lotfi Mansouri, then COC chief, recalled the six performances had a more than 85 percent attendance. But Vickers's refusal was upsetting for Mansouri, who had felt that the tenor's prestige would have been beneficial. He recalled a bit grimly that in spring 1984, when the Met took *Grimes* with Vickers to Toronto, also at the O'Keefe, it was far from a full house.[7]

Arthur Vickers, the younger brother of Jon, was killed on September 16, 1980, in a crash on the TransCanada Highway, between Kamloops, British Columbia, and Calgary, where he taught high school. A University of Calgary graduate, he was forty-eight and the father of three children. Arthur also had been working as a transport truck driver to make more money for his family. Jon went to the service at a Calgary funeral home but did not sing a solo, telling Arthur's widow, Lillian, that he didn't want to distract from Arthur.[8] But all were aware of his presence as his voice rose above the rest in the hymns. This left Jon with six living siblings.

In November 1980 he was at Covent Garden for seven *Otello*s, led by Davis, with Teresa Zylis-Gara and Renato Bruson. And newer faces had moved into the Royal Opera House, with the flashy German tenor Peter Hofmann singing Siegmund. Albert Remedios took both Siegfrieds in the *Ring*, also with Davis. José Carreras was Edgardo in *Lucia di Lammermoor*, and Domingo starred in *Les Contes d'Hoffmann*.

The Met's 1980–81 season was disrupted by a labor dispute, and casualties included the planned fall opening, *Turandot* with Caballé and Pavarotti, and the new *Pique Dame* planned for Domingo. *Lulu* began December 12, with Stratas; there was a *Tristan* beginning in January, with Spas Wenkoff partnering Gwyneth Jones. *Mahagonny* came in March, but Cassilly was the lumberjack singing with Stratas, not Vickers, who disliked the political implications of the piece. Cassilly also took the *Samson et Dalila* that season.

The rescheduling included several concerts, and Vickers sang in one of the Met's two Wagner programs in April, his only appearance that season. On April 11 he did *Parsifal*, Act 2, and, with Nilsson, "O sink' hernieder" from *Tristan*, Act 2.

With the beginning of the 1981–82 season, Anthony A. Bliss became general manager. Levine remained as music director and principal conductor and exerted much more influence in artistic decisions. Vickers would not be back at the house until fall 1983.

Vickers sang seven performances of *Peter Grimes* at the Paris Opéra in January and February 1981, under John Pritchard's baton, in the Covent Garden production staged by Elijah Moshinsky. Patricia Wells was Ellen Orford, Benjamin Luxon Balstrode. His colleagues from *Poppea*, Jocelyne Taillon and Michel Sénéchal, turned up as Mrs. Sedley and the Rector. And the young baritone Gino Quilico, a son of Louis Quilico, was Ned Keene.

Grimes was back at Covent Garden for six performances in June and July 1981. With Vickers finally settling with the BBC-TV that June, it was broadcast on June 30, and the production was taped for a video.

August found the tenor in an odd *Tristan* in Rio de Janeiro, his only appearance there, singing with an Isolde (Janice Yoes) in identical silver tunics. The five performances beginning August 16 were his last work with a member of the Wagner family. Wolf-Siegfried Wagner, the son of Wolfgang, directed, and Franz-Paul Decker conducted. Roberta Knie, then Vickers's Isolde of choice, had flown down but had to drop out after a vocal problem arose in rehearsal. Ruth Hesse was Brangäne, and Thomas Stewart was Kurwenal.

The Royal Opera opened a new production of *Samson et Dalila* on September 29; it hadn't been seen on that stage since 1928. Shirley Verrett was Samson's betrayer in a staging by Moshinsky. Another run was to be repeated in 1982. Vickers wore a full-length, roughly woven robe and a wig that fell past his shoulders. He lay on his back as Verrett seduced him. (The production has been available on a commercial video.)

In an interview in London, Vickers, then almost fifty-five, was asked, as happened frequently, when he would sing *Les Troyens* again. He said: "It's a great sadness to me that it's kicked around now in the press that I've dropped these roles from my repertoire. The truth of the matter is that I've dropped nothing from my repertoire, in terms of Otello, Tristan or Aeneas. But the truth of the matter is also that they don't ask me. They just don't do it!"[9] In fact, he never would sing Énée again, sad indeed for the many who never had the opportunity to see him in the part. The Davis recording remains a landmark, but there is no film of Vickers in the role, though one had been talked of in 1971.

From London he was off to do the United Nations Day celebration on October 24, repeating it in Washington, D.C., with Orquesta Filharmonica de la Ciudad de Mexico, Fernando Lozano conducting. Vickers and Scotto sang the *Otello* love duet, and Vickers did the "Winterstürme." And in November 1981 Vickers was in Chicago for *Fidelio* with Johanna Meier and Eva Marton as his Leonores.

That December another tenor proved again that Vickers wasn't the only singer to raise issues of principle. René Kollo was locked in combat with director Giorgio Strehler over La Scala's season-opening *Lohengrin*. Kollo didn't like his heavy armor and helmet, but he also let the media know he opposed Strehler's concept of the hero as a political warrior instead of a Christian knight. He left Milan, returned to sing the premiere (after his costume was changed) when no replacement could be found, but departed after one performance.[10]

With his Grimes preserved for posterity, his twenty-fifth anniversary with the Royal Opera House coming up, and his knees giving him arthritic pain, Vickers was looking ahead to retirement. But he also had in mind more work on *Die Winterreise*, which would display his special talents, if idiosyncratically.

Vickers was still in demand in Paris as well as London, even as he wondered how many years he would continue and found some roles becoming more of a strain. Beginning February 27, 1982, he sang a run of nine *Fidelios* at the Paris Opéra. In April and May he sang seven Canios and six Tristans at the ROH. The April 27 *Pagliacci* fell on the twenty-fifth anniversary of his Covent Garden house debut, and he was honored on May 27 with an ROH lunch. John Tooley, Harold Rosenthal, the editor of *Opera* magazine, the critic David Cairns, Mrs. John Coast, the arts minister, and Hetti and their son Ken Vickers were among the guests.

This Canio was "as anguished and naturalistic as it always has been," Alan Blyth reported in *Opera* of the April 8 performance, and Vickers was in superb voice. He "is able to arouse compassion as much by the position of his shoulders as by the expansive thrill of his overwhelmingly intense tones; what other tenor would dare sing Vesti la giubba almost with his back to the audience?" Vickers "was free with his music, straining rapport with the conductor, James Conlon, in 'No, pagliaccio non son.'"[11]

But Conlon said later the performances went well, and as far as he knew nothing was wrong to make Vickers as sullen as he was about the usual twenty-fifth anniversary presentation made onstage after the April 27 performance. Conlon described Vickers's unhappy response to the house's recognition of the date, and it's a revealing story with an odd coda.

Vickers "was not having any of it. He was, for whatever reason, angry. It had to do with his feelings about Covent Garden and the administration, nothing to do with the performance," Conlon recalled. "He had told them not to come onstage and do this, but there they were." Conlon was taking his bow when the curtain opened and out came John Tooley. "I looked over at [Vickers] during the speech. He had on a grim smile that looked like the cyanide smile. He made some very short statement, something to do with a dentist, and a curt thank you.

"Backstage, he put his arm around me. 'You know, Jimmy, tell you a story,'" and the conductor did a good imitation of the Vickers–James Cagney voice. "'When I started out, I had a farm, and I didn't make much money in those days. Now I make a lot of money. At a certain point, I figured out each performance I sang was worth one cow.'" Conlon was all ears. "'When I don't like what's been going on all night, I console myself—tonight I bought a cow.'"

Conlon, who would become head of the Paris Opéra, remembered this often "at the end of the night when I'm not happy, frustrated . . . things are out of control, three people are sick. . . . I can't tell you how many nights I come offstage and tell myself I bought a cow."[12]

But when Vickers was told years later by the author how much this story had meant to Conlon, he put on his chilly face. He brushed it off as insignificant, perhaps simply not wishing to recall a night when he had been somewhat churlish, or again, unable to see another's viewpoint.

Vickers's temper had not much improved as he went into *Tristan und Isolde* in May 1982, with Gwyneth Jones, Yvonne Minton, Donald McIntyre as Kurwenal, and Gwynne Howell as the king. Davis had asked a répétiteur to take Vickers some notes after the dress rehearsal; Vickers had sharp words with the man and threw him out of the dressing room. McIntyre recalled that Davis went in next and a big blow-up followed between the two, "the only time I really heard Colin lose his top. I think Colin's voice was as loud as Vickers's, just an absolute shouting match." McIntyre said he knew that Vickers apologized to the conductor later. The baritone couldn't pass up a chance, at a dinner given by Jones after the first night, to twit them about the fun he had had in the next dressing room, hearing it all. "I think they were both very embarrassed about it." This could have been the occasion after which Davis gave Vickers some handsome cufflinks, but Davis didn't recall in which *Tristan* run that occurred. He did recall to the author a "flaming row" over "who got lost in the 5/4 section" of Act 3. Later Vickers called him to say, "We're still friends, aren't we?" "He liked people to stand up to him," said Davis.[13]

Vickers by now was feeling the burden of *Tristan*. Before a performance, a weariness like that after "loading a big truck with gravel" came over him, with seven and a half hours ahead from the time he sat down to make up until the evening's end. And he had said that six years earlier.[14]

Family remained a Vickers keystone. He finished the *Tristans* on Wednesday, June 2, 1982, and flew immediately to join five of his remaining six siblings in Prince Albert. The occasion was the dedication of a $2.5 million grade school to be named for the entire Vickers clan. Their late father, William, was recalled on June 4 as "an outstanding educator, beloved and remembered," and Jon's fame was noted. But the naming of the school was "family recognition for every single one of you," said the mayor.[15]

Each Vickers sibling introduced his or her children and grandchildren, more than fifty of them all told. David, the eldest of Vickers's brothers, worked in real estate and retailing (and like his father had eight children); Wesley, the father of seven, worked in accounting with General Motors. Three of the other siblings had made lives connected with religion: Albert (Ab) was a United Church minister who also was a prison chaplain, echoing his father's work; the oldest sister, Margaret, and her husband, the Reverend Alf Bayne, founded a missionary camp in British Columbia; and Ruth married a Baptist minister.

Then it was back to Europe for the Vickers known by the world. His first Paris Canio came very late, in July 1982, with Catherine Malfitano as Nedda. He was indisposed for the first night, June 26, and James King, in strong voice, stepped in. On June 29 Vickers's artistry was evident, but so were illness and fatigue, as reported by *Opera*. On July 2 Amadeo Zambon took over, and on July 5 Richard Cassilly, dramatic but nasal. Finally, on July 5, Vickers was back on form, and Sergio Segalini noted that while the performance was less precise than his overwhelming Canios at La Scala ten years previous, his unique intensity remained, and his was still one of the great interpretations of the role.[16]

As with so many of his leading ladies, Vickers drew a vivid reaction from Malfitano: "It was pretty scary to be onstage with him . . . but his scariness was based in a solid technique. . . . When he exploded onstage, it all came from a very controlled place. But it never seemed calculated—that was his gift."[17]

Teresa Stratas sang in *Pagliacci* with Vickers in London, and she recalled that he always "questioned his every sound after the performances. He was a perfectionist, still whittling away" at the role. Backstage, he would lift up this sparrow of a soprano and ask her, "Was it okay? It wasn't bad, was it? I felt a little gravelly in that spot, was it okay?"[18]

Late in summer 1982 Vickers had to cancel a *Winterreise* at Wolf Trap Farm Park, in Virginia, in order to have surgery on both knees. They had become increasingly painful with arthritis, and the cartilage had worn away. Hetti blamed it on the kneeling he did onstage, in *Tristan,* for instance. For two years beforehand he had taken cortisone so that he could sing when his throat was in bad shape. His heroic body was showing its age and the wear of life onstage.[19]

Two weeks after surgery he made two rare appearances at Toronto's new, yet-to-open Roy Thomson Hall. Both were private affairs, closed to the public and media, one a recital on August 29 for the Canadian Bar Association, the other a government-organized gala for a meeting of the International Monetary Fund and International Bank. The Toronto writer and theater director Urjo Kareda recorded the awkwardness of the September 8 gala in telling detail that summarized the failure of Canadians to truly recognize, appreciate, and honor one of their few great international artists. Vickers, driving his own car as usual, was told to move on when he tried to park in his assigned spot, and he wasn't recognized by one of the "Ottawa cultural mandarins" who arranged the concert and intercepted Vickers backstage, fearing an interloper.[20]

The tenor had to follow the Canadian Brass, a female pop singer, and the jazz pianist Oscar Peterson. Sweetly noting that Peterson was a hard act to follow, he launched into deeply serious arias, from Handel's *Samson, Die Walküre,* and *Otello*'s death scene. "No crowd-pleasing, no yielding even to middle-of-the-road operatic tastes. One could feel the audience edging away from the intensity of the music even as the singer declaimed it. Vickers, his own man always, had made no concessions, had simply given his best."[21]

Vickers was still using two canes for his knees when he arrived in early September for *Tristan* in Chicago. Lyric Opera's Bill Mason thought the tenor could never get through all the performances; the production had a raked stage, always difficult for the most fit of singers. Vickers sang all seven *Tristan*s, with Janis Martin, but, according to Mason, said he would have done it for nobody else but Ardis Krainik, of whom he was so fond.[22]

Ernst Poettgen directed, with Ferdinand Leitner in the pit. Harold Rosenthal wrote in *Opera* that on October 15, when he was "in sovereign voice, he repeated the successes of his London performances and gave a searing last act."[23] And as it turned out, those were his final complete *Tristan*s, chiefly because, as he said, he didn't get offers for the role. And there was always the issue of an Isolde, and one with whom Vickers would agree to sing.

Vickers returned to Chicago for *Pagliacci,* seven performances beginning November 3 that kept him there most of the month, with Josephine Barstow as Nedda and Cornell MacNeil as Tonio. It was the Met's Zeffirelli production, staged for Chicago by Fabrizio Melano, and was paired with Francis Poulenc's *La Voix Humaine,* also with Barstow. Carlo Felice Cillario conducted, replacing Bruno Bartoletti, who was ill. Cillario was unfamiliar with the Poulenc and had not done *Pagliacci* in some time.[24]

Kareda, also for his Canadian article, recorded Vickers dealing with a messy Chicago rehearsal period. At the dress rehearsal he sang out, although he had said he would only mark. He was so subtle "that he had hurled himself into ['Vesti la giubba'] before anyone realized it.

"Stooped, clinging to the white silk clown's jacket as if it embodied all his disappointments, Vickers sang as if he were discovering the music for the first time. He didn't shape the scene as a show-stopper but as something painful and private, a harrowing insight into a broken man."[25]

The tenor took on *Die Winterreise* in concert and on a recording, and critics had a field day discussing his interpretation. Many were eager to hear him, because while Schubert wrote this most demanding cycle originally for a high voice, it is unusual to hear a tenor attempt it. It is mostly territory for baritones and the occasional daring soprano. Vickers discussed his interpretation beforehand with Christa Ludwig, a lieder expert, and said she had told him, "You're making too much of it."[26] Vickers wouldn't have been Vickers if he had not, but certainly there were some who felt the German song was not suitable for him.

As noted in the previous chapter, he sang it first in Guelph, Ontario, in 1979, then at Tanglewood in 1980 (he had first studied it at age twenty-four in Toronto). He wanted to do it at the Royal Opera House and was quite upset when house director Sir John Tooley wouldn't agree to a recital. Tooley said later he knew he could not get a large enough audience for it, and Vickers told him, "You don't have faith in me." Tooley said it was rather a question of whether Vickers should be singing a song cycle of any kind.[27]

Tooley went to Vickers's 1983 *Winterreise* in Paris. This also upset Vickers, ostensibly because of Tooley's rejection of a concert. But Tooley felt the truth was that Vickers wasn't very good in the piece, that the four fast songs went well but the slower songs were ponderous in that large voice. "I didn't want Jon to be shown up in a bad light. That was my motive [for rejecting a concert]. I wanted the [London] public to have a particular memory of Jon, not one that was a reflection of Jon not at his best."[28]

This appeared to be accurate, not self-serving on Tooley's part. Others close to Vickers confirmed that Tooley and others at Covent Garden had always tried to protect Vickers simply because they thought so highly of him.

Vickers was in Paris to record *Winterreise,* between July 9 and 13 at the Salle Wagram. Vickers said later that he did not get on with his accompanist, Geoffrey Parsons, and was not happy with the results of the collaboration.[29] John Tooley confirmed that Parsons had problems with Vickers. "I know [Parsons] was struggling to catch him a lot of the time. Either [Vickers] was early or he was late."[30]

Alain Lanceron, director of EMI Classics France, said it was his idea to record Vickers after hearing him do the work in February 1983 with Parsons at the Théâtre des Champs-Élysées in Paris. French critics praised the result, even one who likened it to a boxing match, with Vickers trying for the twenty-five-year-old title held for the cycle by Dietrich Fischer-Dieskau and Alfred Brendel. This critic had thought it was a mission impossible, with the forceful Vickers totally unsuited to the Lied, but admitted that, amazingly, the tenor triumphed with the pure passion of music. The "mad" scene of *Peter Grimes,* it was suggested, was the twenty-fifth song of the Winter's Journey.[31]

Lanceron, who had admired Vickers in Liebermann's Paris productions, saw this *Winterreise* as an approach outside the tradition of Fisher-Dieskau or Hermann Prey. Rather than pure German lieder, he agreed it was more like an operatic character: "You could find traces of the character of Otello, of Canio, Parsifal, all the great parts Jon sang onstage, with great intensity and emotion." The recording was quite slow, longer than any *Winterreise* on disk. "Some hated it, but a lot loved it," he said; the record didn't sell well, perhaps two thousand copies in France and few elsewhere. EMI in London wasn't happy about the recording, asking why it should be done, since Vickers was no Schubert specialist. But Lanceron felt, rightly, that it was a unique interpretation that should be preserved. "It was so like a painful dream of somebody looking back at his life . . . he was really involved, it was a moving, suffering interpretation."[32]

Vickers always enjoyed singing the cycle. In his liner notes for the French release he likened it to a great piece of sculpture, of which "the viewing from many angles reveals new and different aspects of beauty." He seemed to believe that it had (like *Peter Grimes*) a universal message, as a nostalgic journey that anyone could take, attaching any meaning particular to that listener.[33]

A most thoughtful review was that of Will Crutchfield on the EMI recording: "The sheer strangeness of the singing strikes one first, as it often does in the tenor's recordings. His voice at this point is a grainy, smoke-colored instrument, often unwieldy, and the beauty that is sometimes breathtaking in the opera house is elusive at microphone range." Vickers does not give a tenoral reading; he transposes most of the songs down as baritones do, but still does not sound like a baritone. "There is the puzzling realization that Mr. Vickers is going to let any number of great changes and events within these songs go by without finding a changed tone color, without any apparent shift of feeling." He has made *Winterreise* universal "without first making it particular."[34]

Conrad Osborne had the most fun with the recording: "What a weird time this unquestionably important artist has put us through these thirty years past! . . . Always the ambivalent feeling—admiration for sticking to his guns, for daring to have his druthers and be his own man, but a speck of resentment for this conservationist, retentive attitude, for not quite fulfilling us. The last time I heard him in recital, he strode onto the Carnegie Hall stage with his full polar-bear presence, talked about John Wayne, and proceeded to sing like, oh, Noel Coward." On the record, "Vickers is a power pitcher giving us soft stuff. It's infuriating." His tempi creep, with "ample occasion for slowdowns and coffee breaks"; No. 7 has "much mincing half voice (how would John Wayne have reacted?)," and in No. 16 "where Vickers should by rights tear us apart [he] sounds like an Irish tenor telling his colleen to never worry. . . . Dammit, Jon—move it and sing out."[35]

In another context, John Steane had written similarly, though more soberly: "Unique among heroic tenors in this respect, he may even leave one wishing for less restraint, for more unabashed opening-up and letting-fly." He added, "But of course Vickers is not 'a tenor' any more than Caruso was. Both are voices unlike any other, and simply share their range and repertoire with the world's tenors."[36]

Of a 1984 Los Angeles performance, Martin Bernheimer noted that Vickers sang all twenty-four songs with no break. (There exists an anecdote of a San Francisco performance at which the philanthropist and composer Gordon Getty clapped alone after the twelfth song, where many singers do break; Vickers smiled, no doubt realizing this was one person familiar with the cycle.)[37]

Every Vickers performance of this cycle, like so much of his opera work, would be different; appreciation of his handling of Schubert's work is dependent on how much one enjoys his wonderfully idiosyncratic sound.

19

Final Grimes, Otello *in South Africa*

T HE AMERICAN SOPRANO CAROL VANESS HAD THE CHANCE TO SING
with Vickers in March and April 1983 when he did a run of ten
*Pagliacci*s with the Paris Opéra. The tenor had wanted someone who
had never sung Nedda, one with original thoughts, and Vaness's experience
reveals how Vickers could inspire other singers.

"He's not a normal-type character in any way. He thinks very psychologically about the roles and relationships between characters," she said. "During one of the first performances, after 'No, pagliaccio non son,' he was
supposed to grab me and kind of shove me, and I was supposed to fall. He
practically threw me fifteen feet to the edge of the commedia platform. I
landed flat on my back." Some of the chorus men looked worried and made
as if to defend her, although their doing so was not in the directions. "I
motioned them no, no, because I thought Jon had always told me, if I come
at you with the knife you better really move! But Jon had the most gentle
heart. He was really caring about his performance. He thinks the audience
should believe it, and not only that, but the singers should believe it."

Another time, Vickers was supposed to sink to the floor to begin "No,
pagliaccio" and stay there. But he looked at Vaness, also on the floor, then
walked over to her. "I thought, 'Wait a minute, I don't remember this in the
original staging.' He straddled me as he was singing, looking down right into
my face, and reached around behind my neck and lifted me off the floor, six
inches. I thought, 'Oh, my God, he really is going to kill me,' I was so
convinced by the intense look in his eyes. He was so lost in the character."

He finished the aria, Vaness jumped up, and the scene continued to its
tragic end, with Vaness feeling, "'Okay, you want to fight, let's fight.' It
started to really feel for the first time like we were living the scene. . . .
It incited in me so much emotion and rage. For that instant, we were those
two characters. He made me into that character. I thought, 'I don't care how
I sing, I don't care how I look. He's pissed me off, kill me, get it over with.'
It was really fascinating.

"After the scene, I just looked at him and said, 'That was for real, wasn't it?' He said, 'Come on, kid, get up off the floor.' He was totally wonderful."[1]

Tax problems arose again for Vickers, this time stemming from an accountant who had cheated many performers. The situation affected his appearances with the Seattle Opera, where he sang *Peter Grimes* in May 1983, just before Speight Jenkins took over the company from Glynn Ross. The U.S. government was claiming that Vickers hadn't paid some taxes, when he believed he had. But the opera company was told to garnish his fees. It was the kind of thing that would really set Vickers off, and Jenkins recalled, "He was screaming and bellowing. He said, 'I know you, I can get mad at you. I don't know the rest of them.'"

Jenkins told Vickers he didn't think the company had any choice but to comply with the IRS demand. Vickers threatened never to set foot on the stage again if his money was taken. "He was in such a rage. We talked to Washington, to congressmen, senators. Finally, two hours before the performance, the government resolved it. And he was right"—he owed nothing. Typically, when Jenkins called to tell Vickers that the matter was settled, the tenor's rage had blown itself out and he just said, "Oh fine."

Jenkins regretted that Vickers never sang again in Seattle, but there were problems in paying the fees he would ask, and Jenkins was still green at the art of negotiating. But he always felt that in his fifty years of operagoing, no other singer had given as much consistent pleasure as Vickers.[2]

This *Grimes* was a production also staged, with a different cast, in Chicago and San Francisco; Vickers's friend Ande Anderson directed. Vickers had a bad cold and missed the first Seattle performances, which were the last for Ross to see as director of the house. Edward Sooter subbed, and Vickers made the last three performances, with a standing ovation the final night, May 14. Although he was so closely identified with the role, "there was never a hint of tired routine," and he was in sovereign voice, reported *Opera*. Ellen was Teresa Kubiak, Balstrode Archie Drake.[3]

Vickers returned to *Tristan und Isolde*, for the second act only, on July 21, 1983, in a concert performance led by Zubin Mehta at Philadelphia's Mann Music Center. The Isolde was Ute Vinzing. It was his last singing of this role, upon which he had made an indelible impact. After the concert, he talked to the music critic Robert Baxter about the decline in opera standards, a theme that by now was troubling him ever more deeply. Baxter saw the white-haired tenor as authoritative but also radiating kindness and gentleness. "Please don't tell your readers that Jon Vickers is angry or bitter," he said. "Tell them that I am sad for an art form that I love deeply, an art form for which I despair."

He noted immense improvement in the technical capabilities of musicians over the past twenty-five years. But "there is not the love, not the preparation, not the analysis and the attempt to go deep into the work to find out not just the surface, the notes, the rhythm and so on, but what is being said. And I don't only mean the text. I mean the profound meaning of what a composer is saying in his music." And he spoke of how his feelings had changed about the Metropolitan Opera: "I can tell you I felt like taking off my hat when I came through the back door because it was an honor to be there. It was like being a painter who had the privilege of having his painting hung in the Louvre. That atmosphere has gone now. We are in the business of merchandising the classics."[4]

Vickers had given up a 1978 Met season-opening night when he canceled *Tannhäuser,* and he never did open the season at that house. In 1983, for its centennial season, the Met passed up the chance to round off a piece of history and present Vickers, the greatest and only contemporary interpreter, in *Les Troyens.* Instead, it cast Plácido Domingo, who went public with his nervousness about the part just ten days before the September 26 opening.

As far back as 1978 the Met had talked with Domingo about 1983. At an October meeting, Domingo, his managers Gerard and Marianne Semon, and the Met's Rodzinski and Ingpen discussed *Troyens* and *Francesca da Rimini* as possible September 26 gala openers. Domingo then doubted very much if Énée was a role for him. "I do not believe that Domingo will ever sing it," Joan Ingpen wrote on November 9, 1978, to Serge Baudo, who sought an Énée for his 1980 Berlioz festival in Lyons. But by January Domingo had agreed with Levine to do it.[5]

In July 1979, however, Vickers's agent, John Coast, was cheerily positing *Peter Grimes* as a centennial season opener for Vickers, who himself noted that he'd never had that prestigious position at the Met.[6] (This was in part because of his repertoire limitations where an opening choice was concerned. Ingpen said the quirky, downbeat *Grimes* would never have been an opener.) But it was already too late; the Met, Ingpen confirmed, never asked Vickers, and never considered him for the opening once Domingo became a possibility. Domingo was the new star, Vickers was in twilight, and indeed had planned to make 1983–84 the final season of his career, which the Met then knew.[7]

Levine recalled that *Les Troyens* had been his idea to begin with, and that it was a tough sell for opening night. Domingo at forty-three was already essential to the Met's box office in a way Vickers never had been. The Domingo-Pavarotti rivalry, however media-driven and not based in reality, would heat up soon and gain headlines for opera that it couldn't refuse. It was not a scenario Vickers would ever approach, let alone embrace. But in a strange fashion he seemed almost to envy the attention paid the other two tenors, while privately deploring many of their actions. Levine admitted he would have thought first of Vickers for *Troyens,* but said negotiations had been totally the job of Ingpen and Anthony Bliss. He did not indicate whether he had ever recommended Vickers to them.[8]

It would seem not, and on March 16, 1980, the Met prepared Domingo's contract to sing eight performances of *Troyens,* including the opening, for eight thousand dollars a night.[9] It must have been a blow to Vickers when he learned of this; he had said that Énée is the role by which he will be remembered. Difficult as the part is, Vickers would no doubt have found ways to accommodate his aging voice to it, had the role been offered for the centennial.

In summer 1983 Domingo was walking around his New York apartment with Vickers's *Troyens* recording on his headphones, puzzling how he himself, also never secure with high notes and additionally not a classic heroic tenor, could manage the part. He later said he'd never do it onstage again, but regretted not recording it.[10] The tenor William Lewis, who was asked to cover Domingo and who sang many rehearsals with Domingo sitting in the audience, said later he didn't see why Vickers couldn't have sung it at the time. Remarkably, Vickers was asked by the Met to step in if Domingo bowed out.

Ingpen was furious when she learned, on holiday in England that summer, that Domingo had told Levine he hadn't completely prepared the role. She reluctantly asked Coast about the possibility of getting Vickers. Even the formidable Ingpen admitted she wouldn't have had the courage to ask Vickers directly. She fully expected that, like Grimes, he'd have sent her away with a flea in her ear. Coast told her Vickers hadn't done the role in some time (not since 1974) and would not sing it on such short notice. "If I'd been Jon, I would have gone up in smoke too," Ingpen said.[11]

That October and November Vickers sang a series of eight *Grimes*es at the Met, led by the recently knighted Sir John Pritchard, with Elisabeth Söderström as Ellen Orford and Thomas Stewart as Captain Balstrode. They ended with the November 19 matinee, and then he went into *Fidelio* in December and January, led by Klaus Tennstedt, with Eva Marton and Hildegard Behrens.

Although he was available, Vickers chose not to join in the Met's Centennial Gala, which ran all afternoon and evening of October 22, 1983. Jess Thomas sang Act 1 of *Die Walküre* with Jessye Norman; McCracken did Otello's "Dio! mi potevi," and Domingo and Freni sang the *Otello* love duet; Pavarotti was on hand for the love scene from *Ballo,* with Leontyne Price; and José Carreras for *Andrea Chénier*'s "Vicino a te," with Montserrat Caballé.

Honored guests included Ferruccio Tagliavini, Cesare Valletti, and Ramón Vinay. So many tenors, but no Vickers. He canceled at the last minute, citing personal reasons. Quite probably he was still smarting from the *Troyens* situation, as Domingo continued his nervous run, succeeded by Lewis.

In November, no doubt urged on by Lyric Opera and its leader, Ardis Krainik, the University of Illinois at Chicago awarded Vickers an honorary doctor of music degree, at a convocation noting the centenary of the death of Richard Wagner.

The Handel *Samson* plans were moving along at the Royal Opera House, although the Dallas Opera had bowed out. Ingpen suggested Michael Geliot to direct it. Vickers, realizing his career had not many more years to run, sought more money from Covent Garden on grounds that he had helped to get the coproduction with Chicago and the Met. On December 9, 1983, Coast wrote Tooley that the tenor had suggested his fee be raised from twenty thousand Swiss francs to twenty-two thousand per performance, but Coast was sure Covent Garden would not agree to that. Instead he suggested that Vickers receive an additional rehearsal fee of twenty thousand Swiss francs (which finally was budgeted as a production expense). Coast referred to the *Samson* as a "long and hazardous negotiation."

He also reported that "Jon's mind is set firmly against Capt. Vere. I think he finds him a bit of a non-entity and feels that he can't do over much with him, apart from anything else." That "else" surely was Vickers's view that Vere also lusted after Billy Budd.[12] Tooley responded on December 15 that he was sad that Vere had been turned down. "I understand his reservations but I think it is a role out of which a lot could have been made by him."[13]

Coast also told Tooley that Vickers didn't want the *Samson*s to be in any way advertised as his farewell performances. The tenor would consider future work with Davis or Bernard Haitink with pleasure, and the operas he was interested in at the end of 1983 were *Parsifal, Die Walküre, L'Incoronazione di Poppea, Samson et Dalila, Salome, Norma, Pique Dame, Pagliacci,* and *Lady Macbeth of Mtsensk.*[14] It is perhaps surprising that at fifty-seven Vickers still was game for the high-lying Pollione and difficult Nerone; this willingness supports the idea that, had he been properly approached, he would have sung *Troyens* at the Met in 1983.

Tooley hedged to Coast about a Covent Garden farewell performance: "We really will have to see what the future brings." And he told the agent he was immensely grateful for his having handled "this difficult affair," the Handel *Samson* plans, with such good humor. Tooley added wryly that he was "glad we have a solution until the next crisis looms," which the administrator knew with Vickers could not be far away.[15]

In January 1984 Vickers bade the Houston Grand Opera farewell with *Peter Grimes*. William Albright reported, "His granite voice was sometimes balky, and he had to resort to forte to avoid cracking in high lyrical passages."[16] Another critic, Frank Gagnard, wrote, "His voice was slightly husky and on one occasion subject to accident, but the tenor has lost none of his dramatic authority and his communicative vocal skill."[17]

Indeed, Vickers was still adding strokes to his portrait. During rehearsals of the revived 1977 production, director Ande Anderson recalled, the tenor halted in the middle of the duet with Ellen, who was Josephine Barstow, Anderson's wife. "He said something had changed, something that never happened before, and he had to change his concept. . . . You never get the impression she actually loves the man, and there could be a relationship of some sort. He felt there was a real future and she took it away from him. So [Grimes] was completely alone even with Ellen."[18] Barstow expanded to the author that she felt Ellen doesn't love Grimes enough, doesn't support him, when she tells him they have failed. Vickers was a little ambivalent about Grimes's raising his hand to Ellen, but in Barstow's interpretation, "she deserves to be hit by him." Vickers changed his portrayal somewhat "because he felt my withdrawal, Ellen's failure to go along with him, to really trust him," notably when Ellen sees the bruise on the apprentice.[19]

In March 1984 Vickers pulled on his seaboots for the last time as Grimes on the stage at Covent Garden, although he would sing it during that company's visit to the Olympics in Los Angeles that summer. He no doubt was unhappy that the voice would not perform as it used to, and this expressed itself in criticism of the chorus. When the hunt for Grimes begins, the chorus is offstage, accompanied by a drum. John Tooley recalled that they were not together, and Vickers blamed the chorus. In the final scene also, Vickers would say he couldn't understand why the chorus was out of tune. "Now, Jon was wrong and the chorus was right," said Tooley, who suggested as much to the tenor. But Vickers would never accept that.[20]

In spring 1984 Vickers sang his final Siegmunds and Grimeses with the Met, on tour from Atlanta to Cleveland. They were not announced as such, and indeed this was not set in stone at the time. The tenor was still angry about not having sung *Les Troyens* the previous fall, and growled about it that April to strangers in his dressing room at the Kennedy Center in Washington, D.C. He wanted it known by his public that he had eventually been asked by the Met to step in if needed.[21]

Leighton Kerner of the *Village Voice* wrote in the program for the Met tour of Vickers's *Grimes*: "The meeting of character and singer has proved to be one of the mightiest collisions in twentieth-century opera, and today's audiences must count themselves lucky to witness it whenever and wherever Vickers puts on that black slicker and thrusts his hands angrily, grievingly into the pockets."[22]

And that spring, another chilly episode with a friend occurred. Roberta Knie, who was on warm terms with both Jon and Hetti, was to sing Brünnhilde in the Met's *Die Walküre* in April. She ran into difficulties with the house and was dropped. She and the American Guild of Musical Artists took the matter up with the Met. Knie wanted Vickers to testify that she had been in good voice, and that he had been delighted to sing with her. To her shock, he declined to become involved.

"I am so glad to have my Bobbie back!" he had told her, picking her up as was his style after she rehearsed the second act. But the Met decided that although she had sung well, she was not a suitable Brünnhilde for them, Knie recalled. (Met records on the incident were not released, but Knie said Hildegard Behrens already had been hired to take over the part.) AGMA wanted her to sue the Met because it felt other artists also had been treated shabbily. As part of the process, many months later Knie left a message for Vickers. "I was sure Jon would go to the arbitration table to testify [for me]."

Hetti called and Knie told her the situation. Jon would not come to the phone. Hetti explained that because he was still singing at the Met, he felt getting involved could be detrimental to his career. So that time at the rehearsal, Knie said in 1998, in tones of regret and some bitterness, "was the last time I've spoken to Jon. It just killed me," she added, "because Jon had been so full of principle about a lot of things." Knie, who had suffered various health and financial trials, was deeply hurt. "I thought of all people in this world Jon would at least speak up for me" and follow his Christian principles. She did hear that Vickers had raised a ruckus at the Met about her absence but to no avail, and he never spoke with her about it.

But she still felt warmly toward him: "We had something special together," and she had been his Isolde of choice in Chicago and Canada, and at Covent Garden. She recalled, "I pulled Jon out of a lot of performances, we pulled each other along. . . . Sometimes Jon would turn to me and say, sing loud tomorrow, 'cause I can't sing piano, all I've got is falsetto."[23]

Vickers's ferocious approach to his roles continued to punctuate his career. That summer, he refused to take a bow and exploded in his dressing room at the Los Angeles Music Center after *Peter Grimes*. It was a Royal Opera presentation (three performances, July 11, 16, 19) as part of the Olympic Arts Festival.

In the final scene, Grimes is accompanied by the voices of villagers, without orchestra. The Royal Opera chorus missed some cues, and Vickers was thrown off in his monologue. Gwyneth Jones, singing *Turandot* at the festival, had been in the audience and went backstage. She was met by Katharine Wilkinson, ROH public relations chief, who warned that Vickers was enraged. A warning might not have been necessary because his shouts could be heard by fans waiting outside for autographs. Tooley had tried to calm the tenor, who was said to have been yelling at, possibly even hitting, a hapless underling, a dresser.

Those in the hallway could hear Jones asking Vickers just what he was doing. "He was in a terrible state, everybody was in a panic," Jones recalled. "They knew how close we were, and I said I would go in there. He was raving. . . . I thought the whole place would be demolished. I was really quite scared. He really is a powerful man, and he was mad. I thought, 'I must try to calm him down.' . . . We just talked a few minutes. . . . I thought a chair might come crashing out." She soothed Vickers by telling him that he had been heard "fantastically well. When he came on, he was so powerful, so wonderful. I said to him it was so fantastic that I never thought of performing in this opera, but I was so thrilled I decided that if someone asked me, I would adore to sing it with him. Maybe this helped put him in a better mood." She later told John Ardoin that Vickers was like a little boy who came to her crying, saying, "Did you hear what they did to me?" She took him in her arms, like a child. That broke his rage.[24]

Three and a half years from retirement, at fifty-eight, Vickers still cared passionately about every detail, about giving his best. It is possible that some part of his fury had been fueled by the pain in his deteriorating knees. Grimes was kneeling in that production for much of the last scene.

Earlier, at the dress rehearsal, Vickers also had been feisty. Stafford Dean was standing in as the lawyer/coroner Swallow for a bass who was ill. In the first act, Vickers strode to the front to take the oath, and Dean stepped forward two paces to interrogate him. "Vickers said in a very loud voice, 'Back off, Stafford, don't get too near!'" recalled the tenor Kim Begley, who was singing the Rector.[25]

Such angry responses certainly have parallels in the careers of other singers. With Vickers, some observers found them egocentric and even irrational; indeed, such incidents were the source of the frequent use of the adjective "crazy" to describe this tenor. But self-centered though some of his reactions were, they also were intrinsic to Vickers's rigid character and to his beliefs about his art and the world. They are inseparable from his achievements.

There were lighter moments that week in Los Angeles as Vickers took time to eye the ladies. The soprano Helen Donath, who sang Pamina at the festival, recalled, "Jon was watching me one day as I was getting my [hotel] breakfast and he said, 'My goodness, Helen, you do have beautiful legs!'" She demurred, but he said, "My legs aren't so hot, and I always notice if other people have especially nice legs. If I say you do, you do!"[26]

In a 1984 Olympics Arts Festival review, Alan Rich decided to place Vickers historically: "[He] is still astonishing as the fury-ridden fisherman Peter Grimes; his performance is a landmark on the level, say, of the Olivier Oedipus or the Isolde of Kirsten Flagstad."[27]

In fall of 1984 Vickers recorded an album of songs by Canadian composers, accompanied by Richard Woitach, for the Canadian Music Center. It was made at the farm, Spruce Winds, after Vickers decided he didn't want to go into Toronto to do it. A grand piano and engineering team were dispatched to Alton for five days of work. This had to be interrupted when the sound equipment trucks had to leave to be used for the visit of Pope John Paul II to Toronto. "Jon doesn't like this Pope—too political," Woitach noted.[28]

The album included three West Coast native tribal songs arranged by Ernest MacMillan, with a beautiful lullaby, "Na Du-Na Du Du," and then Vickers very much in character as a tribesman scolding "old maids and housewives" whose chatter disturbed him. Six Medieval Love Songs, with music by Jean Coulthard, displayed Vickers singing exquisite poetry in an erotic mood, "dying, dying of desire."

Many of the songs were written in the 1940s, noted the Toronto critic William Littler: "Vickers has never been known for his advocacy of the avant-garde in music." But Littler called the disk "a landmark event in Canadian recording," with the voice of the nation's most famous opera singer at the service of its own music.[29]

Vickers did a concert that included some of the songs on September 20, 1985, at Toronto's Roy Thomson Hall and commented between numbers. He sang the "Winterstürme," noting how Wagner had challenged taboos and "the bases on which civilization is built" by incorporating themes of illegitimacy and incest into his operas. Die Walküre is about a love affair between a brother and sister, Vickers noted, cautioning an audience member, "Don't hide your head like that!"

He also sang a favorite, Vaughan Williams's "Song of the Road" from Hugh the Drover, and the Grimes "mad" scene, of which he said, "It all takes place in the mind." His encores were two of the Canadian songs, "New Love," by Coulthard, and the Indian lullaby, which must have resonated because his first grandson had been born earlier in the year.

Vickers received some home province recognition on October 14, 1984. A recital was sponsored in Saskatoon's Centennial Auditorium by the Saskatchewan Arts Councils and Music Festival Association, with Margaret Galloway aiding in the event. Peter Schaaf accompanied Vickers. The next night, Saskatchewan government officials gave a dinner for him, and he spoke at the music department of the University of Saskatchewan.

Vickers sang *Winterreise* twice in fall of 1984, on September 30 at Orchestra Hall in Chicago, presented by Lyric Opera, with Peter Schaaf as accompanist. And in his first Los Angeles recital, he appeared on October 3 at the Dorothy Chandler Pavilion of the Los Angeles Music Center. In Los Angeles, the critic Martin Bernheimer noted, he wore a plain black business suit, not white tie, although it was an evening concert. He was greeted at his entrance by a storm of applause, which appeared to surprise him. "It must be *Peter Grimes*," he was heard to say as he bowed, presumably referring to his Olympics appearances. Dubbing the cycle the *Hamlet* of singers, Bernheimer concluded that in time Vickers could be in the class of Fischer-Dieskau, Peter Pears, and Hans Hotter.

The house was much too big for such an art song recital, but Vickers sustained the tension through the eighty-five-minute marathon (he again used no break after the first twelve songs). While praising his urgency and beauty of tone, the critic said Vickers "has not yet mastered the art of instant poetic definition. He does not yet color the words with great impact," so that the varied irony, whimsy, bitterness, are blurred. "In the sad songs he correctly reduces his awesome roar to a delicate whisper, but what should be a supported pianissimo tone sometimes emerges as a breathy croon." And he noted that an inadvertent crack of the voice brought "genuine terror to the line, 'Ich wein' auf meiner Hoffnung Grab'—I *weep* on the grave of my hope."[30]

Vickers got a standing ovation at the end.

In December 1984 Vickers sang the final *Otello*s of his career in Cape Town, South Africa, a city off the major opera circuit. Hetti accompanied him for the stay of several weeks in the turn-of-the-century Mount Nelson Hotel. Vickers had been invited by his old friend Murray Dickie, the Scots comprimario tenor who was now running the Cape Town opera company. One important reason he accepted was that he had known Dickie when the older man was married to his first wife, who died after a long struggle with cancer. Vickers had been extremely impressed that Dickie had stayed at her side during her illness.[31] It was an example that he himself was to follow.

Those final *Otello*s were a striking experience for the tenor, as he sang in a country where racial apartheid was still much in evidence. At the end of his career it changed the way in which he thought about this most intellectually demanding of his roles. His idea of Otello had never been simply that of a black man poisoned by jealousy who, as some productions have it, reverts to barbarism. Vickers was very conscious of the suffering of this hero, of his complex relationship with his wife, of his physical prowess, and of the trials of leadership that in part led to his downfall.

Vickers's thirty-first and final Met *Otello* had come on June 6, 1979, on the tour at Wolf Trap Farm Park, in Virginia. But in the pointed racial context of the Cape Town atmosphere, new insights came to the tenor, who had sung the role for twenty years and thought he had a solid view of it. But he wished he had been able to sing it there twenty years earlier so he could have melded these insights to his portrayal. It seems he would have stressed much more the fact of Otello's race.

Murray Dickie, who had sung for thirty-three years at the Vienna Staatsoper and six at the Met, beginning in 1962, two years after Vickers's debut there, presented it as a challenge to his friend to sing the Moor in that chiefly black country. The opera had been performed in the Nico Malan Opera House for the first time on May 14, 1977. Dickie went to some lengths to get a bank sponsorship for the production and would not reveal the amount, probably because it chiefly covered Vickers's fee.

Vickers's first response was that he would not sing for a segregated audience, but Dickie said the audience had been integrated for more than a decade and the company itself was integrated. In fact, he said, his best tenor, who would have been ideal for Cassio, was colored. (Color-blind casting had yet to rear its head to muddle Shakespeare's drama, and Dickie and that tenor agreed it would have been unworkable.)

Nicolai Gedda had run into problems on a South African tour about this time. Dickie said he had cut short the tour after his mother's death, but also that Gedda had received abusive calls at his Cape Town hotel. On his return to Sweden, he was forced by public pressure to denounce the trip he had made. And he never went back for opera appearances that Dickie had in mind. Asked by a journalist about Gedda's experience, Vickers gave a typically broad reply. He expressed concern about the view that the arts should become involved in causes, political and otherwise. "Religion is confused with politics, art with politics, sport with politics. . . . Art can only be judged as art inasmuch as it reflects ultimate reality. We deal in essences, universality and beauty, not in negatives."[32]

Whatever this may have meant, Vickers was generally color-blind himself, having worked with some of the greatest artists who were black. He made a naive error when he set off for Cape Town and laughed at himself, recalling that it never occurred to him that black makeup might not be a staple there. The makeup provided turned out not to be dark enough for the fair Canadian, and he was slightly allergic to it. He placed an emergency call to his old friend Ron Freeman, the ROH makeup chief, who sent him a kit with Negro 2, as it is called, and his Otello wig.[33]

But Vickers didn't receive them in time for the dress rehearsal, so that the colored cast members hadn't seen him as a black man. "I just wish that for all my performances I could have had the reaction that I had [the first] night." When he stepped out of the darkness onstage to sing his first lines, "Esultate," there were gasps onstage. The cast reacted strongly. In the love duet, when Otello seeks *un bacio* from his wife, sung by the Italian soprano Rosanna Rocca in a long blond wig, Vickers took her face in his hands and kissed her. The chorus in particular sucked in its breath. This was still daring in the charged political atmosphere of the time.

In the third act, Otello reacts as Iago (the American baritone Wayne Long) tells of Cassio's dream, saying the man whom Otello fears his wife loves calls out her name in sleep. Vickers had always sung in anger at that point. "I could *not* do it," he recalled. "I was just overcome with sorrow." Instead, he sang softly and sadly. "That was dictated to me by the suffering in South Africa!" he said emphatically.[34]

Christine Crouse, assistant director to Dickie, recalled the soft singing and at first it was thought Vickers simply was marking—not singing out. Crouse, whose mother, the South African soprano Nellie du Toit, had sung Desdemona in the 1977 *Otello*, said Vickers had a few vocal difficulties. But they were balanced by the electric sense of occasion about his being there and his forceful personality. He had pitch problems in the love duet, but it wasn't a real detraction.[35]

Sally Presant, the mezzo singing Emilia, said Vickers was very aggressive, even angry at times, with the mild-mannered Italian guest conductor Bruno Aprea (who had studied with Seiji Ozawa at Tanglewood). Vickers enjoyed the rehearsals tremendously but was less enthusiastic about the stress of performance. But when she came to a piano rehearsal with acute laryngitis, Vickers told her severely that she was being unprofessional, seemingly taking umbrage at her being ill. "He gave me a terrible blast. I felt like an absolute nobody," said Presant, who had sung character parts at the English National Opera before going to Cape Town.

At a *sitzprobe* a week later, however, Aprea kept correcting the orchestra on a section for Emilia that begins with a high note. Vickers spoke up: "He said that is an incredibly cruel place to keep bringing a singer in on," said Presant. She saw in the paradoxical Vickers "incredible intolerance under a heart of pure gold." She laid it to his Scorpio birth sign, which she shared: contradictory, living on nerves, having trouble dealing with real-world pressures. "I think the hard side comes out as a result of some inner hurt, a defensive mechanism."

Aprea apparently had never conducted *Otello*, which obviously would be problematic for Vickers. At one point, the tenor told the story of the opera to the orchestra, so frustrated was he with their dealings with the score. "He wasn't doing it to be a great prima donna, it's just the way he was, the artistry and a huge anger that went with it," said Presant.[36]

Vickers sang six times from December 1 to December 21. His performance was truly moving, "full of light and shade . . . made even more remarkable by the many and varied shades of gray between those two extremes," wrote Julius F. Eichbaum in the South African magazine *Scenaria*. He was in fine voice, "despite the fact that the years have inevitably taken their toll here and there."[37]

The South African experience apparently would have changed some of the views Vickers had expressed to Alan Blyth just before his first London *Otello*, in May 1972. His interpretation was then "less fussy," but his fundamental idea had not changed. To him, Otello was not a savage, and the relationship with Desdemona went beyond pure eroticism, "even though the psychiatrists today have adopted a phrase known as the Othello syndrome." As with *Peter Grimes*, Vickers saw the larger picture:

> The tragedy of Otello could be that of any man elevated to a high position—he's lonely and because of all the fawning, he is uncertain about who his friends are.
>
> Otello must be related to all of life, and not just to the relationship of a black man and a white woman who fell in love. It's far too limiting, and also too insulting to Shakespeare—and to every black man on the face of the earth. The fact that he's black is only one element in the situation.

Otello's age and perhaps the waning of his sexual drive are factors in his fear that his wife is unfaithful, Vickers said.[38]

During the twenty-one years in which he sang Otello, Vickers preferred to take it on at most eight times a year. This was the case even in the late 1960s and 1970s, when, following Del Monaco and before Domingo's Moor, he and James McCracken were the major tenors singing the role and thus were in heavy demand. (The Russian Vladimir Atlantov also made much of the part in those years.) Vickers told Blyth he liked to think of Otello as the Julius Caesar of the Venetian empire. It was like Vickers to seek nobility in his characters. He also believed that Iago must be a man easy to like, since Otello's role is so deeply tied to that of his captain, and the relationship is even more crucial than that with Desdemona. Vickers likened the characters of Otello and Carmen, in that her relationship depends so much upon the interpretation of Don José. The Moor's jealousy had been difficult for Vickers to assume because he himself, he said, had not a jealous bone in his body.

Vickers had been familiar with the music since he understudied the role in a 1955 production by the CBC in his Toronto days. He felt it to be the most difficult role in the Italian repertory. Radames may be more technically difficult and more exposed, but with Otello, "you have this enormous contrast between the big declamatory passages and the lyrical ones, such as the love duet, monologue and death. Then there is the emotional strain of portraying this continually seething volcano." Tristan is a much longer role, but Vickers saw him as an extrovert and always said that he found it much more tiring to project the introverted Moor, as he played him.[39]

Otello performances by various singers may be excellent in many differing ways, since the character and his music are so rich in shadings. Vickers always said no performance was ever the same for him, because he could never encompass this ever-changing, flawed hero in an evening. And so there are many *Otello* tenors who can be admired. But Tullio Serafin, who was eighty-two when he recorded it with Vickers in 1960, told Vickers he was better than Francesco Tamagno, who had created the role for Verdi in 1887.[40] (Tamagno retired in 1902 and Serafin could well have heard him onstage; some recordings remain.)

Karajan had spoken of the individuality Vickers brought to his Otello and Tristan.[41] And Teresa Stratas's eyes filled with tears as she recalled this uniquely tragic Moor. "He had nobility and dignity that he carried, and when he crumbled it was distressing to see this great man disintegrate . . . into small pieces of torn flesh and soul. . . . You saw him on the ground, cowering in a corner. As a colleague watching, you felt you had to look away. . . . It broke my heart [to see] that noble person a broken man."[42]

20

The Trials of Samson

Vickers's last appearance in a major new production came with Handel's *Samson*, shared for the Handel tercentenary in 1985 and 1986 by Covent Garden, Lyric Opera of Chicago, and the Metropolitan Opera. (He also appeared in Lyric's first-ever *Parsifal* in 1986.) This controversial *Samson* caused the furies to rage around Vickers for reasons that reverberated with so many of the qualities that set him apart throughout his career. Handel performance views had changed greatly since the 1958 *Samson* in which Vickers had sung, under Raymond Leppard. The new Elijah Moshinsky–Timothy O'Brien staging was conducted by Julius Rudel, in a large-house version, although without the additional orchestration Beecham had insisted upon, and with little ornamentation by the singers. It caught the full blast of the authentic-music battle, then at its height.

As Vickers described it: "We were praised to the skies or we were carved to ribbons" by the critics.[1] In *Opera* Stanley Sadie personified the negative response: "The performance represented an ostrich-like unawareness of all that has been going on in Handel performance over the last decades. . . . In sum, Covent Garden have conspicuously failed to do due honour to the greatest composer having historical links with the house."[2]

Sir John Tooley, ROH general director at the time of the *Samson*, and with the house since 1955, told the author bluntly, speaking his mind for the first time: "It was a mistake for Jon to have done it." Tooley had foreseen the firestorm that lay ahead. But, he said in his clipped tones,

> What else could I do at that point? Performing Handel's *Samson* once more meant everything to Jon. And Jon is a great artist, has given a great deal of time to Covent Garden, been immensely loyal to Covent Garden. And I believed that in fact it was right to go along with this, and let the public once more have the chance of hearing this artist [in the role], although I knew musically it would be out of keeping with

current performance practice. But what I did not believe was that it would be quite so out of step.

Tooley became quite worked up as he recalled this period and his opposition to Vickers's request, his warnings to the tenor of what lay ahead. "Do you honestly think I would have put Jon into *Samson* at that point, with that style of musical performance? No. Never. I really put my head on the block for that man at that point, and my God, I got slated for it. Really slated."

Tooley was sad for Vickers that the tenor failed to understand that much opinion would be against the performance style Vickers wanted. Over the years, he had suffered through many arguments with Vickers about Handel performance. "Jon never believed that any Handel should ever be decorated. He believed that the [Charles] Mackerrases, the [Roger] Norringtons, the [John] Eliot Gardiners were just recreating things for their own financial advantage. He always used to say to me, 'Come on, they're just doing this—new editions, new money . . . that's the only reason they're doing it. It's not what Handel ever wanted.'"

Vickers would offer to sing for Tooley "Where'er you walk," from Handel's *Semele,* "trying to explain to me how Handel wanted it performed." Tooley's voice was full of wry exasperation as he recalled this Vickers theme. "And I had to say to Jon, 'Well, look, there's documentary evidence to prove you wrong.' 'Oh, that's rubbish,' he said. 'I know! This is the way it is.'"[3]

ROH plans to revive *Samson* had fallen through in the early 1970s, a disappointment for Vickers, who may have wanted a new production then. But he told Alan Blyth even in 1974 that "they wanted to revert to embellished Handel, which I think is old-fashioned. The music and Milton's Agonistes have a stark strength without all that." He also complained that the Micah was to have been sung by a countertenor, not a contralto. He noted "all my admiration for countertenors," not a sentiment he was to repeat, but said that even so "I don't want to appear on the operatic stage with them."[4] Later he would be even more scornful of them.

Tooley finally acquiesced to the 1985 production. But he remained very heated as he remembered, "We had a performance of Handel's *Samson,* conducted by Julius Rudel, whom I did not want."[5] But Vickers did. It could have been because Rudel, with whom he had worked well on *Poppea* in 1978 in Paris, was one of the few conductors who would agree to deal with the tenor at that point. Vickers's wayward tempi and demanding ways had alienated a number of men in the pit.

Rudel came into the picture after Mackerras, for one, had discussed the proposal with Tooley and Vickers in 1982. Mackerras, known for his Handel work as well as his Janáček expertise, said he and Vickers simply did not see eye to eye on Handel performance. Vickers wanted it done as it had been in 1958, with Leppard's arrangements, which came under heavy fire from the early music movement. The style had changed, and Mackerras also agreed that Vickers could well have objected because by the 1980s his voice no longer had the agility for the faster, more flexible performance in fashion.[6]

As Tooley recalled the meeting in his office, Vickers arrived with the Leppard score and began to glower as Mackerras laid out his preferences, including the use of a countertenor. Finally, Vickers flung the score down on Tooley's table, dashing papers onto the floor, and declared, "This is the only version I will sing!"

But Tooley had already spoken with Leppard, who told him that under no circumstances would he allow that version to be performed again, because it was not how Leppard himself would do Handel in the 1980s. Later that day Tooley saw Vickers, who roared with laughter and said, "I was a bit noisy this afternoon, wasn't I?" As often happened, he was a little ashamed of his outburst.[7]

So Vickers chose Rudel, and although they fell out for a time toward the end of the run in the three houses, "Julius was immensely patient with Jon," Tooley recalled. "On the last aria ['Thus when the sun'], for example, they were at odds with each other, and between the general rehearsal and the first night, the whole thing was reversed. Jon said it was too slow, then he decided that in fact it was—I don't know, the thing was chaotic. But it was Jon again in his obstinate frame of mind, saying, 'I know, the rest of you don't!'" Tooley voiced these words of Vickers's with great emphasis.[8]

It was Vickers who first called Rudel to ask him to conduct the opera. And it was Vickers who insulted Rudel in front of the entire cast and orchestra at a Chicago Lyric rehearsal. Rudel viewed this as so catastrophic that he offered to quit (the sensible Lyric chief Ardis Krainik, who had weathered countless such storms, never considered the idea). And it was Rudel who took chief blame from London critics who disliked the performances there.

In the beginning, Vickers clearly had good memories of working with Rudel, dating from a 1960s *Die Walküre* in Philadelphia, and continuing through the 1978 Paris *Poppea*. Rudel himself said in a 1990 interview that he was "scared stiff. I knew I had let myself in for a terrible thrashing. Everybody in London is a cousin of Handel! Every musicologist, certainly." But Rudel was attracted by the idea of conducting at Covent Garden, where he had never before been invited. Indeed, he also was asked to conduct *Die Fledermaus* and *Andrea Chénier* during the *Samson* period. In March 1984 Rudel was confirmed to conduct.

He recalled that when Vickers phoned him, "He said, 'I warn you . . . I hate these sissified versions with all that fancy ornamentation. I sing it straight, as Beecham taught me.'" Rudel looked at the score, "and I thought, 'Okay, if I can get him to do a few appoggiaturas, one can manage.'" Rudel realized that all the other vocal performances would have to be minimally ornamented if that was the way Vickers planned to do it.[9]

Vickers told the critic Tom Sutcliffe during the London run, "I am astounded that from Beecham—a giant, a man of such musical capacity and integrity—Britain should have degenerated into asking fiddlers to play without vibrato."[10]

Rudel did make attempts to talk Vickers out of his anti-ornamentation position and buried himself in the British Museum, studying Handelian manuscripts to gather ammunition. It was useless. Rudel recalled having dinner with Vickers and his wife. "Even she told him, 'Come on, get off it.' Sweet lady, but totally ineffectual. But I remember I tried so much to help him and still to make it something that I could put my name to."

Rudel had to allow Vickers to go his own way while the conductor helped some other singers who wanted to add a little to their parts. He prided himself on being able to add natural-sounding ornaments for those who wished to show off their trills and roulades. He had done a great deal of this for Beverly Sills in New York. Still, Vickers "would practically have a seizure when he heard anybody else doing a little ornamentation." In one instance, the Scottish soprano Marie McLaughlin saw fit in London to allow Vickers to know she was ornamenting, with Rudel's aid. "He hit the roof," said Rudel.[11]

McLaughlin later claimed, perhaps disingenuously, to be unaware of any such situation: "I had no confrontation with Tooley, with Rudel or with [Vickers]." She said she was supportive of Vickers's style, and that many persons involved had been surprised at the choice of Rudel to conduct this opera, knowing of his departures from the score, changes, and cuts in his *Giulio Cesare* recording with Beverly Sills and Norman Treigle.[12] However, Tooley confirmed Rudel's account about McLaughlin's decorating some arias, offending Vickers. Tooley asked her to tone it down.

Vickers also was upset when the soprano June Anderson, singing in the Chicago performances, wanted to add a da capo in the show-stopping final-act "Let the bright seraphim." Vickers had told Rudel he wanted no da capos, or repeats, because they weren't written. When Anderson asked Rudel about it, he warned her, "I don't think Mr. Vickers will go for it." But Anderson had it in her Lyric contract, agreed to before Vickers arrived in Chicago, that she could ornament as she wished. She said later she hadn't known in advance about Vickers's opposition.[13]

William Mason, then assistant to Krainik and now Lyric general director, was present when Krainik turned her formidable powers of persuasion on Vickers. "It was pure Ardis. She appealed to his better instincts, for a young singer in a showcase role. She reminded him of his Lyric debut, and that June had been the Second Niece in *Grimes* in 1977, and that [June] looked up to Jon." It worked.[14]

Rudel also recalled Carol Vaness's troubles as Dalila, which she sang in London (at the Met she sang the Israelite and Philistine women in some performances). When she importuned Samson onstage, "She told me sometimes [Vickers] would mutter about what I was supposedly doing to her—while she was singing, and he would rattle his chains and stomp about." Rudel laughed ruefully at the memory. "Instead of letting the poor girl sing—and hear the orchestra, which was not very loud!—he was carrying on about what I was doing to her, not to him, about how I was distorting or whatever."[15]

Vaness recalled that Vickers "would sit there [onstage] and say, 'Can you believe how slow that aria was?' . . . I would say, 'Jon, shut up, I'm singing now.' . . . Jon could say, 'Poor Carol, poor Carol,' and that didn't affect me so much; it made me laugh sometimes." Vaness did in fact use ornamentation.

> It was none of his business, but he had fingers into everything because he wanted to be sure the characters would mesh. I ornamented heavily, once I could show the emotional value of it . . . and Jon never said don't.
>
> We never had an argument. We'd be in the middle of something and he'd say, "By the way, I don't think these ornaments you are doing [belong]." . . . I didn't ask him if I would do it. I said, "Let me show you something, Jon." And we would do the scene and I would show him why. All I had to do was be there with him. He didn't like fakes, anybody just saying something to say it. He would just as soon look at you and say, "Bullshit! Don't bullshit me."

She confirmed that Vickers and Rudel had fought over tempi. Rudel could be a strong-minded conductor, "and it was like World War III, getting them together." The role of Samson, Vaness felt, "was not super-easy for him." He was "certainly good up to A," but age had taken its toll on the voice.[16]

The Welsh bass Gwynne Howell, who sang Manoah, Samson's father, in London and Chicago, agreed. "Jon's voice, although it had tremendous character and power and charisma, in order to do ornamentation it needed to be youthful and flexible. So why should Jon expose himself, try to do something that the voice at that time wasn't really at its best to do? Singers never want to expose that kind of a limitation."[17] One conclusion must be that Vickers's concerns ran along those lines, not solely on what he felt was right for Handel performance in general.

Rudel tried his best.

> I would go to him in his dressing room in London, and try to find out [what he wanted], and he would sing it, and the funny thing is, he was inconsistent with himself. . . . For example, he said a steady tempo, and he would start, and after two beats the tempo would not be steady and he would never notice. There were times when the concertmaster or orchestra members and I exchanged smiling glances because of what I had to do to make it seem as if it was a steady tempo, but it wasn't. And they were right with me, and it was wonderful, both in London and Chicago, and New York, everywhere.[18]

Chicago's Bruno Bartoletti, who had been an assistant to Serafin, believed that tempo in general is not absolute. He viewed Vickers as a dramatic tenor, and "to have these beautiful phrases, with Jon you must go a little slow."[19]

In London, Vickers expressed some dissatisfaction with Rudel to Tooley, feeling the conductor was leaning too much to the early music performance side. And for reasons Rudel said he never understood, Vickers evinced strong resentment about the conductor's playing of the harpsichord in the pit (commonplace in Handel's day, and again today in early music performances). Perhaps the tenor felt it distracted from his own work onstage. Rudel said Tooley told him, "Do yourself a favor in Chicago—let somebody else play the harpsichord." Rudel did, although this did not forestall the blowup there in autumn 1985.

That incident occurred at a stage rehearsal when Vickers shouted at Rudel for all to hear: "I can't teach you how to conduct!" and stalked off. It was a moment of extreme mortification for the dignified Viennese veteran, although he carried on bravely with the rehearsal. Rudel offered to resign, but Krainik arranged an apology by Vickers. Rudel recalled with faint bitterness, "He apologized in his dressing room," where nobody else could hear. Mixed with the bitterness was the tinge of astonishment that accompanied so many colleagues' anecdotes of Vickers. "It was the nadir of my career, frankly speaking."[20]

Krainik, typically, downplayed the incident. "He gave a little speech to the chorus, but that's Jon, that's his way. . . . There might have been a couple of rocky minutes."[21] Howell, who was present, said, "Jon always livened up a dull rehearsal. God, if you can't have insults flying around, it gets a bit boring." He said Rudel hadn't said much. "I think Jon needs a response."[22]

Moshinsky, having himself survived Vickers's wrath on several occasions, felt that Rudel had overreacted.[23] But Rudel recalled having a drink with John Coast at the Waldorf bar in London and hearing Coast voice concern that "the man is ruining himself, spouting off and saying he won't sing, and then he complains that he doesn't get any offers."[24]

The situation had settled down by the time of the Met performances of *Samson*, beginning in February 1986. Moshinsky, who also had directed Vickers in *Tristan* and *Grimes*, as well as the Saint-Saëns *Samson*, believed that the Handel hero was an ideal role for the tenor. "He always felt that his character had to somehow be purified . . . and justified of some terrible sin. . . . No one else could portray that, this man laboring under some great sin, which came upon him like a curse."[25]

Samson is a dramatic oratorio rather than an opera, and the title role is the first major heroic part that Handel wrote for a tenor instead of a castrato. This would have pleased Vickers, who had virulent criticism for the castrati and their peacock techniques. Freaks, he called them. Their vocal tradition "was an aberration poor Handel had to cope with," Vickers told Tom Sutcliffe.[26] Based in large part on Milton's *Samson Agonistes*, *Samson* portrays the inner development of the hero as he becomes an instrument of divine will. The destruction of the Philistine temple occurs offstage (unlike the crowd-pleasing Saint-Saëns work).

Vickers spent most of the production chained in a wheeled, platform-like cart; Harapha, the giant, faced off with him in his own cart in one scene that some likened to playing at bumper cars. Vickers wore a ragged, soiled robe, a startling departure from the eighteenth-century garb of the rest of the Israelites, as well as the Philistines. But when Robert Tear later took over the part, he reverted to knee breeches and tied-back wig. Some thought Vickers had insisted on the robe. Tear himself said Vickers had balked at the eighteenth-century dress.[27] But Moshinsky said the situation was just the opposite. "We never wanted to put him in eighteenth-century costume. You can't put Jon Vickers into an eighteenth-century costume. Tear you had to, because he has no mythic quality."

The production was conceived with the idea that Vickers would play a great prophet, "as seen from the point of view of the eighteenth century that wrote about him. It was an oratorio, and the idea was poetic, not realistic," said Moshinsky. When Tear did the revival, "I didn't want him to wear Vickers's costume, because I thought it was too individual" to Vickers, said the director. Whatever the rationale, the robe must have pleased Vickers because it camouflaged his bowed legs as knee breeches could never have done, and he wanted to appear at his best for this major event in his home house.

Moshinsky, who came in after the death of the original director, Michael Geliot, admitted,

> I didn't care two hoots about Handelian style. . . . What's interesting, important is what you feel when someone sings "Total eclipse." If you're only aware of style, then it's a total bore. What I cared about most was that Jon could express what was inside the music—however he did it. It was a personal venture, it was a vehicle . . . and I thought that was terribly important and validated the whole evening. I've never experienced anything like his singing of "Total eclipse."[28]

In an interview during the Lyric broadcast of *Samson*, Moshinsky compared Vickers to Marlon Brando, calling him "the only singer who can play subtext." Moshinsky said "Total eclipse" was meant to be sung with deep expression, although some detached Handelians would have us believe otherwise.[29]

Vickers told Tom Sutcliffe: "The true strength of Samson was in his commitment, his fidelity to his calling" (and this description covered the tenor's calling as well). "His strength was spiritual. He broke faith, and what a price he paid." When Samson sings "My strength returns," he is filled with Jehovah's strength, made manifest in Samson's weakness. "Those are the things you have to convey—not whether you can sing trills and roulades," Vickers declared. But he admitted that his singing had changed with his life experiences since he first had done the role at age thirty-one. "I've had heartbreaks with colleagues. I've had moments of tremendous—almost exaltation."[30]

At the London opening, on February 20, 1985, Vickers was mostly well received. John Higgins of the *Times* wrote, "Jon Vickers has returned in triumph to the title role he first sang at Covent Garden in 1958. . . . The tones may be as grainy as well-weathered oak, but the power of the characterization—another Florestan arisen from the depths—is unquestioned."[31] Peter Stadlen said, "Here was singing of extreme expressionism, shunning all tenoral vanity and no matter if these drawn-out agonised recitatives hardly sounded like period Handel."[32]

In *Opera*, Stanley Sadie sniffed, regarding Rudel, that "there is something slightly bizarre about inviting an Austrian-born American to conduct Handel at Covent Garden." Vickers's Samson, he wrote, was too much like his

Florestan, Otello, and Grimes. "The sound is unrivaled: generous, warm, craggily masculine. And the lumbering stage presence works well for a blind man. But the price is high. The recitative is ponderous and distorted; and the aria lines are constantly violated by Mr. Vickers' way of scooping up to every main note. One wants cleaner singing and more vitality . . . this Samson seemed practically the same age as his father."[33] But in Chicago, where *Samson* opened on October 12, the *Tribune's* John von Rhein insisted that "what was lost in musical fidelity was more than gained in dramatic truth."[34]

When Rudel and Vickers got to the Met, opening February 3, 1986, Alan Rich wrote: "At 59, the Canadian tenor is a volcanic force and seldom, if ever, in better voice than now," singing with a vibrancy "that makes most other tenors sound like wimps. . . . His English diction is an artwork in itself."[35] Martin Mayer noted in *Opera*, "Vickers' sound was mannered, hollow, baritonal—but he never seemed tired or old . . . at all times a dominant figure. I was unhappy with exclusive use of a crooned mezza-voce in the farewell aria, but otherwise I would not find fault. No doubt they sang it differently in the 18th century, but they didn't have a 4,000-seat house to fill."[36]

Andrew Porter, who earlier had found Vickers's "Total eclipse" to be "the most stirring phrases I have ever heard him utter," found much fault in 1986: Vickers "wallows in the role. It is a self-indulgent performance, without subtlety—violent and extreme. He roars, snarls, croons, moans. . . . One can think it a tremendous performance or an unbearable one, or both."[37] And Peter G. Davis noted that Vickers remained "a vocal law unto himself. It is impossible not to be moved by a performer of such craggy integrity, but it is also impossible to enjoy Handel singing that now sounds so labored, mannered, and compromised. I first heard Vickers 27 years ago, at Covent Garden in the same part, and the comparison between then and now is too painful to make."[38]

When this *Samson* was to be revived in London in 1986, Tooley told Vickers that in no way was he willing to repeat it musically as it had been done in 1985. Vickers was lined up for the revival, if not contracted, but Tooley gave Vickers's agent, Coast, two options for him: to come along with the different performance style or to drop out. Vickers opted out.

Tooley's perception of Vickers's career, focused by the *Samson* problems, was that Vickers could have gained even greater artistic heights if he had not refused to see others' ideas and to be influenced by them. Tooley felt strongly that Vickers, who brought many wonderful things to a work, should have relented enough to use new ideas in ways that would have been still his own.

Jon throughout his life had always been too dictatorial with conductors and producers. This was partly born out of Jon's own convictions, but those convictions in my judgment were often too narrow, were too narrowly based, because Jon was blinkered, and Jon could only see things in a certain manner.

That's not to say you didn't get the most phenomenal performances out of Jon, which you did. Absolutely incredible. But sometimes I felt with Jon . . . if he'd allowed his own imagination to be stimulated more by others. . . . Because this is what performance is about—it's not only the possession of an extraordinary instrument, it's obviously the way you use it, and people don't go along too much alone. They're subject to the influences of other people—conductors, producers.

Jon certainly was open to suggestions in the early days, but as he got older, more and more he would row with conductors and say, "I've sung Tristan a hundred and fifty times, ten times more than you've conducted it," and all this sort of stuff. "And I know this is how this should be."[39] [Actually he sang it about sixty times.]

In his later years, Vickers became ever more certain that he knew not only how Tristan should be sung but indeed how much of the world should conduct itself. With the windup of *Samson*, he was just two years from retirement from the stage, but there would be no retiring of the Vickers worldview. This was to offer moments as fiery as any behind the scenes in the opera world.

21

Parsifal *and Farewell to the Met*

A MONTH AFTER THE LONDON *SAMSON* OPENING, VICKERS WAS among twenty-one charter honorees inducted into the Hall of Fame for Great American Opera Singers, launched by Philadelphia's Academy of Vocal Arts on March 30, 1985. He took part in a panel discussion, and at the dinner he mingled with old friends including Regina Resnik, Lili Chookasian, Eleanor Steber, John Macurdy, and John Alexander.

Steber may have been slightly tipsy when she went onstage for her dinner speech. She wound up, startlingly and unsteadily, with Brünnhilde's battle cry, and the applause was mixed with laughter. Some in the audience whispered about her conduct, but Vickers steadfastly saw nothing but a wonderful colleague. He applauded at his table, murmured fondly, "What a character!" and called for someone to help her down from the stage. When his turn came, he read a favorite poem by Arthur O'Shaughnessy, which he had used in other speeches, beginning: "We are the music makers, And we are the dreamers of dreams." It went on to call those music makers the movers and shakers of the world, which Vickers certainly hoped to be with his art.[1]

On April 22 and 23 he was Siegmund for apparently the final time, but only in Act 1, with Ontario's Kitchener-Waterloo Symphony under Raffi Armenian. Lynn Vernon was Sieglinde, William Wildermann was Hunding.

Parsifal is an opera Vickers called "the most blasphemous work ever." Although he shunned *Tannhäuser* on moral grounds, he sang the wise fool many times. He must have come to terms with the messianic Parsifal; in a 1986 Chicago interview, he said the opera is about "the joy of giving, not taking."[2]

Leonie Rysanek emphasized how seriously Vickers took the part. "He is possessed! He believes he *is* Parsifal now when we do it. He's absolutely a saint, a priest, after Kundry's kiss," she told Robert Jacobson in 1986.[3]

Andrew Porter saw this in the spring 1985 Met *Parsifal*, Vickers's last in that house. He gave the tenor what must be seen as the highest accolade (although Porter had not hesitated to be critical of Vickers on occasion, despite his general admiration):

> Mr. Vickers's and Miss Rysanek's reenactment of Christ and the Magdalen and his mystic celebration of the Last Supper were so vivid as to make their presentation in a common playhouse almost unseemly. . . . Mr. Vickers is a tenor who avowedly "carries the responsibility of revealing Christ's continuing redemptive power to the world" [Porter is quoting the *Cambridge Opera Handbook*], and he does so here in a performance that transcends mere aesthetic appraisal.

Such a phrase could be used of few if any other singers. Porter noted, "Today there are no other tenors, and few singers, who interpret with such intensity."[4] Of course, Vickers found Parsifal blasphemous precisely because he feared any identification with Christ.

The German soprano and mezzo soprano Christa Ludwig also spoke highly of Vickers as Parsifal. Of the second act, with the emotional scene between Parsifal and Kundry, she said: "He really had, how shall I put this, not this sexy tenor voice like Domingo or Tauber" —the "creamy voice," she called it—"but he had the type of voice for the Wagnerian parts. When he sang Parsifal, the voice was not sexy; he was neutral. He was a man, but he didn't know love. With Domingo, nobody would believe he didn't know women."

She continued: "I remember . . . when I [as Kundry] wanted to kiss [Vickers], he has to sing "Amfortas, die Wunde." I was in tears on the stage. . . . This outburst for him was so real. He never took care about the voice; he gave always his best. He didn't say, 'I have to sing tomorrow.'" In *Fidelio*, she said, "He really was Florestan, not a fat singer in chains. . . . He was a modern singer. You believed him onstage, as Otello, Aeneas. A very, very rare species, especially of tenors. They are all in love with themselves."[5]

Despite receiving generally outstanding reviews, as with some for *Parsifal*, Vickers remained prickly on the subject of critics. Longtime colleague Shirley Verrett said of him in 1987: "He has that thing about critics . . . many [singers] become so upset they want to punch them out, and it's nerve-wracking." Critics, said the American mezzo, "take swipes at you, when you get to a certain point in your career. They start knocking the pins from under you and some people cannot take this very well. They become very, very defensive." Verrett said that "in the not too distant past," at the Met, Vickers had told her one day, "You know, Shirley, when they write crazy, stupid things . . . they don't know what they're talking about most of the time, and

I just don't come back. And then they miss me." Shrugged Verrett, "That's the way he is."[6]

The agent Merle Hubbard had a lighter recollection of those final *Parsifals* at the Met with Rysanek—as Hubbard put it fondly, "the two old dinosaurs showing the whole world how to do *Parsifal*." Hubbard took Carol Vaness, who had sung often with the tenor, backstage after the second act to see Vickers.

> We went into his dressing room, and he was taking a shower, humming away. And he came out, and he was so happy to see her, and kissy-kissy, wasn't this great. As he's talking to her, he slips on his clothes, and, finally his little homburg, and his umbrella. He says, "Great to see you," and walks out of his dressing room. This was after the second act of *Parsifal*. There's another act. And he was down the hall. And we sat there, and Carol looked at me and said, "Shall we tell him? Shall we go get him?" Well, we decided to go out in the hall, and he came back. He said, "Holy God, there's another act!" This was a broadcast (April 20); he was halfway out of the theater!

Hubbard laughed warmly at the memory.[7]

The Covent Garden production of Handel's *Samson* opened at Chicago Lyric on October 12, 1985, with the American soprano Ellen Shade as Dalila. It was the twenty-fifth anniversary of the tenor's Lyric debut, as Siegmund. The run ended November 1. Domingo had been in the house on October 21 for *Otello*, but dashed off when the Mexican earthquake hit, leaving the rest of the performances to William Johns.

On November 19, 1985, Vickers began a run of six *Pagliaccis* at the Met, replacing Domingo, who was still in Mexico, where he had lost several relatives. The Spaniard, who grew up in Mexico, would cancel many performances to do benefits for the relief effort. These were Vickers's final Canios in the house, where he sang this, one of his most intense roles, only thirteen times.

Hetti was not well, and Vickers said later that he hadn't wanted to leave her, "but she said, 'You are going,' and I agreed on condition I could fly back and forth to be with her between performances." He also recalled his ever-growing disappointment with the opera world. "As I stood in the wings . . . Sherrill Milnes walked out to sing the Prologue and was interrupted three times [by applause] because he hit a high note. I said to myself, what in the name of heaven are you singing for? They have filled the auditorium with people who have come to witness a circus."[8]

In January 1986 Vickers did a week-long stint at the University of Toronto as the music faculty's first Wilma and Clifford Smith Visitor in Music series. He worked closely with students and wound up with a public lecture on *Peter Grimes*.

That February he backed out of a commitment to sing the tenor solo in Andrew Lloyd Webber's Requiem at Centre-in-the-Square in Kitchener, Ontario, in May. The conductor Howard Dyck said Vickers made an oral agreement but then decided the music wasn't right for his voice. Chris Merritt was signed to replace him.

The Met's *Samson* premiered on February 3 and ran for eight performances. In March 1986 at the Metropolitan Opera House Vickers received the Arturo Toscanini Association Artistic Achievement Award, given by the Central Opera Service. The other awardees were Marilyn Horne and James Levine.

In July 1986 the Met offered Vickers a new production of *Salome* for spring 1989, directed by Nikolaus Lehnhoff, with Eva Marton. Klaus Tennstedt was to have conducted, but it fell to Marek Janowski. This turned out to be a striking production, leaving a memory of long curtains blowing eerily on a high gallery, shunning the decadence below. Vickers was offered eight performances and asked to cover one, at ten thousand dollars a performance, three thousand for the cover. The Met's Jonathan Friend made an urgent plea for a decision the following October, but Vickers sent a "no" on November 21.[9] He had sung Herod at Orange in 1974. Hetti didn't care for the role, and he was increasingly concerned about her.

The Royal Opera House toured the Far East again in September 1986. Vickers sang *Samson et Dalila* on September 10 and 13 at Seoul's Sejong Cultural Centre, despite being stricken with laryngitis between the dress rehearsal and first performance. Bruna Baglioni was Dalila in Seoul and continued in the role when Elena Obraztsova apparently was held up by Moscow production requirements.

He was back in shape for the same opera on September 20, 22, and 25 in Tokyo. The company's Korean Airlines charter flight had left Seoul one hour ahead of the airport bomb that exploded there on September 14. Another unfortunate incident intervened on the tour; José Carreras became ill and had to be replaced in *Carmen* by Franco Bonisolli.

Hetti joined her husband on this tour, looking well and no doubt recalling her Far East birthplace, China. Younger daughter Wendy also made the trip, and they joined in lavish parties given by hosts in both countries.

These were to be Vickers's final performances with the company with which his international career had begun in 1957, almost thirty years previous. It is fitting that he was Samson, a religious hero and a fighter to the end.

A plan to have Vickers star in a new opera about the last years of Sitting Bull, chief of the Teton Sioux, at a Calgary Olympic Arts Festival production, turned into another fiasco involving the tenor and his homeland. It would have been an opportunity for him to create a role, something he never did achieve in his career. The opera, titled *Ghost Dance*, with music by American-born Gregory John Levin, then a professor at the University of Calgary, was commissioned by the philanthropist and history buff Floyd S. Chalmers. The producer, John Miller, who had left the Canadian Music Centre, asked Vickers to do it.

Chalmers was pleased, Miller recalled, because Vickers was a man like Sitting Bull, a kind of charismatic elder. Physically, the Sioux leader, also a former shaman and something of a prophet, was short and stocky, and, it was believed, had had a slight limp, like Vickers at the time because of his bad knees. Sitting Bull, who died in 1890 at age fifty-six, had helped defeat General Custer at the Battle of Little Bighorn in 1876, and after the general Sioux defeat had escaped to Canada for five years.

Vickers wanted the English soprano Josephine Barstow to play Catharine Weldon, a New York socialite, do-gooder, and painter who reportedly made her way to the American West and infiltrated Sitting Bull's family. She became a defender of the Indian cause and was welcomed into the chief's tent, although there was ambiguity as to whether he took her as a wife.

Mavor Moore, the author of more than one hundred plays and three musicals, and of the libretto for Harry Somers's 1966 opera *Louis Riel*, had written a libretto ideal for Vickers, said Miller. The ghost dance referred to in the title was a part-Christian, part-Indian cult focused on an Indian messiah who would restore their lands to the Indians. Sitting Bull refused to bar the ghost dance from his region, although Weldon begged him to do so. He was murdered by native police in government employ.

Culminating three years of effort on *Ghost Dance*, a workshop with two performances was conducted November 13 and 15, 1986, at St. Andrew's United Church in Toronto. Vickers's longtime colleague Franz-Paul Decker, just appointed conductor emeritus of the Barcelona Symphony, was interested in taking that orchestra for the opera's premiere at the Winter Olympics in Calgary. Chalmers told Miller that the family would guarantee Vickers's (large) international fee.

Vickers had spent considerable time on the project and at the first workshop was out of sight in the church balcony, poring over the score with

Decker. But "I think he absolutely intimidated the composer," said Miller. "He came on with all guns blaring," to say what was wrong with the work. Miller had been through this and knew it was Vickers's way of dealing with creative propositions.[10]

Richard Woitach, who probably would have coached Vickers for the part, was even more blunt. He told the author that Levin clearly didn't know how to write for the voice, particularly the operatic voice. "Jon did rip into this guy! He said, 'You just don't know anything. How dare you present something like this to [me]?'" Woitach agreed with Vickers, from reading the score.[11] The music was not at all modernistic, but surprisingly lyrical, said Eric Dawson, now entertainment editor of the *Calgary Herald*, who was at the workshop. It did have elements that Dawson thought bordered on kitsch, such as stereotyped Indian rhythms and ululating sounds.[12]

Levin took furious notes on what Vickers said. The Canadian assessors, ill equipped to consider such an opera, seem to have lost their nerve. Vickers's lack of enthusiasm could not have helped. Eight days after the workshop, the Olympic music committee told festival manager Michael Tabbitt they had voted against showcasing the opera's premiere. Federal agencies that would have financially supported the production backed away, and opera companies to whom Tabbitt spoke weren't interested in taking it on.

Tabbitt told Dawson, "There really wasn't an opera there. People commented that if you forgot the music, you'd have a damn good play." It was felt that rewriting couldn't be accomplished in time for the Olympics. Miller, however, told the author, "They decided it was too daunting for them to do. They focused on the weaknesses of the music. Instead of giving us a chance to do [another] workshop, the [artistic] head pulled his support."[13] Dawson also heard that Vickers hated the score, although all he wrote at the time was that the tenor wasn't ready to sign a contract.

The American directors encouraged Miller and Levin to push ahead. But the project never transpired, "another bureaucratic example of this Canadian insecurity with big, risky projects," said Miller.[14] The Canadian Opera Company had never expressed real interest, and in the 1980s it was not looked to as a proponent of Canadian works.

Talk of the new opera was in the air when, shortly afterward, Vickers sang *Die Winterreise* on November 19, 1986, at Calgary's Singer Hall, with Schaaf accompanying. He warned the audience, "I don't do it very well," reported Dawson, who gave him an excellent review, saying he ranged "from the most intimate aside to heroic expressions of the wanderer's pain." At the climax of "Die Kraehe," when Vickers unexpectedly stepped away from the piano and unleashed his voice for the first time, the effect was "devastatingly potent."[15]

In October 1986 Vickers sang Chicago Lyric's first-ever *Parsifal*, a Pier Luigi Pizzi production. Vickers had planned the role there in 1982, but Lyric found the year before that it couldn't afford to mount a production. The tenor agreed to repeat the 1979 *Tristan* instead.

Bill Mason recalled that Vickers could well have been killed on opening night of the *Parsifal*, October 6. At the end of Act 1 a metal pipe fell from above, missed the trim mark, and crashed to the floor just a couple of feet downstage from Vickers. Mason rushed backstage, but Vickers laughed off the incident.[16]

He hadn't laughed about his insistence that Lyric not use the supertitles that soon would become commonly deployed in most houses. He said to the writer Will Crutchfield after a *Parsifal* performance; "I told them it would break my heart if they used supertitles, and they agreed. But if it had come down to it, I would have refused to sing with them." Crutchfield, who also disliked titles, noted, "Anyone who has seen Mr. Vickers in the role will understand how trivializing it would be to make him share the stage with a running commentary."[17]

There is another view. Matthew Epstein, who became Lyric artistic advisor in 1980 (and artistic director in 1999), said that Krainik agreed to skip the titles because of her long relationship with Vickers. "He was very strong about it. They took away the focus from the performer, he felt." But Epstein viewed titles as "a necessary evil," and while he admitted they can distract, there is the compensation of providing the text. "An artist like Vickers who was so text-oriented may or may not have been right in those early days. Anybody who understood the words better got more pleasure out of his performance."[18] Certainly *Parsifal*, with far more talk than action, qualifies as a work for which audiences may be especially grateful for such help.

In this production, John von Rhein credited Vickers with displaying Parsifal's maturation:

> At his first entry this Parsifal was very much the naive child of nature, growing in heroic depth and stature through the epiphany of Kundry's kiss to his final act of healing. Vickers' craggy tenor soared with intensity, rarely sacrificing lyricism to force; his outburst *Amfortas! Die Wunde!* became the dramatic crest of the opera. In his singing and acting, he limned the human, as opposed to the mythic, aspects of the

character. . . . That such a performance should come from an artist who is nearing 60 is astonishing."[19]

Crutchfield called Vickers's performance "startlingly athletic," since in that production Parsifal must fight Klingsor's demons onstage and then dance with the Flower Maidens.[20] In fact, although Vickers did step amid the Maidens, a double who never faced the audience was used for the sword fight, normally offstage.

Vickers's final Met performances came in spring 1987, in the same role as with the Royal Opera House, Samson in Saint-Saëns's *Samson et Dalila*, with Marilyn Horne in four performances and the Bulgarian Alexandrina Milcheva in one, her debut. No announcement was made about Vickers because it wasn't known that these would be his last moments of agonizing misery at the millstone, his final Met struggles to reach that climactic, temple-toppling B-flat.

At the March 28 opening Vickers hugged Horne at the bows, and she put her head on his chest, seeming relieved. At another bow, Horne had murmured to him that nobody in the cast was under fifty. Vickers looked to both sides and said, "Honey, you're the only one under sixty!"[21] He had turned sixty the previous fall.

Ken Vickers, who had talked his father out of retiring a decade earlier, said at the time that these were probably Vickers's last Met appearances. Hetti and Ken were present for the final one on April 18, a broadcast matinee.

As rehearsals began, Vickers had demonstrated once again his remarkable commitment. A year from retirement, the tenor still cared passionately about the details of a performance and about making it convey the emotion that he felt it should. At the first stage rehearsal, Vickers halted everything and for ten or fifteen minutes lectured cast and chorus about the story, the Book of Judges, and Samson's relationship with his fellow Hebrews. "Nobody challenged him, no stage manager told him to stop, everyone was 'spellbound," recalled the writer Cori Ellison, who was in the chorus. They were indeed seeing a legend in action, gaining an insight into just what drove this singer and what might be learned from him.[22]

Peter G. Davis wrote that he hadn't expected a lot from Horne or Vickers, doing strenuous roles late in their careers. "Wrong again. Vickers, of course, has always committed himself to every part he sings with ferocious intensity . . . and so he does here. That brief, wordless inner struggle before he follows Dalila into her tent—pure cornball silent-movie stuff in most tenors' hands—is an unforgettable moment, the tragic climax of a deeply moving, fervently sung interpretation." He liked Horne's haughty temptress too.[23]

Will Crutchfield devoted two lengthy paragraphs to Vickers in his review, reflecting his knowledge and appreciation of the tenor:

> Mr. Vickers was at his best. The idiosyncratic grace and strength of line in his movement are at one with the uniquely personal timbre and strength of his voice. Gestures as simple as kneeling in reverence or making a fist in defiance are imbued with a certainty of meaning that can only be explained by the singer's own inner conviction. The pride of a fierce religious sentiment unbent by captivity rang through his tones in the first act, and the grainy, anguished sound of his voice in the last embodied the weight of knowing his weakness had brought misfortune not only on him, but also on his people.
>
> Mr. Vickers is 60 years old, and to a generation that has heard many tenors far younger falter, the continued potency and security of his voice are remarkable. He can put its full strength behind long, sustained phrases in the region of upper F, G and A flat without strain or apparent fatigue, and he can soften it (to haunting effect in the first-act trio) without fading into insubstantiality. This should come as no surprise: Mr. Vickers has an enormous voice, but does not sing as though a special effort at bigness is the point. And it has been clear for at least four years now that he is going to be one of those singers who approaches the final phase of his career with his wits about him, his choice of roles sound and his vocal technique consolidated rather than flung to the four breezes.[24]

But that career was almost over. After those *Samson*s, Levine had lunch with Vickers. "All Jimmy talked about was the problems he was having with Plácido," said Thomas Pellaton, then with Harold Shaw Concerts, booking Vickers. One can well imagine how that sat with Vickers.

Pellaton said that the only work the Met had offered Vickers for the future was *Salome:* "He was not pleased with that suggestion." Vickers at that point had withdrawn little from his repertory and would have done any of several big roles for the Met.[25]

Emerson Buckley probably was the last orchestra leader whose troops felt the Vickers wrath, during the four performances of *Samson et Dalila* the tenor sang that May with Opera Colorado, Denver, beginning May 9. He had problems with Buckley's orchestra, which seemed uninterested in this opera. Denver's Boettcher Concert Hall has a thrust stage with the musicians partly underneath it. Vickers related, "I was very naughty. I went to the front of the stage and bent down and told them I've sung this many times with the Vienna Philharmonic and they didn't seem to have any trouble playing it."[26]

Viorica Cortez was Dalila, and both she and Vickers were praised. The tenor still brought "stunning conviction and ringing, commanding voice," reported the *Denver Post*'s Glenn Giffin.[27] And Vickers knew these would be his final performances as this hero he had first sung twenty-four years before.

He did a Fourth of July concert, a bit of an odd man out, singing "The Star-Spangled Banner" under James Conlon for the Washington National Symphony's annual "Capital Fourth" concert on the grounds of the Capitol building. His "Winterstürme" was not a piece many visitors lounging on the grass had ever heard, nor was Vickers's name familiar, although he was extolled as "the greatest Wagnerian tenor alive today."

In August 1987, Levine sent Vickers a telegram in which the conductor clung to the hope of Vickers's return in the 1989 Ring Cycle.

> I was very sorry to hear from [agent] Caroline Woodfield of your decision to make the *Samson*s your last performances here, and I hope very much that you will reconsider. I hope you know that all the performances we did together (66, I think) of *Walküre* on the tour, *Otello*, *Parsifal*, *Forza* and *Bartered Bride* were among the high points of my time here; you are really one of the artists with whom I have always felt a close emotional tie. It was also wonderful for me as an audience member to see you so often in *Grimes*, *Fidelio*, *Pagliacci*, *Jenůfa*, the two *Samson*s and the others.
>
> As those two performances of *Walküre* in April/May 1989 are the first time in 50 years that the Met will do the cycle in a complete week, and my first integral cycle, it would specially mean a lot to me if you would come back for these two Siegmunds. Will you think again? I look forward to hearing from you.

Levine added a postscript: "It would also give us a chance to have a discussion (which I had hoped to have during the *Samson*s . . .) about where this crazy art form of ours is going!"

Vickers's personal response was not available. It's possible he felt he was invited only because no other tenor was available for those dates (Gary Lakes and Robert Schunk later were scheduled).

With their five children grown and scattered, the Vickerses found their Bermuda home, Blue Horizons, far too large. On May 29, 1987, Vickers sold the property to the Italian financier Silvio Berlusconi for $4,250,000, a handsome profit over what the tenor had paid. Jon and Hetti moved to Random Rocks, a much smaller but still spacious home on Spanish Point with a private beach but less than an acre of land. It would be the scene of Hetti's last battle.

22

Canadian Coda and a Worldview

VICKERS, SEEKING MORE CONCERT WORK, IN 1985 HAD ASKED Toronto-based General Arts Management, Inc., to book him in North America, although he remained on John Coast's roster for opera. The pianist and photographer Peter Schaaf had suggested GAMI president Peter J. Sever, for whom Schaaf had done some artist photos. Sever opened a New York office in 1985, and Vickers made a deal with him in the back of a limousine on the way to the airport from the Met. Vickers wasn't flexible on his high fees, Sever recalled. "I think at that point it was twenty-five thousand dollars for a concert. For a recital, that was a minimum. Which was high, given that he wasn't known except by the real cognoscenti."[1]

Sever's staff worked the phones daily to book Vickers, often a hard sell. But GAMI got a dozen dates for Vickers in the United States and Canada in the fall of 1987; Laurelle Favreau booked what would be an important one in May 1988 in Kitchener, Ontario.

It was Sever who suggested the program titled "A Retrospective on the History of the Tenor Role in Opera" for Vickers; it served much better for bookings in the United States than did unfamiliar German lieder. And Vickers never wanted to do a series of arias, feeling that few stand up out of context. Other singers later did similar themed concert programs, such as Samuel Ramey's popular "Date with the Devil."

Sever recalled the first concert he booked for Vickers, November 23, 1986, at the six-hundred-seat Performing Arts Center of Montgomery College, in Rockville, Maryland:

> These people—they didn't even know who he was. One of my other
> artists, a chamber orchestra, had cancelled, and they wanted to have
> something Canadian. I said, "Have you heard of Jon Vickers?" No. I
> said, "I tell you what"—because I'm not going to sell him—"you go

and ask around who Jon Vickers is, and we'll talk. Call a few knowledgeable friends."

They did, and they were just fainting who he was—Wow! Von Karajan's favorite tenor! So we booked this concert, and I heard *Winterreise* in a six-hundred-seat hall by Jon Vickers. It was incredible, one of the great concerts of my life.[2]

Sever gave up his New York office in spring 1987, and the company was bought by his staffer Laurelle Favreau. Just after the *Samson*s in Denver, Harold Shaw and Tom Pellaton of Shaw's agency went to Toronto to meet with Vickers. Favreau continued to represent Vickers in Canada, and Shaw signed to handle the tenor for U.S. concerts. But in the year he was on their roster, Shaw was never able to get him a booking. The question of age arose, of whether he was up to a concert. And there was always the fee issue. Shaw handled Hermann Prey, who also was baffled that he could not get more than fifteen thousand dollars for a *Winterreise,* "which I thought was a lot!" said Pellaton.[3]

As for Vickers's other concert possibilities, unimaginative orchestra programmers weren't interested in the *Peter Grimes* final scene. Doing *Das Lied von der Erde* meant a mezzo also had to be paid. (He sang it on January 10, 1987, with the Detroit Symphony under Gunther Herbig, with Stefania Toczyska, and with Giulini in Los Angeles in 1984. He still had *Parsifal* Act 2 and *Walküre* Act 1 on his list.

The Ambassador Auditorium in Pasadena, California, complained about the tenor retrospective program he gave on March 9, 1988. It wasn't a full house. The critic Martin Bernheimer said that the recital was oddly organized, that Vickers's banter was improvised and reminiscent of opera parodist Anna Russell, and that his large talents weren't suited to intimate settings.[4]

Indeed, Vickers had no reputation as a concert artist, a different animal from an opera singer, and Pellaton thought that he would have had to build a concert career. But it was just too late. And Vickers would never understand why the much-marketed Pavarotti and Domingo could command the offers and dollars that he could not, because he thought in such vastly different terms about the value of an artist. But Pellaton said there was no discussion of taking lower fees. "He wasn't interested. He would rather not sing at that point in his career." Vickers told Pellaton that since he wasn't performing as much, it was hard to get the voice up to the level he wanted. It had taken until the middle of the run of the Denver *Samson* to get it in shape. He was sixty-one and now had long gaps between engagements.

Clearly the end was in sight, Pellaton recalled: "There was some bitterness about the way it was ending, and sadness for the state of the art, and a bit of tiredness. He had tilted at all those windmills, a bit of a Don Quixote. . . . He was always on the outside a bit. He never would buy into the sleazy ethics of [the music business]."[5]

Vickers became interested in Mussorgsky's *Songs and Dances of Death*, a work to which he was well suited. He sang the four songs, in English, for the first time in May 1987 at the Guelph Spring Festival, with Richard Woitach at the piano. In September of that year he sang the songs in three performances with the Toronto Symphony under Andrew Davis. But he would cancel a Canadian tour and a Carnegie Hall performance with the same forces.

Robert Everett-Green complained that Vickers "sang the Mussorgsky at roughly the same level as he had with the piano at Guelph, resorting early and often to his dramatic sotto voce. It was an impressive display of Vickers' artistic integrity, except that with so much integrity to worry about, he could scarcely make himself heard. The second song suffered most, as the orchestra gently folded the tenor into its bosom, where he could still be seen mouthing the words."[6]

William Littler noted that "he wasn't afraid to rein in that big sound of his. . . . Instead of trying to make beautiful music with these songs, he concentrated on evoking mood, etching character and projecting meaning. What a remarkable singing actor."[7] A changed critic from the one who saw that "middle-aged tenor" in 1969!

The author attended the September 11 performance and noted that the second song, with the tenor as Death wooing an invalid, was the most striking of the four. Inherent in the music and emphasized by Vickers's presentation was a heavily hypnotic quality. The audience was utterly still as Death stalked lovingly; at the last line, after a brief further silence, it was shocked—the only applicable word—into brief applause; this was a crowd that clearly knew it is not the custom to clap between songs of a cycle. The first song, with the tenor as both Death and a mother, was moving, the two characters clearly delineated vocally and dramatically; the last two songs, dealing with peasants, soldiers, and cavalry in faster tempos, left Vickers a little breathless and visibly happy to have galloped to the end.

The Toronto Symphony was scheduled, with Vickers in the Mussorgsky, for November 1, 1987, at Carnegie Hall. But at the last minute, the tenor canceled. He was in town but was actually ill. Even his Shaw agents in the hall didn't know of his decision. It would have been his final New York concert appearance.

On December 19, 1987, Vickers was announced to sing Jason in Sarah Caldwell's Boston production of *Médée,* scheduled to open January 22, 1988. It was verse in a new Greek translation, with actors miming the action and English surtitles. But on January 12 Vickers's cancelation was announced and a new March 24 opening was given. The *Boston Herald* story suggested the tenor had decided it wasn't wise to sing it that late in his career. On January 29 the *Christian Science Monitor* wrote that Vickers had withdrawn at the last minute because he was not "physically or emotionally or vocally able to do the role," quoting James Morgan, the Boston Opera publicist.[8]

The last half-year of Jon Vickers's career was marked by sacrifice, by a gratifying farewell appearance not planned as such, and by the sad miscarriage of what would have been a Canadian farewell tour.

He had some major bookings for the first half of 1988, runs of *Peter Grimes* at the Maggio Musicale in Florence and in May and June at Covent Garden. But Tom Pellaton took the call when Vickers told the Harold Shaw office that spring that he was finally going to stop singing. Pellaton told him they would keep him on the roster for another year in case something exceptional came along.[9]

The posters went up for the Covent Garden *Grimes* and that spring Vickers, worried about Hetti's condition, flew to New York to coach with Richard Woitach. "He was up on the part . . . but he said, 'I don't know if I'm going to be able to go through with this,'" Woitach recalled. "He said, 'Hetti wants me to do it, but I feel I should be by her side.' And that's what happened."[10]

Vickers canceled the Florence *Grimes* and was replaced by Jacque Trussel, who also was his Covent Garden alternate. Josephine Barstow and Victor Braun were in the ROH cast (their debuts there in *Grimes*) for six performances scheduled with Trussel on May 17 and 21, and with Vickers on June 1, 4, 9, and 11. Vickers let Covent Garden's John Tooley know the situation with Hetti, very straightforwardly, when he canceled his appearances in May, although it was given out at one point by Covent Garden that Vickers had ear problems and couldn't fly.

The same week, a poster went up outside the Royal Opera House saying that Domingo had bowed out of June performances of *Lohengrin,* withdrawing it from his repertoire for the time being because he didn't have time to "re-prepare" it. Patrons would receive partial refunds because the tenors they would hear would not be Domingo. No such poster was up about *Grimes,* nor was there any price cut because it was not Vickers in the role.

And so Vickers sacrificed for the sake of his wife what he knew would have been his final portrayal of Peter Grimes, a role with which he would be forever identified. And he clung to his family privacy to the end, never giving the real reason he had bowed out, although it could have been face-saving for him.

When Vickers canceled in Florence, he then was free to accept an invitation closer to home and Hetti. On May 27 and 28, 1988, Vickers sang *Parsifal*, Act 2, with the Kitchener-Waterloo Symphony, led by Raffi Armenian, in Kitchener, Ontario. Gail Gilmore was Kundry and Claude Corbeil was Klingsor, with a chorus of Flower Maidens.

Kitchener lies in an area of farmland, small homes, lilac bushes, and Lutheran cemeteries, not far from Vickers's farm. The audience was appreciative, although one had to wonder what some made of Amfortas's wound, of Kundry's strange cries. But Vickers himself had come out of a small Canadian town and had conquered this intellectually sophisticated masterwork.

Armenian, born in Egypt and Vienna-trained, had long been a Wagnerite. He helped design the Kitchener Center, with the orchestra pit styled akin to that of Bayreuth, partly under the stage. Three committed singers, an excellent orchestra, and the intimate house made these performances memorable, with Vickers the high point in his "Amfortas! Die Wunde." He was in excellent voice (the author was present for both); it was clear his recent cancelations had not had to do with vocal problems. The voice was as powerful as ever, with only one small break noted, and his soft tones, as on "Die Mutter," were as heartrending.

He was again matchless in his intensity. Elements included the very tension of the body, sometimes poised on one foot, the other heel raised; the head turned in pain, the face downturned in grief, transfigured when uplifted, twisted in contemplation of Amfortas's sufferings; the use of the arms—as much in concert opera as in fully staged performance—held out from the body, raised slowly, hands spread on chest, showing the wound "here"; and at "Love's delirium," arms raised to encircle a lover. When Kundry grasped his arms, they did not respond, as they should not; later, he grasped her arms when offering her salvation. The confident, dominant stride toward Kundry was the same as his stride toward Isolde and Desdemona. The tension was there even in the beginning of the act when he faced the chorus at the rear, his back to the audience for quite some time, or when turning to and from Kundry during her sections.

How does the singer work up to expose so much of himself in a single act of an opera? Such intensity and freshness of feeling go far beyond the repetition of a role sung many times. Courage and confidence may be gained by repetition, but reaching that point cannot be easy with less time to prepare onstage. Such a performance makes clear once again that the sound of this voice was totally individual. It cannot be overstated: Other voices are more beautiful, but few if any voices have been able to convey such passion and meaning. It is a question how much of this singer's art rested on the God-given fact of that sound quality, which can be separated from technique and from the years of mastering the performance of demanding repertoire.

At the bows Vickers was generous as ever, kissing the mezzo, urging the chorus to rise, his back to the audience, and clapping for them. Many of his family were there, and a longtime Canadian friend of Vickers's, Dr. Clive Mortimer, also went backstage. "He said, 'I'm glad you're here. You heard my final concert. You heard me perform for the last time,'" Mortimer recalled. "This was our first inkling. . . . He always said he'd quit 'before anybody tells me to.' We chatted with him about how he felt. He just said, 'It's over. It's finished. It's not been bad, has it?' I think he has that incredible strength. He said he'd walk away from it, and he did."[11]

Armenian, however, didn't learn he had conducted Vickers's final public appearance until about a month later, when he received a letter from the tenor. "He said he didn't want to tell me then. He started in a small town in Canada, and wanted to end in a small town in Canada."[12] One of Vickers's first concert dates in the 1950s had been a Verdi Requiem in Kitchener, with Lois Marshall, Maureen Forrester, and James Milligan.

And so a career ended quietly, amid the Ontario farmlands, the roots from which this tenor had sprung. If Vickers was at all disappointed in this finale, he would have but to think of a story he was fond of telling about the Roman general Cincinnatus. Following great victories, the general had felt unneeded by his country and had retired to raise cabbages. After serving the empire yet once more, the soldier-farmer again took up his gardening with pride, knowing, as Vickers said, that "there is no defeat if one holds on to the ultimate in honesty and seeks ever to relate his life to it." Such a retirement holds only simplicity and dignity.[13] And that is how it was with Jon Vickers.

That *Parsifal* might have been followed by a series of Canadian farewell concerts. Peter Sever had worked on a fifty-concert eastern Canadian tour for Vickers, to take place in 1988. It was, Sever said, disastrously subverted by the Canada Council, a final blow to Vickers by his homeland at a time when he should have been retiring full of honors. The council is Canada's national funding agency for the arts and, like most bureaucracies, no stranger to petty bickering, as Maureen Forrester noted in her autobiography.[14]

Said Sever: "The Canada Council, for purely political reasons, turned it down. And the reason, bottom line—they didn't like Jon Vickers. The bureaucrats didn't like Jon Vickers because he's outspoken and he's difficult and he's all the things he is." Forrester was chairman at the time, and may not have been involved in details of the tour. But Sever says she told him of Vickers, "He's not a nice man, you know."

The council rejected the first tour proposal by GAMI, then, according to Sever, offered a grant intentionally low enough that the council knew the tour couldn't be financed. "Jon and I were both *furious* about it. And the fee that he was asking was reasonable. He came down to [something] like five thousand dollars a concert . . . which for him is very reasonable. Plus pianist, plus . . . I had worked out that he'd walk away with five thousand dollars a concert."[15] That was remarkably reasonable for Vickers, fifteen or twenty thousand dollars less than what he had asked for concerts outside Canada.

Laurelle Favreau, having taken over GAMI from Sever in spring 1987, continued to work on council-related tour dates that fall for Vickers in provinces including New Brunswick, Quebec, and Nova Scotia. Favreau, like Vickers a Prince Albert native, recalled that GAMI had worked to line up presenters for about two years. When the council first turned down the idea, which proposed a large grant that would have given Vickers his regular fee, it said its mandate was to fund younger artists. It is possible that Forrester took some offense at that fee, since she had toured Canada for much less. (The council said it had no files on the first proposal.) Favreau asked presenters to write the council, saying this was a unique opportunity to hear a great artist in their communities, one they would not have without a grant.[16]

Vickers agreed to lower his fee, and GAMI made another request to the council, which wrote back in March 1988 that the grant would be for just $41,425, with the first installment forwarded in August 1988. And the council wanted Vickers to appear with a young Canadian pianist, although Vickers could have some choice in that. He had wanted his frequent accompanist Peter Schaaf, who would have been much more appropriate for a farewell tour than a young player unused to working with a singer now legendary. (There was also discussion of using Catherine Vickers, a pianist who was a daughter of Vickers's brother Wesley.)

In 1991 Vickers recalled the tour episode this way. He had agreed to sing for one-seventh of his fee. "Then all of a sudden I got a letter informing me that I could do ten concerts, only on the condition that I took along with me another young *aspiring* Canadian artist to share the platform. . . . Right or wrong, I would not tolerate that for one second." This was not, he insisted, because it would have taken anything away from his own performance. But

"I turned it down for the same reason as when the Lauritz Melchior Heldentenor Foundation contacted me [in 1990] and wanted me to chair the massive, world competition to find . . . a successor to Melchior. Prize money was to be a minimum of fifty thousand dollars," he said, sounding amazed at the amount. He had asked if there must be a winner. Told yes, he said, "I won't touch it!" He told the foundation, "First of all you are exploiting the name of Melchior, and second of all you are setting up somebody else to be exploited. . . . Sure, for two or three years he'll probably make a lot of money, whether he can sing or not. I could sell a fish on the name of Melchior! It's a cruelty." Vickers seemed to be speaking yet again for excellence, not wanting to name an undeserving winner.

Jumping back to the aborted Canadian tour, he said, "I don't mean to say I'm . . . too big to share a platform with a young Canadian person. But I like to flatter myself to think it would be a badge of honor for some youngster to come on the platform and share the stage with me. And I don't think that's arrogance."[17] From the way he spoke, it seemed clear the council episode was still painful to him.

He was asked at that 1991 lecture if he believed the saying that a prophet is without honor in his own country. He brushed that off: "Who cares." He noted that Benjamin Britten had "a problem" with acceptance. And "Birgit Nilsson was always second-rate in Sweden."[18]

Favreau and Sever, who continued to work together on Vickers's engagements, went to the *Parsifal* in Kitchener in May 1988, but the tenor said nothing to them about its being his last appearance. Favreau said the accompanist issue was resolved, and Vickers could have Schaaf. Contracts had been made with a dozen presenters and venues. In mid-July Favreau got a call from Vickers, who was in Bermuda. He told her the *Parsifal* had been his final concert, and he was going to retire. "It was a very deep voice, very calm, very slow, stating that was going to be his last concert, how he wanted to end his career," and he was not going to do the Canadian recitals.

Favreau was stunned, on a personal level because she had just taken over GAMI and the tour was financially important to her. As for Vickers, "He got burned so many times coming to Canada, and this compounded it again. In no way can I blame him," said Favreau. "I'm just so sorry it had to end the way it did. We wanted to make it a great experience for him. The country type of guy he is, he would have enjoyed those [small] halls."

But she knew that the *Parsifal* concert had been a high point for the tenor, and she realized how hard it was for him to get his voice up to his standards when he was singing so infrequently. She knew that his wife's health was a continuing concern and had caused him to cancel other GAMI dates, including a televised 1987 Montreal Symphony concert and the Toronto Symphony tour.

The council was shocked at his withdrawal, she said, and the presenters were deeply disappointed. Favreau, who had hoped for a western Canada tour for Vickers the following year, could not bring herself to bill him for expenses incurred in the planning. Ironically, Forrester replaced Vickers on the tour. She was delighted to do so, said Favreau, and appeared with a soprano on the GAMI roster, Rosemarie Landry, and a Canadian pianist, André Laplante. Favreau lost two presenters, but Forrester did the other ten dates.

Had the Canada Council approved the tour earlier, without a two-year fight, said Favreau with a tinge of bitterness, Vickers's voice as well as his wife's health might both have been in better condition.[19] And Vickers would have had the farewell tour that he, and Canada, richly deserved.

Jon Vickers's personality was so powerful, he was so eager to put across his views, and he had such physical and mental stamina that many thought he could have done well on the stage of the real world.

He could have been a prime minister, a world leader rising from populist roots on his farm. He most certainly would have been a magnate had he remained in the retail business field where he began. But in a way he did have a second career even as he attained the highest rank in opera: He was a preacher, without ordination, as his father had been, and humbly proud of it. He had his father's orotund speaking voice. If you closed your eyes when Vickers was lecturing, or simply in passionate conversation, as his phrases rolled out, rising and falling dramatically, you could well imagine him in cleric's garb, thundering from the pulpit.

He loved to talk, and he knew the impact he could have. "It's strange to stand here in front of you people and preach, because I feel that's what I do," he told a London audience in 1981. "But," he intoned with rising drama, "I would not be an opera singer, I would not walk onto an opera stage unless I was convinced that when I did it, I was trying to reach through the proscenium arch and taking ahold of each one of you people emotionally and intellectually, and trying to raise your eyes and your feelings and your emotions to look at the Divine."[20]

That was certainly an audience-stopper; singers didn't talk this way. Many (especially tenors) were thought to have little in those cavities whence their sound emanated, and most didn't broach topics like the Almighty or the downfall of Western civilization, another favorite topic of this tenor. They were content with "And then I sang . . ." But to many, Vickers was the

Old Testament incarnate, onstage and off. He wore Samson's rags instead of cleric's collar and spoke directly to his Lord and Savior. Andrew Porter and Sir Edward Downes both regretted that Vickers never sang the title role of *Stiffelio*, Verdi's minister who pardons his adulterous wife from the pulpit after much soul-searching.

Many friends, colleagues, and acquaintances of Vickers's would tell of their brushes, in varying degrees, with his convictions. Most respected them, and it was difficult not to do so, although in later years some found him veering to the pompous. His memorial remarks in Toronto on the soprano Lois Marshall in 1997 were criticized as such.

One story, possibly apocryphal, had a soprano at the Met fleeing the lecherous clutches of a baritone, who was warned off by Vickers. Having rescued the woman, in his dressing room he asked her (a Jew) whether she had recognized Jesus as her savior. The soprano's response: "Better I had gone with the baritone!"

From the daily Bible teachings of his boyhood, and from the books of philosophy, theology, history, and psychology that he devoured in hotel rooms around the globe, Vickers crafted a worldview that was devoutly Christian and anticommunist, dipped in Freudian and Jungian theories in the days before those came into question. He was also, in the 1990s phrase, politically incorrect, because he believed deeply in a meritocracy. Excellence was almost a deity to him; he had no room for mediocrity, however "diverse." "We are living in a society in which this absurd contradiction of equality has crept in. There isn't equality, there never will be, and to pretend there is, is an insult," he said, using Plato as a reference.[21]

He admired Jewish contributions and abhorred Hitler; he often quoted from works by the psychiatrist Viktor E. Frankl, a concentration camp survivor who focused on man's search for meaning. Black singers were among his best friends and colleagues, and nobody rooted harder for the African-American boxer Evander Holyfield. But Vickers's fundamental lack of sympathy with homosexuals popped out from time to time, although some played major roles along his career path. The bass-baritone Sir Donald McIntyre came from a strong Methodism and had no such bias; he suggested something psychological was at work with Vickers.[22]

Vickers spoke out for the needs of art, as he saw them, deploring the spread of commercialism and marketing that reached a peak with the Three Tenors syndrome in the 1990s. In later years he castigated gifted people who "seize upon the opportunity their talents have given them to enrich themselves, while they degrade art in contributing to the decline of our culture and civilization." It is no leap to see he had especially in mind those other tenors. "If you can't dazzle them with brilliance, then you blind them with bullshit," was a favorite Vickers lecture comment on image-making in the arts. He always remembered that Herbert Breslin had told him 95 percent of audiences can't recognize a good singer from a bad one. He believed that true art comprises "beauty, truth and love—and if any one of them is missing there is no work of Art."[23]

He was fond of quoting Picasso, whom he often reviled as a fake, though an admitted one. "When art ceases to be the food that feeds the best minds, the artist can use his talents to perform all the tricks of the intellectual charlatan," wrote Picasso in a quote Vickers repeated in his talks. And for Vickers the term *art* must never be applied to sports, buildings, or other mundane works. This was an abuse, a lowering of the word to banality. He was appalled when some Canadian festival organizers put forth an exhibit of hockey masks as art. (He was disinvited to that Vancouver festival.) However, in his view, even conductors, singers, and other performers are not artists; they merely serve the true creative artists, the composers. This was a favorite theme.

Vickers's religious beliefs rode in tandem with his art, almost served it, though he might call that blasphemous. His voice was "God-given," he told many. This was not a strange thing to say, because he had been told that was so since he was a small child, by the parents he revered. He felt close to God, and colleagues were made quite aware of this. The producer Humphrey Burton recalled negotiating with Vickers in his agent's office and having the tenor tell him, "I have a pipeline to God." Responded Burton, "I'm sure you have."[24]

When Vickers was recording *Les Troyens*, David Cairns recalled, "Somebody was saying, '"Why is Vickers doing such and such,' and someone said, rather bitterly, 'I expect it's because God told him.'"[25]

Vickers was deeply impressed by the late United Nations Secretary General Dag Hammarskjöld and his book, *Markings*. The Swede thought deeply about his relationship to God and felt himself an instrument thereof, as did Vickers. However, W. H. Auden notes in his foreword to that book, "The man who says, 'Not I, but God in me' is always in great danger of imagining that he *is* God." This can lead to a refusal to listen to those who disagree with him and to paranoia, he wrote, adding that neither could be proven of Hammarskjöld.[26]

Dr. R. Maurice Boyd is an Irish-born Presbyterian minister, a onetime actor, and an opera lover who became friendly with the Vickers family while living in London, Ontario. In 1989, after his retirement, Vickers sang two solo hymns at Boyd's church at the time, New York's Fifth Avenue Presbyterian. Boyd admired what he called the enormous integrity that Vickers brought to his work. "No one is more aware that he is under the authority of the art, of what it is that he represents . . . a noble succession. If he speaks of Otello, it's to speak of all those who have attempted to realize [the role], and with a sense almost of incredulity that he's been allowed to be part of this."

And Boyd noted that the person who is under authority is the person who *has* authority. "If you're under the authority of art, then you have standards; you won't prostitute your art. You will have a sense of integrity towards the composer and the music." Of Vickers's specific religion, Boyd said he is fairly conservative but not a Bible literalist or a fundamentalist, and he has "a wonderful sense of the transcendent, of the Divine expectation and of the Divine grace and mercy."[27]

A recollection by Teresa Stratas gives insight into Vickers's view of the world. In February and March 1979 she was singing Berg's *Lulu* in Paris, directed by Rolf Liebermann. Vickers was finishing his second run of *Poppea*. He told her, "You look terrible!" and went on to comment that it must be because of "that dirty role" she was playing, the amoral Lulu. In fact, he disapproved of the liberal Stratas's lifestyle, she felt. His was a far more straitlaced, conservative philosophy, whatever his own failings may have been.

She also recalled an *Otello* rehearsal in Montreal, attended by her niece. Vickers was throwing her to the ground as the Desdemona he suspected of faithlessness, calling her "that dirty thing," the harlot—*cortigiania*—Otello fears she has become. Stratas had to reassure her niece that it was just acting, but she felt that Vickers in fact might have been deploring whatever he saw as Stratas's own flaws.

Robert Duvall as a hellfire Pentecostal preacher in the 1997 movie *The Apostle* reminded Stratas strongly of Vickers. And he was a lot like John the Baptist to her. The Baptist may have been lustful for Salome, but he kept those fires damped down as best he could, seeking refuge in his faith.[28]

Vickers sang Tristan but scorned the faithlessness to his king. He sang Siegmund but was critical of the incestuous love of that hero for his twin sister. He shunned any suggestion that Parsifal could be the Savior. And of course he declined to sing Tannhäuser, citing moral grounds.

In his public talks Vickers spoke out against general moral decline and lack of love for children, against rock music's siren song to the senses, against drug use. He espoused the moral views of the American conservative William Bennett. His closeness to the soil—chopping wood, birthing calves on his farm—kept him in touch with fundamentals, he often said. He felt that calling evil men animals was an insult to the animal world. In his later years, Vickers enjoyed lecturing at colleges; sometimes they were billed as lecture-demonstrations, but he rarely sang more than a line or two. Audiences as yet unexposed to his speaking style would be startled to hear him launch wholeheartedly into discussions of the Holocaust, of the nature of man, of his view of the spread of evil in the land (noting cat food commercials using Mozart, as well as drug problems and homosexuality), or on occasion, on genetic engineering involving changing the estrus cycles of cows.

After hearing a few of these talks, one can see how much Vickers put his soul into them. One talk in particular yielded some clues as to how he saw these efforts. "We've got to abandon the concept of big television-coverage solutions. It has to start with you and me. I believe with all my heart in a little yeast in the loaf." Vickers relished a quote from Laurens van der Post: "He said Jesus only addressed the crowd once, and spent all the rest of his time with twelve ordinary men." He noted that he had been invited to do a series of master classes and lectures in Banff, Canada, that would be broadcast. He declined, preferring to meet with smaller groups that he could see were interested deeply in his interests: art and its salvation, and Jesus and the salvation of the world.[29]

The tenor offered a homely farm metaphor about his life and gift. "Sometimes when you're digging up potatoes, you find the most beautiful one, but on the side, there's a little bump. . . . If that bump is bruised, it will go rotten and contaminate the whole potato. So you take a knife and just nicely slice it off. I always say that the potato is me, and the little bump on my side is my talent. I think if I could cut it off, I'd still be a whole potato."

He said this wearily in January 1978, the year he almost retired, adding, "I don't think I should sing any more. I think I have made my contribution" to what he called the revolution in opera led by Wieland Wagner and Callas. But that revolution was spent, and he was tired of fighting.[30]

Vickers wrestled with himself and his convictions. He fought hubris, although he believed himself to be among the best, if not the best, of the tenors of his time. He spoke of his contributions as tiny, but, paradoxical as always, he clearly was aware that they were huge. "I have involved audiences over and over again with my Tristan, my Grimes and my *Fidelio*—I'm not bragging, it's fact."[31] Some said he battled sexual temptation, always a musky companion for performers on the lonely road. He exhausted himself in weighing the moralities of all his business and artistic dealings.

And he never did conquer his stubbornness, perhaps his most enduring quality. "I never bluff" was a favorite warning. Jon Vickers rarely changed his mind, once he had made it up.

Epilogue

"Will you please just play my tunes once in a while?"
— Jon Vickers, 1991, on the organ grinder
in *Die Winterreise* as representing every artist

THE CRITIC JOHN STEANE, IN NOTES FOR AN IMPORTANT 1997 video release, *The Art of Singing: Golden Voices of the Century*, once again placed Vickers "in a class of his own." Steane ranked his Florestan as "one of the supreme portrayals of the age, a distinction shared with Christoff's Boris Godunov, Gobbi's Scarpia, and Callas's Tosca.[1] Vickers appears on the video in Florestan's aria and speaks about Callas.

"They can't touch me now," the tenor had said in a dinner table conversation in 1985, at an Academy of Vocal Arts dinner in Philadelphia. He meant, of course, the critics; he knew his place in history was secure.[2] But still there would remain that nagging ambivalence about the recognition of his own art.

His demons continued to torment him well after he had left the stage. By October 1993 he still had not begun his own book, and when I asked about it, he said, "Who cares! Who cares? Nobody's going to remember. You mention my name today and they don't know who I am! . . . If I walked into the Metropolitan Opera company today, nobody would know who I was!" He amended, "The chorus would know."[3]

Martin Bernheimer had written of similar dismay on Vickers's part in the 1980s when the tenor told how he had called the Met business office to be greeted by a person who did not recognize his name.[4]

This time, despite reassurances, he continued, "I'm just a teeny, weeny, weeny, weeny, weeny little blip in the history of opera, and I know that." Mollified slightly by further assurances of his place in the operatic annals, he said, "Well, I would like to think that maybe I had made a little statement. But I don't have the ability of a Mozart to have the last laugh!"

This conversation occurred the day before his sixty-seventh birthday. Vickers could turn vehement on many topics, and this was a theme I had heard from him before. Still, it was troubling to hear this sense of unfulfillment expressed by such a great artist. He did add, "Don't misunderstand me. I'm not bitter. I had a phenomenal career. I had a phenomenal life. I have no bitterness. The operatic world was good to me!" Clearly, he still was brooding about past battles when he added, "But I fought, not for Jon Vickers, and that's what the press said about me, that I was a difficult crotchety man who fought for himself." He believed he had fought to offer the best of his art.[5]

Fortunately, after his retirement the Vickers legacy was to be confirmed for posterity by a number of re-releases and new releases of some of his earlier work, notably by Video Artists International, owned by Ernest Gilbert. The red tape of various bureaucracies, including Canada's CBC, was negotiated skillfully by Gilbert, so that many audio and video treasures could be released. The videos included early CBC-TV productions of portions of *Manon Lescaut, Tosca,* and *Il Trovatore,* operas Vickers never sang in full, and a complete 1955 CBC *Pagliacci,* Vickers's first Canio; a group of scenes (*Samson et Dalila, Otello, Fidelio, Grimes*), taped in 1984 at the Ottawa National Arts Centre; the CBC telecast of the 1965 Toronto concert with Böhm; and a 90-minute *Tristan* in Montreal, with Knie. As of this writing, a video of Vickers in a real gem, *H.M.S. Pinafore,* a tight T-shirt revealing the tenor's youthful musculature, awaited release.

VAI audio releases included the 1967 Carnegie Hall concert, a live 1968 Buenos Aires *Pagliacci,* and his first *Tristan* in Buenos Aires. Gilbert tried unsuccessfully to get Vickers to make some new recordings. A Christmas album was talked of in the early 1990s, but Vickers was too busy with family visits, although he had been vocalizing.

Vickers picked up another honorary degree, a Doctor of Letters, on May 31, 1990, from the University of British Columbia, from which his wife had graduated. He very much enjoyed giving lectures, indeed preferred them to master classes, and did little such work after he left the stage. He had talked of directing and even conducting, and of establishing music programs in Bermuda or Canada, but never took up those careers.

He did encourage several younger tenors, including the late Timothy Jenkins, and another young American, Ian DeNolfo. But it seemed that his gifts were not really ones that could be passed on to students; his voice and his methods were so individual that they stood apart. This is not to say that young singers were not eager to question him, as they did after his lectures, and to hear his stories. He stressed strongly that they should never be themselves onstage but should always demonstrate the emotions of their characters.

Younger talents in the opera world looked to him. Said the controversial director Peter Sellars, whose updated productions Vickers probably disliked:

"I think a great mistake has been made in a lot of the opera world, that voices [should be] pretty. To me, that's like only wanting to marry a dumb blonde! To me, a voice also can possess intelligence, soulfulness, a kind of moral force. A voice contains so many qualities, and prettiness of sound is not the primary one, actually." He suggested, "You have Jon Vickers, or you have Shirley Verrett, certain singers who—the sound isn't pretty, it's expressive and [emotionally] deep. And that's what you're looking for."[6]

Meanwhile, among tenors of Vickers's time, Franco Corelli, several years Vickers's senior (how many is at issue), was making more public appearances. Lured by the New York opera radio talk show host Stefan Zucker, Corelli took part in lectures; he talked vaguely in the early 1990s of another recording. Carlo Bergonzi gave a New York concert as late as 1999, sounding as committed and enthusiastic as in youth, his warm tone and remarkable breath control intact.

In December 1990 Jon and Hetti's Christmas card together showed them with all their children (a tradition each year) and the children's spouses: Allison and then-husband Kym Anthony; Bill Vickers and wife Karen; young Jonathan Vickers, who would become a United Church minister, and wife Mary; Ken Vickers and wife Jane; and Wendy and husband Andrew Roughton (they had married in 1989); plus Allison's three children, one cradled on Hetti's lap, and two with their grandfather.

Vickers gave three lectures in July 1991 at the Royal Conservatory of Music in Toronto and began one by saying he would illustrate "man as a spiritual being," a favorite Vickers phrase. This turned out to be a description of helping a heifer give birth on his farm, where for thirty years he had run a cow-calf operation. He told of trying to subdue the terrified animal, in pain with a breech presentation. Using a rope hooked to the back of a truck, Vickers and helpers made her lie down and finally pulled out the calf.

"We dragged it around to the mother's nose, and instantly, all struggle, tension, and fear vanished, replaced by a tender concern it's simply hard to believe an animal such as a cow could demonstrate. We gathered up all of our paraphernalia . . . and left her with her new calf, who was at that moment the whole of her world. Now that is a mystery, a very fundamental, miraculous mystery." Had the calf died, the heifer would have had only "a mild curiosity" about it. But, Vickers said, man "ponders the mystery of life, relationships, everything." And he segued, typically, into mention of Laurens van der Post on a visit to African bushmen.

The lectures included Vickers's usual defense of Western culture and classical art, as he thundered that "multiculturalism is no culture!" For more than twenty years "beloved Canada" has been subjected to "a steady stream of clowns and mountebanks," he said. "Those who shout the loudest about our culture cannot begin to define it. . . . . The search for truth is being subjugated to Canadian content. The wrong culture is being cultivated; cancer is being cultivated, if you will." Canada, he said, faces the danger of choosing a mosaic, not a melting pot. "We are tearing ourselves apart." And he quoted the author Robertson Davies to note that the Bible used to be shorthand for all, but no longer. "Western civilization has a foundation more stable than anything in history."[7]

As usual, there was fallout of a very Canadian kind. Toronto had become a much more diverse city than in Vickers's early days there. After the first lecture, the conservatory received a number of letters complaining about what were perceived as Vickers's ethnic and sexist biases. At the second talk, Vice Principal Robert Creech said that Vickers invited any who wished to dispute him to speak out. None did, although a soprano who had written was one of several women who became embroiled in a discussion with Vickers about changing mores in the light of birth control advances and new perceptions of female sexuality. Vickers, as might be expected, remained unmoved by their arguments.

Vickers spoke of the final song in *Die Winterreise*, the organ grinder's lonely lament, reading an unusual meaning into it. He said the grinder was like an old singer, hoping that his tunes would be played once in a while.

The singer Ian Garratt talked with Vickers by phone a week after the lectures, and after a critical article in the *Toronto Globe and Mail*. Vickers said he was upset because he felt he had been misunderstood. So was Hetti, who had not been strong enough to attend the talks. "But she wasn't so ill that I couldn't hear her in the background yelling 'There was no truth in it,' about the *Globe* story," said Garratt.[8]

Jon and Hetti returned to their Bermuda home, and in October 1991 Hetti was so ill that her children were called to see her. Vickers himself was in quite some pain with his arthritic knees; he was taking Prednisone and had put up a good front at the July lectures when he strode onto the stage and up auditorium steps with no visible discomfort. He had stood greeting admirers after all three talks. He planned to have both knees replaced that very month, but then his wife reached her last days.

Hetti Vickers's agonizing battle with cancer came to an end on the evening of November 24, 1991, when she died quietly at home in her husband's arms. She was just sixty-four years old. She would never have lived so long, the family believed, but for her husband's attentive care. He had, without ever making public the real reason, canceled a number of important performances in his last years of singing to be with her.

She had had many operations after the diagnosis of breast cancer in the late 1970s, and Vickers would take her home to the farm afterward, as she wanted, in the RV in which she could have a bed. Toward the end he personally attended to her needs and changed her dressings.

She left her husband and children admiring her bravery and spiritual fortitude but ravaged with grief. It was as if all the suffering Vickers had ever portrayed on the stage, as Siegmund, Samson, Florestan, Tristan, had gathered in bitter chorus around him.

She died on the first birthday of granddaughter Erin, child of Ken and Jane. All were present; Hetti had wanted to have a little party in her room for Erin, and they did. Then she slipped away, her family around her. It was in important ways a good death. Vickers must have recalled the death of his mother, who also had expressed contentment and no fear, with faith in eternity.

The funeral was delayed till Thursday, November 28, so that sons Billy and Jonathan could arrive in Bermuda. On Wednesday night the family had visiting hours at Random Rocks. Hetti was in an open coffin, surrounded by flowers. One Bermuda friend said, "The family was very proud of how serene she looked." Vickers was outwardly jovial as usual, but he was marked by sorrow. He seemed more stooped, his collar bigger, his white hair in unusual disarray, his eyes and cheeks seeming worn by tears. Typically, he spoke only of what an amazing woman his wife had been.

Friends marveled at the faith that clearly sustained him and his children. But some wondered how well Vickers would survive without his wife. He had traveled so much over the years that his roots were less deep in Bermuda than Hetti's. Many people were in awe of him and afraid to approach him in friendship.

The funeral was in Christ Church in Warwick parish, across Hamilton Harbor from the city of Hamilton. It was the Scottish church of Hetti's family. Founded in 1719, the small white building boasted of being the oldest Presbyterian church in the Western Hemisphere.

It rained steadily from gray skies that Thursday afternoon. Hetti's coffin was covered in white flowers and greens. The family sat in the front pews, and some could hear Vickers's voice raised in the hymns. The minister told the mourners that Hetti had been to church just two weeks before, to an 8 A.M. service, even though she was on oxygen. Her husband had carried her into the church.

When the minister had visited her in the days before her death, "She said, 'It's a gift.'" She meant, he said, that God had allowed her to be able to bear the burden of her illness. When she learned of her "virulent" form of cancer, she decided not to be a victim, but to live with it as fully as she could. "She never spoke a word of resentment, of why did this happen to me?"

The readings were the Ninety-first Psalm: "Thou shalt not be afraid . . . for the pestilence that walketh in darkness"; Paul's Epistle to the Romans, chapter 8; Revelation; and John on betrayal. The minister echoed what all her friends would say of Hetti Vickers: She was a woman of radiant strength and unfailing faith, whose family was her most important priority. "She was happiest when all of them could be together," he said.

The mourners followed coffin and family out the side door to the rear of the cemetery that surrounds the church. Hetti was laid inside one of the flat white marble tombs. There also would be a memorial service for her in Ripley, Ontario, where her parents were buried.

Ken and Jane were to stay with Vickers through the following April. That spring he faced the postponed surgery for total replacement of both his knees; his arthritis had become continuously painful. Ken and his wife were to be with him in Bermuda for the arduous recuperation period, during which Ken would renovate a house on St. George's. Perhaps if Vickers could take some part in that, the work of the hands of which he had done so much, it could help restore him. He would stay in Bermuda, certainly in the winter. He was no longer fond of the cold that clamped down on Canada for so many months of the year.

To the surprise of some friends, Vickers married Judith Panek Stewart on March 27, 1993, at her home in Arcadia, California, near Pasadena. A Presbyterian minister performed the ceremony. At fifty-three, she was thirteen years younger than Vickers; she was born October 1, 1939. She was a flight attendant and the mother of a daughter, Piper, nineteen, and a son, Justin, seventeen, by her previous marriage, which had ended in divorce in February 1984. Her parents were Ralph W. Panek, born in Kentucky, and Illinois-born Evelyn Bode.

Jon had known her for thirty-one years, since he met her on a plane. Hetti also knew her and had urged that after her death they marry. She knew that her husband was not a man who would do well without a wife.

Judy, as she is known, continued to fly for United Airlines until her retirement date at fifty-five, after flying for more than thirty-three years. The couple seemed well suited to one another; dark-haired Judy was petite, sweet-faced, and serene as Hetti had been, and held similar values. They took a two-week Tall Ships honeymoon cruise in the Caribbean.

Vickers, with two stepchildren making him patriarch now to a brood of seven, became much involved with his new wife's family. He spoke of helping tutor his stepdaughter in an assignment on Oedipus; she had quite a resource in a man who had portrayed great heroes onstage. The marriage added to his ever-peripatetic life, as for the next several years they traveled not only between Bermuda and the farm but also to her home and to visit her parents in the Midwest. They also made trips to Prince Albert for Vickers's school reunions.

By 1994 Vickers was settled into his comfortable second marriage and devoting time to his family. That June he and Judy flew to Italy, where Vickers was a judge in Giuseppe di Stefano's voice competition. Peter Glossop, to whom Vickers still referred as "my Iago," talked Vickers into taking part, despite the tenor's disdain of such contests. As Vickers told it, di Stefano and the organizers told Glossop, "Work on Jon!" Vickers had known Pippo, as di Stefano was called, for decades, and liked him.

Vickers was his energetic, realistic self in the role of judge; on the panel was Felicia Weathers, with whom he had sung in *The Queen of Spades* at the Met. The contest included some seventy-three singers, an unusually large number, and Vickers said, "From the beginning, I started marking very hard, because when I saw seventy-three people, I said, 'This is crazy.' . . . Some of my other judges thought I was being heartless . . . but I said, 'You're going to have to do the same thing anyway.'"

No Italian tenors won. Vickers lamented that the contest showed that "the standard of Italian singing teachers . . . is terrible. . . . [The Italian singers] had good voices, but they didn't know how to sing."[9]

As Vickers judged the young singers, three tenors not so much younger than he were preparing for the Three Tenors Encore concert at Dodger Stadium in Los Angeles, the night before the World Cup soccer championship finals. The Carreras-Domingo-Pavarotti concert, led by Zubin Mehta, was widely telecast, but Vickers said he didn't watch. He did take time to read about this tenoral three-ring circus, which to him was another downgrading of his art. About this time, Domingo took on the artistic directorship of the Washington Opera, effective 1996, when he would be fifty-five (by most accounts). This would be in addition to his singing and conducting career, as well as his artistic consultancy with the Los Angeles Music Center Opera. As of this writing, Vickers has never held any administrative post in the music world.

Vickers traveled to the Tanglewood Music Center, in Lenox, Massachusetts, on July 28, 1996, as a guest at the fiftieth-anniversary revival of *Peter Grimes*, in the newly restored Tanglewood Theater. In summer 1946 *Grimes* had been presented at Tanglewood, after the 1945 London premiere. The opera had been commissioned by Serge Koussevitzky, the Boston Symphony Orchestra music director, who in 1942 gave Britten one thousand dollars to compose it.

The critic Richard Dyer wrote that Vickers could be seen at intermission, "now white-haired, as he stared wild-eyed across the green lawn and declaimed, 'The whole sea's boiling!'"—a line from *Grimes*.[10]

Singing Grimes was the Canadian tenor Thomas Doherty, a former clergyman from London, Ontario. Vickers visited with the cast and particularly liked the singing of the Balstrode, the African-American baritone Stephen Salters.

A hale Vickers celebrated his seventieth birthday on October 29, 1996, at an emotion-filled surprise party. The tenor, who had expected a small family dinner, was stunned after being greeted by the large group of friends. Son Bill, who has a good lyric tenor and has become a fine Shakespearean actor (chiefly in Canada), led the singing of "For He's a Jolly Good Fellow." "We know you're a good actor," somebody joked to Vickers of his surprise. "Is this an act?" Guests included Martina Arroyo. Teresa Stratas accepted, then canceled at the last minute. About forty telegrams had been sent from Sir Colin Davis, Thomas Allen, Renata Tebaldi, Christa Ludwig, Régine Crespin, and more.

The dinner at the Toronto Hunt Club was hosted by all five Vickers children. Ken, an excellent photographer as well as a building contractor, arranged a video made from old home movies. A large poster with photos of Vickers and the unkempt American country singer Willie Nelson announced slyly, "The Two Tenors—World Tour." Stratas sent perhaps the most extravagant telegram: "I want to hold you, kiss you," she wrote.

Vickers, with his wife, Judy, seated next to him, told his friends, "I want to toast to someone not here tonight, the woman who gave me these five wonderful children and who asked me before she died to take this wonderful woman as my wife." Hetti Vickers certainly was present in spirit. She was seen in the home movies as a beautiful young mother romping with her children and, most touchingly, dancing outdoors with her husband in a slow-motion sequence.

VAI's Ernest Gilbert, also at the dinner, was still mining the trove of unreleased Vickers material, learning from guest Peter Schaaf about a videotape of Vickers's 1988 concert in Pasadena with Schaaf. Gilbert at the time was working with Vickers on the release of four more videos. One was the CBC *A Man and His Music* documentary, about which the tenor was unhappy because legal restrictions had prevented the original from fully documenting his career, leaving out certain performances. Gilbert planned an insert stating this. He had smoothed over a rift between Schaaf and Vickers over the pianist's percentage payment for VAI's release of *Die Winterreise*. Gilbert thought he had arranged for Vickers to pay Schaaf his fee, but when Schaaf asked Vickers about it, he told him to talk to Gilbert, who then arranged a separate agreement to pay Schaaf himself.[11] Vickers was always the businessman as well as the artist.

In England, the Berlioz Society marked Vickers's seventieth with an evening of music dubbed "Je suis Énée," organized by David Cairns. Cairns's piece on Vickers from his book *Responses* was reprinted in *Opera* magazine, with photos of Vickers in many roles.

In 1996 Canada's CBC Radio celebrated its sixtieth birthday with a four-and-a-half-hour program on November 2, a Saturday when the Met broadcast didn't air. It concentrated on the 1950s years of the CBC Opera Company, in which Vickers sang seventeen roles. Many artists were invited, and to the astonishment of the producers, Vickers turned up. "He looked absolutely marvelous, in a handsome suit, white hair, healthy, and he was charming on the radio," said Stuart Hamilton, who interviewed the tenor. Vickers was enthusiastic about how his CBC work had stood him in good stead when he went to Europe. A segment of the 1956 *Troilus and Cressida* was played—"hair-raising," Hamilton called it. Vickers had a reunion with the woman with whom he had sung. "He was gallant with her, kissed her hand. It was all very satisfying and lovely."

Afterward, Vickers introduced Hamilton to his wife and said, "I've never been happier in my life." Hamilton mentioned the happiness Vickers had given to audiences, but the tenor explained, "I'm really happy because I don't have to sing anymore." Hamilton felt this was indicative of what his whole career had meant. "For him it was a torture, not a pleasure. . . . He was put on this earth to do it. He was very religious and it was his cross to bear. He did make a lot of money, and he was very smart with it." But Hamilton could think only of the anguish of one of the greatest of the century's singers during his life onstage.[12]

That may be overstating Vickers's feelings. Certainly it must have been a relief not to have to meet the extraordinarily high expectations audiences had for him. Famous singers generally feel that they are expected to put forth not just 100 percent but 120 percent, and that is simply not possible on every night of singing. Still, Vickers had had an extraordinary career, which gave him a life of world travel, recognition, and financial security beyond anything he could have dreamed of as a poor boy peddling yeast in Prince Albert.

In 1997 Vickers sold Random Rocks, the Bermuda house where Hetti had died, and bought a smaller home for himself and Judy, next to the golf club at Riddell's Bay in Warwick, the parish in which Hetti was buried. In July he and Judy flew to London for the Royal Opera House gala marking the closing of the building for major renovation, amid headline-making administrative turmoil.

Vickers had been asked to sing in the *Grimes* Pub Scene, which would accommodate many in the large cast of gala artists. Of course, he declined. "When I quit, I quit," he reaffirmed to the author.

Other singers at the gala suggested it was symptomatic of the ignorant leadership of Covent Garden at the time that Vickers, at his age and retired for a decade, was offered such an exposed and difficult piece of music. Further, he and other historically important singers in the audience weren't asked to go onstage for a finale. Nor was their presence announced or even made known to those performing or to other acquaintances in the audience.

After the curtain fell, Vickers finally was able to mount the stage and greet old friends. The event marked the end of an era in English opera, and Vickers had been part of the best of it. On an October 1998 London visit to give a lecture, he lambasted in the press what he called the stupidity and ignorance of those who had decided to shut down ROH performances during the renovation.

In 1998 the farm, Spruce Winds, was put on the market, listed at $985,000, more than twice what it was valued at a decade earlier. That May, David Vickers, eldest of Jon's brothers, died at age seventy-nine, in Nainaimo, British Columbia. Jon attended the funeral but, as at Arthur's death, declined to sing. He had only one brother left, Wesley, and three sisters.

In June 1998 Vickers was onstage again, in a nonsinging role. He narrated the Richard Strauss piece *Enoch Arden*, at the Montreal Chamber Festival, and enthusiastically planned further performances of it for 1999.

In November 1998, in Ottawa, Vickers received the prestigious Governor General's Performing Arts Award, a ten-thousand-dollar cash prize, with other honorees including the Royal Canadian Air Farce, a comedy group, and the director of the Royal Winnipeg Ballet. Stratas spoke onstage at the gala about Vickers's communication of the transcendance of the human spirit. Her prepared notes called him "my favorite colleague, my stage soulmate."[13] She also noted the eleven honorary degrees he had received around the world, because this had been left out at the awarding of medals the previous night.

Sadly, Canada had yet another wound to inflict on Vickers. The gala show's segment on him included a lovely cello performance after Stratas's remarks and CBC film clips. But when the show was edited for TV that December, a grossly tasteless segment performed earlier, with a soprano aping Pavarotti, singing "Nessun dorma," gobbling spaghetti and gargling red wine, was substituted for the cello piece. Stratas was horrified to think audiences might believe that she and Vickers had approved of such a thing. The tenor's homeland had disappointed him once more.

The eminent Canadian author Robertson Davies knew Vickers as an Ontario neighbor, living in Caledon, a little south of the Vickers farm. Davies, who referred cynically to Canada in one of his books as "the Home of Modified Rapture,"[14] recalled in a letter to the author in 1995, the year he died:

> When Mr. Vickers began his career in Canada he was rather roughly treated by some of the Toronto critics. I could never understand why because I saw the performances they criticized and it never seemed to me that Vickers deserved the patronizing things they said about him. This continued for a great many years, even after he had gained an international reputation. . . . As so often happens, however, the critics who were so mean to him are all either dead or retired—in any case they are forgotten, whereas he has become a singer of the highest international repute.[15]

Many Canadian singers became known beyond that nation in the 1990s. Gino Quilico, son of Louis Quilico, progressed admirably, and the younger Russell Braun, son of another famous baritone, Victor Braun, unfurled baritone talents under the wing of the Marilyn Horne Foundation. Tenors abounded: Paul Frey, Richard Margison, Michael Schade. But Ben Heppner, from British Columbia, led the pack, to many the best tenor anywhere of his generation. He took on Grimes, to excellent reviews, and sang an acclaimed Tristan for Seattle Opera in 1998.

A review of the 1996 RCA Victor Red Seal *Fidelio*, with Heppner and Deborah Voigt, compared Heppner favorably to Vickers.[16] But the timbres are completely different, and Heppner has a free high range. Vickers said generously in 1995, "He's got a better voice than I had. It's true!"[17]

Many voices may appear that are "better" than Jon Vickers's. But the glories of this most singular tenor sound, and the achievements of a man rooted in the familiar fields and ordinary streets of Canada, have found a safe harbor in the history of singing.

Performance History

NSO	National Symphony Orchestra
NYO	National Youth Orchestra
NYP	New York Philharmonic
OBA	Opera de Bellas Artes
OCO	Opera Colorado
OCB	Opera Company of Boston
POP	Paris Opéra
POC	Pasadena Opera Company
RCS	Royal Conservatory Symphony Orchestra
ROC	Royal Opera
RPO	Royal Philharmonia Orchestra
SLZ	Salzburg Festival
SFO	San Francisco Opera
SFP	San Francisco Performances
SNO	Scottish National Orchestra
SOP	Seattle Opera
STF	Stratford Festival
SCA	Teatro alla Scala
TCL	Teatro Colón
TMC	Toronto Mendelssohn Choir
TOF	Toronto Opera Festival
TSO	Toronto Symphony Orchestra
VST	Vienna Staatsoper
WSO	Winnipeg Symphony Orchestra

1951

| April 17 | RCS | Toronto (Massey Hall) | Concert |

1952

| November 26 | CBR | Toronto | *The School for Fathers:* Filipeto |

1953

| April 22 | CBR | Toronto | *The Rake's Progress:* Sellem |
| November 25 | CBR | Toronto | *Così fan tutte:* Ferrando |

1954

February 25	TOF	Toronto	*Rigoletto:* Duke
February 27	TOF	Toronto	*The School for Fathers:* Filipeto
March 1	TOF	Toronto	*Rigoletto:* Duke
March 3	TOF	Toronto	*The School for Fathers:* Filipeto
March 4	TOF	Toronto	*Rigoletto:* Duke
March 5	TOF	Toronto	*The School for Fathers:* Filipeto
March 6	TOF	Toronto	*Rigoletto:* Duke
March 9	TOF	Hamilton	*Rigoletto:* Duke
March 13	TOF	London	*Rigoletto:* Duke

April 27	TMC	New York	*Messiah:* Soloist
May 5	CBR	Toronto	*A Tale of Two Cities:* Darnay
May 16	CBT	Toronto	*Die Fledermaus:* Alfred
August 1	CBT	Toronto	*Down in the Valley:* Brack Weaver
October 13	CBR	Toronto	*A Tale of Two Cities:* Darnay
November 17	CBR	Toronto	*Eugene Onegin:* Lenski
December 30	CBT	Toronto	*Manon Lescaut,* Act 2: Des Grieux

1955

March 1	TOF	Toronto	*La Traviata:* Alfredo
March 2	TOF	Toronto	*Die Fledermaus:* Alfred
March 3	TOF	Toronto	*La Traviata:* Alfredo
March 5	TOF	Toronto	*La Traviata:* Alfredo
March 7	TOF	Toronto	*La Traviata:* Alfredo
March 9	TOF	Toronto	*La Traviata:* Alfredo
March 11	TOF	Toronto	*Die Fledermaus:* Alfred
March 12	TOF	Toronto	*La Traviata:* Alfredo
March 15	TOF	Kitchener	*La Traviata:* Alfredo
March 16	TOF	Hamilton	*La Traviata:* Alfredo
May 26	CBT	Toronto	*Tosca,* Act 1: Cavaradossi
November 3	CBT	Montreal	*Pagliacci:* Canio
November 30	CBR	Toronto	*The Ruby:* Albert

1956

January 5	CBT	Toronto	*Il Trovatore,* Act 4: Manrico
January 22	CBT	Toronto	*Le Nozze di Figaro:* Don Basilio
January 25	CBR	Toronto	*Le Nozze di Figaro:* Don Basilio
February 6	CBR	Toronto	*Die Walküre,* Act 1: Siegmund
February 24	TOF	Toronto	*Carmen:* Don José
February 27	TOF	Toronto	*Carmen:* Don José
February 29	TOF	Toronto	*Carmen:* Don José
March 3	TOF	Toronto	*Carmen:* Don José
March 6	TOF	Toronto	*Carmen:* Don José
March 8	TOF	Toronto	*Carmen:* Don José
March 10	TOF	Toronto	*Carmen:* Don José
March 12	TOF	Kitchener	*Carmen:* Don José
July 7	STF	Stratford	*The Rape of Lucretia:* Male Chorus
July 10	STF	Stratford	*The Rape of Lucretia:* Male Chorus
July 12	STF	Stratford	*The Rape of Lucretia:* Male Chorus
July 17	STF	Stratford	*The Rape of Lucretia:* Male Chorus
July 19	STF	Stratford	*The Rape of Lucretia:* Male Chorus
July 24	STF	Stratford	*The Rape of Lucretia:* Male Chorus
September 5	CBR	Toronto	*The Yeomen of the Guard*
October 10	CBR	Toronto	*Troilus and Cressida:* Troilus
October 31	CBT	Toronto	*H.M.S. Pinafore:* Ralph Rackstraw
November 17	AOS	Philadelphia	*Médée:* Jason (In concert)
November 20	AOS	New York	*Fidelio:* Florestan (In concert)
December 26	CBT	Toronto	*Gianni Schicchi:* Rinuccio

1957

March 4	ROC	Cardiff	*Un Ballo in Maschera:* Riccardo
March 6	ROC	Cardiff	*Un Ballo in Maschera:* Riccardo
March 23	ROC	Manchester	*Carmen:* Don José
March 26	ROC	Manchester	*Un Ballo in Maschera:* Riccardo
March 28	ROC	Manchester	*Un Ballo in Maschera:* Riccardo
April 6	ROC	Southampton	*Carmen:* Don José
April 9	ROC	Southampton	*Un Ballo in Maschera:* Riccardo
April 11	ROC	Southampton	*Un Ballo in Maschera:* Riccardo
April 24	ROC	London	*Carmen:* Don José
April 27	ROC	London	*Un Ballo in Maschera:* Riccardo
April 29	ROC	London	*Un Ballo in Maschera:* Riccardo
May 3	ROC	London	*Carmen:* Don José
May 7	BBC	London	Concert
May 15	ROC	London	*Un Ballo in Maschera:* Riccardo
May 18	ROC	London	*Un Ballo in Maschera:* Riccardo
June 6	ROC	London	*Les Troyens:* Énée
June 11	ROC	London	*Les Troyens:* Énée
June 14	ROC	London	*Les Troyens:* Énée
June 20	ROC	London	*Les Troyens:* Énée
June 29	ROC	London	*Les Troyens:* Énée
July 2	ROC	London	*Les Troyens:* Énée
July 4	ROC	London	*Carmen:* Don José
July 8	ROC	London	*Les Troyens:* Énée
July 11	ROC	London	*Les Troyens:* Énée
July 18	ROC	London	*Carmen:* Don José
July 20	ROC	London	*Carmen:* Don José
October 31	ROC	London	*Carmen:* Don José
November 2	ROC	London	*Carmen:* Don José
November 8	ROC	London	*Carmen:* Don José
November 11	ROC	London	*Carmen:* Don José
November 26	ROC	London	*Aida:* Radames
November 30	ROC	London	*Aida:* Radames
December 7	ROC	London	*Un Ballo in Maschera:* Riccardo
December 9	ROC	London	*Un Ballo in Maschera:* Riccardo
December 13	ROC	London	*Un Ballo in Maschera:* Riccardo
December 17	ROC	London	*Un Ballo in Maschera:* Riccardo
December 20	ROC	London	*Un Ballo in Maschera:* Riccardo
December 28	ROC	London	*Aida:* Radames
December 31	ROC	London	*Aida:* Radames

1958

January 9	ROC	London	*Aida:* Radames
January 13	ROC	London	*Un Ballo in Maschera:* Riccardo
January 14	RPO	London	Concert
January 25	ROC	London	*Aida:* Radames
January 30	ROC	London	*Aida:* Radames
March 22	ROC	Manchester	*Aida:* Radames
March 25	ROC	Manchester	*Carmen:* Don José
March 29	ROC	Manchester	*Carmen:* Don José

April 2	ROC	London	*Aida:* Radames
April 7	ROC	London	*Aida:* Radames
April 18	ROC	London	*Aida:* Radames
April 22	ROC	London	*Aida:* Radames
May 9	ROC	London	*Don Carlos:* Don Carlos
May 12	ROC	London	*Don Carlos:* Don Carlos
May 15	ROC	London	*Don Carlos:* Don Carlos
May 19	ROC	London	*Don Carlos:* Don Carlos
May 21	ROC	London	*Don Carlos:* Don Carlos
May 24	ROC	London	*Don Carlos:* Don Carlos
May 26	ROC	London	*Don Carlos:* Don Carlos
May 28	ROC	London	*Don Carlos:* Don Carlos
June 6	LSO	London	Messa da Requiem (Verdi): Soloist
June 10	ROC	London	Gala performance
June 16	ROC	London	*Les Troyens:* Énée
June 19	ROC	London	*Les Troyens:* Énée
July 10	ROC	London	*Les Troyens:* Énée
July 17	ROC	London	*Les Troyens:* Énée
July 19	ROC	London	*Les Troyens:* Énée
July 28	BAY	Bayreuth	*Die Walküre:* Siegmund
August		Vancouver	Messa da Requiem (Verdi): Soloist
August 14	BAY	Bayreuth	*Die Walküre:* Siegmund
September 24	ROC	London	*Die Walküre:* Siegmund
October 7	ROC	London	*Die Walküre:* Siegmund
October 14	ROC	Leeds	*Samson:* Samson
October 15	ROC	Leeds	*Samson:* Samson
October 17	ROC	Leeds	Gala performance
October 18	ROC	Leeds	*Samson:* Samson
November 6	DCO	Dallas	*Médée:* Jason
November 8	DCO	Dallas	*Médée:* Jason
November 15	ROC	London	*Samson:* Samson
November 19	ROC	London	*Aida:* Radames
November 22	ROC	London	*Aida:* Radames
November 24	ROC	London	*Samson:* Samson
November 27	RPO	London	Concert
November 30	RPO	London	Symphony no. 9 (Beethoven): Soloist
December 4	RPO	London	Symphony no. 9 (Beethoven): Soloist
December 12	ROC	London	*Samson:* Samson
December 20	ROC	London	*Samson:* Samson
December 26	ROC	London	*Aida:* Radames
December 30	ROC	London	*Aida:* Radames

1959

January 3	ROC	London	*Samson:* Samson
January 8	VST	Vienna	*Die Walküre:* Siegmund
January 11	VST	Vienna	*Carmen:* Don José
January 13	VST	Vienna	*Un Ballo in Maschera:* Riccardo
January 15	VST	Vienna	*Aida:* Radames
January 19	VST	Vienna	*Die Walküre:* Siegmund
January 28	VST	Vienna	*Don Carlos:* Don Carlos

February 12	VST	Vienna	*Die Walküre:* Siegmund
February 15	VST	Vienna	*Don Carlos:* Don Carlos
February 19	VST	Vienna	*Aida:* Radames
February 22	VST	Vienna	*Aida:* Radames
February 27	VST	Vienna	*Carmen:* Don José
March 3	VST	Vienna	*Carmen:* Don José
March 8	VST	Vienna	*Pagliacci:* Canio
March 12	VST	Vienna	*Pagliacci:* Canio
March 16	ROC	Manchester	*Samson:* Samson
March 18	VST	Vienna	*Pagliacci:* Canio
March 22	VST	Vienna	*Aida:* Radames
March 27	ROC	Manchester	*Samson:* Samson
March 30	VST	Vienna	*Die Walküre:* Siegmund
April 3	ROC	London	*Un Ballo in Maschera:* Riccardo
April 9	ROC	London	*Un Ballo in Maschera:* Riccardo
April 22	ROC	London	*Don Carlos:* Don Carlos
April 24	ROC	London	*Don Carlos:* Don Carlos
April 28	ROC	London	*Don Carlos:* Don Carlos
May 1	ROC	London	*Don Carlos:* Don Carlos
May 4	ROC	London	*Don Carlos:* Don Carlos
May 19	ROC	London	*Aida:* Radames
May 22	ROC	London	*Aida:* Radames
May 28	ROC	London	*Parsifal:* Parsifal
June 1	ROC	London	*Parsifal:* Parsifal
June 8	ROC	London	*Samson:* Samson
June 12	ROC	London	*Samson:* Samson
June 17	ROC	London	*Médée:* Jason
June 22	ROC	London	*Médée:* Jason
June 24	ROC	London	*Médée:* Jason
June 27	ROC	London	*Médée:* Jason
June 30	ROC	London	*Médée:* Jason
September 5	SFO	Portland	*Pagliacci:* Canio
September 11	SFO	San Francisco	*Aida:* Radames
September 19	SFO	San Francisco	*Pagliacci:* Canio
September 24	SFO	San Francisco	*Aida:* Radames
September 29	SFO	San Francisco	*Carmen:* Don José
October 1	SFO	San Francisco	*Carmen:* Don José
October 2	SFO	San Francisco	*Aida:* Radames
October 11	SFO	Berkeley	*Aida:* Radames
October 15	SFO	San Francisco	*Pagliacci:* Canio (Student performance)
October 19	SFO	San Francisco	*Pagliacci:* Canio (Student performance)
October 20	SFO	San Francisco	*Pagliacci:* Canio (Student performance)
October 23	SFO	Los Angeles	*Carmen:* Don José
October 28	SFO	Los Angeles	*Pagliacci:* Canio
October 29	SFO	San Diego	*Carmen:* Don José
November 1	SFO	Los Angeles	*Aida:* Radames
November 7	SFO	Los Angeles	*Aida:* Radames

November 8	SFO	Los Angeles	*Carmen:* Don José
November 19	DCO	Dallas	*Médée:* Jason
November 21	DCO	Dallas	*Médée:* Jason
November 26	ROC	London	*Carmen:* Don José
November 28	RPO	London	Symphony no. 9 (Beethoven): Soloist
November 30	RPO	London	Symphony no. 9 (Beethoven): Soloist
December 2	ROC	London	*Aida:* Radames
December 5	ROC	London	*Aida:* Radames
December 8	ROC	London	*Carmen:* Don José
December 11	ROC	London	*Carmen:* Don José
December 16	ROC	London	*Pagliacci:* Canio
December 19	ROC	London	*Pagliacci:* Canio
December 22	ROC	London	*Pagliacci:* Canio

1960

January 17	MET	New York	*Pagliacci:* Canio
January 28	MET	New York	*Fidelio:* Florestan
February 2	MET	New York	*Fidelio:* Florestan
February 9	MET	New York	*Die Walküre:* Siegmund
February 13	MET	New York	*Fidelio:* Florestan
February 20	MET	New York	*Die Walküre:* Siegmund
February 26	MET	New York	*Die Walküre:* Siegmund
February 29	MET	New York	*Fidelio:* Florestan
March 7	MET	New York	*Die Walküre:* Siegmund
March 11	MET	New York	*Fidelio:* Florestan
March 16	MET	New York	*Fidelio:* Florestan
March 24	VST	Vienna	*Carmen:* Don José
March 27	VST	Vienna	*Die Walküre:* Siegmund
March 29	VST	Vienna	*Carmen:* Don José
April 2	VST	Vienna	*Aida:* Radames
April 6	VST	Vienna	*Pagliacci:* Canio
April 8	VST	Vienna	*Pagliacci:* Canio
April 19	ROC	London	*Parsifal:* Parsifal
April 29	ROC	London	*Les Troyens:* Énée
May 2	ROC	London	*Les Troyens:* Énée
May 5	ROC	London	*Les Troyens:* Énée
May 10	ROC	London	*Les Troyens:* Énée
May 13	ROC	London	*Les Troyens:* Énée
May 24	ROC	London	*Aida:* Radames
August 26– September 2	CNE	Toronto	Grandstand show
September 17	SFO	San Francisco	*Carmen:* Don José
September 30	SFO	San Francisco	*Aida:* Radames
October 16	SFO	Berkeley	*Carmen:* Don José
October 24	SFO	San Francisco	*Aida:* Radames
October 29	MET	New York	*Carmen:* Don José
November 3	MET	New York	*Carmen:* Don José
November 6	SFO	Los Angeles	*Carmen:* Don José

November 16	LOC	Chicago	*Die Walküre:* Siegmund
November 18	LOC	Chicago	*Die Walküre:* Siegmund
November 21	LOC	Chicago	*Die Walküre:* Siegmund
December 17	SCA	Milan	*Fidelio:* Florestan
December 20	SCA	Milan	*Fidelio:* Florestan
December 22	SCA	Milan	*Fidelio:* Florestan

1961

January 3	SCA	Milan	*Fidelio:* Florestan
January 5	SCA	Milan	*Fidelio:* Florestan
January 8	VST	Vienna	*Die Walküre:* Siegmund
January 13	VST	Vienna	*Andrea Chénier:* Chénier
January 17	VST	Vienna	*Andrea Chénier:* Chénier
January 23	VST	Vienna	*Fidelio:* Florestan
January 28	VST	Vienna	*Pagliacci:* Canio
January 31	VST	Vienna	*Carmen:* Don José
February 3	VST	Vienna	*Aida:* Radames
February 24	ROC	London	*Fidelio:* Florestan
February 27	ROC	London	*Fidelio:* Florestan
March 4	ROC	London	*Fidelio:* Florestan
March 7	ROC	London	*Fidelio:* Florestan
March 11	ROC	London	*Fidelio:* Florestan
March 15	ROC	London	*Fidelio:* Florestan
March 18	ROC	London	*Fidelio:* Florestan
May 14	VST	Vienna	*Aida:* Radames
May 21	VST	Vienna	*Don Carlos:* Don Carlos
May 24	VST	Vienna	*Don Carlos:* Don Carlos
May 30	VST	Vienna	*Carmen:* Don José
June 2	VST	Vienna	*Don Carlos:* Don Carlos
June 5	VST	Vienna	*Aida:* Radames
June 8	ROC	London	*Pagliacci:* Canio
June 9	VST	Vienna	*Die Walküre:* Siegmund
June 18	VST	Vienna	*Aida:* Radames
June 21	VST	Vienna	*Fidelio:* Florestan
June 27	VST	Vienna	*Don Carlos:* Don Carlos
August 6	NOG	Epidaurus	*Médée:* Jason
August 13	NOG	Epidaurus	*Médée:* Jason
September 3	VST	Vienna	*Aida:* Radames
September 6	VST	Vienna	*Die Walküre:* Siegmund
September 18	ROC	London	*Fidelio:* Florestan
September 21	ROC	London	*Fidelio:* Florestan
September 25	ROC	London	*Fidelio:* Florestan
September 29	ROC	London	*Die Walküre:* Siegmund
October 2	ROC	London	*Die Walküre:* Siegmund
October 5	ROC	London	*Die Walküre:* Siegmund
October 9	ROC	London	*Die Walküre:* Siegmund
October 20	LOC	Chicago	*Andrea Chénier:* Chénier
October 25	LOC	Chicago	*Andrea Chénier:* Chénier
October 28	LOC	Chicago	*Andrea Chénier:* Chénier
November 6	MET	New York	*Aida:* Radames

November 13	LOC	Chicago	*Fidelio:* Florestan
November 17	LOC	Chicago	*Fidelio:* Florestan
November 22	LOC	Chicago	*Fidelio:* Florestan
November 23	VST	Vienna	*Fidelio:* Florestan
November 25	MET	New York	*Aida:* Radames
December 11	SCA	Milan	*Médée:* Jason
December 14	SCA	Milan	*Médée:* Jason
December 20	SCA	Milan	*Médée:* Jason
December 23	MET	New York	*Die Walküre:* Siegmund
December 29	MET	New York	*Die Walküre:* Siegmund

1962

January 10	MET	New York	*Die Walküre:* Siegmund
January 23	MET	New York	*Die Walküre:* Siegmund
February 6	AOS	New York	*Samson:* Samson
February 23	ROC	London	*Un Ballo in Maschera:* Riccardo
February 27	ROC	London	*Un Ballo in Maschera:* Riccardo
March 2	ROC	London	*Un Ballo in Maschera:* Riccardo
March 5	ROC	London	*Un Ballo in Maschera:* Riccardo
March 7	ROC	London	*Un Ballo in Maschera:* Riccardo
March 12	ROC	London	*Un Ballo in Maschera:* Riccardo
April 5	ROC	London	*Fidelio:* Florestan
April 16	VST	Vienna	*Die Walküre:* Siegmund
April 21	VST	Vienna	*Pagliacci:* Canio
April 25	VST	Vienna	*Die Walküre:* Siegmund
April 28	VST	Vienna	*Carmen:* Don José
May 25	VST	Vienna	*Fidelio:* Florestan
May 29	SCA	Milan	*Médée:* Jason
June 3	SCA	Milan	*Médée:* Jason
September 6	OBA	Mexico City	*Die Walküre:* Siegmund
September 11	OBA	Mexico City	*Aida:* Radames

1963

January 26	MET	New York	*Fidelio:* Florestan
January 31	MET	New York	*Pagliacci:* Canio
February 15	MET	New York	*Fidelio:* Florestan
February 20	MET	New York	*Fidelio:* Florestan
March 1	MET	New York	*Fidelio:* Florestan
March 6	MET	New York	*Fidelio:* Florestan
March 11	MET	New York	*Fidelio:* Florestan
April 18	DOB	Berlin	*Aida:* Radames
April 28	HS	Hamburg	*Don Carlos:* Don Carlos
May 1	VST	Vienna	*Carmen:* Don José
May 3	HS	Hamburg	*Un Ballo in Maschera:* Riccardo
May 17	TCL	Buenos Aires	*Otello:* Otello
May 19	TCL	Buenos Aires	*Otello:* Otello
May 23	TCL	Buenos Aires	*Otello:* Otello
May 26	TCL	Buenos Aires	*Otello:* Otello
June 2	TCL	Buenos Aires	*Carmen:* Don José
June 6	TCL	Buenos Aires	*Carmen:* Don José

June 8	TCL	Buenos Aires	*Carmen:* Don José
June 12	TCL	Buenos Aires	*Carmen:* Don José
June 15	TCL	Buenos Aires	*Carmen:* Don José
June 18	TCL	Buenos Aires	*Carmen:* Don José
June 28	TCL	Buenos Aires	*Samson et Dalila:* Samson
June 30	TCL	Buenos Aires	*Samson et Dalila:* Samson
July 3	TCL	Buenos Aires	*Samson et Dalila:* Samson
July 6	TCL	Buenos Aires	*Samson et Dalila:* Samson
July 19	NYO	Stratford	Concert
October 10	SFO	San Francisco	*Die Walküre:* Siegmund
October 15	SFO	San Francisco	*Die Walküre:* Siegmund
October 18	LOC	Chicago	*Un Ballo in Maschera:* Riccardo
October 23	LOC	Chicago	*Fidelio:* Florestan
October 26	LOC	Chicago	*Fidelio:* Florestan
November 2	LOC	Chicago	*Otello:* Otello
November 8	LOC	Chicago	*Otello:* Otello
November 13	LOC	Chicago	*Otello:* Otello
November 18	SFO	Los Angeles	*Die Walküre:* Siegmund
November 21	SFO	San Diego	*Die Walküre:* Siegmund
November 30	DCO	Dallas	*Messiah:* Soloist

1964

January 26	GTG	Geneva	*Samson et Dalila:* Samson
January 28	GTG	Geneva	*Samson et Dalila:* Samson
January 30	GTG	Geneva	*Samson et Dalila:* Samson
February 1	GTG	Geneva	*Samson et Dalila:* Samson
February 4	GTG	Geneva	*Samson et Dalila:* Samson
February 8	ROC	London	*Aida:* Radames
February 13	ROC	London	*Aida:* Radames
February 18	ROC	London	*Aida:* Radames
February 21	ROC	London	*Aida:* Radames
February 24	ROC	London	*Aida:* Radames
February 26	ROC	London	*Aida:* Radames
February 29	AMC	Amsterdam	*Samson et Dalila:* Samson (In concert)
March 9	ROC	London	*Fidelio:* Florestan
March 11	ROC	London	*Fidelio:* Florestan
March 13	ROC	London	*Fidelio:* Florestan
March 18	ROC	London	*Fidelio:* Florestan
March 21	ROC	London	*Fidelio:* Florestan
March 24	ROC	London	*Fidelio:* Florestan
April	DOB	Berlin	*Aida:* Radames
April	DOB	Berlin	*Fidelio:* Florestan
May 29	VST	Vienna	*Pagliacci:* Canio
June 2	ROC	Manchester	*Aida:* Radames
June 6	ROC	Manchester	*Aida:* Radames
June 8	ROC	Manchester	*Aida:* Radames
June 19	ROC	Manchester	*Otello:* Otello
June 23	ROC	Manchester	*Otello:* Otello
June 26	ROC	Manchester	*Otello:* Otello

July 21	BAY	Bayreuth	*Parsifal:* Parsifal
July 29	BAY	Bayreuth	*Parsifal:* Parsifal
August 7	BAY	Bayreuth	*Parsifal:* Parsifal
August 13	BAY	Bayreuth	*Parsifal:* Parsifal
September 14	COC	Toronto	*Carmen:* Don José
September 18	COC	Toronto	*Carmen:* Don José
September 23	COC	Toronto	*Carmen:* Don José
September 26	COC	Toronto	*Aida:* Radames
September 30	COC	Toronto	*Carmen:* Don José (Student performance)
October 13	SFO	San Francisco	*Fidelio:* Florestan
October 17	SFO	San Francisco	*Fidelio:* Florestan
October 23	SFO	San Francisco	*Lady Macbeth of Mtsensk:* Sergei
October 31	SFO	San Francisco	*Lady Macbeth of Mtsensk:* Sergei
November 9	SFO	Los Angeles	*Fidelio:* Florestan
November 16	SFO	Los Angeles	*Carmen:* Don José
November 19	SFO	San Diego	*Carmen:* Don José
November 23	SFO	Los Angeles	*Lady Macbeth of Mtsensk:* Sergei
November 25	SFO	Los Angeles	*Carmen:* Don José
November 28	SFO	Los Angeles	*Pagliacci:* Canio

1965

February 22	MET	New York	*Die Walküre:* Siegmund
March 1	MET	New York	*Der fliegende Holländer:* Erik
March 6	MET	New York	*Die Walküre:* Siegmund
March 9	MET	New York	*Die Walküre:* Siegmund
March 17	MET	New York	*Samson et Dalila:* Samson
March 24	MET	New York	*Die Walküre:* Siegmund
March 26	MET	New York	*Samson et Dalila:* Samson
April 2	MET	New York	*Die Walküre:* Siegmund
April 10	MET	New York	*Die Walküre:* Siegmund
April 13	MET	New York	*Der fliegende Holländer:* Erik (Student performance)
April 16	MET	New York	*Samson et Dalila:* Samson
April 19	MET	Boston	*Samson et Dalila:* Samson
April 27	MET	Cleveland	*Samson et Dalila:* Samson
May 7	MET	Atlanta	*Otello:* Otello
May 18	MET	St. Louis	*Otello:* Otello
May 22	MET	Minneapolis	*Der fliegende Holländer:* Erik
May 28	MET	Detroit	*Samson et Dalila:* Samson
July 7	MET	New York	*Pagliacci:* Canio (In concert)
August 31	OBA	Mexico City	*Otello:* Otello
September 4	OBA	Mexico City	*Otello:* Otello
September 28	MET	New York	*The Queen of Spades:* Herman
October 4	MET	New York	*The Queen of Spades:* Herman
October 10	TSO	Toronto	Concert
October 11		Montreal	*Aida:* Radames
October 16	MET	New York	*The Queen of Spades:* Herman
October 18		Montreal	*Aida:* Radames
October 21	MET	New York	*The Queen of Spades:* Herman
October 21		Montreal	*Aida:* Radames

October 23		Montreal	*Aida:* Radames
October 24	NYP	New York	Symphony no. 9 (Beethoven): Soloist
October 26		Montreal	*Aida:* Radames
October 29		Montreal	*Aida:* Radames
October 31		Montreal	*Aida:* Radames
November 3	LOC	Chicago	*Samson et Dalila:* Samson
November 5	LOC	Chicago	*Samson et Dalila:* Samson
November 8	LOC	Chicago	*Samson et Dalila:* Samson
November 13	LOC	Chicago	*Samson et Dalila:* Samson
November 20	MET	New York	*The Queen of Spades:* Herman
November 24	MET	New York	*The Queen of Spades:* Herman
December 3	MET	New York	*The Queen of Spades:* Herman
December 20	MET	New York	*Samson et Dalila:* Samson

1966

January 4	MSO	Montreal	Concert
January 5	MSO	Montreal	Concert
January 29	POC	Pasadena	*Aida:* Radames
February 25	ROC	London	*Parsifal:* Parsifal
March 2	ROC	London	*Parsifal:* Parsifal
March 5	ROC	London	*Parsifal:* Parsifal
March 8	ROC	London	*Parsifal:* Parsifal
March 11	ROC	London	*Parsifal:* Parsifal
March 15	ROC	London	*Parsifal:* Parsifal
April 1	MET	New York	*Fidelio:* Florestan
April 7	MET	New York	*Fidelio:* Florestan
April 12	MET	New York	*Fidelio:* Florestan
April 16	MET	New York	Gala performance
April 22	MET	Boston	*The Queen of Spades:* Herman
April 27	MET	Cleveland	*The Queen of Spades:* Herman
May 1		New York	Recital
May 3	MET	Atlanta	*The Queen of Spades:* Herman
May 11	ROC	London	*Un Ballo in Maschera:* Riccardo
May 14	ROC	London	*Un Ballo in Maschera:* Riccardo
May 16	ROC	London	*Un Ballo in Maschera:* Riccardo
May 21	MET	Minneapolis	*The Queen of Spades:* Herman
May 24	MET	Detroit	*The Queen of Spades:* Herman
May 26	ROC	London	*Un Ballo in Maschera:* Riccardo
May 30	ROC	London	*Un Ballo in Maschera:* Riccardo
June 1	ROC	London	*Un Ballo in Maschera:* Riccardo
July 27	SLZ	Salzburg	*Carmen:* Don José
July 30	SLZ	Salzburg	*Carmen:* Don José
August 10	SLZ	Salzburg	*Carmen:* Don José
August 27	SLZ	Salzburg	*Carmen:* Don José
September 22	SFO	San Francisco	*Don Carlos:* Don Carlos
September 27	SFO	San Francisco	*Don Carlos:* Don Carlos
October 1	SFO	San Francisco	*Don Carlos:* Don Carlos
October 14	LOC	Chicago	*Otello:* Otello
October 16	LOC	Chicago	*Otello:* Otello

October 19	LOC	Chicago	*Otello:* Otello
October 22	LOC	Chicago	*Otello:* Otello
November 4	SFO	San Francisco	*Les Troyens:* Énée
November 8	SFO	San Francisco	*Les Troyens:* Énée
November 12	SFO	San Francisco	*Les Troyens:* Énée
November 15	SFO	San Francisco	*Carmen:* Don José
November 18	SFO	San Francisco	*Carmen:* Don José
November 24	SFO	San Francisco	*Carmen:* Don José
November 27	SFO	San Francisco	*Carmen:* Don José

1967

January 20	MET	New York	*Peter Grimes:* Peter Grimes
January 24	MET	New York	*Peter Grimes:* Peter Grimes
January 30	MET	New York	*The Queen of Spades:* Herman
February 11	MET	New York	*Peter Grimes:* Peter Grimes
February 15	MET	New York	*Peter Grimes:* Peter Grimes
February 18	MET	New York	*The Queen of Spades:* Herman
February 22	MET	New York	*The Queen of Spades:* Herman
February 25	MET	New York	*Peter Grimes:* Peter Grimes
March 1	MET	New York	*The Queen of Spades:* Herman
March 6	MET	New York	*The Queen of Spades:* Herman
March 9	MET	New York	*Peter Grimes:* Peter Grimes
March 19	SLZ	Salzburg	*Die Walküre:* Siegmund
March 23	SLZ	Salzburg	*Die Walküre:* Siegmund
April 3	MET	New York	*Otello:* Otello
April 14	MET	New York	*Otello:* Otello
April 30		New York	Recital
May 11	ROC	London	*Carmen:* Don José
May 16	ROC	London	*Carmen:* Don José
May 19	ROC	London	*Carmen:* Don José
May 24	ROC	London	*Carmen:* Don José
May 27	ROC	London	*Carmen:* Don José
June 1	ROC	London	*Carmen:* Don José
June 5	ROC	London	*Carmen:* Don José
June 9	ROC	London	*Carmen:* Don José
July 14		Montreal	*Otello:* Otello
July 17		Montreal	*Otello:* Otello
July 20		Montreal	*Otello:* Otello
July 23		Montreal	*Otello:* Otello
July 29	SLZ	Salzburg	*Carmen:* Don José
August 1	SLZ	Salzburg	*Carmen:* Don José
August 8	SLZ	Salzburg	*Carmen:* Don José
August 14	SLZ	Salzburg	*Carmen:* Don José
August 25	MET	Newport	*Otello:* Otello
August 28	SLZ	Salzburg	*Carmen:* Don José
October 15	VST	Vienna	*Fidelio:* Florestan
October 18	VST	Vienna	*Don Carlos:* Don Carlos
October 21	VST	Vienna	*Fidelio:* Florestan
October 24	VST	Vienna	*Pagliacci:* Canio
October 29	VST	Vienna	*Aida:* Radames

November 1	VST	Vienna	*Parsifal:* Parsifal
November 9	VST	Vienna	*Don Carlos:* Don Carlos
November 21	MET	New York	*Die Walküre:* Siegmund
November 24	MET	New York	*Die Walküre:* Siegmund
November 27	MET	New York	*Die Walküre:* Siegmund
December 2	MET	New York	*Die Walküre:* Siegmund
December 5	MET	New York	*Die Walküre:* Siegmund

1968

January 24	ROC	London	*Aida:* Radames
January 27	ROC	London	*Aida:* Radames
January 30	ROC	London	*Aida:* Radames
February 2	ROC	London	*Aida:* Radames
February 8	ROC	London	*Aida:* Radames
February 13	ROC	London	*Aida:* Radames
February 17	ROC	London	*Aida:* Radames
February 21	MET	New York	*Die Walküre:* Siegmund
February 24	MET	New York	*Die Walküre:* Siegmund
February 29	MET	New York	*Die Walküre:* Siegmund
March 4	MET	New York	*Die Walküre:* Siegmund
March 14	ROC	London	*Aida:* Radames
March 20	ROC	London	*Aida:* Radames
March 28	ROC	London	*Aida:* Radames
April 1	ROC	London	*Aida:* Radames
April 10	SLZ	Salzburg	*Die Walküre:* Siegmund
April 15	SLZ	Salzburg	*Die Walküre:* Siegmund
June 21	TCL	Buenos Aires	*Pagliacci:* Canio
June 23	TCL	Buenos Aires	*Pagliacci:* Canio
June 26	TCL	Buenos Aires	*Pagliacci:* Canio
June 27	TCL	Buenos Aires	*Pagliacci:* Canio
June 30	TCL	Buenos Aires	*Pagliacci:* Canio
July 5	TCL	Buenos Aires	*Carmen:* Don José
July 7	TCL	Buenos Aires	*Carmen:* Don José
July 10	TCL	Buenos Aires	*Carmen:* Don José
July 13	TCL	Buenos Aires	*Carmen:* Don José
July 16	TCL	Buenos Aires	*Carmen:* Don José
July 23	TCL	Buenos Aires	*Padmâvatí:* Ratan-Sen
July 24	TCL	Buenos Aires	*Carmen:* Don José
July 26	TCL	Buenos Aires	*Padmâvatí:* Ratan-Sen
July 28	TCL	Buenos Aires	*Padmâvatí:* Ratan-Sen
July 30	TCL	Buenos Aires	*Padmâvatí:* Ratan-Sen
August 1	TCL	Buenos Aires	*Padmâvatí:* Ratan-Sen
August 10	CO	Blossom Festival (Ohio)	Concert
September 21	MET	New York	*Carmen:* Don José
September 25	MET	New York	*Carmen:* Don José
September 30	MET	New York	*Carmen:* Don José
October 10	MET	New York	*Carmen:* Don José
October 31	MET	New York	*Die Walküre:* Siegmund
November 8	MET	New York	*Die Walküre:* Siegmund

November 15	DCO	Dallas	*Otello:* Otello
November 18	DCO	Dallas	*Otello:* Otello
December 12	SCA	Milan	*Die Walküre:* Siegmund

1969

January 18	MET	New York	*Carmen:* Don José
January 24	MET	New York	*Carmen:* Don José
February 19	MET	New York	*Die Walküre:* Siegmund
March 1	MET	New York	*Die Walküre:* Siegmund
March 13	MET	New York	*Peter Grimes:* Peter Grimes
March 18	MET	New York	*Peter Grimes:* Peter Grimes
March 21	MET	New York	*Peter Grimes:* Peter Grimes
March 24	SCA	Milan	*Pagliacci:* Canio
March 26	SFO	Los Angeles	*Die Walküre:* Siegmund
March 29	SFO	Los Angeles	*Die Walküre:* Siegmund
April 5	MET	New York	*Peter Grimes:* Peter Grimes
April 10	MET	New York	*Peter Grimes:* Peter Grimes
April 19	MET	New York	*Peter Grimes:* Peter Grimes
May 21	ROC	London	*Peter Grimes:* Peter Grimes
May 24	ROC	London	*Peter Grimes:* Peter Grimes
May 30	ROC	London	*Peter Grimes:* Peter Grimes
June 2	ROC	London	*Peter Grimes:* Peter Grimes
June 5	ROC	London	*Peter Grimes:* Peter Grimes
June 10	MSO	Montreal	Concert
June 14	ROC	London	*Aida:* Radames
June 17	ROC	London	*Aida:* Radames
June 20	ROC	London	*Aida:* Radames
September 17	ROC	London	*Les Troyens:* Énée
September 20	ROC	London	*Les Troyens:* Énée
September 23	ROC	London	*Les Troyens:* Énée
September 30	ROC	London	*Les Troyens:* Énée
October 3	ROC	London	*Les Troyens:* Énée
October 7	ROC	London	*Les Troyens:* Énée
October 10	ROC	London	*Les Troyens:* Énée
October 18	SFO	San Francisco	*Aida:* Radames
October 21	SFO	San Francisco	*Aida:* Radames
October 24	SFO	San Francisco	*Aida:* Radames
October 29	SFO	San Francisco	*Aida:* Radames
October		Guelph	Concert
November 23	SFO	Sacramento	*Aida:* Radames
November 26	SFO	San Francisco	*Aida:* Radames
November 30	SFO	San Francisco	*Aida:* Radames

1970

January 2	BSO	Boston	*Das Lied von der Erde* (Mahler)
January 3	BSO	Boston	*Das Lied von der Erde* (Mahler)
January 6	BSO	Boston	*Das Lied von der Erde* (Mahler)
January 14	ROC	London	*Fidelio:* Florestan
January 17	ROC	London	*Fidelio:* Florestan
January 20	ROC	London	*Fidelio:* Florestan

January 23	ROC	London	*Fidelio:* Florestan
January 26	ROC	London	*Fidelio:* Florestan
February 21	WSO	Winnipeg	Concert with Stratas
February 24		Montreal	Concert
May	SCA	Milan	*Pagliacci:* Canio
June 30	ROC	London	Gala performance
August 10	SLZ	Salzburg	*Otello:* Otello
August 13	SLZ	Salzburg	*Otello:* Otello
August 18	SLZ	Salzburg	*Otello:* Otello
August 25	SLZ	Salzburg	*Otello:* Otello
August 29	SLZ	Salzburg	*Otello:* Otello
September 11	TCL	Buenos Aires	*Fidelio:* Florestan
September 13	TCL	Buenos Aires	*Fidelio:* Florestan
September 16	TCL	Buenos Aires	*Fidelio:* Florestan
September 19	TCL	Buenos Aires	*Fidelio:* Florestan
September 24	TCL	Buenos Aires	*Fidelio:* Florestan
September 29	MSO	Montreal	*Fidelio:* Florestan (In concert)
December 16	MET	New York	*Fidelio:* Florestan
December 21	MET	New York	*Fidelio:* Florestan
December 26	MET	New York	*Fidelio:* Florestan
December 29	MET	New York	*Fidelio:* Florestan

1971

January 2	MET	New York	*Fidelio:* Florestan
January 9	MET	New York	*Fidelio:* Florestan
January 22	MET	New York	*Fidelio:* Florestan
January 26	MET	New York	*Carmen:* Don José
January 27	MET	New York	*Fidelio:* Florestan
February 8	MET	New York	*Fidelio:* Florestan
February 10	MET	New York	*Carmen:* Don José
February 13	MET	New York	*Carmen:* Don José
February 23	MET	New York	*Fidelio:* Florestan
February 26	MET	New York	*Carmen:* Don José
March 1	MET	New York	*Carmen:* Don José
March 6	MET	New York	*Carmen:* Don José
April 3	SLZ	Salzburg	*Fidelio:* Florestan
April 7	SLZ	Salzburg	*Fidelio:* Florestan
April 12	SLZ	Salzburg	*Fidelio:* Florestan
April 21	ROC	London	*Parsifal:* Parsifal
April 27	ROC	London	*Parsifal:* Parsifal
May 1	ROC	London	*Parsifal:* Parsifal
May 4	ROC	London	*Parsifal:* Parsifal
May 8	ROC	London	*Parsifal:* Parsifal
May 12	ROC	London	*Parsifal:* Parsifal
May 19	MET	Minneapolis	*Carmen:* Don José
July 1	ROC	London	*Peter Grimes:* Peter Grimes
July 5	ROC	London	*Peter Grimes:* Peter Grimes
July 8	ROC	London	*Peter Grimes:* Peter Grimes
July 12	ROC	London	*Peter Grimes:* Peter Grimes
July 18	STF	Stratford	Concert

July 30	SLZ	Salzburg	*Otello:* Otello
August 3	SLZ	Salzburg	*Otello:* Otello
August 12	SLZ	Salzburg	*Otello:* Otello
August 16	SLZ	Salzburg	*Otello:* Otello
August 27	SLZ	Salzburg	*Otello:* Otello
August 30	SLZ	Salzburg	*Otello:* Otello
September 25	TCL	Buenos Aires	*Tristan und Isolde:* Tristan
September 30	TCL	Buenos Aires	*Tristan und Isolde:* Tristan
October 3	TCL	Buenos Aires	*Tristan und Isolde:* Tristan
October 6	TCL	Buenos Aires	*Tristan und Isolde:* Tristan
October 10	TCL	Buenos Aires	*Tristan und Isolde:* Tristan
October 14	TCL	Buenos Aires	*Tristan und Isolde:* Tristan
October 27	MET	New York	*Carmen:* Don José
October 30	MET	New York	*Carmen:* Don José
November 12	DCO	Dallas	*Samson et Dalila:* Samson
November 14	DCO	Dallas	*Samson et Dalila:* Samson
November 18	DCO	Dallas	*Fidelio:* Florestan
November 21	DCO	Dallas	*Fidelio:* Florestan
November 23	DCO	Dallas	*Fidelio:* Florestan
November 28	DCO	Dallas	*Samson et Dalila:* Samson
December 13	MET	New York	*Carmen:* Don José
December 29	MET	New York	*Samson et Dalila:* Samson

1972

January 1	MET	New York	*Samson et Dalila:* Samson
January 6	MET	New York	*Samson et Dalila:* Samson
March 25	SLZ	Salzburg	*Tristan und Isolde:* Tristan
March 29	SLZ	Salzburg	*Tristan und Isolde:* Tristan
April 2	SLZ	Salzburg	*Tristan und Isolde:* Tristan
April 20	LAP	Los Angleles	*Das Lied von der Erde* (Mahler)
April 22	MET	New York	Gala performance
April 28	MET	Boston	*Fidelio:* Florestan
May 3	MET	Cleveland	*Fidelio:* Florestan
June 1	ROC	London	*Otello:* Otello
June 5	ROC	London	*Otello:* Otello
June 10	ROC	London	*Otello:* Otello
June 14	ROC	London	*Otello:* Otello
June 17	ROC	London	*Otello:* Otello
June 26	ROC	London	*Otello:* Otello
July 16	IPO	Tel Aviv	*Samson et Dalila:* Samson
July 18	IPO	Tel Aviv	*Samson et Dalila:* Samson
July 22	IPO	Tel Aviv	*Samson et Dalila:* Samson
July 24	IPO	Tel Aviv	*Samson et Dalila:* Samson
July 26	IPO	Tel Aviv	*Samson et Dalila:* Samson
July 31	SLZ	Salzburg	*Otello:* Otello
August 12	SLZ	Salzburg	*Otello:* Otello
August 22	SLZ	Salzburg	*Otello:* Otello
September 21	ROC	London	*Les Troyens:* Énée
September 25	ROC	London	*Les Troyens:* Énée
October 3	ROC	London	*Les Troyens:* Énée

October 7	ROC	London	*Les Troyens:* Énée
October 11	ROC	London	*Les Troyens:* Énée
November 3	DCO	Dallas	*Dido and Aeneas:* Aeneas
			Pagliacci: Canio
November 10	DCO	Dallas	*Dido and Aeneas:* Aeneas
			Pagliacci: Canio
November 24	MET	New York	*Die Walküre:* Siegmund
December 2	MET	New York	*Die Walküre:* Siegmund
December 5	MET	New York	*Otello:* Otello
December 9	MET	New York	*Otello:* Otello
December 13	MET	New York	*Otello:* Otello
December 16	MET	New York	*Die Walküre:* Siegmund
December 20	MET	New York	*Otello:* Otello
December 23	MET	New York	*Otello:* Otello

1973

February 26	MET	New York	*Peter Grimes:* Peter Grimes
March 8	MET	New York	*Peter Grimes:* Peter Grimes
March 14	MET	New York	*Peter Grimes:* Peter Grimes
March 20	MET	New York	*Peter Grimes:* Peter Grimes
March 24	MET	New York	*Peter Grimes:* Peter Grimes
March 30	MET	New York	*Peter Grimes:* Peter Grimes
April 17	SLZ	Salzburg	*Tristan und Isolde:* Tristan
April 22	SLZ	Salzburg	*Tristan und Isolde:* Tristan
June 8	MET	New York	*Otello:* Otello
June 16	MET	New York	*Otello:* Otello
June 20	MET	New York	*Otello:* Otello
July 7	COR	Orange	*Tristan und Isolde:* Tristan
September 21	MSO	Montreal	*Otello:* Otello (In concert)
October 22	MET	New York	*Les Troyens:* Énée
October 27	MET	New York	*Les Troyens:* Énée
October 30	MET	New York	*Les Troyens:* Énée
November 2	MET	New York	*Les Troyens:* Énée
November 5	MET	New York	*Les Troyens:* Énée
November 9	MET	New York	*Les Troyens:* Énée
November 12	MET	New York	*Les Troyens:* Énée
November 15	MET	New York	*Les Troyens:* Énée
November 30	DCO	Dallas	*Andrea Chénier:* Chénier
December 4	DCO	Dallas	*Andrea Chénier:* Chénier
December 8	DCO	Dallas	*Andrea Chénier:* Chénier
December 13	MSO	Montreal	Concert

1974

January 26	MET	New York	*Tristan und Isolde:* Tristan
January 30	MET	New York	*Tristan und Isolde:* Tristan
February 9	MET	New York	*Otello:* Otello
February 12	MET	New York	*Otello:* Otello
February 15	MET	New York	*Otello:* Otello
February 21	MET	New York	*Otello:* Otello
February 27	MET	New York	*Otello:* Otello

March 16	MET	New York	*Les Troyens:* Énée
April 4	ROC	London	*Fidelio:* Florestan
April 8	ROC	London	*Fidelio:* Florestan
April 11	ROC	London	*Fidelio:* Florestan
April 17	ROC	London	*Fidelio:* Florestan
April 19	ROC	London	*Fidelio:* Florestan
May 4	GSF	Guelph	*The Rape of Lucretia:* Male Chorus
May 6	GSF	Guelph	*The Rape of Lucretia:* Male Chorus
May 8	GSF	Guelph	*The Rape of Lucretia:* Male Chorus
May 21	VST	Vienna	*Fidelio:* Florestan
July 13	COR	Orange	*Salome:* Herodes
July 20	COR	Orange	*Norma:* Pollione
September 30	LOC	Chicago	*Peter Grimes:* Peter Grimes
October 4	LOC	Chicago	*Peter Grimes:* Peter Grimes
October 7	LOC	Chicago	*Peter Grimes:* Peter Grimes
October 10	LOC	Chicago	*Peter Grimes:* Peter Grimes
October 12	LOC	Chicago	*Peter Grimes:* Peter Grimes
October 15	LOC	Chicago	*Peter Grimes:* Peter Grimes
November 15	MET	New York	*Jenůfa:* Laca
November 20	MET	New York	*Jenůfa:* Laca
November 30	MET	New York	*Jenůfa:* Laca
December 5	MET	New York	*Jenůfa:* Laca
December 12	MET	New York	*Jenůfa:* Laca
December 17	MET	New York	*Jenůfa:* Laca
December 21	MET	New York	*Jenůfa:* Laca

1975

January 17	MET	New York	*La Forza del Destino:* Alvaro
January 21	MET	New York	*La Forza del Destino:* Alvaro
January 27	MET	New York	*La Forza del Destino:* Alvaro
February 4	MET	New York	*La Forza del Destino:* Alvaro
February 6		New York	Concert
February 8	MET	New York	*La Forza del Destino:* Alvaro
February 20	MET	New York	*Die Walküre:* Siegmund
February 25	MET	New York	*Die Walküre:* Siegmund
March 1	MET	New York	*Die Walküre:* Siegmund
March 11	MET	New York	*Die Walküre:* Siegmund
March 17	MET	New York	*La Forza del Destino:* Alvaro
March 22	MET	New York	*La Forza del Destino:* Alvaro
March 26	MET	New York	*La Forza del Destino:* Alvaro
April 2	MET	New York	*Die Walküre:* Siegmund
April 11	LAP	Los Angeles	*Fidelio:* Florestan (In concert)
April 13	LAP	Los Angeles	*Fidelio:* Florestan (In concert)
April 15	LAP	Los Angeles	*Fidelio:* Florestan (In concert)
April 27	GSF	Guelph	*The Diary of One Who Vanished* (Janáček)
May 3	OCB	Boston	*Benvenuto Cellini:* Cellini

May 6	OCB	Boston	*Benvenuto Cellini:* Cellini
May 9	OCB	Boston	*Benvenuto Cellini:* Cellini
July 9	ROC	London	*Peter Grimes:* Peter Grimes
July 14	ROC	London	*Peter Grimes:* Peter Grimes
July 17	ROC	London	*Peter Grimes:* Peter Grimes
July 19	ROC	London	*Peter Grimes:* Peter Grimes
July 22	ROC	London	*Peter Grimes:* Peter Grimes
July 25	ROC	London	*Peter Grimes:* Peter Grimes
August 2	COR	Orange	*Otello:* Otello
August 23	LAP	Los Angeles	Concert
September 3	ROC	London	Concert
September 6	VST	Vienna	*Carmen:* Don José
September 12	VST	Vienna	*Fidelio:* Florestan
September 19	VST	Vienna	*Don Carlos:* Don Carlos
September 24	MU	Munich	*Tristan und Isolde:* Tristan
September 28	MU	Munich	*Otello:* Otello
October 1	VST	Vienna	*Otello:* Otello
October 29	LOC	Chicago	*Fidelio:* Florestan
November 1	LOC	Chicago	*Fidelio:* Florestan
November 4	LOC	Chicago	*Fidelio:* Florestan
November 7	LOC	Chicago	*Fidelio:* Florestan
November 10	LOC	Chicago	*Fidelio:* Florestan
November 14	LOC	Chicago	*Fidelio:* Florestan
December 6	DCO	Dallas	*Tristan und Isolde:* Tristan
December 9	DCO	Dallas	*Tristan und Isolde:* Tristan
December 13	DCO	Dallas	*Tristan und Isolde:* Tristan

1976

January 17	GMO	Miami	*Otello:* Otello
January 21	GMO	Miami	*Otello:* Otello
January 24	GMO	Miami	*Otello:* Otello
February 6		New York	Recital
March 4	ROC	Milan	*Peter Grimes:* Peter Grimes
March 6	ROC	Milan	*Peter Grimes:* Peter Grimes
March 8	ROC	Milan	*Peter Grimes:* Peter Grimes
March 11	ROC	Milan	*Peter Grimes:* Peter Grimes
March 23	ROC	London	*Carmen:* Don José
April 6	ROC	London	*Carmen:* Don José
April 9	ROC	London	*Fidelio:* Florestan
April 12	ROC	London	*Carmen:* Don José
April 14	ROC	London	*Fidelio:* Florestan
April 17	ROC	London	*Fidelio:* Florestan
April 19	ROC	London	*Carmen:* Don José
April 24	ROC	London	*Carmen:* Don José
April 27	ROC	London	*Carmen:* Don José
May 14	POP	Paris	*Parsifal:* Parsifal
May 18	POP	Paris	*Parsifal:* Parsifal
May 22	POP	Paris	*Parsifal:* Parsifal
May 27	POP	Paris	*Parsifal:* Parsifal
June 7	DOB	Berlin	*Tristan und Isolde:* Tristan

June 12	DOB	Berlin	*Tristan und Isolde:* Tristan
June 17	DOB	Berlin	*Tristan und Isolde:* Tristan
July 17	NAC	Ottawa	*The Queen of Spades:* Herman
July 20	NAC	Ottawa	*The Queen of Spades:* Herman
July 22	NAC	Ottawa	*The Queen of Spades:* Herman
July 24	NAC	Ottawa	*The Queen of Spades:* Herman
July 26	NAC	Ottawa	*The Queen of Spades:* Herman
September 11	SFO	San Francisco	*Die Walküre:* Siegmund
September 14	SFO	San Francisco	*Die Walküre:* Siegmund
September 17	SFO	San Francisco	*Die Walküre:* Siegmund
September 22	SFO	San Francisco	*Die Walküre:* Siegmund
September 26	SFO	San Francisco	*Die Walküre:* Siegmund
October 2	SFO	San Francisco	*Die Walküre:* Siegmund
October 6	SFO	San Francisco	*Peter Grimes:* Peter Grimes
October 9	SFO	San Francisco	*Peter Grimes:* Peter Grimes
October 13	SFO	San Francisco	*Peter Grimes:* Peter Grimes
October 17	SFO	San Francisco	*Peter Grimes:* Peter Grimes
October 22	SFO	San Francisco	*Peter Grimes:* Peter Grimes
November 5	DCO	Dallas	*Samson:* Samson
November 7	DCO	Dallas	*Samson:* Samson
November 9	DCO	Dallas	*Samson:* Samson
November 23	VST	Vienna	*Die Walküre:* Siegmund
November 27	VST	Vienna	*Fidelio:* Florestan
November 30	VST	Vienna	*Pagliacci:* Canio
December 5	VST	Vienna	*Tristan und Isolde:* Tristan

1977

January 28	HGO	Houston	*Peter Grimes:* Peter Grimes
January 30	HGO	Houston	*Peter Grimes:* Peter Grimes
January 31	HGO	Houston	*Peter Grimes:* Peter Grimes
February 1	HGO	Houston	*Peter Grimes:* Peter Grimes
February 5	HGO	Houston	*Peter Grimes:* Peter Grimes
February 28	ROC	London	*Otello:* Otello
March 4	ROC	London	*Otello:* Otello
March 8	ROC	London	*Otello:* Otello
March 12	ROC	London	*Otello:* Otello
March 16	ROC	London	*Otello:* Otello
March 19	ROC	London	*Otello:* Otello
April 9	POP	Paris	*Otello:* Otello
April 13	POP	Paris	*Otello:* Otello
April 20	POP	Paris	*Otello:* Otello
April 25	POP	Paris	*Otello:* Otello
April 29	POP	Paris	*Otello:* Otello
June 8	ROC	London	*Jenůfa:* Laca
June 11	ROC	London	*Jenůfa:* Laca
June 14	ROC	London	*Jenůfa:* Laca
June 17	ROC	London	*Jenůfa:* Laca
June 20	ROC	London	*Jenůfa:* Laca
July 17	IPO	Tel Aviv	*Fidelio:* Florestan
July 20	IPO	Tel Aviv	*Fidelio:* Florestan

July 24	IPO	Tel Aviv	*Fidelio:* Florestan
July 27	IPO	Tel Aviv	*Fidelio:* Florestan
July 30	IPO	Tel Aviv	*Fidelio:* Florestan
August 6	IPO	Orange	*Fidelio:* Florestan
August 8	IPO	Tel Aviv	*Fidelio:* Florestan
September 14	NYP	New York	Concert: *Parsifal,* Act 2
October 15	LOC	Chicago	*Peter Grimes:* Peter Grimes
October 19	LOC	Chicago	*Peter Grimes:* Peter Grimes
October 22	LOC	Chicago	*Peter Grimes:* Peter Grimes
October 25	LOC	Chicago	*Peter Grimes:* Peter Grimes
October 28	LOC	Chicago	*Peter Grimes:* Peter Grimes
October 31	LOC	Chicago	*Peter Grimes:* Peter Grimes
November 3	LOC	Chicago	*Peter Grimes:* Peter Grimes
November 5	LOC	Chicago	*Peter Grimes:* Peter Grimes
November 21	MET	New York	*Peter Grimes:* Peter Grimes
November 26	MET	New York	*Peter Grimes:* Peter Grimes
November 29	MET	New York	*Peter Grimes:* Peter Grimes
December 3	MET	New York	*Peter Grimes:* Peter Grimes
December 10	MET	New York	*Peter Grimes:* Peter Grimes

1978

January 2	MET	New York	*Pagliacci:* Canio
January 14	MET	New York	*Pagliacci:* Canio
January 16	MET	New York	*Pagliacci:* Canio
January 19	MET	New York	*Pagliacci:* Canio
January 30	MET	New York	*Otello:* Otello
February 4	MET	New York	*Otello:* Otello
February 8	MET	New York	*Otello:* Otello
February 11	MET	New York	*Otello:* Otello
March 17	POP	Paris	*L'Incoronazione di Poppea:* Nerone
March 20	POP	Paris	*L'Incoronazione di Poppea:* Nerone
March 22	POP	Paris	*L'Incoronazione di Poppea:* Nerone
March 25	POP	Paris	*L'Incoronazione di Poppea:* Nerone
March 29	POP	Paris	*L'Incoronazione di Poppea:* Nerone
April 1	POP	Paris	*L'Incoronazione di Poppea:* Nerone
April 4	POP	Paris	*L'Incoronazione di Poppea:* Nerone
April 17	POP	Paris	*L'Incoronazione di Poppea:* Nerone
April 19	POP	Paris	*L'Incoronazione di Poppea:* Nerone
April 22	POP	Paris	*L'Incoronazione di Poppea:* Nerone
May 16	RPO	London	Concert
May 25	ROC	London	*Tristan und Isolde:* Tristan
May 29	ROC	London	*Tristan und Isolde:* Tristan
June 1	ROC	London	*Tristan und Isolde:* Tristan
June 7	ROC	London	*Tristan und Isolde:* Tristan (Act 3 omitted)
August 12	BSO	Tanglewood (Lenox, Mass.)	Concert
September 21	MET	New York	*Otello:* Otello
September 25	MET	New York	*Otello:* Otello

October 3	MET	New York	*Otello:* Otello
October 7	MET	New York	*Otello:* Otello
October 25	MET	New York	*The Bartered Bride:* Vašek
October 30	MET	New York	*The Bartered Bride:* Vašek
November 3	MET	New York	*The Bartered Bride:* Vašek
November 6	MET	New York	*The Bartered Bride:* Vašek
November 11	MET	New York	*The Bartered Bride:* Vašek
November 16	MET	New York	*The Bartered Bride:* Vašek
November 18	MET	New York	*The Bartered Bride:* Vašek
November 21	MET	New York	*The Bartered Bride:* Vašek
November 25	MET	New York	*The Bartered Bride:* Vašek
November 29	MET	New York	*The Bartered Bride:* Vašek
December 2	MET	New York	*The Bartered Bride:* Vašek

1979

January 24	POP	Paris	*L'Incoronazione di Poppea:* Nerone
January 27	POP	Paris	*L'Incoronazione di Poppea:* Nerone
January 29	POP	Paris	*L'Incoronazione di Poppea:* Nerone
January 31	POP	Paris	*L'Incoronazione di Poppea:* Nerone
February 3	POP	Paris	*L'Incoronazione di Poppea:* Nerone
February 6	POP	Paris	*L'Incoronazione di Poppea:* Nerone
February 9	POP	Paris	*L'Incoronazione di Poppea:* Nerone
March 5	GMO	Miami	*Samson et Dalila:* Samson
March 7	GMO	Miami	*Samson et Dalila:* Samson
March 10	GMO	Miami	*Samson et Dalila:* Samson
April 2	MET	New York	*Parsifal:* Parsifal
April 6	MET	New York	*Parsifal:* Parsifal
April 10	MET	New York	*Parsifal:* Parsifal
April 14	MET	New York	*Parsifal:* Parsifal
April 17	MET	Cleveland	*Otello:* Otello
May 9	GSF	Guelph	*Die Winterreise* (Schubert)
May 12	MET	Dallas	*The Bartered Bride:* Vašek
May 15	MET	Minneapolis	*Otello:* Otello
May 19	MET	Minneapolis	*The Bartered Bride:* Vašek
May 23	MET	Detroit	*Otello:* Otello
May 26	MET	Detroit	*The Bartered Bride:* Vašek
June 2	MET	Philadelphia	*Otello:* Otello
June 6	MET	Vienna, Va.	*Otello:* Otello
June 9	MET	Vienna, Va.	*The Bartered Bride:* Vašek
June 27	ROC	London	*Pagliacci:* Canio
June 30	ROC	London	*Pagliacci:* Canio
July 2	ROC	London	*Pagliacci:* Canio
July 5	ROC	London	*Pagliacci:* Canio
July 9	ROC	London	*Pagliacci:* Canio
July 12	ROC	London	*Pagliacci:* Canio
July 14	ROC	London	*Pagliacci:* Canio
July 17	ROC	London	*Pagliacci:* Canio
July 20	ROC	London	*Pagliacci:* Canio
September 11	ROC	Seoul	*Peter Grimes:* Peter Grimes

September 13	ROC	Seoul	*Peter Grimes:* Peter Grimes
September 19	ROC	Tokyo	*Peter Grimes:* Peter Grimes
September 22	ROC	Tokyo	*Peter Grimes:* Peter Grimes
September 27	ROC	Osaka	*Peter Grimes:* Peter Grimes
October 2	ROC	Tokyo	*Peter Grimes:* Peter Grimes
October 5	ROC	Tokyo	*Peter Grimes:* Peter Grimes
October 14	LOC	Chicago	Gala performance
November 15	LOC	Chicago	*Tristan und Isolde:* Tristan
November 20	LOC	Chicago	*Tristan und Isolde:* Tristan
November 26	LOC	Chicago	*Tristan und Isolde:* Tristan
December 1	LOC	Chicago	*Tristan und Isolde:* Tristan
December 5	LOC	Chicago	*Tristan und Isolde:* Tristan
December 10	LOC	Chicago	*Tristan und Isolde:* Tristan
December 14	LOC	Chicago	*Tristan und Isolde:* Tristan

1980

January 14	MET	New York	*Fidelio:* Florestan
January 18	MET	New York	*Fidelio:* Florestan
January 21	MET	New York	*Fidelio:* Florestan
January 25	MET	New York	*Fidelio:* Florestan
January 29	MET	New York	*Fidelio:* Florestan
February 2	MET	New York	*Fidelio:* Florestan
February 11	MET	New York	*Fidelio:* Florestan
May	MM	Florence	*Die Winterreise* (Schubert)
May 16	ROC	London	*Tristan und Isolde:* Tristan
May 20	ROC	London	*Tristan und Isolde:* Tristan
May 24	ROC	London	*Tristan und Isolde:* Tristan
May 29	ROC	London	*Tristan und Isolde:* Tristan
June 4	ROC	London	*Tristan und Isolde:* Tristan
June 9	ROC	London	*Tristan und Isolde:* Tristan
June 16	MM	Florence	*Die Winterreise* (Schubert)
June 19	MM	Florence	*Die Winterreise* (Schubert)
June 29	BSO	Tanglewood (Lenox, Mass.)	*Die Winterreise* (Schubert)
July 4	BSO	Tanglewood (Lenox, Mass.)	Concert
November 3	ROC	London	*Otello:* Otello
November 7	ROC	London	*Otello:* Otello
November 11	ROC	London	*Otello:* Otello
November 14	ROC	London	*Otello:* Otello
November 18	ROC	London	*Otello:* Otello
November 22	ROC	London	*Otello:* Otello
November 25	ROC	London	*Otello:* Otello
November 30		Montreal	Concert

1981

January 26	POP	Paris	*Peter Grimes:* Peter Grimes
January 29	POP	Paris	*Peter Grimes:* Peter Grimes
January 31	POP	Paris	*Peter Grimes:* Peter Grimes
February 4	POP	Paris	*Peter Grimes:* Peter Grimes

February 7	POP	Paris	*Peter Grimes:* Peter Grimes
February 10	POP	Paris	*Peter Grimes:* Peter Grimes
February 12	POP	Paris	*Peter Grimes:* Peter Grimes
March 13	LSO	London	*Das Lied von der Erde* (Mahler)
April 11	MET	New York	Concert
May 2	HS	Hamburg	*Fidelio:* Florestan
May 6	HS	Hamburg	*Fidelio:* Florestan
May 10	HS	Hamburg	*Fidelio:* Florestan
May 14	HS	Hamburg	*Fidelio:* Florestan
June 23	ROC	London	*Peter Grimes:* Peter Grimes
June 26	ROC	London	*Peter Grimes:* Peter Grimes
June 30	ROC	London	*Peter Grimes:* Peter Grimes
July 3	ROC	London	*Peter Grimes:* Peter Grimes
July 7	ROC	London	*Peter Grimes:* Peter Grimes
July 10	ROC	London	*Peter Grimes:* Peter Grimes
July 21	LAP	Los Angeles	Concert: *Parsifal*, Act 2
August 2	BSO	Tanglewood (Lenox, Mass.)	Concert
August 16		Rio de Janeiro	*Tristan und Isolde:* Tristan
August 19		Rio de Janeiro	*Tristan und Isolde:* Tristan
August 23		Rio de Janeiro	*Tristan und Isolde:* Tristan
August 27		Rio de Janeiro	*Tristan und Isolde:* Tristan
August 30		Rio de Janeiro	*Tristan und Isolde:* Tristan
September 28	ROC	London	*Samson et Dalila:* Samson
October 1	ROC	London	*Samson et Dalila:* Samson
October 3	ROC	London	*Samson et Dalila:* Samson
October 6	ROC	London	*Samson et Dalila:* Samson
October 9	ROC	London	*Samson et Dalila:* Samson
October 12	ROC	London	*Samson et Dalila:* Samson
October 15	ROC	London	*Samson et Dalila:* Samson
October 17	ROC	London	*Samson et Dalila:* Samson
October 24		New York	Concert
November 7	LOC	Chicago	*Fidelio:* Florestan
November 11	LOC	Chicago	*Fidelio:* Florestan
November 14	LOC	Chicago	*Fidelio:* Florestan
November 17	LOC	Chicago	*Fidelio:* Florestan
November 20	LOC	Chicago	*Fidelio:* Florestan
November 23	LOC	Chicago	*Fidelio:* Florestan
November 28	LOC	Chicago	*Fidelio:* Florestan
December 1	LOC	Chicago	*Fidelio:* Florestan
December 12	DCO	Dallas	*Peter Grimes:* Peter Grimes
December 14	DCO	Dallas	*Peter Grimes:* Peter Grimes
December 17	DCO	Dallas	*Peter Grimes:* Peter Grimes

1982

February 4	GTG	Geneva	*Parsifal:* Parsifal
February 8	GTG	Geneva	*Parsifal:* Parsifal
February 11	GTG	Geneva	*Parsifal:* Parsifal
February 27	POP	Paris	*Fidelio:* Florestan
March 2	POP	Paris	*Fidelio:* Florestan

March 6	POP	Paris	*Fidelio:* Florestan
March 9	POP	Paris	*Fidelio:* Florestan
March 12	POP	Paris	*Fidelio:* Florestan
March 15	POP	Paris	*Fidelio:* Florestan
March 18	POP	Paris	*Fidelio:* Florestan
March 23	POP	Paris	*Fidelio:* Florestan
March 26	POP	Paris	*Fidelio:* Florestan
April 8	ROC	London	*Pagliacci:* Canio
April 12	ROC	London	*Pagliacci:* Canio
April 15	ROC	London	*Pagliacci:* Canio
April 19	ROC	London	*Pagliacci:* Canio
April 21	ROC	London	*Pagliacci:* Canio
April 24	ROC	London	*Pagliacci:* Canio
April 27	ROC	London	*Pagliacci:* Canio
May 13	ROC	London	*Tristan und Isolde:* Tristan
May 17	ROC	London	*Tristan und Isolde:* Tristan
May 21	ROC	London	*Tristan und Isolde:* Tristan
May 25	ROC	London	*Tristan und Isolde:* Tristan
May 29	ROC	London	*Tristan und Isolde:* Tristan
June 2	ROC	London	*Tristan und Isolde:* Tristan
June 29	POP	Paris	*Pagliacci:* Canio
July 8	POP	Paris	*Pagliacci:* Canio
July 10	POP	Paris	*Pagliacci:* Canio
July 13	POP	Paris	*Pagliacci:* Canio
August 29		Toronto	Concert
September 2		Toronto	Concert
September 20	LOC	Chicago	*Tristan und Isolde:* Tristan
September 25	LOC	Chicago	*Tristan und Isolde:* Tristan
September 29	LOC	Chicago	*Tristan und Isolde:* Tristan
October 4	LOC	Chicago	*Tristan und Isolde:* Tristan
October 8	LOC	Chicago	*Tristan und Isolde:* Tristan
October 12	LOC	Chicago	*Tristan und Isolde:* Tristan
October 15	LOC	Chicago	*Tristan und Isolde:* Tristan
November 3	LOC	Chicago	*Pagliacci:* Canio
November 6	LOC	Chicago	*Pagliacci:* Canio
November 9	LOC	Chicago	*Pagliacci:* Canio
November 13	LOC	Chicago	*Pagliacci:* Canio
November 16	LOC	Chicago	*Pagliacci:* Canio
November 19	LOC	Chicago	*Pagliacci:* Canio
November 22	LOC	Chicago	*Pagliacci:* Canio
December 3	HGO	Houston	*Pagliacci:* Canio
December 7	HGO	Houston	*Pagliacci:* Canio
December 10	HGO	Houston	*Pagliacci:* Canio
December 12	HGO	Houston	*Pagliacci:* Canio

1983

January 11	ROC	London	*Samson et Dalila:* Samson
January 14	ROC	London	*Samson et Dalila:* Samson
January 17	ROC	London	*Samson et Dalila:* Samson

January 20	ROC	London	*Samson et Dalila:* Samson
January 26	ROC	London	*Samson et Dalila:* Samson
January 29	ROC	London	*Samson et Dalila:* Samson
February 2	NYP	New York	Symphony no. 9 (Beethoven): Soloist
February 4	ROC	London	*Samson et Dalila:* Samson
February 7	ROC	London	*Samson et Dalila:* Samson (Student performance)
February 9	ROC	London	*Samson et Dalila:* Samson
March 28	POP	Paris	*Pagliacci:* Canio
March 30	POP	Paris	*Pagliacci:* Canio
April 1	POP	Paris	*Pagliacci:* Canio
April 4	POP	Paris	*Pagliacci:* Canio
April 7	POP	Paris	*Pagliacci:* Canio
April 12	POP	Paris	*Pagliacci:* Canio
April 15	POP	Paris	*Pagliacci:* Canio
April 18	POP	Paris	*Pagliacci:* Canio
April 21	POP	Paris	*Pagliacci:* Canio
April 23	POP	Paris	*Pagliacci:* Canio
May 11	SOP	Seattle	*Peter Grimes:* Peter Grimes
May 14	SOP	Seattle	*Peter Grimes:* Peter Grimes
June 14	ROC	London	*Fidelio:* Florestan
June 17	ROC	London	*Fidelio:* Florestan
June 20	ROC	London	*Fidelio:* Florestan
June 24	ROC	London	*Fidelio:* Florestan
June 27	ROC	London	*Fidelio:* Florestan
June 30	ROC	London	*Fidelio:* Florestan
July 4	ROC	London	*Fidelio:* Florestan
July 21	MMC	Philadelphia	Concert: *Tristan und Isolde,* Act 2
October 13	MET	New York	*Peter Grimes:* Peter Grimes
October 18	MET	New York	*Peter Grimes:* Peter Grimes
October 26	MET	New York	*Peter Grimes:* Peter Grimes
October 29	MET	New York	*Peter Grimes:* Peter Grimes
November 4	MET	New York	*Peter Grimes:* Peter Grimes
November 9	MET	New York	*Peter Grimes:* Peter Grimes
November 15	MET	New York	*Peter Grimes:* Peter Grimes
November 19	MET	New York	*Peter Grimes:* Peter Grimes
December 11	LOC	Chicago	Callas celebration
December 17	MET	New York	*Fidelio:* Florestan
December 21	MET	New York	*Fidelio:* Florestan
December 31	MET	New York	*Fidelio:* Florestan

1984

January 4	MET	New York	*Fidelio:* Florestan
January 7	MET	New York	*Fidelio:* Florestan
January 19	HGO	Houston	*Peter Grimes:* Peter Grimes
January 22	HGO	Houston	*Peter Grimes:* Peter Grimes
January 24	HGO	Houston	*Peter Grimes:* Peter Grimes
January 27	HGO	Houston	*Peter Grimes:* Peter Grimes

March 5	ROC	London	*Peter Grimes:* Peter Grimes
March 9	ROC	London	*Peter Grimes:* Peter Grimes
			(Student performance)
March 14	ROC	London	*Peter Grimes:* Peter Grimes
March 17	ROC	London	*Peter Grimes:* Peter Grimes
March 20	ROC	London	*Peter Grimes:* Peter Grimes
March 29	LAP	Los Angeles	*Das Lied von der Erde* (Mahler)
March 30	LAP	Los Angeles	*Das Lied von der Erde* (Mahler)
April 1	LAP	Los Angeles	*Das Lied von der Erde* (Mahler)
April 23	MET	Washington, D.C.	*Peter Grimes:* Peter Grimes
April 26	MET	Washington, D.C.	*Die Walküre:* Siegmund
April 30	MET	Washington, D.C.	*Die Walküre:* Siegmund
May 4	MET	Washington, D.C.	*Peter Grimes:* Peter Grimes
May 7	MET	Atlanta	*Peter Grimes:* Peter Grimes
May 10	MET	Atlanta	*Die Walküre:* Siegmund
May 14	MET	Memphis	*Die Walküre:* Siegmund
May 17	MET	Dallas	*Die Walküre:* Siegmund
May 21	MET	Minneapolis	*Peter Grimes:* Peter Grimes
May 24	MET	Minneapolis	*Die Walküre:* Siegmund
May 28	MET	Detroit	*Peter Grimes:* Peter Grimes
May 31	MET	Detroit	*Die Walküre:* Siegmund
June 4	MET	Toronto	*Peter Grimes:* Peter Grimes
June 7	MET	Toronto	*Die Walküre:* Siegmund
June 11	MET	Cleveland	*Peter Grimes:* Peter Grimes
June 15	MET	Cleveland	*Die Walküre:* Siegmund
July 11	ROC	Los Angeles	*Peter Grimes:* Peter Grimes
July 16	ROC	Los Angeles	*Peter Grimes:* Peter Grimes
July 19	ROC	Los Angeles	*Peter Grimes:* Peter Grimes
September 30	LOC	Chicago	*Die Winterreise* (Schubert)
October 3	LAP	Los Angeles	*Die Winterreise* (Schubert)
December 1	CAP	Cape Town	*Otello:* Otello
December 5	CAP	Cape Town	*Otello:* Otello
December 10	CAP	Cape Town	*Otello:* Otello
December 14	CAP	Cape Town	*Otello:* Otello
December 18	CAP	Cape Town	*Otello:* Otello
December 21	CAP	Cape Town	*Otello:* Otello

1985

February 20	ROC	London	*Samson:* Samson
February 23	ROC	London	*Samson:* Samson
February 28	ROC	London	*Samson:* Samson
March 5	ROC	London	*Samson:* Samson
March 8	ROC	London	*Samson:* Samson
March 11	ROC	London	*Samson:* Samson
March 16	ROC	London	*Samson:* Samson
April 8	MET	New York	*Parsifal:* Parsifal
April 11	MET	New York	*Parsifal:* Parsifal
April 17	MET	New York	*Parsifal:* Parsifal
April 20	MET	New York	*Parsifal:* Parsifal
April 22	KWS	Kitchener	Concert: *Die Walküre,* Act 1

April 23	KWS	Kitchener	Concert: *Die Walküre*, Act 1
September 7	SNO	Glasgow	Concert
September 20		Toronto	Concert
October 12	LOC	Chicago	*Samson:* Samson
October 16	LOC	Chicago	*Samson:* Samson
October 19	LOC	Chicago	*Samson:* Samson
October 22	LOC	Chicago	*Samson:* Samson
October 25	LOC	Chicago	*Samson:* Samson
October 28	LOC	Chicago	*Samson:* Samson
November 1	LOC	Chicago	*Samson:* Samson
November 19	MET	New York	*Pagliacci:* Canio
November 23	MET	New York	*Pagliacci:* Canio
November 27	MET	New York	*Pagliacci:* Canio
November 30	MET	New York	*Pagliacci:* Canio
December 3	MET	New York	*Pagliacci:* Canio
December 7	MET	New York	*Pagliacci:* Canio

1986

February 3	MET	New York	*Samson:* Samson
February 7	MET	New York	*Samson:* Samson
February 10	MET	New York	*Samson:* Samson
February 15	MET	New York	*Samson:* Samson
February 19	MET	New York	*Samson:* Samson
February 26	MET	New York	*Samson:* Samson
March 1	MET	New York	*Samson:* Samson
March 6	MET	New York	*Samson:* Samson
March 19	SFP	San Francisco	*Die Winterreise* (Schubert)
September 10	ROC	Seoul	*Samson et Dalila:* Samson
September 13	ROC	Seoul	*Samson et Dalila:* Samson
September 20	ROC	Tokyo	*Samson et Dalila:* Samson
September 22	ROC	Tokyo	*Samson et Dalila:* Samson
September 25	ROC	Tokyo	*Samson et Dalila:* Samson
October 6	LOC	Chicago	*Parsifal:* Parsifal
October 10	LOC	Chicago	*Parsifal:* Parsifal
October 14	LOC	Chicago	*Parsifal:* Parsifal
October 18	LOC	Chicago	*Parsifal:* Parsifal
October 22	LOC	Chicago	*Parsifal:* Parsifal
October 25	LOC	Chicago	*Parsifal:* Parsifal
October 30	LOC	Chicago	*Parsifal:* Parsifal
November 23	MOC	Rockville, Md.	*Die Winterreise* (Schubert)

1987

January 10	DS	Detroit	*Das Lied von der Erde* (Mahler)
January 26	VST	Vienna	*Pagliacci:* Canio
January 30	VST	Vienna	*Pagliacci:* Canio
February 3	VST	Vienna	*Pagliacci:* Canio
March 28	MET	New York	*Samson et Dalila:* Samson
April 3	MET	New York	*Samson et Dalila:* Samson
April 8	MET	New York	*Samson et Dalila:* Samson
April 13	MET	New York	*Samson et Dalila:* Samson

April 24	GLS	Guelph	Concert: *Songs and Dances of Death* (Mussorgsky)
May 9	OCO	Denver	*Samson et Dalila:* Samson
May 12	OCO	Denver	*Samson et Dalila:* Samson
May 15	OCO	Denver	*Samson et Dalila:* Samson
May 17	OCO	Denver	*Samson et Dalila:* Samson
July 4	NSO	Washington, D.C.	Concert
September 9	TS	Toronto	Concert: *Songs and Dances of Death* (Mussorgsky)
September 10	TS	Toronto	Concert: *Songs and Dances of Death* (Mussorgsky)
September 11	TS	Toronto	Concert: *Songs and Dances of Death* (Mussorgsky)

1988

March 9	AAP	Pasadena	Concert: Tenor retrospective
March 11	MOC	Rockville, Md.	Concert: Tenor retrospective
November 3	MOC	Rockville, Md.	*Die Winterreise* (Schubert)
May 27	KWS	Kitchener	Concert: *Parsifal,* Act 2
May 28	KWS	Kitchener	Concert: *Parsifal,* Act 2

1998

June 2	MCM	Montreal	*Enoch Arden* (R. Strauss): Narration

Opera Roles and First Performances

1. Filipeto, *The School for Fathers*, 1952, Toronto (radio)
2. Sellem, *The Rake's Progress*, 1953, Toronto
3. Ferrando, *Così fan tutte*, 1953, Toronto
4. Duke of Mantua, *Rigoletto*, 1954, Toronto
5. Charles Darnay, *A Tale of Two Cities*, 1954, Toronto (radio)
6. Alfred, *Die Fledermaus*, 1954, Toronto (TV)
7. Brack Weaver, *Down in the Valley*, 1954, Toronto (TV)
8. Lenski, *Eugene Onegin*, 1954, Toronto (radio)
9. Alfredo, *La Traviata*, Toronto, 1955
10. Don José, *Carmen*, 1955, Toronto
11. Canio, *Pagliacci*, 1955, Montreal (TV)
12. Albert, *The Ruby*, 1955, Toronto (radio)
13. Don Basilio, *Le Nozze di Figaro*, 1956 (TV and radio)
14. Male Chorus, *The Rape of Lucretia*, 1956, Stratford Festival, Ontario, Canada
15. Troilus, *Troilus and Cressida*, Toronto, 1956 (radio)
16. Jason, *Médée*, 1956, Philadelphia (concert)
17. Florestan, *Fidelio*, 1956, New York (concert)
18. Rinuccio, *Gianni Schicchi*, 1956, Toronto (TV)
19. Riccardo, *Un Ballo in Maschera*, 1957, Cardiff, England
20. Énée, *Les Troyens*, 1957, ROH, London
21. Radames, *Aida*, 1957, ROH, London
22. Don Carlos, *Don Carlos*, 1958, ROH, London
23. Siegmund, *Die Walküre*, 1958, Bayreuth
24. Samson, *Samson*, 1958, Leeds
25. Parsifal, *Parsifal*, 1959, ROH, London
26. Chénier, *Andrea Chénier*, 1961, Vienna
27. Otello, *Otello*, 1963, Buenos Aires
28. Samson, *Samson et Dalila*, 1963, Buenos Aires
29. Sergei, *Lady Macbeth of Mtsensk*, 1964, San Francisco
30. Erik, *Der fliegende Holländer*, 1965, Metropolitan Opera, New York
31. Herman, *The Queen of Spades*, 1965, Metropolitan Opera, New York
32. Peter Grimes, *Peter Grimes*, 1967, Metropolitan Opera, New York
33. Ratan-Sen, *Padmâvatî*, 1968, Buenos Aires
34. Tristan, *Tristan und Isolde*, 1971, Buenos Aires
35. Aeneas, *Dido and Aeneas*, 1972, Dallas Civic Opera
36. Herodes, *Salome*, 1974, Orange
37. Pollione, *Norma*, 1974, Orange
38. Laca, *Jenůfa*, 1974, Metropolitan Opera, New York
39. Alvaro, *La Forza del Destino*, 1975, Metropolitan Opera, New York
40. Cellini, *Benvenuto Cellini*, 1975, Boston
41. Nerone, *L'Incoronazione di Poppea*, 1978, Paris
42. Vašek, *The Bartered Bride*, 1978, Metropolitan Opera, New York

Selected Discography and Videography

Operas

Aida (Verdi)
RCA 1962. Price, Gorr, Merrill, Tozzi; Solti.

Carmen (Bizet)
EMI 1970. Bumbry, Freni, Paskalis; Frühbeck de Burgos.

Don Carlos (Verdi)
Paragon 1980 [Live, Royal Opera, May 12, 1958]. Brouwenstijn, Barbieri, Gobbi, Christoff; Giulini.

Fidelio (Beethoven)
EMI 1962. Ludwig, Hallstein, Frick, Berry, Crass; Klemperer.
EMI 1972. Dernesch, Donath, Laubenthal, Kelemen, Ridderbusch; Karajan.
Melodram 1983 [Live, Royal Opera, March 7, 1961]. Jurinac, Morrison, Robinson, Hotter, Frick; Klemperer.

L'Incoronazione di Poppea (Monteverdi)
Legendary Recordings [Live, 1978]. Jones, Ludwig, Masterson, Taillon, Sénéchal, Burles, Stilwell, Ghiaurov; Rudel.

Médée (Cherubini)
Melodram 1987 [Live, Royal Opera, June 30, 1959]. Callas, Cossotto, Carlyle, Zaccaria; Rescigno.
Melodram 1988 [Live, Dallas Civic Opera, December 6, 1958]. Callas, Carron, Berganza, Zaccaria; Rescigno.

Otello (Verdi)
RCA 1961. Rysanek, Gobbi; Serafin.
EMI 1974. Freni, Glossop; Karajan.

Pagliacci (Leoncavallo)
VAI Video [Live, Canadian Broadcasting Corporation, November 3, 1955]. Likova, Savoie, Quilico.
VAI 1992 Video [Live, Teatro Colón, June 1968]. Carlyle, MacNeil, Tomasetti; Bartoletti.
London Video [1968] Kabaivonska, Lorenzi, Glossop, Panerdi; Karajan

Parsifal (Wagner)
Melodram 1984 [Live, Bayreuth Festival, 1964]. Ericson, Stewart, Hotter, Neidlinger; Knappertsbusch.

Peter Grimes (Britten)
Philips 1978. Harper, Bainbridge, Summers, Robinson; Davis.
EMI/HBO Video [Live, Royal Opera]. Harper, Payne, Bainbridge, Bailey; Davis.

Salome (Strauss)
HRE [Live, Chorégies d'Orange, July 13, 1974]. Rysanek, Hesse, Stewart, Laubenthal; Kempe.

Samson et Dalila (Saint-Saëns)
EMI 1963. Gorr, Blanc, Diakov; Prêtre.

Tristan und Isolde (Wagner)
VAI [Live, Teatro Colón, September 24, 1971]. Nilsson, Hoffman, Mittelmann; Stein.
EMI 1972. Dernesch, Ludwig, Berry, Weikl, Ridderbusch; Karajan.
HRE 1973 [Live, Chorégies d'Orange, July 7, 1973]. Nilsson, Hesse, Laubenthal, Berry, Rundgren; Böhm.
VAI Video [Excerpts; Canadian Broadcasting Corporation, 1976]. Knie, Forrester, Braun; Decker.

Les Troyens (Berlioz)
Philips 1970. Lindholm, Veasey, Begg, Glossop, Soyer; Davis.

Die Walküre (Wagner)
London 1962. Nilsson, Brouwenstijn, Gorr, London, Ward; Leinsdorf.
DG 1967. Crespin, Janowitz, Veasey, Stewart, Talvela; Karajan.
Melodram 1981 [Live, Bayreuth Festival, 1958]. Rysanek, Varnay, Gorr, Greindl, Hotter; Knappertsbusch.

Other Works

Das Lied von der Erde (Mahler)
Philips 1982. Norman; Davis.

The Dream of Gerontius (Elgar)
Arkadie 1991. [Live, Rome, 1967]. Shacklock, Nowkowski; Barbirolli.

Enoch Arden (R. Strauss)
VAI 1999. [Live, Montreal, 1998]. Narration; Hamelin, piano.

Messa da Requiem (Verdi)
EMI 1970. Caballé, Cossotto, Raimondi; Barbirolli.

Messiah (Handel)
RCA 1957. Marshall, Palmateer, Milligan; MacMillan.
RCA 1959. Vyvyan, Sinclair, Tozzi; Beecham.

Symphony no. 9 in D Minor (Beethoven)
CBS 1979. Popp, Obraztsova, Talvela; Maazel.
RCA 1983 [Live, Avery Fisher Hall, February 2, 1983]. M. Price, Horne, Salminen; Mehta.

Die Winterreise (Schubert)
EMI 1984. Parsons, piano.
VAI 1992. Schaaf, piano.

Collections

Jon Vickers. Unique Opera Records. Songs, arias, hymns; various sources.

Jon Vickers. Radio Canada International, 1972. Irish folk songs, and songs by Scarlatti, Purcell, Dvořák, Beethoven; Barkin, piano.

Jon Vickers: Four Operatic Portraits. VAI 1984 Video. Scenes from *Samson, Fidelio, Peter Grimes, Otello*. Canadian Broadcasting Corporation.

Jon Vickers in Concert. VAI. Selections by Schumann, Handel, Scarlatti, Purcell, Dvořák; Woitach, piano.

Jon Vickers Sings Verdi and Puccini. VAI Video [Live, Canadian Broadcasting Corporation, 1954–56]. Scenes from *Manon Lescaut, Tosca, Il Trovatore*.

Jon Vickers. Met Legends, 1997. Arias, selections from *Die Winterreise* and Verdi Requiem.

In Concert: Karl Böhm and Jon Vickers. VAI 1965 Video. Canadian Broadcasting Corporation. Arias from *Fidelio, Die Walküre*; Böhm.

Italian Arias. RCA 1964. Selections from *La Gioconda, Martha, Don Carlos, L'Arlesiana, Pagliacci, Andrea Chénier, Tosca, Il Trovatore, Otello*. Rome Opera Orchestra; Serafin.

Srul Irving Glick. Radio Canada International 1989. Two Landscapes (Glick); Woitach, piano.

Vickers. Centrediscs 1985. Canadian songs; Woitach, piano.

Notes

Preface

1. Birgit Nilsson, telephone interview by author, March 24, 1987.
2. Regina Resnik, interview by author, New York, March 17, 1989.
3. Richard Cassilly, interview by author, New York, February 18, 1989.
4. Francis Robinson, quoted in Adrian Waller, "Bravo Jon Vickers," *Reader's Digest,* April 1977 (Canadian ed.), 40–44.
5. Carl Jung, ed., *Man and His Symbols* (New York: Laurel/Dell, 1968), 101.

Prologue

1. Jon Vickers, CBC Radio interview by Lorna Jackson, Prince Albert, Sask., September 1977.
2. Vickers, tribute dinner remarks, Prince Albert, Sask., September 27, 1977.
3. Vickers, quoted in Urjo Kareda, "The Tenor of His Times," *Saturday Night* (Toronto), March 1983, 37.
4. Robertson Davies, *Maclean's,* September 1972.

1. Prince Albert

1. Vickers, lecture series, Royal Conservatory of Music, Toronto, July 17, 1991.
2. Ibid.
3. Vickers, quoted in John Ardoin's chapter in Herbert H. Breslin, ed., *The Tenors* (New York: Macmillan, 1974), 48. (Many quotes in Ardoin's chapter are taken from a 1974 CBC documentary, "A Man and His Music.")
4. Jean Turnbull, interview by author, Prince Albert, Sask., June 1993.
5. Vickers, in Kareda, "The Tenor of His Times," 38.
6. Vickers, in Breslin, *The Tenors,* 48.
7. Vickers, in Kareda, "The Tenor of His Times," 40.
8. Vickers, RCM lecture series, Toronto, July 17, 1991.
9. Eva Payne Furniss, telephone interview by author, October 1991.
10. Turnbull interview.
11. Vickers, interview by Jim Becker, The Wagner Society, London, October 13, 1981 (tape).
12. Furniss interview.
13. H. A. Loucks, 1982 Vickers School dedication program.
14. William Powell, telephone interview by author, 1998.
15. Vickers, in Breslin, *The Tenors,* 52.
16. John V. Hicks, telephone interview by author, October 12, 1991.
17. Vickers, quoted in Robert Jacobson, *Reverberations* (New York: Morrow, 1974), 279 (with Erika Davidson).
18. Vickers, interview by Becker, 1981.
19. Vickers, in Breslin, *The Tenors,* 53–54.
20. Vickers, in Kareda, "The Tenor of His Times," 40.
21. Vickers, in Breslin, *The Tenors,* 54.

22. Vickers, graduation address, Royal Conservatory of Music, Toronto, November 13, 1969.
23. Robert Morrow, telephone interview by author, July 1997.
24. Vickers, interview by David Cairns, "The Power and the Passion," *Sunday Times* (London), May 9, 1982.
25. Vickers, interview by Becker, 1981.
26. Ibid.
27. Robert Motherwell, telephone interview by author, August 1997.
28. Vickers, in Kareda, "The Tenor of His Times," 40.
29. Vickers, in "A Man and His Music," CBC documentary, 1974.
30. Frank White, in ibid.
31. Vickers, in Kareda, "The Tenor of His Times," 40.
32. Vickers, Prince Albert tribute, 1977.
33. Vickers, in "A Man and His Music."
34. Vickers, interview, *Winnipeg Tribune*, December 4, 1959.
35. R. D. Kerr, interview by author, Prince Albert, August 1993.
36. W. Powell interview.
37. John Hicks, tribute dinner remarks, Prince Albert, Sask., September 27, 1977.
38. Turnbull interview.
39. Arnold Friesen, tribute dinner remarks, Prince Albert, Sask., September 27, 1977.
40. Vickers, remarks to National Association of Symphony Women, Montreal, June 4, 1973.
41. Vickers, interview, "Desert Island Discs," BBC Radio, 1968.
42. Vickers, in "A Man and His Music."
43. Vickers, interview, *Winnipeg Tribune*, December 4, 1959.
44. Vickers, interview, *London Sunday Telegram*, July 7, 1957.
45. Vickers, interview by Becker, 1981.
46. Ibid.
47. John V. Hicks, telephone interview by author, April 30, 1997.
48. Vickers, Prince Albert tribute, 1977.

2. Footloose
1. Vickers, interviews.
2. Vickers, in Waller, "Bravo Jon Vickers."
3. Vickers, interview, *Maclean's*, August 27, 1960.
4. Vickers, interview, "Desert Island Discs," 1968.
5. Vickers, interview, *Opera*, April 1962, 236.
6. Richard Bocking, telephone interview by author, November 15, 1997.
7. Winnifred Harpell Bocking, telephone interview by author, November 15, 1997.
8. J. Patrick Boyer, *A Passion for Justice* (Toronto: Osgood Society for Canadian History, 1994), 385–86.
9. Mary Seaman Copeland, telephone interview by author, 1997.
10. Flin Flon history courtesy Joyce Guymer Henderson.
11. Ron Price, telephone interview by author, February 16, 1997.
12. James Goodman, telephone interview by author, February 1997.
13. Dorothy Young Liss, telephone interviews by author, February and March 1997.
14. Goodman interview.
15. Liss interview.
16. Kit Cole, telephone interview by author, July 1997.
17. Price interview.

18. Liss interview.
19. Ibid.
20. Cecelia Sukke Allen, interview by author, April 19, 1997.
21. Liss interview.
22. Goodman interview.
23. Joyce Guymer Henderson, telephone interview by author, February 15, 1997.
24. Liss interview.
25. Allen interview.
26. Goodman interview.
27. Doris Hunt, telephone interview by author, March 1998.
28. Vickers, interview, *Toronto Star*, October 13, 1958.
29. Vickers, interview by Thurmond Smithgall, New York Wagner Society, April 26, 1998.
30. Liss interview.
31. Robert Publow, telephone interview by author, September 2, 1997.
32. Vickers, interview by Becker, 1981.
33. Ibid.
34. Stewart MacMillan Thomson, telephone interview by author, May 28, 1990.
35. Phyllis Cooke Thomson, interview by author, Winnipeg, August 30, 1993.
36. S. Thomson interview.
37. Ibid.
38. Ed Thomson, interview by author, Winnipeg, August 30, 1993.
39. Cairns, "The Power and the Passion."
40. Kathleen Morrison Brown, interview by author, Winnipeg, August 30, 1993.
41. S. R. M., review, *Winnipeg Tribune*, December 10, 1948.
42. Brown interview.
43. Rene Hoole, interview by author, Winnipeg, August 30, 1993.
44. Brown interview.
45. Mary Morrison, interview by author, Toronto, February 4, 1989.
46. Review, *Winnipeg Tribune*, November 16, 1949.
47. Brown and Morrison interviews.
48. Nan Shaw, interview by author, Toronto, February 4, 1989.
49. Vickers, graduation address, RCM, 1969.
50. Hoole interview.

3. Beginnings at the Conservatory
1. Rudolf Bing, remarks on fifth Toronto Opera Festival opening, National Club, February 20, 1954.
2. Shaw interview.
3. Victor Feldbrill, telephone interview by author, September 1991.
4. Shaw interview.
5. Vickers, interview, *Toronto Star*, August 18, 1956, and interview by Noël Goodwin, "Jon Vickers," *Opera*, April 1962, 236.
6. Vickers, interview, *Prince Albert Daily Herald*, October 27, 1952.
7. Guttman interview.
8. Shaw interview.
9. George Lambert, CBC radio interview by Ruby Mercer, 1963.
10. Vickers, in Breslin, *The Tenors*, 55.
11. Ezra Schabas, telephone interview by author, August 11, 1991.
12. Ian Garratt, telephone interview by author, August 2, 1991.

13. Stuart Hamilton, telephone interview by author, January 24, 1998.
14. Vickers, lectures.
15. Shaw interview.
16. Leo Barkin, telephone interview by author, 1989.
17. Nicholas Goldschmidt, interview by author, Toronto, February 5, 1989.
18. Morley Meredith, interview by author, New York, September 23, 1991.
19. Maureen Forrester, telephone interview by author, April 7, 1991.
20. Vickers, in Breslin, *The Tenors*, 60.
21. Franz Kraemer, interview by author, Toronto, August 23, 1993.
22. Ibid.
23. Shaw interview.
24. Robert Goulet, telephone interview by author, June 20, 1993.
25. Edith Milligan Binnie, interview by author, New York, November 8, 1991.
26. Ibid.
27. United Church of Canada, Victoria University Archives, biographical file.
28. Interviews with Hetti Vickers's relatives by author.
29. Hetti Vickers, interview, London, June 27, 1959, unidentified Canadian newspaper.
30. May Hambly, telephone interview by author, 1997.
31. Richard and Winnifred Bocking interviews.
32. Vickers, interview, "Desert Island Discs," 1968.
33. Hambly interview.
34. Vickers, interview, "Desert Island Discs," 1968.
35. Hambly interview.
36. Teresa Stratas, interview by author, New York, March 1, 1998.
37. Peter Glossop, telephone interview by author, April 25, 1997.
38. Roberta Knie, interview by author, New York, August 13, 1997.
39. Sir John Tooley, interview by author, London, May 23, 1990.
40. John Miller, telephone interview by author, August 7, 1991.

4. A Tenor in Toronto
  1. Binnie interview; wedding article, *Toronto Globe & Mail*, undated clipping [August 1953].
  2. Shaw interview.
  3. Morrison interview.
  4. Liss interview.
  5. Metropolitan Opera Archives, auditions file.
  6. Garratt interview.
  7. Schabas interview.
  8. University of Toronto, Fisher Archive, RCM Concert Bureau correspondence, 1950s.
  9. John Kraglund, review, *Toronto Globe & Mail*, November 9, 1953.
 10. Vickers, interview by Blaik Kirby, *Toronto Daily Star*, January 20, 1962.
 11. Herbert Tinney, telephone interview by author, 1998.
 12. Feldbrill interview.
 13. Canadian Opera Company, Joan Baillie Archives, performance contracts file.
 14. Hugh Thomson, review, *Toronto Star*, February 26, 1954.
 15. John Kraglund, review, *Toronto Globe & Mail*, February 26, 1954.
 16. Kraemer interview.
 17. Binnie interview.
 18. Vickers, interview, *Ottawa Journal*, July 17, 1976.

19. Olin Downes, review, *New York Times*, April 1954.
20. Vickers, interview by author for VAI *Pagliacci* video release, August 1993.
21. Eva Likova, interview by author, New York, April 24, 1992.
22. Vickers, interview, VAI *Pagliacci*.
23. Vickers, lecture, 92nd Street Y, New York, April 26, 1998.
24. Guttman interview; Vickers, in Kareda, "The Tenor of His Times," 41; Schabas interview.
25. Resnik interview.
26. Joanne Ivey Mazzoleni, telephone interview by author, August 14, 1997.
27. Hugh Thomson, review, *Toronto Star*, February 25, 1956; George Kidd, review, *Toronto Telegram*, February 25, 1956.
28. Resnik interview.
29. Vickers, in Waller, "Bravo Jon Vickers."
30. Schabas interview.
31. Ibid.
32. University of Toronto, Fisher Archive, RCM Concert Bureau correspondence.
33. Resnik interview.
34. Vickers, in Kareda, "The Tenor of His Times," 41; Vickers, interview by Becker, 1981.
35. Guttman interview.
36. Montague Haltrecht, *The Quiet Showman: Sir David Webster and the Royal Opera House* (London: Collins, 1975), 223.
37. Shaw interview.
38. According to ROH Archivist Francesca Franchi, Webster's diary shows that on November 25, 1955, he flew to Montreal. No date is listed for Vickers's audition in Toronto, but it seems to have followed very shortly after the Montreal audition for other singers. Haltrecht's book on Webster gives November 17 as Vickers's audition date (p. 223), but this cannot be correct, because the diary shows Webster in London on that date, a Thursday. November 27 was a Sunday, apparently the "rainy Sunday" to which Vickers later referred (Haltrecht, *The Quiet Showman*, 222).
39. Lambert, interview by Mercer, 1963.
40. Goldschmidt interview.
41. Haltrecht, *Quiet Showman*, 223.
42. Webster to Vickers, cable, Royal Opera House Archives (hereafter cited as ROH Archives).
43. Stein to Webster, cable, May 8, 1956; Webster to Stein, cable, May 11, 1956, ROH Archives.
44. Vickers, interview, *London Observer*, May 18, 1980.
45. Haltrecht, *Quiet Showman*, 224.
46. Ibid.
47. Vickers interviews.
48. Vickers, interview by Becker, 1981.
49. Tooley interview.
50. ROH Archives.
51. ROH Archives.
52. John Coast letters.
53. ROH Archives.
54. Howard Taubman, review, *New York Times*, November 21, 1956.
55. Vickers lectures.
56. Edwin H. Schloss, review, *Philadelphia Inquirer*, November 30, 1956.

57. ROH Archives.

58. Vickers, interview by Becker, 1981.

59. Vickers, in Kareda, "The Tenor of His Times," 41.

60. Vickers, various lectures.

5. Covent Garden and Battling the BBC

1. Vickers, telephone remarks to author, July 29, 1994.

2. Morrison interview.

3. ROH Archives.

4. Tooley interview.

5. Edward Downes, quoted in Jon Tolansky, "Anniversary Portrait," *About the House,* no. 13, autumn 1997, 54.

6. Ande Anderson, telephone interview by author, May 27, 1989.

7. Ron Freeman, interview by author, London, May 15, 1997.

8. Vickers, interview by Becker, 1981.

9. Ibid.

10. Downes, in Tolansky, "Anniversary Portrait," 52.

11. Vickers, interview by Becker, 1981.

12. John Lucas, *Reggie: The Life of Reginald Goodall* (London: Julia MacRae/Random House, 1993), 142–43.

13. Lord Harewood, telephone interview by author, October 15, 1997.

14. Downes, in Tolansky, "Anniversary Portrait."

15. ROH Archives.

16. Vickers to Herman Geiger-Torel, May 8, 1957, Canadian Opera Company Archives (hereinafter cited as COC Archives).

17. Ramón Vinay, interview, *Manchester Guardian,* March 17, 1957.

18. Review, *Financial Times,* March 6, 1957.

19. Desmond Shawe-Taylor, review, *Statesman and Nation* (London), May 4, 1957.

20. Harold Rosenthal, review, *Opera,* June 17, 1957, 390.

21. Downes, in Tolansky, "Anniversary Portrait"; Noël Goodwin, review, *Daily Express,* April 1957.

22. Haltrecht, *Quiet Showman,* 224.

23. Canadian Opera Company, Joan Baillie Archives, correspondence files.

24. Hector Berlioz, *Memoirs of Hector Berlioz,* trans. and ed. David Cairns (reprint, London: Cardinal, 1990), 423.

25. David Cairns, *Responses* (New York: Knopf, 1973), 147.

26. Vickers, interview, CBC Radio Tuesday Night Series, October 1973.

27. Blanche Thebom, telephone interview by author, November 1994.

28. Rafael Kubelik, interview, *Opera News,* March 16, 1974.

29. Haltrecht, *The Quiet Showman,* 255.

30. Vickers to Geiger-Torel, March 14, 1958, COC Archives.

31. Vickers, interview, *Opera News,* October 1973, 38.

32. Anderson interview; Sir John Gielgud, interview, *Opera News,* February 12, 1966, 9.

33. Jacques Bourgeois, review, *Opera,* September 1957, 585–86; review, *Scotsman,* June 1957.

34. Vickers, interview, *Toronto Telegram,* June 28, 1957.

35. Feldbrill interview.

36. Vickers, lecture, University of Toronto, November 1995.

37. Vickers, quoted in Jacobson, *Reverberations,* 279.

38. Vickers to Geiger-Torel, February 27, 1958, COC Archives.

39. Vickers, Toronto lecture, 1995.
40. Vickers to Geiger-Torel, March 14, 1958, COC Archives.
41. Vickers interview, 1969.
42. Fred Weidner, interview by author, December 23, 1997.
43. Lionel Salter, telephone interview by author, August 18, 1997.
44. Vickers to Webster, September 22, 1957, ROH Archives.
45. Salter interview.
46. Vickers to Webster, ROH Archives.
47. ROH Archives.
48. John Ardoin, telephone interview by author, July 10, 1997.
49. Coast to Gillian Jones, ROH contracts manager, May 23 and December 9, 1980, ROH Archives.
50. Agency source prefers anonymity.
51. Vickers to Wieland Wagner, January 9, 1958, Bayreuth Festspiele Archives.
52. Adler office to Stein, December 19, 1957, San Francisco Opera Archives, San Francisco Performing Arts Library and Museum (PALM).
53. Metropolitan Opera Archives.
54. Russell Braddon, *Joan Sutherland* (London: Collins, 1962), 77–78.

6. A Don Carlos *Triumph and Bayreuth Debut*

1. Review, *Times* (London), January 1958; Sir Colin Davis, telephone interview by author, May 1990.
2. ROH Archives.
3. Vickers to Geiger-Torel, COC Archives.
4. Ibid.
5. Haltrecht, *Quiet Showman*, 235.
6. Harold Rosenthal, review, *Opera*, October 1958, 396.
7. William Lewis, interview by author, Philadelphia, November 29, 1986.
8. Vickers, Toronto lecture, 1995.
9. Frederic Spotts, *Bayreuth: A History of the Wagner Festival* (New Haven, Conn.: Yale University Press, 1994), 246.
10. Bayreuth Archives.
11. Ibid.
12. Régine Crespin, lecture, Alliance Française, New York, November 14, 1997.
13. Vickers, interview, *Scenario,* January 1985.
14. Vickers, Toronto lecture, 1995.
15. Ralf Steyer, review, *Opera*, October 1958, 719.
16. *Wiesbaden Courier,* review, undated, used in William Stein ad for Vickers.
17. Vickers, Toronto lecture, 1995.
18. Bayreuth Archives.
19. Vickers, Toronto lecture, 1995.
20. Vickers to Geiger-Torel, COC Archives; Gerhard Hellwig to Vickers, Bayreuth Archives.
21. Wieland Wagner to Vickers, June 4, 1964, Bayreuth Archives.
22. Hans Hotter, telephone interview by author, 1997.
23. Vickers, quoted in Heinz Ludwig, "Of the Nibelung Faith in Salzburg," 1975, publication name unavailable.
24. Vickers, in Kareda, "The Tenor of His Times," 43–44.
25. Vickers, interview by Smithgall, 1998.
26. Andrew Porter, review, *Opera*, November 1958, 743.

27. Goodwin, "Jon Vickers," *Opera*, 239.
28. Stone Widney, telephone interview by author, 1997.
29. Metropolitan Opera Archives.
30. Ingpen to Bing, ROH Archives; Joan Ingpen, telephone interview by author, 1998.
31. Haltrecht, *Quiet Showman*, 240.
32. Vickers, various interviews.
33. Stein to Webster, March 19, 1958, ROH Archives.
34. Coast to Webster, July 19, 1958, ROH Archives.
35. Haltrecht, *Quiet Showman*, 239.
36. Coast to Webster, ROH Archives.
37. Haltrecht, *Quiet Showman*, 239.
38. Ingpen interview.
39. Vickers, 92nd Street Y lecture, 1998.
40. Bliss Hebert, telephone interview by author, July 11, 1997.
41. Arianna Stassinopoulos, *Maria Callas: The Woman behind the Legend* (New York: Simon and Schuster, 1981), 191–92; Haltrecht, *Quiet Showman*, 182; Vickers, interview, *Toronto Star*, August 25, 1960.
42. John Rosenfield, review, *Dallas Morning News*, November 7, 1958.
43. Vickers, interview, "A Life in Music," CBC radio, October 23, 1973.
44. Rosenfield, review, *Dallas Morning News*, November 7, 1958.
45. Vickers, interview by Tom Sutcliffe, "Strongman," *Opera News*, March 1, 1986.
46. Geoffrey Tarran, review, *Morning Advertiser*, June 20, 1959.
47. C.W., review, *Musical Times*, August 1959.
48. Ardoin interview.
49. Vickers, Toronto lecture, 1995.
50. George Jellinek, *Callas: Portrait of a Prima Donna* (1960; reprint, New York: Dover, 1986), 317.

7. *New Roles, New Houses*
1. William Mann, review, *Opera*, December 1958, 806.
2. Glossop interview.
3. Jeryl Metz Woitach, interview by author, New York, January 11, 1997.
4. Vickers, interview, *Yorkshire News*, October 6, 1958.
5. Vickers to Webster, January 7, 1959, ROH Archives.
6. Christopher Raeburn, fax to author, September 21, 1998.
7. Richard Bletschacher, telephone interview by author, February 1, 1998.
8. Ibid.
9. Joseph Wechsberg, review, *Opera*, March 1959, 159.
10. Wechsberg, review, *Opera*, June 1960, 412.
11. Vickers, graduation address, RCM, 1969.
12. Metropolitan Opera Archives, contracts file.
13. Vickers profile, *Time*, February 22, 1960.
14. Vickers, interview, *Toronto Globe & Mail*, April 10, 1959.
15. Vickers to Geiger-Torel, COC Archives.
16. Geiger-Torel to Vickers, February 14, 1959, COC Archives.
17. Evan Senior, review, *Music and Musicians*, July 1959, 19.
18. Goodwin, "Jon Vickers," 234.
19. Vickers, interview by Smithgall, 1998.
20. Ibid.

21. Charles Reid, *Thomas Beecham: An Independent Biography* (New York: Dutton, 1962), 241–42.
22. Vickers, interview by Smithgall, 1998.
23. Ibid.
24. Arthur Bloomfield, review, *Musical America*, October 1959, 3.
25. Arthur Jacobs, review, *Reynold's News*, December 20, 1959.
26. Sheila Porter, interview by author, New York, December 28, 1992.
27. Vickers, quoted in Breslin, *The Tenors*, 281.
28. Vickers, telephone interview by author, August 1993.
29. Vickers, interview, *Prince Albert Herald*, July 10, 1959.
30. S. Porter interview.
31. A. Anderson interview.

8. The Met
1. Merle Hubbard, interview by author, New York, July 10, 1992.
2. Walter Taussig, interview by author, New York, January 23, 1998.
3. Richard Woitach, interview by author, New York, December 23, 1996.
4. Vickers, interview by Robert Angus, *Weekend* Magazine (Toronto), August 20, 1960.
5. Robert Sabin, review, *Musical America*, February 1960; John Briggs, review, *New York Times*, January 18, 1960; Herbert Breslin, preface to *The Tenors*, xiv.
6. Irving Kolodin, review, *Saturday Review*, February 1960; Kolodin, *The Metropolitan Opera, 1883–1966: A Candid History* (New York: Knopf, 1966), 622.
7. James Levine, interview by author, New York, September 17, 1998.
8. Howard Taubman, review, *New York Times*, January 29, 1960, 15.
9. Theodor Uppman and Jean Uppman, interview by author, New York, November 1, 1997.
10. Speight Jenkins, telephone interview by author, January 24, 1998.
11. Vickers profile, *Time*, February 22, 1960.
12. Howard Taubman, review, *New York Times*, February 10, 1960.
13. Vickers to Bing, ROH Archives.
14. Coast to Webster, May 5, 1960, ROH Archives.
15. Ibid.
16. Alan Kayes, telephone interview by author and letter, July 1993.
17. Nancy Swift, BMG Records, telephone conversation with author, July 1993.
18. Vickers, in Breslin, *The Tenors*, 65.
19. Richard Mohr, interview by author, New York, May 27, 1993.
20. Ibid.
21. Harold Rosenthal, review, *Opera*, January 1962, 50.
22. Vickers, telephone interview by author, April 20, 1993.
23. Terence McEwen, telephone interview by author, 1996.
24. Ibid.
25. Regina Resnik, interview by author, May 1999.
26. Vickers, interview, *Prince Albert Herald*, September 11, 1963.
27. Vickers interview, Hugh Thomson, *Toronto Globe & Mail*, May 18, 1964.
28. Vickers, interview by Blaik Kirby, *Toronto Star*, 1963.
29. Don Henahan, review, *Chicago Daily News*, November 17, 1960.
30. Claudia Cassidy, review, *Chicago Tribune*, November 17, 1960.
31. H. D. Rosenthal, review, *Opera*, April 1961, 101.
32. Reg Suter, letter to author, July 1997.

33. H. D. Rosenthal, review, *Opera*, April 1961, 273.
34. Andrew Porter, review, *Opera*, November 1961, 728–29.
35. Walter Legge, EMI proposal letter, March 8, 1961, EMI Archives.
36. Alan Blyth, *Opera on CD* (London: Kyle Cathie, 1992), 25.
37. Mohr interview.

9. The Solti Debacle
1. Bruce Burroughs, telephone interview by author, September 1990.
2. Tooley interview.
3. Valerie Solti, book luncheon remarks, New York, October 27, 1997.
4. John Copley, telephone interview by author, June 13, 1997.
5. Solti to Vickers, November 2, 1960, ROH Archives.
6. Coast to Muriel Kerr (assistant to Webster), January 3, 1961, ROH Archives.
7. Mohr interview; Breslin, *The Tenors*, 69.
8. Haltrecht, *Quiet Showman*, 289; S. Porter interview.
9. Vickers interview, *Opera News*, December 23, 1961, 31.
10. Copley interview.
11. Hans Hotter, telephone interview by author, 1997.
12. Tooley interview.
13. Solti to Vickers, quoted in Haltrecht, *Quiet Showman*, 289–90.
14. Ingpen interview.
15. A. Anderson interview.
16. Harewood interview.
17. Vickers interview, May 16, 1968, CBC Radio, CBC Archives.
18. S. Porter interview.
19. Roberta Knie, interview by author, New York, August 13, 1997.
20. Sir Georg Solti, *Memoirs* (New York: Knopf, 1997), 133.
21. V. Solti, book luncheon remarks, 1997.
22. Roger Dettmer, review, *Opera*, December 1961, 790; Claudia Cassidy, review, *Chicago Tribune*, October 21, 1961; Don [Donal] Henahan, review, *Chicago Daily News*, October 21, 1961; Dettmer, review, *Chicago American*, October 1961.
23. Galina Vishnevskaya, *Galina: A Russian Story* (New York: Harcourt Brace Jovanovich, 1984), 291–94.
24. Ibid., 322–23.
25. Coast to Victor Olaf, November 8, 1961, EMI Archives.
26. J. D. Bicknell to P. V. de Jongh, January 5, 1962, EMI Archives.
27. ROH Archives.
28. Vickers, graduation address, RCM, 1969.
29. Vickers, interview by Blaik Kirby, *Toronto Star*, January 20, 1962.
30. Memo to Bing, 1962, Metropolitan Opera Archives.
31. Porter review, 1969.
32. ROH Archives.
33. Coast to Ingpen, August 24, 1962, ROH Archives.
34. Source prefers anonymity.
35. William Littler, interview by author, Toronto, July 16, 1991.
36. Diefenbaker Canada Centre, University of Saskatchewan, Saskatoon, correspondence files.
37. Littler interview.
38. Vickers, in Kareda, "The Tenor of His Times," 38.

39. Sir Colin Davis, letter to author, September 2, 1998.
40. Hugh Thomson, interview by author, 1998.
41. Woitach interview.
42. Margaret Atwood, interview, *New York Times*, December 30, 1996.
43. Vickers, interview, *Toronto Star*, July 17, 1963.

10. Lonely Hotels
 1. David Cairns, interview by author, Purchase, N.Y., August 4, 1989.
 2. New York Philharmonic, videotape, Museum of Television and Radio, New York.
 3. Sylvie de Nussac, booklet for Camille Saint-Saëns, *Samson et Dalila*, EMI Angel, 3639 (1963).
 4. Review, *Opera*, September 1962, 615.
 5. Curt Weinstein, review, *Opera*, November 1963, 744.
 6. Vickers, interview by John Kraglund, *Toronto Globe & Mail*, July 17, 1963.
 7. Vickers, interview, *Prince Albert Herald*, September 11, 1963.
 8. Lotfi Mansouri, telephone interview by author, April 10, 1998.
 9. Claudia Cassidy, review, *Chicago Tribune*, 1963.
 10. Stein to Robinson, January 7, 1964, Metropolitan Opera Archives.
 11. Wieland Wagner to Vickers, cable, January 7, 1964, and Vickers to W. Wagner, cable, January 8, 1964, Bayreuth Archives.
 12. Telegram, January 8, 1964, Bayreuth Archives.
 13. Ibid.
 14. Vickers, interview by Hugh Thomson, *Toronto Globe & Mail*, May 18, 1964.
 15. Cairns, *Responses*, 148.
 16. Vickers, quoted in Breslin, *The Tenors*, 64.
 17. Freeman interview.
 18. Peter Diggins, review, *Opera*, autumn festival issue, 1964, 19–26.
 19. Vickers, quoted in Ludwig, "Of the Nibelung Faith in Salzburg."
 20. Ibid.
 21. Mansouri interview.
 22. Garratt interview.
 23. McEwen interview.
 24. Martin Bernheimer, review, *Opera*, May 1965, 337.
 25. John Ardoin, review, *Opera*, December 1965, 876.
 26. Kraemer interview.
 27. Bayreuth Archives.
 28. Kraemer interview.
 29. Zubin Mehta, interview by author, March 1998.
 30. Yvonne Minton, interview by author, Chicago, October 31, 1992.
 31. Allen Hughes, review, *New York Times*, May 2, 1966; George Movshon, *Hi Fidelity*, July 1966, 31.
 32. Bayreuth Archives.
 33. Arthur Bloomfield, *The San Francisco Opera, 1922–1978* (Sausalito, Calif.: Comstock, 1978), 230, 241.
 34. Kenneth Dean Wallace, review, *Musical America*, January 1967, 22.
 35. Vickers, "Working with Herbert von Karajan," *Opera Canada*, no. 4, 1969, 13.
 36. Vickers, quoted in Ulla Colgrass, *For the Love of Music* (Toronto: Oxford University Press, 1988), 179.
 37. Nina Lawson, interview by author, New York, September 12, 1997.

11. Peter Grimes

1. Leighton Kerner, *Stagebill*, Kennedy Center, Washington, D.C., April 1984.
2. Gwynne Howell, telephone interview by author, May 2, 1997.
3. Vickers, 92nd Street Y lecture, 1998.
4. Sir Charles Mackerras, interview by author, New York, April 14, 1998.
5. Elijah Moshinsky, interview by author, New York, November 9, 1990.
6. Max Loppert, "Jon Vickers on *Peter Grimes*," *Opera*, August 1984, 840.
7. Jacobson, *Reverberations*, 278–79.
8. Levine interview.
9. Jacobson, *Reverberations*, 278.
10. Uppman interview.
11. Loppert, "Vickers on *Grimes*," 842.
12. Levine interview.
13. Philip Brett, telephone interview by author, July 9, 1999, on Pears article, "Neither a Hero nor a Villain," in Brett, ed., *Benjamin Britten: Peter Grimes* (Cambridge, Eng.: Cambridge University Press, 1983), 152.
14. Philip Hope-Wallace, *Time and Tide*, quoted in Humphrey Carpenter, *Benjamin Britten: A Biography* (New York: Macmillan, 1992), 223.
15. Andrew Porter, notes for *Albert Herring*, New York City Opera, October 1971.
16. Brett, fax to author, September 17, 1997.
17. Woitach interview; Lawson interview.
18. Loppert, "Vickers on *Grimes*," 835–36.
19. Colgrass, *For the Love of Music*, 176.
20. Vickers interview by William Albright, *Houston Post*, January 16, 1977.
21. Vickers, lecture, Montgomery College, Rockville, Md., November 24, 1986; Vickers, 92nd Street Y lecture, 1998.
22. Mackerras interview.
23. Vickers, interview by David Cairns, Arts Liaison, South Bank, July 1981; Donald Mitchell, telephone interview by author, August 18, 1997.
24. Vickers, interview by Cairns, 1981.
25. Ben Heppner, telephone interview by author, January 1995; Woitach interview.
26. Breslin, *The Tenors*, 59–60.
27. C. Davis interview.
28. Vickers, Tanglewood Festival program, July 1996.
29. Littler interview.
30. Colin Graham, telephone interview by author, October 21, 1998; Graham, e-mail to author, October 20, 1998.
31. Britten quoted in Desmond Shawe-Taylor, *Sunday Times* (London), December 5, 1976.
32. Robert Tear, interview by author, Washington, D.C., June 8, 1987.
33. Tooley interview.
34. C. Davis interview.
35. Moshinsky interview.
36. Tooley interview.
37. Richard Dyer, interview by author, Boston, May 15, 1993.
38. Levine interview.
39. Anthony Dean Griffey, telephone interview by author, April 30, 1999.

12. A Prophet in His Own Country

1. Peter G. Davis, review, *Musical America*, June 1967, 7.

2. Allen Hughes, review, *New York Times,* April 5, 1967.

3. John Ardoin, review, *Dallas Morning News,* November 16, 1968.

4. Olin Chism, review, *Dallas Times Herald,* November 16, 1968.

5. Eric McLean, review, *Montreal Star.*

6. Source prefers anonymity.

7. Source prefers anonymity.

8. Review, *Wien Zeitung,* November 3, 1967.

9. Vickers, interview by Philip Anson, *Toronto Globe & Mail,* May 30, 1998.

10. Taussig interview.

11. Horst Kogler, review, *Opera,* March 1968, 249.

12. Vickers interview, CBC Radio, no date available.

13. Bruno Bartoletti, interview by author, Chicago, August 28, 1996.

14. Richard Woitach on "Metropolitan Opera Quiz," February 19, 1994.

15. Robert Merrill, interview by author, New York, May 10, 1993.

16. Vickers, remarks to National Association of Symphony Women, 1973.

17. Howell interview.

18. Lucine Amara, quoted in Bruce Burroughs, "Serene Lucine," *Opera Quarterly* 9, no. 1 (autumn 1992): 90.

19. William Littler, review, *Toronto Star,* May 2, 1969.

20. Vickers, interview by Blaik Kirby, *Toronto Globe & Mail,* March 6, 1971.

21. Adler to Vickers, August 12, 1969, San Francisco Opera Archives, PALM.

22. Coast to Adler, July 25, 1969, San Francisco Opera Archives, PALM.

23. Robert Tuggle and John Pennino of the Met Archives, conversation with author, 1999.

24. Coast to Adler, San Francisco Opera Archives, PALM.

25. Cairns interview.

26. Alan Blyth, *Colin Davis* (New York: Drake, 1973), 40.

27. Cairns interview.

28. Glossop interview.

29. Blyth, *Colin Davis,* 41.

30. Cairns, *Responses,* 150.

13. A Unique Tenor Repertoire and a Tristan *Debut*

1. Vickers, interview, "Desert Island Discs," 1968.

2. Coast, letter to Adler, April 1, 1970, San Francisco Opera Archives, PALM.

3. James Helme Sutcliffe, review, *Opera News,* October 10, 1970, 26.

4. Vickers, interview by Becker, 1981.

5. Measurements list, April 4, 1970, San Francisco Opera Archives, PALM.

6. Coast to Adler, June 19, 1970, San Francisco Opera Archives, PALM.

7. Woitach interview.

8. Glossop interview.

9. Coast to Tooley, November 13, 1970, ROH Archives.

10. James Conlon, telephone interview by author, January 14, 1995.

11. K. H. Adler memo, October 22, 1970, San Francisco Opera Archives, PALM.

12. K. H. Adler, San Francisco Opera Archives, PALM.

13. Richard Rodzinski, telephone interview by author, July 16, 1997.

14. Bloomfield, *San Francisco Opera,* 280.

15. EMI Archives.

16. Otto Schenk, interview by author, New York, March 4, 1991.

17. Kiri Te Kanawa, interview, *Musical America,* May 1974, 9.

18. Coast to Tooley, May 17, 1971, ROH Archives.
19. Woitach interview.
20. Vickers, quoted in Renée Maheu, "Vickers: Heldentenor," *MusicCanada*, October 1977; Vickers, Toronto lecture, 1995; Vickers, interview by Bernard Levin, BBC Radio, 1982.
21. Vickers, interview by Blaik Kirby, *Toronto Globe & Mail*, March 6, 1971.
22. Harold Brodkey, "Dying: An Update," *New Yorker*, February 7, 1994, 71.
23. Woitach interview.
24. Ernest Newman, *The Wagner Operas*, vol. 1 (New York: Harper Colophon, 1983), 233; Vickers, Toronto lecture, 1995.
25. Vickers, interview, *London Observer*, May 18, 1980.
26. Birgit Nilsson, *My Memoirs in Pictures* (New York: Doubleday, 1981; reprint, New York: Da Capo Press, 1982), 46.
27. Oscar Figueroa, review, *Opera*, March 1972, 251–52.
28. Moshinsky interview.
29. Max Loppert, review, *Financial Times*, London, May 19, 1980.
30. Thomas Allen, telephone interview by author, July 25, 1997.
31. Cairns interview.
32. Sir Donald McIntyre, interview by author, New York, February 1, 1993.
33. Vickers, interview by Nancy Malitz, *Ovation*, October 1986, 20.
34. Helga Dernesch, telephone interview by author, December 12, 1997.
35. Conlon interview.
36. Richard Osborne, *Conversations with Karajan* (London: Oxford University Press, 1989), 77.

14. A Moor Does Battle, Énée and Tristan at the Met
1. Vickers, interview, *London Standard*, May 26, 1972.
2. C. Davis interview.
3. Vickers, interview, *London Standard*, May 26, 1972.
4. Vickers, interview by Alan Blyth, *Times* (London), May 2, 1972.
5. Tom Sutcliffe, review, *Music and Musicians*, August 1972.
6. Review, *Musical Times*, August 1972.
7. Andrew Porter, *A Musical Season* (New York: Viking Press, 1974), 89.
8. Gerald Fitzgerald, review, *Opera News*, January 27, 1973, 22.
9. John Ardoin, review, *Dallas Morning News*, November 5, 1972.
10. Vickers, telephone conversation with author, October 28, 1993.
11. Louis Quilico, interview by author, New York, February 10, 1990.
12. Fabrizio Melano, telephone interview by author, July 11, 1999; Schuyler Chapin, *Musical Chairs: A Life in the Arts* (New York: Putnam, 1977), 313.
13. Quilico interview.
14. Franco Zeffirelli, interview by author, New York, May 2, 1999.
15. Chapin, *Musical Chairs*, 317–18.
16. Victor Callegari, telephone interview by author, July 1998.
17. Vickers, interview, *London Observer*, May 18, 1980.
18. J. J. Outerbridge, telephone interview by author, 1998.
19. William Duncan, telephone interview by author, September 6, 1997.
20. Davies, quoted in John Kraglund, report, *Toronto Globe & Mail*, May 15, 1973.
21. Alan Rich, review, *New York*, November 5, 1973, 89.
22. Levine interview.
23. Lewis interview.

24. John Ardoin, review, *Dallas Morning News,* December 2, 1973.
25. Chapin, *Musical Chairs,* 363–64.
26. Schuyler Chapin, interview, *New York Times,* January 11, 1974, 16.
27. Chapin, *Musical Chairs,* 361, 363.
28. Klara Barlow, telephone interview by author, January 26, 1992.
29. Chapin, *Musical Chairs,* 362.
30. Mignon Dunn, interview by author, New York, March 31, 1997.
31. Chapin, *Musical Chairs,* 365; *New York Times,* January 11, 1974.
32. Chapin, *Musical Chairs,* 365.
33. Speight Jenkins, review, *New York Post,* January 12, 1974.
34. Erich Leinsdorf, interview by Speight Jenkins, *New York Post,* January 15, 1974; Barlow interview.
35. Harold Schonberg, review, *New York Times,* January 12, 1974.
36. Barlow interview.
37. Speight Jenkins, review, *New York Post,* January 28, 1974.
38. Raymond Ericson, review, *New York Times,* January 28, 1974.
39. Donal Henahan, review, *New York Times,* February 22, 1974; George Movshon, review, *Opera,* June 1974, 498–500.
40. Source prefers anonymity.
41. Vickers and Te Kanawa, interview by Michael Owens, *London Evening Standard.*
42. Chapin, *Musical Chairs,* 369–70.
43. Metropolitan Opera Archives.
44. Metropolitan Opera Archives.
45. Metropolitan Opera Archives.

15. A Man and His Music

1. Colin Graham, e-mail to author, October 20, 1998.
2. Eric McLean, review, *Montreal Star,* May 6, 1974.
3. Knie interview.
4. Monique Barichella, review, *Opera News,* October 1974, 60.
5. Charles Pitt, review, *Opera,* autumn festival issue, 1974, 58.
6. R. Bocking interview.
7. Bartoletti interview.
8. Graham interview.
9. Vickers, notes, *Opera News,* December 21, 1974.
10. Cairns interview.
11. Levine interview.
12. Bruce Burroughs, telephone interview by author, fall 1989.
13. Terence Shawn, telephone interview by author, January 21, 1996.
14. Bruce Burroughs, review, *Music Journal,* March 1975, 35–36.
15. Porter, *Music of Three Seasons,* 89.
16. Metropolitan Opera Archives.
17. Ardoin interview.
18. William Fred Scott, telephone interview by author, December 30, 1984.
19. Porter, *Music of Three Seasons,* 169.
20. Paul Hume, review, *Washington Post,* May 12, 1975.
21. Sarah Caldwell, interview by author, Boston, May 15, 1993.
22. Janet Stubbs, telephone interview by author, 1998.
23. Metropolitan Opera Archives.
24. Vickers, interview by Alan Blyth, *Times* (London), October 24, 1974.

25. Knie interview.
26. Olin Chism, review, *Dallas Times Herald*, December 8, 1975.
27. Ardoin, review, *Dallas Morning News*, December 8, 1975.
28. Nicola Rescigno, telephone interview by author, January 1985.
29. Vickers, 92nd Street Y lecture, 1998.
30. Roger Carroll, telephone interview by author, 1998.
31. Vickers, interview by John Ardoin, quoted in *Opera*, April 1976, 337.
32. Charles Reid, *John Barbirolli: A Biography* (New York: Taplinger, 1971), 194.
33. Knie interview.
34. F. W. O'R., review, *Musical America*, May 1976, 27.
35. Review, *Variety*, undated clipping [February 1976].
36. John Rockwell, review, *New York Times*, February 8, 1976.
37. Jack Diether, review, *The Westsider*, February 12, 1976.
38. Coast to Rodzinski, May 17, 1976, Metropolitan Opera Archives.
39. Ibid.
40. Vickers, interview by Alan Blyth, *Grammophone*, September 1976, 402.
41. Mackerras interview.
42. Coast to Tooley, June 3, 1976, ROH Archives.
43. Kraemer interview.
44. Ruby Mercer, review, *Opera Canada*, no. 3, 1976, 37.
45. Robert Jacobson, review, *Opera News*, October 1976, 50.
46. Mario Bernardi, telephone interview by author, July 10, 1998.
47. Ibid.
48. Vickers, interview, *Ottawa Citizen*, July 10, 1976.

16. The Tannhäuser *Scandal*

1. Knie interview.
2. Ernest Newman, *The Wagner Operas*, vol. 1 (New York: Harper Colophon, 1983), 63.
3. Victor Gollancz, *Journey towards Music* (New York: Dutton, 1965), 77, 105.
4. Vickers, interview by Alan Blyth, *Times* (London), May 24, 1972.
5. Tooley interview.
6. Metropolitan Opera Archives, contracts file.
7. Knie interview.
8. Vickers, Montgomery College lecture, 1988.
9. Metropolitan Opera Archives.
10. Metropolitan Opera Archives, transcript of telephone conversation.
11. Tooley interview.
12. Metropolitan Opera Archives.
13. Metropolitan Opera Archives.
14. Metropolitan Opera Archives.
15. Metropolitan Opera Archives.
16. McEwen interview.
17. ROH Archives.
18. John Cunningham, "Unsung Hero," *Manchester Guardian*, January 16, 1977.
19. James McCracken, interview by author, New York, March 11, 1987.
20. Cassilly interview.
21. Glossop interview.
22. William Wildermann, interview by author, Washington, D.C., February 5, 1988.
23. Jerome Hines, telephone interview by author, June 16, 1998.

24. Vickers, Toronto lecture, 1995.
25. Dorothy Kirsten, *A Time to Sing* (New York: Doubleday, 1982), 88.
26. Taussig interview.
27. Kraemer interview.
28. Levine interview.
29. Moshinsky interview.
30. Lorne Watson, telephone interview by author, February 27, 1998.
31. Mansouri interview.
32. Vickers, interview by Bernard Levin, BBC Radio, 1982.
33. Vickers, interview by CBC Radio.
34. Ingpen interview.
35. Sherrill Milnes, telephone interview by author, December 28, 1997.
36. Ingpen interview.
37. Milnes interview.
38. Ingpen interview.

17. From Moose Jaw to Monteverdi
1. Sir Charles Mackerras, letter to author, April 1998.
2. Wildermann interview.
3. Ibid.
4. Cairns, "The Power and the Passion."
5. Margaret Galloway, telephone interview by author, December 13, 1992.
6. Jean Macpherson, interview with Vickers, *Saskatoon Star Phoenix,* September 29, 1977.
7. Coast to Betty Scholar, September 19, 1977, ROH Archives.
8. June Anderson, interview by author, October 29, 1998.
9. Jenkins interview.
10. Jenkins, review, *New York Post,* January 3, 1978.
11. Jenkins interview.
12. Leonie Rysanek, telephone interview by author, January 1996.
13. Rolf Liebermann, *En Passant par Paris* (Paris: Gallimard, 1980), 265.
14. Ingpen interview.
15. Gwyneth Jones, telephone interview by author, June 14, 1991.
16. Julius Rudel, interview by author, New York, July 13, 1990.
17. Charles Pitt, review, *Opera,* May 1978, 469–71.
18. Benjamin Ivry, "Monteverdi Arrives—in Milwaukee," *Opera News,* October 1988, 10–13.
19. Elizabeth Forbes, review, *Opera Canada,* no. 3, 1978, 34.
20. Howell interview.
21. Garner to Rodzinski, July 5, 1978, Metropolitan Opera Archives.
22. Richard Dyer, review, *Boston Globe,* August 1978.
23. Cairns, "The Power and the Passion."
24. Vickers, RCM lecture series, July 1991.
25. Vickers, RCM lecture series, July 19, 1991.
26. Dyer interview.
27. Vickers, interview, *Opera News,* December 2, 1978.
28. Patrick J. Smith, review, *Opera,* January 1979.
29. Rudel interview.
30. Anthony Laciura, telephone interview by author, June 17, 1998.
31. Coast to Ingpen, February 8, 1979, Metropolitan Opera Archives.

32. John Gage, telephone interview by author, July 1997.
33. John Kraglund, review, *Toronto Globe & Mail*, May 19, 1979.
34. Jacob Siskind, review, *Ottawa Citizen*, May 10, 1978.
35. David Gockley, interview by author, Houston, November 3, 1989.
36. Luciano Pavarotti, telephone interview by author, February 28, 1989.
37. Knie interview.

18. A Winter's Journey
 1. Fred Plotkin, various conversations with author.
 2. Levine interview.
 3. Ingpen interview.
 4. Donal Henahan, review, *New York Times*, July 1, 1980.
 5. Andrew Porter, review, *New Yorker*, July 21, 1980.
 6. Richard Dyer, review, *Boston Globe*, July 7, 1980.
 7. Mansouri interview.
 8. Lillian Vickers, telephone interview by author, November 8, 1998.
 9. Vickers, interview by Becker, 1981.
10. *Opera.*
11. Alan Blyth, review, *Opera*, June 1982, 650–52.
12. Conlon interview.
13. McIntyre interview; Davis interview.
14. Vickers, in Breslin, *The Tenors*, 67.
15. *Prince Albert Herald*, June 5, 1982.
16. Sergio Segalini, review, *Opera*, October 1982, 1067.
17. Catherine Malfitano, telephone interview by author, February 10, 1991.
18. Stratas interview.
19. Woitach interview.
20. Kareda, "Tenor of His Times," 38.
21. Ibid.
22. William Mason, telephone interview by author, November 14, 1997.
23. Harold Rosenthal, review, *Opera*, January 1983, 24.
24. Kareda, "Tenor of His Times," 40.
25. Ibid., 47.
26. Vickers, interview by Jacob Siskind, *Ottawa Journal*, May 9, 1979.
27. Tooley interview.
28. Ibid.
29. Vickers, conversation with author.
30. Tooley interview.
31. Jean Cotte, review, *France Soir*, February 10, 1983.
32. Alain Lanceron, telephone interview by author, 1998.
33. Vickers, liner notes, *Le Voyage d'Hiver*, French EMI, 1984.
34. Will Crutchfield, review, *New York Times*, February 10, 1985.
35. Conrad Osborne, review, *Opus*, June 1985, 20.
36. John Steane, *The Grand Tradition* (New York: Duckworth, 1974), 431.
37. Allan Ulrich *(San Francisco Examiner)*, interview by author, July 6, 1999.

19. Final Grimes, Otello *in South Africa*
 1. Carol Vaness, telephone interview by author, June 20, 1992.
 2. Jenkins interview.

3. F. B. St. Clair, review, *Opera*, October 1983, 1124–25.
4. Vickers, interview by Robert Baxter, *Camden* (N.J.) *Courier Journal*, July 31, 1983.
5. Metropolitan Opera Archives.
6. Coast to Ingpen, July 11, 1979, Metropolitan Opera Archives.
7. Ingpen interview.
8. Levine interview.
9. Metropolitan Opera Archives, contracts file.
10. Domingo interview.
11. Ingpen interview.
12. ROH Archives.
13. ROH Archives.
14. ROH Archives.
15. ROH Archives.
16. William Albright, review, *Opera*, October 1984, 1108.
17. Frank Gagnard, review, *New Orleans Times-Picayune*, January 24, 1984, 6.
18. A. Anderson interview.
19. Josephine Barstow, interview by author.
20. Tooley interview.
21. Vickers, remarks to author, Washington, D.C., April 1984.
22. Leighton Kerner, *Stagebill*, Kennedy Center, Washington, D.C., April 1984.
23. Knie interview.
24. Jones interview; Ardoin interview.
25. Kim Begley, telephone interview by author, July 24, 1997.
26. Helen Donath, telephone interview by author, 1988.
27. Alan Rich, review, *Newsweek*, July 23, 1984.
28. Woitach interview.
29. William Littler, review, *Toronto Star*, October 18, 1985.
30. Martin Bernheimer, review, *Los Angeles Times*, October 5, 1984.
31. Danuta Dickie, telephone interview by author, December 9, 1997.
32. Garth Verdal, coverage of press conference, *Cape Argus*, November 23, 1984.
33. Vickers, RCM lecture series, July 19, 1991.
34. Ibid.
35. Christine Crouse, telephone interview by author, November 8, 1997.
36. Sally Presant, telephone interview by author, November 8, 1997.
37. Julius F. Eichbaum, review, *Scenaria*, January 1985.
38. Vickers, interview by Alan Blyth, *Times* (London), May 24, 1972.
39. Ibid.
40. Vickers, conversation with author, 1985.
41. Richard Osborne, *Conversations with Karajan*, 77.
42. Stratas interview.

20. The Trials of Samson
1. Vickers, interview by Tom Sutcliffe, February 1985.
2. Stanley Sadie, review, *Opera*, April 2, 1985, 368.
3. Tooley interview.
4. Vickers, interview by Alan Blyth, *Times* (London), October 24, 1974.
5. Tooley interview.
6. Mackerras interview.
7. Tooley interview.

8. Ibid.
9. Rudel interview.
10. Vickers, in Sutcliffe, "Strongman," 20.
11. Rudel interview.
12. Marie McLaughlin, interview by author, New York, October 10, 1990.
13. J. Anderson interview.
14. Mason interview.
15. Rudel interview.
16. Vaness interview.
17. Howell interview.
18. Rudel interview.
19. Bartoletti interview.
20. Rudel interview.
21. Ardis Krainik, interview by author, November 1990.
22. Howell interview.
23. Moshinsky interview.
24. Rudel interview.
25. Moshinsky interview.
26. Vickers, in Sutcliffe, "Strongman," 19.
27. Robert Tear, interview by author, Washington, D.C., June 8, 1987.
28. Moshinsky interview.
29. Elijah Moshinsky, interview on WFMT radio, Chicago, during Lyric Opera broadcast, 1985.
30. Vickers, in Sutcliffe, "Strongman," 20.
31. John Higgins, review, *Times* (London), February 22, 1985.
32. Peter Stadlen, review, *London Daily Telegraph*, February 2, 1985.
33. Stanley Sadie, review, *Opera*, April 1985, 368–71.
34. John von Rhein, review, *Chicago Tribune*, October 14, 1985.
35. Alan Rich, review, *Newsweek*, February 17, 1986.
36. Martin Mayer, review, *Opera*, May 1986, 525–27.
37. Andrew Porter, review, *New Yorker*, February 17, 1986.
38. Peter G. Davis, review, *New York*, February 17, 1986.
39. Tooley interview.

21. Parsifal and Farewell to the Met
1. Vickers, conversation with author, Philadelphia, March 30, 1985.
2. Vickers, interview by Becker, 1981 (Vickers is quoting Will and Ariel Durant); Vickers, interview by Norman Pellegrini, WFMT radio, Chicago, autumn 1986.
3. Leonie Rysanek, interview by Robert Jacobson, *Opera News*, March 15, 1986, 10–14.
4. Andrew Porter, review, *New Yorker*, April 22, 1985.
5. Ludwig interview.
6. Shirley Verrett, interview by author, Chicago, September 28, 1987.
7. Hubbard interview.
8. Vickers, interview by William Littler, *Toronto Star*, July 14, 1991.
9. Metropolitan Opera Archives.
10. Miller interview.
11. Woitach interview.
12. Eric Dawson, telephone interview by author, 1998.
13. Miller interview.

14. Ibid.
15. Eric Dawson, review, *Calgary Herald,* November 29, 1986.
16. Mason interview.
17. Vickers, interview by Will Crutchfield, in "On Supertitles . . . ," *New York Times,* November 27, 1986.
18. Matthew Epstein, telephone interview by author, February 20, 1998.
19. John von Rhein, review, *Chicago Tribune,* October 8, 1986.
20. Will Crutchfield, review, *New York Times,* October 27, 1986.
21. Plotkin interview.
22. Cori Ellison, interview by author, 1998.
23. Peter G. Davis, review, *New York,* April 13, 1987.
24. Will Crutchfield, review, *New York Times,* March 30, 1987.
25. The Reverend Thomas Jean-Pierre Pellaton, interview by author, New York, January 11, 1992.
26. Vickers, lecture, Montgomery College, 1988.
27. Glenn Giffin, review, *Denver Post,* May 11, 1987.

22. Canadian Coda and a Worldview
1. Peter Sever, interview by author, Toronto, July 19, 1991.
2. Ibid.
3. Pellaton interview.
4. Martin Bernheimer, review, *Los Angeles Times,* March 11, 1988.
5. Pellaton interview.
6. Robert Everett-Green, review, *Toronto Globe & Mail,* September 10, 1987.
7. William Littler, review, *Toronto Star,* September 10, 1987.
8. *Boston Herald,* January 29, 1988; *Christian Science Monitor,* January 29, 1988.
9. Pellaton interview.
10. Woitach interview.
11. Dr. Clive Mortimer, telephone interview by author, August 30, 1991.
12. Raffi Armenian, telephone interview by author, September 28, 1991.
13. Vickers, graduation address, RCM, 1969. (The historian Livy makes no mention of cabbages.)
14. Maureen Forrester, *Out of Character* (Toronto: McClelland and Stewart, 1986), chapter 28.
15. Sever interview.
16. Laurelle Favreau, telephone interview by author, October 5, 1991.
17. Vickers, RCM lecture series, July 19, 1991.
18. Ibid.
19. Favreau interview.
20. Vickers, interview by Becker, 1981.
21. Vickers, interview by Ulla Colgrass, *Music Magazine,* December 1986.
22. McIntyre interview.
23. Vickers, program notes, Christian School event, Canada (date, place unavailable).
24. Humphrey Burton, telephone interview by author, August 18, 1997.
25. Cairns interview.
26. W. H. Auden, foreword, *Markings,* by Dag Hammarskjöld (reprint; New York: Ballantine Books, 1983), xv.
27. The Reverend R. Maurice Boyd, interview by author, New York, November 19, 1991.

28. Stratas interview.
29. Vickers lectures.
30. Vickers, interview by Stephen E. Rubin, *Newsday* (New York), January 22, 1978.
31. Vickers, interview by Colgrass.

Epilogue
1. John Steane, notes, *The Art of Singing: Golden Voices of the Century,* Warner Music Vision, NVC Arts, 1997.
2. Vickers, conversation with author, Philadelphia, March 30, 1985.
3. Vickers, telephone conversation with author, October 1993.
4. Vickers, interview by Martin Bernheimer, *Los Angeles Times,* July 8, 1984.
5. Vickers, conversation with author, October 28, 1993.
6. Peter Sellars, telephone interview by author, July 1998.
7. Vickers, RCM lecture series, July 1991.
8. Ian Garratt, telephone interview by author, August 2, 1991.
9. Vickers, telephone conversation with author, July 29, 1994.
10. Richard Dyer, review, *Boston Globe,* July 30, 1996.
11. Ernest Gilbert, telephone interviews by author, 1998, 1999.
12. Stuart Hamilton, telephone interview by author, January 24, 1998.
13. Teresa Stratas, from her text, Ottawa, November 1998.
14. Robertson Davies, *The Lyre of Orpheus* (New York: Viking, 1988), 454.
15. Robertson Davies, letter to author, February 14, 1995.
16. Anthony Tommasini, review, *New York Times,* October 24, 1996.
17. Vickers, conversation with author, 1995.

Selected Bibliography

Books

Berlioz, Hector. *The Memoirs of Hector Berlioz.* Trans. and ed. by David Cairns. Reprint, London: Cardinal, 1990.

Bloomfield, Arthur. *The San Francisco Opera, 1922–1978.* Sausalito, Calif.: Comstock Editions, 1978.

Blyth, Alan. *Colin Davis.* New York: Drake, 1973.

Breslin, Herbert H., ed. *The Tenors.* New York: Macmillan, 1974. (Vickers chapter by John Ardoin uses much material from the CBC documentary "A Man and His Music.")

Brett, Philip, comp. *Peter Grimes.* Cambridge Opera Handbooks. Cambridge: Cambridge University Press, 1983.

Cairns, David. *Responses.* New York: Knopf, 1973.

Carpenter, Humphrey. *Benjamin Britten: A Biography.* New York: Scribner, 1992.

Chapin, Schuyler. *Musical Chairs: A Life in the Arts.* New York: Putnam, 1977.

Colgrass, Ulla. *For the Love of Music.* Toronto: Oxford University Press, 1988.

Conrad, Peter. *A Song of Love and Death: The Meaning of Opera.* New York: Poseidon Press, 1987.

Davies, Robertson. *The Enthusiasms of Robertson Davies.* Ed. by Judith Skelton Grant. New York: Penguin Books, 1991.

———. *The Lyre of Orpheus.* New York: Viking, 1988.

Emmons, Shirlee. *Tristanissimo: The Authorized Biography of Heroic Tenor Lauritz Melchior.* New York: Schirmer Books, 1990.

Fingleton, David. *Kiri.* New York: Atheneum, 1983.

Forrester, Maureen, with Marci McDonald. *Out of Character.* Toronto: McClelland and Stewart, 1986.

Gollancz, Victor. *Journey towards Music.* New York: Dutton, 1965.

Haltrecht, Montague. *The Quiet Showman: Sir David Webster and the Royal Opera House.* London: Collins, 1975.

Hammarskjöld, Dag. *Markings.* 1966. Reprint, New York: Ballantine Books, 1983.

Jacobson, Robert, *Reverberations.* New York: Morrow, 1974.

Jellinek, George. *Callas: Portrait of a Prima Donna.* 1960. Reprint. New York: Dover, 1986.

Jung, Carl G., ed. *Man and His Symbols.* New York: Laurel/Dell, 1968.

Kolodin, Irving. *The Metropolitan Opera, 1883–1966: A Candid History.* New York: Knopf, 1966.

Liebermann, Rolf. *En Passant par Paris.* Paris: Gallimard, 1980.

Lowe, David A. *Callas As They Saw Her.* London: Robson, 1987.

Lucas, John. *Reggie: The Life of Reginald Goodall.* London: Random House, 1993.

Malcolm, Andrew H. *The Canadians.* New York: Times Books, 1985.

Mansouri, Lotfi, with Aviva Layton. *Lotfi Mansouri: An Operatic Life.* Oakville, Ont.: Mosaic Press; Toronto: Stoddard, 1982.

Mercer, Ruby. *The Quilicos.* Oakville, Ont.: Mosaic Press, 1990.

Newman, Ernest. *The Wagner Operas.* Vol. 1. New York: Harper Colophon, 1983.

Nilsson, Birgit. *My Memoirs in Pictures.* New York: Doubleday, 1981.

Osborne, Richard. *Conversations with Karajan*. Oxford: Oxford University Press, 1989.

Rasponi, Lanfranco. *The Last Prima Donnas*. New York: Limelight, 1985.

Reid, Charles. *John Barbirolli: A Biography*. New York: Taplinger, 1971.

———. *Thomas Beecham: An Independent Biography*. New York: Dutton, 1962.

Ripley Historical Group. *Huron's Hub: A History of the People and Homes in Ripley, Ontario, 1875–1992*. Ripley, Ont.: Friesen Printers, 1994.

Rosenthal, Harold. *Opera at Covent Garden: A Short History*. London: Gollancz, 1967.

Schabas, Ezra. *Sir Ernest MacMillan: The Importance of Being Canadian*. Toronto: University of Toronto Press, 1994.

Silversides, Brock V. *Gateway to the North: A Pictorial History of Prince Albert*. Saskatoon, Sask.: Western Producer Prairie Books, 1989.

Spotts, Frederic. *Bayreuth: A History of the Wagner Festival*. New Haven, Conn.: Yale University Press, 1994.

Steane, John. *The Grand Tradition*. New York: Duckworth, 1974.

Vishnevskaya, Galina. *Galina: A Russian Story*. New York: Harcourt Brace Jovanovich, 1984.

Magazine Articles

Blyth, Alan. Vickers interviews. *Times* (London), May 24, 1972, October 24, 1974.

Brodkey, Harold. "Dying: An Update." *New Yorker*, February 7, 1994.

Burroughs, Bruce. "Serene Lucine: Lucine Amara." *Opera Quarterly*, autumn 1992, 24–106.

Goodwin, Noël. "Jon Vickers." *Opera*. April 1962, 233–39.

Kareda, Urjo. "The Tenor of His Times." *Saturday Night* (Toronto), March 1983, 38–47.

Loppert, Max. "Jon Vickers on *Peter Grimes*." *Opera*, August 1984, 835–43.

Malitz, Nancy. "Jon Vickers: A Tough-Minded Tenor." *Ovation*. October 1986, 14–20.

Porter, Andrew. "Hero." *New Yorker*, July 21, 1980.

Sutcliffe, Tom. "Strongman." *Opera News*, March 1, 1986.

Tolansky, Jon. "Anniversary Portrait." Interview with Edward Downes. *Opera House* (Royal Opera House, Covent Garden) 13 (autumn 1997).

Vickers, Jon. Interview. *Scenaria* (Pretoria, South Africa), January 1985.

"The Vickers Creed." *Opera News*, March 16, 1974, 14.

Williams, Jeannie, "A Sense of Awe: The Career of Jon Vickers as Seen in Reviews." *Opera Quarterly*, autumn 1990, 36–73.

Television

Carmen. 1965 Salzburg production, Herbert von Karajan, Vienna Philharmonic. Bumbry, Freni, Vickers, Diaz. Aired July 24, 1982, CBS-TV. Museum of Television and Radio, New York.

Impressions of Herbert von Karajan: A Film by Vojtech Jaoney. 1978. Excerpt of Karajan's *Pagliacci* film with Vickers. Aired October 31, 1981, CBS Cable. Museum of Television and Radio, New York.

"Live from the Met: *Otello*." September 25, 1978. WNET-TV. Museum of Television and Radio, New York. Intermission interview of Vickers by Francis Robinson.

"A Man and His Music." CBC documentary, produced and directed by Richard Bocking. 1974.

"Opening Night at Lincoln Center." September 23, 1962. CBS-TV. Museum of Television and Radio, New York.

Video

"The Art of Singing: Golden Voices of the Century." John Steane, notes. Warner Music Video, NVC Arts, 1997.

"Dief," 26½-minute memento of Canadian Prime Minister John George Diefenbaker, comprising scenes from his life and funeral. Directed by William Canning. National Film Board of Canada.

Radio

"Desert Island Discs." Aired 1968, BBC, London.

"Jon Vickers: A Life in Music." Aired October 23, 1973, CBC Radio.

Acknowledgments

Many people in several countries were most generous with their help on my odyssey of many years preparing this book. I made a number of Canadian friends and must mention in Prince Albert John V. Hicks, Frances Short, William Smiley, and Ronald Smith. Jean A. Turnbull, Douglas Wallace, and Jack Matheson also were most helpful. In Winnipeg, Kathleen Morrison Brown was an invaluable tour guide, and the Thomson family in entirety, notably Stewart, Phyllis, and Ed, were gracious hosts and sources. Thanks also to collector Charlie Hooey.

For the Flin Flon years, thanks to Jean Guymer Henderson, Dorothy Young Liss, and Cecelia Allen. Richard and Winnifred Bocking were helpful on Vickers's time in Port Arthur, now part of Thunder Bay, Ontario. Mr. Bocking's CBC Vickers documentary, "A Man and His Music," is the only existing filmed document on the tenor's life and as such has been extremely valuable.

In Toronto I was helped by Mary Morrison; William Littler; the late Robert Binnie and his late wife, Edith Milligan Binnie; Franz Kraemer; Ezra Schabas; Louis Applebaum; and Nan Shaw, now of Prince Edward Island. Thanks to Janet Stubbs and Stuart Hamilton, and to Susan Burton for outstanding genealogical research. Also in Canada, Irving Guttman, Eric Dawson of Calgary, and Bob Cooney of Brandon were most helpful.

In Bermuda, John Adams, Sue Judah, William Duncan, Anthony and Marjorie Pettit, Yeaton Outerbridge, and J. J. Outerbridge provided valuable assistance. Thanks as well to Herbert Tinney of Buffalo.

Regina Resnik was of inestimable help on the early years of Vickers's career.

Many archives were invaluable sources. At the Royal Opera House at Covent Garden, Francesca Franchi and her staff gave continual aid. The indefatigable Margaret Nicholson, a onetime orange deliverer for Vickers, as an ROH Archives volunteer compiled an utterly invaluable chronology of Vickers's roles at the ROH. She also did excellent photo research. My thanks to Robert Tuggle and John Pennino at the Metropolitan Opera Archives, as well as Peter Clark of the Met Press Office; at the New York City Opera, Susan Woelzl; at Lyric Opera of Chicago, Susan Mathieson, Elizabeth Connell, Roger Pines, and the estimable Danny Newman; at the

Dallas Opera, Rebecca Sherman; at the Bayreuth Festspielhaus, Peter Emmerich; Dr. Eike Rathgebe of the Herbert von Karajan Centrum, Vienna; and from the Wagner Society of New York, special thanks to Kit Gill, Verena Kossodo, Nathalie and Harry Wagner; at the Royal Festival Hall, London, Mala Jones; at the CNE, Amber Timmons; Birthe Jorgensen and Joan Baillie of the Canadian Opera Company Archives; Gail Donald and Barbara Clark of the CBC Radio Archives; Marcia Childs of the United Church Archives; Richard Warren at the Toronto Symphony Archives; John Davis at the BBC Written Archives, Reading, England; Jerry Grace, National Arts Center, Ottawa; Gill Louw of the Cape Town Performing Arts Board; S. Ben-Aroyo in Tel Aviv; Orrin Howard of the Los Angeles Philharmonic; Kirsten Tanaka at the San Francisco Performing Arts Library and Museum; Ava Jean Mears, Houston Grand Opera; and Tina Ryker at the Seattle Opera.

Thanks as well to Charles Rodier of EMI Classics in London and Alain Lanceron of French EMI Classics; Sylvie de Nussac in Paris; Joanne Morrow of the Canada Council; Richard Mohr and Alan Kaye, formerly of RCA; Hernan Luis Vigo Suarez in Buenos Aires; Eugenio Scabo at Teatro Colón; Robert Hudson at Carnegie Hall; Savannah Whaley in Miami; and Dr. Michael Cordovana of Catholic University, Washington, D.C.

Also special thanks to Joan Ingpen, David Cairns, Donald Mitchell, Philip Brett, Humphrey Burton, John Lucas, Peter Conrad, Peter G. Davis, John Ardoin, Fred Plotkin, Merle Hubbard, Gregory Mowery, Albert Innaurato, Martin Bernheimer, and Robert Sutherland at the Met Music Library.

Manuela Hoelterhoff, Sir John Tooley, Richard Woitach and Jeryl Metz Woitach, and Edgar Vincent merit special mention.

For the discography and performance history, my thanks to Geoffrey Peterson of Thorne Thomas Co. My gratitude goes to Friedrich Danielis, Susan Salm, and Roberta Knie for translation help; my agent, Susan Schulman, for her support over many years, and my London agent, Serafina Clarke, for her optimism; William Frohlich, Ann Twombly, and Barbara Lenes of Northeastern University Press, for invaluable aid on my first book; editor Larry Hamberlin; and my sister, Stephanie Russell, and brother, Peter Craig, for urging me on.

And I would like to thank Jon Vickers. Although he did not cooperate with this book, over several years he helped me with liner notes for some of his VAI re-releases and aided in the lengthy 1990 article I wrote for *Opera Quarterly* on his career as seen in reviews. He shared many of his views in conversation and introduced me to much magnificent music. It has been a privilege to explore the life of this feisty artist, who is in his totality a once-in-a-century experience.

Index

Academy of Music (Philadelphia), 60
Academy of Vocal Arts (Philadelphia), 276, 300
Adam, Theo, 193, 206
Adler, Kurt, 106, 128, 151
Adler, Kurt Herbert, 67, 79, 153, 159, 167, 168–69, 219
Africaine, L' (Meyerbeer), 46
Aida (Verdi), 12, 32, 58, 60, 79, 86, 88–89, 95, 97, 99–100, 109, 112, 114, 115, 116, 120, 121–22, 123, 127, 129, 132, 134, 145, 154, 160, 232, 241, 265
Albright, William, 145, 257
Aldeburgh (England), 142, 144
Alexander, John, 276
Allen, Cecelia Sukke, 22–24
Allen, Thomas, 174, 307
Alton, Ont.: site of JV farm, 124, 260
Amara, Lucine, 99, 157
Ambassador Auditorium (Pasadena, Calif.), 288
American Guild of Musical Artists, 258
American Opera Society (New York), 59–60
An die ferne Geliebte (Beethoven), 35, 137, 205
Anderson, Alan Stanley (Ande), 63, 66, 73, 101, 118, 195, 225, 235, 253, 257
Anderson, June, 227–28, 269
Andrea Chénier (Giordano), 99, 109, 120, 185, 255, 268
Anthony, Charles, 106
Anthony, Kym, 302
Apostle, The (film), 298
Applebaum, Louis, 54
Aprea, Bruno, 263–64
Arcadia, Calif., 305
Ardoin, John, 10, 78, 90, 92, 109, 117, 135, 146, 151–52, 179, 185, 198, 202
Arlesiana, L' (Cilea), 46, 47, 74
Armenian, Raffi, 276, 291
Arroyo, Martina, 307
Art of Singing, The: Golden Voices of the Century (video recording), 300
Artistes Internationaux, 166
Arturo Toscanini Association Arstistic Achievement Award, 279

Ash, Dorothy, 23
Athens (Greece) festival, 18
Atlanta, 257
Atlantov, Vladimir, 165, 264
Atwood, Margaret, 126
Auden, W. H., 297
Augustine United Church (Winnipeg), 26, 30
Avery, Lawrence, 59
Avery Fisher Hall (orig. Philharmonic Hall), 127, 137

Bach, Johann Sebastian: arias, 42, 139
Bacquier, Gabriel, 151
Baglioni, Bruna, 279
Baker, Janet, 160
Ballad of Heroes, The (Britten), 50
Ballo in maschera, Un (Verdi), 61, 67–70, 82, 95, 109, 116, 123, 197, 235, 255
Banff, Alta., 299
Barbieri, Fedora, 82
Barbirolli, Sir John, 80
Barcelona Symphony, 280
Barkin, Leo, 37, 158
Barlow, Klara, 185–86, 187–88, 189, 190
Baron, Dr. Shirley, 168
Barrett, Herbert, 137
Barstow, Josephine, 249, 257, 280, 290
Bartered Bride, The (Smetana), 145, 206, 233, 235, 285
Bartoletti, Bruno, 136, 154, 195, 249, 271
Baudo, Serge, 254
Baum, Kurt, 60, 137
Baxter, Robert, 253
Bayne, Rev. Alf, 247
Bayreuth Festival, 33, 54, 59, 68, 74–75, 79, 84–85, 91, 109, 119, 128, 131, 133, 138, 169, 176, 213; Festspielhaus, 133
BBC. *See* British Broadcasting Corporation
Beacon Concerts Ltd. (London), 166
Beecham, Sir Thomas, 98–99, 203, 266, 269
Beethoven, Ludwig van: songs and arias, 47, 158
Begley, Kim, 259
Behrens, Hildegard, 241, 255, 258

Orquesta Filharmonica de la Ciudad de Mexico, 245
Osborne, Conrad, 251
Osborne, Richard, 176
Otello (Verdi), 4, 18, 37, 58, 68–69, 75, 99, 108, 116, 118, 123,127, 129, 130–31, 132, 135, 138, 141, 151–52, 166, 167, 168, 169, 171, 178–80, 181, 183, 189, 191, 194, 197, 204–5, 206, 212, 215, 216, 222–23, 232–33, 235, 242–43, 245, 248, 255, 261–62, 264–65, 278, 298, 301; recordings, 109–10, 111, 183, 265
Ottawa National Arts Center, 301
Outerbridge, Christena (Tena) Henrietta Martyn (mother-in-law), 40
Outerbridge, Henrietta Elsie (wife). *See* Vickers, Henrietta (Hetti) Elsie Outerbridge
Outerbridge, Ian Worrall (brother-in-law), 41–42, 108, 228
Outerbridge, Joseph John, 40, 182
Outerbridge, Dr. Leonard Mallory (father-in-law), 40, 42, 108
Outerbridge, Lydia, 41
Outerbridge, Patricia. *See* Wickstrom, Patricia
Outerbridge, William, 40
Oxenburg, Allen Sven, 59
Ozawa, Seiji, 232, 263

Padmâvatî (Roussel), 155
Pagliacci (Leoncavallo), 48, 51, 58, 95, 96, 97, 98, 99, 100–101, 105, 107, 128, 154, 158, 166, 179, 185, 194, 228, 235, 236, 245, 247, 249, 252, 256, 278, 285
Palais Garnier (Paris), 223
Panek, Ralph W., 305
Papineau-Couture, Jean, 158
Paris, 70, 249
Paris Opéra, 132, 176, 206, 222, 229, 234, 244, 245, 246, 247, 252
Park, Dr., 34
Park, Helen, 34
Parly, Ticho, 151
Parsifal (Wagner), xiv, 32, 37, 53, 75, 82, 83, 84, 85, 86, 98, 109, 123, 131, 133, 137, 153, 170–71, 206, 213, 227, 235, 244, 256, 266, 276–78, 282–83, 285, 288, 291–92, 294, 298
Parsons, Geoffrey, 250
Pasadena, Calif., 305
Patanè, Giuseppe, 228
Patchen, Kenneth, 195
Patzak, Julius, 224

Pavarotti, Luciano, xiv, 101, 129, 165, 195, 199, 215, 217–18, 234, 236, 241, 243, 254–55, 288. *See also* Three Tenors
Peabody Conservatory of Music (Baltimore), 48
Pears, Sir Peter, 54–55, 81, 84, 142, 144, 145, 147, 148, 170, 195, 232, 261
Pease, James, 67
Peerce, Jan, 20, 60, 131, 137
Pellaton, Thomas, 284, 288–89, 290
People, 204
Performing Arts Center (Montgomery College, Rockville, Md.), 287
Perón, Juan, 173
Perot, Ross, 181
Peter Grimes (Britten), 4, 25, 38, 51, 71, 78–79, 84, 88, 127, 135, 139, 141–50, 151, 156, 157, 166, 174, 183, 184, 194, 195, 206, 212, 214, 219, 227, 235, 243, 244, 250, 253, 254, 255, 257–59, 260, 270, 272, 279, 285, 288, 290, 301, 306–7, 309, 310; 1981 recording, 145
Peterson, Oscar, 248
Philadelphia, 54, 60, 131, 235, 276
Philadelphia Inquirer, 60
Philharmonia Orchestra (London), 81, 95
Philharmonic Hall (Berlin), 183
Philharmonic Hall (New York). *See* Avery Fisher Hall
Philips records, 161
Picasso, Pablo, 297
Pilarczyk, Helga, 76
Pilgrim's Progress, The (Vaughan Williams), 158
Pique Dame (Tchaikovsky), 130, 135, 142, 151, 181, 185, 207, 235, 241, 243, 256, 306
Pirates of Penzance, The (Gilbert & Sullivan), 22–23
Pitt, Charles, 193, 231
Pittsburgh, 18
Pizzi, Pier Luigi, 282
Place des Arts (Montreal), 200, 209
Playhouse Theater (Winnipeg), 29
Plotkin, Fred, 241
Plymouth Brethren, 13
Poettgen, Ernst, 173, 200, 201, 248
Poliuto (Donizetti), 112
Ponnelle, Jean-Pierre, 236
Port Arthur. *See* Thunder Bay, Ont.
Port Credit High School (Spadina, Ont.), 41
Porter, Andrew, 86, 113, 123, 144, 178, 197, 199, 242, 274, 276–77, 296

broadcasts and recordings: *Aida* (recording), 114; *The Art of Singing: Golden Voices of the Century* (video recording), 300; *The Bartered Bride* (Met telecast), 233; Canadian music (CBC radio recording), 194; Canadian songs (recording), 260; Canadian TV documentary, 132; 1967 Carnegie Hall concert (VAI audio recording), 301; CBC Radio 60th anniversary program, 308; Weill's *Down in the Valley* (televised), 38; *Fidelio* (recording), 113; Fidelio (scenes; video recording), 301; *H.M.S. Pinafore* (video recording), 301; *L'Incoronazione di Poppea* (video recording), 229–30; *Jon Vickers: A Life in Music* (CBC radio special), 183; *A Man and His Music* (CBC-TV documentary), 194, 307; *Manon Lescaut* (scenes for CBC-TV), 301; *Otello* (Met telecast), 232; *Otello* (scenes; video recording), 301; *Otello* (recording), 265; *Otello* (second recording), 183; *Pagliacci* (Buenos Aires; VAI audio recording), 301; *Pagliacci* (CBC recording), 302; 1988 Pasadena concert (video recording), 307; *Peter Grimes* (BBC-TV recording), 79; *Peter Grimes* (scenes; video recording), 301; *Peter Grimes* (video recording), 244; *Samson et Dalila* (recording), 128; *Samson et Dalila* (video recording), 244; *Samson et Dalila* (scenes; video recording), 301; 1965 Toronto concert (CBC telecast), 301; *Tosca* (scenes for CBC-TV), 301; *Il Trovatore* (scenes for CBC-TV), 301; *Les Troyens* (recording), 160–62; *Tristan und Isolde* (recording), 175; *Tristan und Isolde* (VAI video recording), 200; *Tristan und Isolde* (Montreal; recorded scenes), 301; *Die Walküre* (recording), 139; Schubert's *Die Winterreise* (recordings), 250, 307

career: early professional engagements, 45–61; Met audition in Montreal, 46; audition with Webster, 57; plan to quit music, 56–57; audition with Karajan, 74; audition with Wieland Wagner, 75; dispute with BBC-TV, 76–79; alterations to *Peter Grimes*, 146–47, 150; Carnegie Hall recitals, 152; controversy over Met *Tristan*, 185, 187–91; coughing incident in Dallas, 203–4; refusal to sing *Tannhäuser*, 210–19, 229; Paris Opéra production of *Otello*, 222–23; as Otello in Cape Town, 261–64; dispute with Julius Rudel, 271–72; JV's interpretation of

Handel's *Samson*, 266–68; final performances, 283; University of Toronto Wilma and Clifford Smith Visitor in Music series, 279; final public appearance, 291–92; Royal Conservatory of Music (Toronto) lectures, 302–3; judge in di Stefano voice competition, 306; *Peter Grimes* anniversary celebration at Tanglewood, 306–7

debuts: Bayreuth Festival, 82–84, 87; Carnegie Hall, 50; Covent Garden, 68; La Scala, 112; Lyric Opera of Chicago, 112; Metropolitan Opera, 105; recital at Philharmonic Hall, 137; Salzburg Festival, 137; San Francisco Opera, 99; Vienna State Opera, 95–96

degrees and awards: inducted into Academy of Vocal Arts Hall of Fame for Great American Opera Singers, 276; Brandon University Honorary Doctorate of Music, 219–20; Canadian Governor General's Performing Arts Award, 309; Central Opera Service Arturo Toscanini Association Artistic Achievement Award, 279; made a Companion of the Order of Canada, 158, 227; London *Evening Standard* Opera Award, 234; Molson prize, 207; scholarships to Royal Conservatory of Music (Toronto), 30, 34; University of British Columbia Honorary Doctor of Letters, 301; University of Illinois (Chicago) Honorary Doctorate, 256

personal life: birth, 10; boyhood, 11–18; high school graduation, 16, 19; early employment, 19–20, 21, 24–25, 26; marriage to Hetti Outerbridge, 42; birth of children, 51, 55, 112, 120, 134; Toronto residence, 42, 55; move to London, 65; farm at Alton, Ont., 124–25; tax troubles, 123, 253; auto accident in Salzburg, 168; move to Bermuda, 181; Hetti's death, 303; marriage to Judith Panek Stewart, 305

training: lessons with Wood, 24, 25, 35; lessons with Thomson, 25–26, 27, 35; with Hudson Bay Company chorus, 25; with Kelvin Grads Glee Club, 28–30; at Royal Conservatory of Music (Toronto), 33–39; studies with George Lambert, 35–37, 51–52

Vickers, Judith Panek Stewart (second wife), 305, 307, 308–9

Vickers, Karen (daughter-in-law), 302

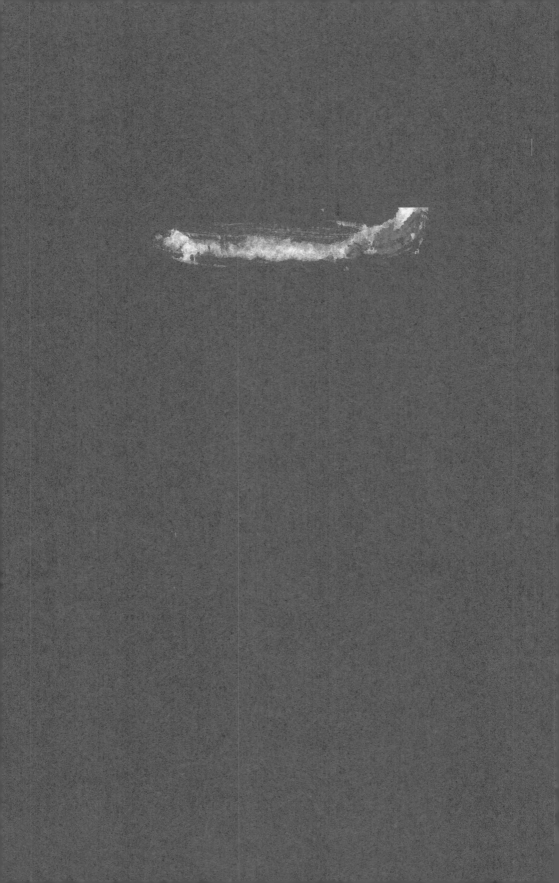